Praise for *In for Life*

This is the story of two remarkable journeys, one by a young Black man who was wrongly imprisoned for killing a Boston cop, the other by a middle-aged suburban White woman who fought for his freedom. In Elaine Murphy's masterful account, In for Life is both a searing indictment of the criminal "justice" system and a testament to the power of human connection and personal resilience.

> —Eileen McNamara, Pulitzer Prize-winning *Boston Globe* journalist (retired); Professor of Journalism, Brandeis University; author, *Eunice: The Kennedy Who Changed the World*

Over the course of my career as an investigative reporter, rarely have I come across research so thorough and probing as the questions and answers raised and dug up by Elaine Murphy in pursuit of truth in the case of Sean Ellis. His freedom is in large part owed to the woman who got to know him as a youth and decided not to stand idly by when he was implicated in the notorious murder of a Boston detective.

Murphy provided us with the core information that helped journalists like me burrow beneath the surface of elaborate lies and fabrications that led to an innocent man being placed behind bars for twenty years. Her exquisitely written memoir explains in finely woven detail why this suburban mom would spend nearly two decades of her life zeroing in on the contradictions of this case. In for Life: A Journey into Murder, Corruption, and Friendship is an important read for anyone seeking justice in our system of law and punishment, which leans heavily in the direction of injustice for Black and brown men and women. Sean Ellis was one of them.

> —Phillip Martin, Senior Investigative Reporter, GBH News Center for Investigative Reporting, Boston

Elaine Alice Murphy's In for Life *is a riveting and inspiring story that is hard to put down. Part investigative journalism, part memoir, and part murder mystery, her powerful accounting of the Sean Ellis story provides a realistic view of the uphill battle to achieve justice when faced with prosecutorial misconduct and the proverbial "blue shield." Her excellent narrative intertwines a beautiful story of friendship, family, and connection between two people from opposite sides of the economic divide with her passion for justice and her deeply impactful journey of personal growth.*

In this time of racial reckoning, In for Life *serves as a North Star for white allyship, providing a clear example of how to truly live your values in solidarity and leverage your privilege to work for justice. Elaine and Sean's story is an inspiration for us all.*

— Jackie Jenkins-Scott, President, Wheelock College, Boston (retired); author, *The 7 Secrets of Responsive Leadership*

For a lawyer there is no greater satisfaction than being responsible for the exoneration of an innocent person. For a writer who operates in an entirely different world, the thrill must be even greater. Author Elaine Alice Murphy and attorney Rosemary Scapicchio devoted almost a quarter of their lives to freeing Sean Ellis. I know about Murphy personally, because I was witness to the birth of her quest.

I would like to proclaim that the book is evidence of justice being done, which should certainly be celebrated, but it is really about injustice being undone. Taking 22 years to free an innocent man is cause to honor those dedicated persons who accomplished it. It is also condemnation of a system that allowed, indeed caused, it to happen. The importance of this book lies not only in the story it tells about the failures and corruption of our criminal justice system in Boston, but also in its reminder to us all that a similar story can be told every day in every city in America.

— Honorable H. Lee Sarokin, Emeritus, U.S. Court of Appeals, Third Circuit. (In 1985 Judge Sarokin overturned the 1966 triple-murder conviction of former middleweight boxer Rubin "Hurricane" Carter, resulting in Carter's release.)

This is a remarkable story, beautifully told. At a time when too many Black men are incarcerated, nameless and faceless to the wider world, one woman, Elaine Alice Murphy, worked tirelessly and against all odds to free one such man, Sean Ellis. Murphy and Ellis' attorney, Rosemary Scapicchio, spent decades fighting for Ellis, who had been wrongfully convicted of the murder of a police officer, serving twenty-two years in prison.

This is a story of passion and commitment, of confronting and fracturing the blue wall of silence by the police, who stonewalled every effort to reexamine Ellis' conviction even as evidence of its flaws mounted. It is also a story of what it takes to make the criminal legal system fair—dogged determination, years and years of work, and a clear-eyed vision of what is right, no matter what the cost. It is a sad commentary on the ordinary cases that the system processes, the ones without Elaine Murphy's and Rosemary Scapicchio's astonishing commitment.

–Honorable Nancy Gertner, Judge, U.S. District Court, D. Mass. (retired); Senior Lecturer, Harvard Law School

In for Life

A Journey into Murder,
Corruption, and Friendship

Elaine Alice Murphy

Satuit Press
Belmont, MA
SatuitPress.com
Printed in the USA

ISBN 978-0-578-96519-2 (Paperback)
ISBN 979-8-218-13203-3 (E-Book)

Library of Congress Control Number: 2023900353

Cover design: Strick&Williams, Brooklyn, NY
Interior design and typeset: Amanda Gentry, Chicago, IL

Second edition, July 2023

For Rich

1944-2022

CONTENTS

PART 6

Justice (2014-2021)

The Murder

Halfway between midnight and dawn on September 26, 1993, Boston Police Detective John J. Mulligan settled down for a nap in the driver's seat of his red Ford Explorer. It was parked in the fire lane in front of a twenty-four-hour Walgreens drugstore in a strip mall in Boston's Roslindale district. For some time now, the fifty-two-year-old detective had moonlighted as the store's private security cop several nights a week. He needed the extra cash.

Despite the hour, a handful of shoppers came and went through Walgreens' glass entryway. At 3:30 a.m., the drugstore's night clerk, Stephen Bannister, stepped out to fetch coffee at the nearby Dunkin' Donuts. Walking past Mulligan's SUV, he saw the detective reclined in the driver's seat, either reading or sleeping. The driver's side window was slightly open, and the engine was running. Knowing the detective and his habits, Bannister decided not to bother him. He'd bring back Mulligan's usual cup of tea.

Fifteen minutes later Bannister tapped on Mulligan's still-open window to deliver his tea but got no response. Peering in, he saw the detective pale and motionless. Blood and brain matter dotted his face, hair, and orange police-issue rain poncho. The panicked clerk ran into Walgreens shouting, "Call 911! There's something wrong with Officer Mulligan!"

Within moments Boston police and medics arrived to find five gunshot wounds in Mulligan's face: one in the middle of his forehead; another just below it, between his eyebrows; one in each eyebrow; and a fifth up his left nostril.

Some commentators would later discern a cross-like pattern in the shots.

Boston Police Commissioner William "Bill" Bratton, outraged over the "execution-style assassination" of a uniformed officer, created a sixty-five-member task force of the city's best and brightest to hunt down the perpetrator. Bratton established a telephone tip hotline and offered a $25,000 reward for information. "We are going to go the extra mile on this one," he pledged.

On October 1, 1993, two thousand police officers from across New England, on motorcycles and in cruisers, led the hearse carrying Mulligan's remains to Holy Name Church in Boston's West Roxbury district. Hundreds of spectators lined the streets, their respectful silence punctuated by the mournful strains of bagpipes and steady beat of drums. Among the dignitaries attending the funeral Mass were Boston's acting mayor, Thomas M. Menino, and U.S. Senator John F. Kerry. With Mulligan's family and friends, they heard tributes to the veteran detective's courage and dedication to his work, plus a few playful jabs.

The detective's brother, Richard, poked fun at Mulligan's thirst for earnings. "What a beautiful day the Lord has given us for John's retirement party.... I can't think of anything he would have wanted more, other than a paid detail."

After Mass, Mulligan's body was escorted by pipe and drum the four miles to Evergreen Cemetery for interment. Hundreds of detectives and fellow Area E-5 officers stood shoulder to shoulder as his casket was lowered, and three final tributes underscored the loneliness of death: a bugler playing taps, a bagpiper rendering one last hymn, and a state police helicopter dipping in solo salute over his grave.

There for the world to see, Detective John J. Mulligan died blue.

PART I

Playmate to Inmate

CHAPTER 1

Visiting Sean

"All purses and jewelry in the locker!" barked the stout female corrections officer as she bustled me through the visitor inspection routine at Walpole, the maximum-security prison in the Massachusetts town of that name. This was my first visit to a prison. I'd never been anywhere near a convicted killer, let alone a cop killer.

He says he didn't do it, I reminded myself to calm my nerves.

The convict in question was Sean Ellis, my son, Mark's, former elementary school classmate whom we'd known in the 1980s, when our family lived in the tranquil Boston suburb of Needham. Sean, a sweet African American boy, had been bused each day from Boston's inner city to our neighborhood school through METCO, a voluntary school integration program. Sean and Mark had been buddies in the third and fourth grades. Now they were each twenty-four years old. Mark was a software architect; Sean was behind bars.

MISS SANTORO'S GRADE 3 CLASS, MITCHELL ELEMENTARY SCHOOL, NEEDHAM, MA, 1983.
SEAN ELLIS, TOP ROW CENTER; MARK MURPHY, BOTTOM ROW 4TH FROM LEFT.

My stomach lurched. The visitors' locker that the guard was pointing me toward required a quarter to open. This was a problem. My trembling fingers found only Canadian coins. "I live in Montreal," I explained, nearly weeping from anxiety. "I drove down this morning, and I don't have a U.S. quarter."

An open palm of coins appeared under my nose. So, she did have a heart. Five minutes earlier this same guard had ejected Mark from the visitors' line. "You can't go in there dressed like that!" she shouted. "No jeans allowed!"

"Why not?" Mark asked, flummoxed. He'd caught the 6:00 a.m. train up from New York City, and now he wouldn't be admitted?

"We have a dress code here!" the guard bellowed.

"This isn't the Ritz," Mark muttered, but the uniformed official was a stone wall. With minutes slipping away from our allotted one-hour visit, Mark grabbed my car keys and rushed out to buy new pants. I was alone.

"Your wedding ring is OK," the guard said, her tone now gentler. "You can leave it on." She marched me to a metal door with no handle, and an unseen controller rumbled the barrier aside to reveal a male guard seated on a wooden chair in a small room. He handed me a plastic bin. "Shoes off!"

Everybody in here shouts, I thought.

"Raise your arms out to the side!" A second guard skimmed a baton over my body. "Now pull down your collar and show me you don't have any chains on your neck.... OK, ma'am. Proceed through the metal detector."

The alarm stayed silent, and on the other side I squeezed back into my shoes. A second thick metal door slid open, and I found myself outdoors, blinking back sunlight in a barren courtyard surrounded by high walls and barbed wire. The heavy door slammed behind me, leaving me adrift in a no-man's land between two buildings. Suddenly a disembodied voice from a loudspeaker mounted on the second building commanded, "Straight ahead!" Fifty feet on I saw a door in the white concrete wall. I opened it and encountered a seated guard. He looked at me expectantly.

"Sean Ellis," I said.

"That will be booth number two." He motioned me to an empty alcove in a row of a half-dozen identical booths, each fronted on the visitor's side by two blue plastic chairs and two telephone receivers mounted on thick plexiglass. On the inmate's side were a single matching chair and phone receiver.

As I sat down, my nerves returned. Would Sean remember me? I hadn't seen him in a dozen years. Our family lost track of him after we moved from Needham to Canada in 1986. We'd learned of his murder conviction through an extraordinary quirk of fate. Friends from Maine, arriving for a weekend visit to our Montreal home, walked in bearing the day's *Boston Globe*. It was Friday, September 15, 1995, and the front-page headline was "Ellis convicted on 3d try in murder of detective."

Ellis convicted on 3d try in murder of detective

After two mistrials, defendant gets life without parole

By John Ellement
GLOBE STAFF

Sean K. Ellis, tried three times for the 1993 execution-style slaying of Boston Police Detective John J. Mulligan, was convicted yesterday of first-degree murder after prosecutors convinced jurors he participated in a killing designed to steal a police officer's gun.

The guilty verdict – after two mistrials – brought such a sense of relief to Suffolk District Attorney Ralph C. Martin 2d that he was nearly moved to tears. It also prompted Mulligan's brother, Richard, to proclaim that justice finally had been served.

Ellis' parents were not in court, but his girlfriend, Letia Walker, angrily cursed at reporters while insisting Ellis, 21, of Dorchester, was wrongly convicted.

The jury, which deliberated only 4¼ hours over two days, convicted Ellis on the legal theory of "felony murder" – that, because he participated in the robbery of Mulligan, Ellis should be held responsible for the murder that resulted, whether he pulled the trigger or not.

The jury also found that the killing – five bullets fired into the face at point-blank range – was done with "extreme atrocity and cruelty."

ELLIS, Page 52

GLOBE STAFF FILE PHOTO / JANET KNOTT

SEAN K. ELLIS
Linked in testimony to weapon

THE *BOSTON GLOBE*'S FRONT-PAGE HEADLINE ON SEPTEMBER 15, 1995.

My husband, Rich, and I struggled to grasp that this twenty-one-year-old Ellis sentenced to life without parole for killing Boston Police Detective John J. Mulligan was the same Sean Ellis we'd known as a child. The same Sean Ellis who'd played tag with Mark under our shady oaks, attended Mark's birthday parties, and slept overnight in Mark's second twin bed. I had only warm memories of that gentle boy.

Three articles about the verdict were printed in the *Globe* that September day. In shock, I read the reporting over and over. The case had been huge in Boston. Mulligan's 1993 murder was grisly and the ensuing homicide investigation, complicated. Sean had pleaded not guilty. He'd been convicted only at his third trial. His first two trials had ended in mistrials because of hung juries. His lawyers vowed to appeal.

Now, three years after his conviction, Mark and I were paying Sean a first visit, prompted by a recent retrial motion his lawyers had filed on his behalf. When I saw the news report of the motion, I'd dashed off a letter to Sean at Walpole State Prison to reintroduce myself and tell him our family had learned of his case. I asked if he'd like a visit. Right away his mother, Mary "Jackie" Ellis, phoned me to say yes, Sean would like a visit very, very much.

A tall, slim Black man with a shaved head strode into the visiting booth, smiling broadly. He recognizes me after all these years, I thought, as Sean sat down on the inmate's side of the plexiglass. He wore baggy gray prison garb. I noted his perfect white teeth, smooth dark skin, and slight mustache. The adult Sean Ellis was handsome, with high cheekbones and full lips.

"Hi, Sean. So, you remembered the Murphys from Needham?"

"Yeah, I d-d-did. I do. I remember all the p-p-parties at your house."

That stutter. He still had it. On top of his shyness as a child, it had made him seem doubly vulnerable. He'd struggle to get his words out. You'd want to reach in and tug them free.

The birthday parties. I pictured the young Sean, blindfolded and being spun by Rich and me in our kitchen, an excited little boy in a party hat, paper donkey tail in hand, careening straight for the donkey's nose. I'd so wanted Sean to feel comfortable in our home, comfortable in our town. I'd wanted him to become a METCO success story.

"When I got your letter, I'd just gotten out of a church service," Sean said. "I had two letters that day, one from my girlfriend and yours. I couldn't figure out who this could be, writing me from Canada. So I opened it first, and I read and read, and I still couldn't remember. Who knew me from Needham? Then I got to the part about going to Fenway Park with Mark and his dad, and to McDonald's, and I knew."

He smiled at the memory and then grew solemn. "Mrs. Murphy, I know this may sound strange, but I think you learning about me was an act of divine intervention."

The notion jolted me. Had God's hand carried that 1995 issue of the *Boston Globe* to Montreal?

I filled Sean in about Mark being barred because of his jeans. Sean explained, "The jeans thing is left over from when inmates could wear them with their jumper tops. The authorities didn't want visitors getting mistaken for inmates if there was trouble. But then we got these gray jumpers, top and bottom, so the regulation doesn't make sense anymore." He shook his head in disgust. "They make up different rules every day."

"It must be hard for you in here."

"I'm surviving. I do have some trouble sleeping though."

I could only imagine what nights were like on a Walpole cellblock. "How do you pass the time?"

"I go to the library a lot. And I write letters."

"What keeps you going, Sean?"

"My faith," he said instantly, "and my mother and my girlfriend, Pam. She's been in my corner the whole time. I try to stay focused, to think positive, you know? I could get to feeling down, with negative thoughts, but I try not to."

"Are you allowed to contact people outside?"

"Yeah, we can call out collect until 9:30 at night. I talk to Pam a lot, and to my mother, but I don't want to run up her phone bill."

"I heard that you left the Needham schools," I ventured. Needham was our one touchstone.

He hesitated and looked down. "I dunno … Needham was … like … sorta racist, ya know? No big incident happened or anything like that, just lotsa little things. I stayed till tenth grade, and then I went to Dorchester High."

Dorchester was a Boston district of two- and three-decker homes that sprang up in the late 1800s to accommodate Irish immigrants. My great-grandparents had been among them. In the early 1900s my father and his two brothers had grown up in a Dorchester two-decker. But by the 1960s the Irish had been largely displaced by Jewish immigrants, who in turn were displaced by African Americans. Successive waves brought Hispanics into the mix, along with immigrants from Cape Verde, the Caribbean, and South Asia, adding a potpourri of vibrant neighborhoods to the remnant of proud Irish. Yet certain pockets in the district struggled with gang violence and drugs. Sean's neighborhood was one.

Thinking of the violence, I said, "Too bad you didn't stay in Needham" and immediately regretted it. Casting about for something neutral to say, I added, "Did you mind the long bus ride out? It must have gotten old."

"Actually, no. I got so I'd look forward to the ride with my brother, Joseph, and my sister Jeanelle." Sean's voice drifted off.

Gradually we got onto his case and his retrial bid. "The witnesses lied," he said, his eyes filling with tears. "But my lawyers have told me not to talk about it, at least not now."

Just then Mark burst into the visiting room. Grabbing the second phone receiver on Sean's booth, he panted, "Hey, Sean! How ya doin?"

Sean's face lit up, and the two grinned through the plexiglass with their old childhood affection. Mark related how he'd gone to two stores, and how the safari-style pants he'd bought nearly didn't pass muster with the female prison guard. "Army pants, she called them, but she finally let me in!"

They stood up to compare their adult heights. Both were six foot one. Both had muscular builds. Mark's light blue eyes and china-white skin were a counterpoint to Sean's black eyes and walnut tones. My son's once-blond hair was now brown, and Sean's shaved head was shiny. They each patted their head and laughed.

They reminisced about elementary school days. Both admitted to having had a crush on their third-grade teacher, Miss Santoro. They recalled Sean's birthday party at the Archdale housing project in Roslindale, where he'd lived before Dorchester. "I was the only kid who couldn't break dance," Mark said with a laugh.

My own memory of that July party was of my pounding heart as I led eight-year-old Mark across the steaming asphalt courtyard of Sean's housing project. Living as I did in a white suburb and reading daily newspaper accounts of Boston's inner-city crime, I was terrified. On the drive home I questioned my sanity at dropping off Mark—the only white kid at the party—but I banished the thought as unworthy.

Afterward Mark bounded into the car and implored, "Why don't we have a party like that?" Sean's birthday had prompted a joyous, all-neighborhood barbecue featuring music and dancing.

At Mark's birthday party two months later, while the other boys busied themselves changing Transformers—that year's hot toy—from racing cars into robots and back into cars, Mark tore open Sean's present, wrapped in the Sunday comics. It was a used paperback book, an adult sci-fi novel. I held my breath. But Mark simply glanced at the title—*Cloned Lives*—and added the book to the gift pile with a cheery, "Thanks, Sean!"

"Your mother told me you're into computers," Sean now said to Mark. "I liked working with computers, too, at Needham High, but when I moved to Dorchester High the equipment was so old I lost interest."

Sean's demeanor changed abruptly, and he said under his breath, "I know this female, and she knows a cop. And she said the cops know I didn't do it, but they're mad because they think I know something and didn't do anything to cooperate with them." He looked morose and shook his head slowly, as if in disbelief.

"What will you do if you get a new trial, and things go your way?" Mark asked.

"I'll move far away from Massachusetts and get into computers or business," Sean said instantly.

After a few more questions about prison routines, the silences lengthened. There was no getting around the reality: Mark and Sean had finished out their childhoods in different worlds.

"Visit's over!" shouted the corrections officer. Mark jumped up and placed his right palm on the plexiglass and held it in place. At first Sean hesitated, but then he caught on and quickly placed his palm on Mark's, completing the high five.

"If you get a new trial, Sean, I'm coming up," Mark said.

The two of us made our way back to the reception area. The metal doors slammed and locked behind us. Cop killer? Before visiting Sean, I worried that I might find a hardened street kid. Instead I'd found a thoughtful young man.

In the parking lot, a breeze sent brown leaves swirling, and a flock of Canada geese honked overhead. Like them, Mark would soon head south, back to Manhattan and his budding career. But Sean would remain forever locked behind concrete and steel unless he got a new trial—and then convinced twelve jurors he didn't murder John Mulligan.

"I know convicted killers always say they're innocent," Mark said, breaking the silence. "But what if Sean really is?"

CHAPTER 2

Bad News Travels North

When Rich and I learned of Sean's conviction in 1995, we'd been living in Canada for nine years. Rich's career had brought us north. A neuroscientist Ph.D, he taught anatomy and ran a research laboratory at Harvard Medical School when we lived in Needham. In 1986 he was offered the chairmanship of a medical school department at the University of Alberta in Edmonton. Seizing the opportunity and craving adventure, we moved our family across the border.

I was an English teacher in Boston, and after that a program administrator for the Massachusetts Department of Education. In Edmonton, I decided
to try my hand at freelance writing and editing, and my consulting took off.

Six years later, in 1992, Rich was recruited to McGill University to head
the Montreal Neurological Institute (MNI), a teaching and research facility
dedicated to understanding the brain and its diseases. Moving to vibrant
Montreal, Quebec, closer to Massachusetts and our extended family, held
great appeal. I had no trouble finding clients in the city's English-speaking
university and business communities.

After Rich and I digested the distressing news about Sean that September Friday, thoughts of the young boy we'd known swirled in my head all
weekend, making it hard to concentrate on our social visit, let alone sleep.
It upset me deeply to picture Sean behind bars.

When our guests departed on Sunday, I turned to my keyboard for so-
lace. I ended up crafting an essay centering on my memories of the schoolboy Sean: Sean, singing in the school's Christmas concert and then sleeping over, his next day's shirt lovingly pressed and folded in his backpack;
Sean's feet, "oversize anchors weighing down the slimmest of boys"; Sean,
stuttering to get his words out; Sean, a youth with "an uncommon sweetness about him." What happened?

I showed the piece to Rich, and he urged me to send it to the *Boston
Globe*. I faxed it in, and to my surprise an opinion editor called the next day
to say they would run it on Thursday.

I was thrilled to hear from the editor. The *Globe* was Boston's most-read
newspaper, and publishing an article in it had particular resonance for me.
My father, Ray Finnegan, spent his entire career at the paper, rising from
copy boy to sportswriter to day editor. Dad's time overseeing the news coverage was short-lived, however: He was sidelined by debilitating depression and anxiety. One summer day in 1948, when I was three, he collapsed
on Boston's Newspaper Row and was carried home on a stretcher. "Nervous breakdown," people whispered, an invisible ailment not to be spoken
of. Shock treatments at a psychiatric hospital didn't help, and for the next

What went wrong in the life of Sean Ellis?

ELAINE MURPHY

Our weekend guests arrived from Maine with laughter and greetings and tales of getting lost. Along with their bags they plopped down the morning's Boston Globe. I glanced at the familiar nameplate with affection. For displaced Bostonians, the Globe's front page is visual comfort food. I couldn't wait to sit down later and digest the local news.

But what does that headline say? "Ellis convicted on 3d try in murder of detective." Pictured alongside it is a downcast young black face.

Funny. We once knew a Sean Ellis, about a dozen years ago in Needham. He was a quiet, sweet African-American boy from the Boston projects. The Metco Program bused him each day to our local school. That Sean Ellis had become our son Mark's friend in the third and fourth grades.

Who could this Sean Ellis be?

Eyes dart down the column, looking for identifying features. "21, of Dorchester." Omigod! Same age as Mark. Could this convicted cop killer be that polite, painfully shy Sean Ellis? That impeccably clean Sean Ellis, with a mother's love and hopes so evident in his crisply ironed shirts?

By now the young visage looks familiar. Nausea rises as the truth sinks in. The two Sean Ellises are one and the same.

The memories flood back. The Needham Sean Ellis had a disabling speech impediment. His stutter mortified him, and he hardly ventured a word. The statement in the Globe takes on new meaning: "Ellis never testified in any of the trials . . ."

What could have gone wrong in this man's life and mind to transform the agreeable child we knew to a convicted murderer?

My husband and I recall Sean's several visits to our home, occasions the whole family enjoyed. He was a reserved boy. Some details come back: the time Sean slept over so he could sing in the Christmas concert, his next

Sean Ellis   GLOBE STAFF PHOTO / FRANK O'BRIEN

day's clothes neatly folded for school. At Mark's birthday, Sean shyly presenting his gift: a paperback book, clearly used and clearly adult in subject matter – all the family could muster. That paperback is still on our family's bookshelf.

The time Mark went to Sean's birthday party in the projects and came home dazzled. The occasion had given rise to a neighborhood barbecue. There were chicken and ribs and music and dancing. "Why don't we have a party like that?" Mark wanted to know. A loving mother was behind it all.

"Ellis' mother, Mary, had attended each day of the three trials, but was absent yesterday when the verdict was returned . . ."

Our older daughter also knew Sean. With Mark away, she was the first to hear of the ghastly Boston murder and Sean's conviction. She blurted out, "It must have broken his mother's heart!"

We recalled that tragedy had visited Mary Ellis before during those Needham days. Sean's older brother, Joe Moody, was also a Needham-Boston Metco student. One hot June afternoon, a middle school classmate invited his friends over for a pool party. All the kids jumped into the back yard pool, but Joe didn't come back up. He sank like a stone and drowned, too embarrassed to admit he couldn't swim. Nobody thought to ask.

After leaving the Needham schools 10 years ago, Mark lost track of his city friend. Just this summer he mused, "I wonder what ever happened to Sean Ellis. Remember those feet?" Of course we did. They were size 10 even then, oversize anchors weighing down the slimmest of boys.

When he heard the dreadful news from Boston, Mark was stricken. To him, Sean had been a good buddy. He remembered that stand-out day my husband treated them both to a Red Sox game and McDonald's. He also remembered Sean getting into fights at school.

Life imprisonment without parole. How sad the paths of two Needham classmates could diverge so greatly. Though a world apart economically, our own son was no golden boy. He had his difficulties at school but has managed to surmount them, and it looks like he'll be a late bloomer.

Mary's 21-year-old Sean will not be blooming. And yet as a young student he had an uncommon sweetness about him; that, and a caring family, and all the opportunity and hopes the Metco program represented. What turned him to violence?

If we knew the answer and ways to prevent it, the Mulligan family and Mary Ellis might not be grieving.

Elaine Murphy, a free-lance writer, once taught in the Boston schools.

AUTHOR'S OPINION PIECE IN THE *BOSTON GLOBE*, SEPTEMBER 21, 1995.
(FULL TEXT APPEARS IN NOTES, CHAPTER 2.)

two decades he lived a much-diminished life, enduring panic attacks that kept him mainly housebound.

Dad was an accomplished writer, and the *Globe* kept him on, giving him the title correspondent out of compassion and loyalty, not obligation. Sitting at our kitchen table, he wrote obituaries and local stories and the occasional feature article, then phoned them in. When his friends saw his byline they called him to say, "Good to see you in print, Ray." He died in 1970. Now, a quarter-century later, I sensed his spirit out there, swelling with pride at the prospect of his daughter getting a byline.

Throughout Dad's long incapacity, the *Globe* mailed him a small salary. Those paychecks kept our family afloat. The *Globe* had a special place in my heart.

After the editor and I worked out preproduction details for my op-ed, I pummeled him with questions. "The Sean Ellis I knew in Needham was a good kid. He'd been selected for the METCO school integration program. What happened to him?"

The editor didn't know much, but he put me in touch with reporter John Ellement, who'd covered the case from start to finish. Ellement gave me a generous slice of phone time.

"What was the story on this murder?" I asked him.

"The case the prosecutor set out was, three people were in the car outside the Roslindale Walgreens: Sean, his cousin Celine Kirk, and his friend Terry Patterson. They said it was a plan hatched in the moment to get Mulligan's gun."

"Did Sean have a criminal record?"

"There were some pending charges against him," Ellement said, "but it was basically small stuff out of Dorchester District Court."

"What about drugs?"

"According to one motion, a federal informant claimed to have had a conversation with Sean in which he learned Sean was running a drug ring and Mulligan was protecting another, rival drug ring. But this informant was said to be lying, and the prosecution never used him."

Dismayed, I asked, "What about witnesses?"

"Ellis' girlfriend's fingerprints were found on one of the ammo clips. She allegedly helped hide the weapons and faced a charge of accessory, so she cooperated with the authorities."

Hide the weapons? It was hard to wrap my head around this world of Sean's.

"Is there any hope for him?"

"First-degree murder cases are automatically reviewed by the Massachusetts Supreme Judicial Court," he said. "Ellis' trial lawyers, Norman Zalkind and David Duncan, are good folks, reputable Boston attorneys working *pro bono* on the case." (I later learned that as court-appointed public defenders, they received a modest hourly fee plus compensation for expenses.)

"What about motive?" I asked. "I don't get it. A vicious, gangland-style murder just to steal a gun?"

"That was the motive the prosecutor used."

"The kid I knew wasn't the type to shoot someone in the face. Who pulled the trigger?"

"They never got into that. The facts were, Terry Patterson's prints were on Mulligan's car. Ellis had the gun and hung onto it. Why did he? And he didn't cut a deal. If Ellis was innocent, why didn't he tell prosecutors what he knew and cut a deal?"

Some weeks later, still ruminating over Sean's plight, I summoned my courage and phoned Sean's lawyer, Norman Zalkind. When I referenced my recent *Boston Globe* piece, he warmed.

"Should I write additional features or op-eds to help fan interest in Sean's case?" I asked.

Zalkind held me off: "We think we have a very strong case for a retrial, so wait till our motion is submitted to the court. If the ruling is favorable, and we get a new trial, then skills like yours could help. I'll send you the brief when we're done."

After taking down my contact information, Zalkind rattled off instructions for how I could visit Sean at Walpole State Prison.

I froze. Me, visit Sean? Before I'd do that, I'd have to learn a lot more about the case. It was one thing to hold memories of a winsome child. It was quite another if that child had morphed into a murderer.

I figured the best way to catch up on what the Boston public knew about John Mulligan's murder and Sean's conviction was to read the *Globe*'s coverage of the case from 1993 to 1995. This proved a hurdle. It was early days for the internet, and the newspaper's archives were not yet online. I phoned the *Globe*'s librarian to request reprints of articles but was discouraged to learn it would take weeks, maybe months, to get them at a cost of six dollars per page.

Driving the 320 miles from Montreal to Boston to read back copies of the newspaper was impractical. I had little time. I'd taken on several major writing assignments, and my calendar was dotted with deadlines. Many evenings I accompanied Rich to professional dinners geared toward recruiting scientists and physicians to the MNI. Plus, I kept our household running.

Mark was in Edmonton attending the University of Alberta, but our two daughters lived at home. Alison, fourteen, was a middle-schooler at a bilingual French-English school. Janet, twenty-five, had earned a liberal arts degree from McGill three years earlier and subsequently moved to Manhattan to work for a health-care consulting firm. But this past year she'd decided to become a doctor, and she'd quit her job and moved home to take postgraduate science and math courses at McGill.

My research endeavor thus stymied, I pushed thoughts of Sean to the back of my mind, and autumn 1995 turned into winter, and winter melted into spring. My mind occasionally traveled to Sean in his cell, but I stayed in my comfortable groove. After all, the jury had rendered its judgment. What could I do about his situation besides feel dreadfully sad...and wait? Nothing would undo his conviction short of the retrial motion Zalkind had promised.

Learning that the *Boston Globe*'s archives came online in 1996 changed everything. Once I finished my annual-report writing in spring, I pep-talked myself: Sean was still sitting in prison. No word had come about his retrial motion, but when Zalkind submitted it, he'd tap me to write articles. I needed more information about what had led the police to Sean.

And so it was that in the summer of 1996, as dusk fell and relative coolness descended on the stately brick homes and well-kept gardens of our Montreal neighborhood, the lights were burning in my third-floor study. Each evening after my editorial day job, I climbed the stairs and crossed into a world three years earlier and six hours south. My mission: digest every article the *Boston Globe* had printed about Mulligan's 1993 murder and its aftermath.

I told myself that if the evidence pointed to Sean's guilt, I'd stop.

CHAPTER 3

The Victim

Plunging into the *Globe*'s archives, I found a staggering amount of print devoted to the case. I began poring through it all. "City police detective slain execution style," announced the newspaper's front-page headline on Monday, September 27, 1993. Detective John Mulligan's gangland-style execution outside a Walgreens drugstore in Roslindale utterly shocked the region. "Who would shoot a police officer that many times in the head?" stunned authorities asked.

A detective killed in action summons dignitaries, and as word of Mulligan's murder seeped out, three city officials new to their posts hurried to the murder scene at a strip mall on American Legion Highway: acting Mayor Thomas Menino, Suffolk County District Attorney Ralph Martin II, and Boston Police Commissioner Bill Bratton. Joining the men in the predawn mist was Suffolk County's chief of homicide, Assistant District Attorney Phyllis Broker.

Police cruisers holding grim fellow officers began swarming through the Walgreens parking lot; scores of other officers affixed black bands to their badges in solidarity and reported for duty, even those on vacation or with the day off.

A second top-of-fold, page 1 article in Monday's *Globe* was an unvarnished report on Mulligan's troubled history. Titled "A veteran known for toughness, and, lately for trouble," it described the slain detective as "an old-fashioned, bare-knuckles sort of cop—headstrong and street-savvy and blunt."

I learned that Mulligan, an officer of twenty-seven years' service, was alternately admired and loathed. In his nearly three decades on the force, he racked up a sizable record of arrests and convictions. He twice won the department's Medal of Honor for bravery, and his personnel file was stuffed with thirty-three letters of commendation from superiors and grateful citizens. Yet alongside the plaudits were multiple charges of police brutality, civil rights violations, and false arrest.

The charges accumulated, and by the early 1990s Mulligan's "chief notoriety ... was as one of the officers most often investigated by the police Internal Affairs (IA) Division for misconduct." He was the subject of an astonishing twenty-four disciplinary probes. In 1992 his department officially branded him a "problem officer."

Nonetheless, the professional consequences to Mulligan were nearly nil. Accused eight times of physically abusing citizens, he was cleared in all but one incident. Making charges disappear was how police Internal Affairs typically resolved complaints in those days, the *Globe* reported. Three of four federal lawsuits lodged by citizens against Mulligan for violating their civil rights and fixing evidence were settled by the city or dismissed before trial; the fourth was pending at the time of his death.

Mulligan's work also carried a whiff of drug corruption. During a 1986 federal probe of the Boston Police Department, a notorious drug dealer named Jesse Waters testified that he routinely paid off Mulligan and several other officers to "protect his drug operations." Called before the grand jury, Mulligan stonewalled and pleaded his Fifth Amendment right, reportedly gaining the "grudging respect" of prosecutors for not being a snitch.

It appeared Mulligan's past had caught up with him. Five .25-caliber bullets pumped into Mulligan's face in a cross-like pattern looked deliberate—and personal. "It was a message," *Globe* columnist Mike Barnicle opined. Police Superintendent Joseph V. Saia Jr., the chief of detectives and head of the task force, agreed: "That's got us looking at his personal and his professional life."

Mulligan's Area E-5 station house was in Boston's relatively affluent West Roxbury section, but it also encompassed tougher neighborhoods in Roslindale, Hyde Park, and Mattapan. The detective's aggressive policing style reportedly earned him many enemies. Investigators began scrutinizing Mulligan's last three months of detective work. It wasn't hard to dredge up individuals bent on revenge.

Money was another potential motivator: Mulligan was heavily in debt as a result of his overreach in Boston real estate. In the late 1980s, at the height of the city's boom market, he purchased a condo for himself in West Roxbury's Highview Park, and then six more units as investments, all financed by a $1.08 million loan. When the recession hit and Boston's real estate market tanked, Mulligan got a second mortgage and borrowed heavily from friends and even fellow officers to make his payments. Still, he couldn't ward off foreclosure.

He ultimately dumped several units, but in 1993 he still held mortgages on three, with balloon payments coming due. He was also making payments on a Corvette convertible, a Jeep Wrangler, and an Acura Legend, and he owed the city nearly $7,000 in back real estate taxes.

The money problems drove Mulligan to hundred-hour workweeks supplemented by a full schedule of private-security details paying twenty-six dollars an hour. Some days he wore his uniform around the clock. His final paid detail at Walgreens on September 26 was his 190th of the year.

Long considered a loner, Mulligan grew increasingly withdrawn as his investments soured and his police work met legal challenges. Toward the end he "shunned the company of others and became suspicious of even fellow officers." Described as "a domineering person" who "controlled any woman he ever went out with," he'd been married once and divorced. He had a twenty-two-year-old son by his ex-wife and a ten-year-old son by a former girlfriend. For the past two years he'd been seeing a twenty-seven-year-old woman who lived in his condo complex. They shared custody of two cats and took trips together.

"John was the charmer type, with an arsenal of on-the-job stories," this girlfriend, Mary Shopov, told reporters. Calling Mulligan a "hard-working and honest" officer with "unfair blemishes on his record," Shopov expressed bitterness about local TV news reports that were portraying him as a hero: "Up to now there's never been anything but bad things said. He was hurt by it... [but now] everyone wants to know something good about him."

To his death, Mulligan remained an enigma, to some an "avenging officer," to others a rogue cop "on the edge of the blue line." The veteran detective died in uniform, and on October 1, 1993, he was buried in uniform, next to his mother.

CHAPTER 4

Sean's Arrest

The *Globe*'s description of John Mulligan's complicated history was eye-opening, and it raised questions. I'd learned from reporter John Ellement that authorities had concluded Mulligan's murder was a spur-of-the-moment act by teenagers to get his gun. Yet it seemed improbable that a detective as controversial as Mulligan ended up killed by caprice. How did investigators connect Sean and Terry Patterson to his murder? I dove into the *Globe*'s reporting on the homicide investigation to find out.

Forensic testing indicated Mulligan had been shot by a .25-caliber gun wielded by a person sitting next to him in his rented Ford Explorer. This meant the detective either knew his killer, or someone forced their way inside his SUV at gunpoint. The manner of the shooting—"five times in specific parts of his head"—led police to suspect it had been done by "a professional."

An unidentified woman had been seen sitting in Mulligan's passenger seat, talking with the detective just before his murder. Mulligan reportedly had phoned his girlfriend, Mary Shopov, at around 1:00 a.m. Police were said to be interviewing Shopov "extensively." Then, abruptly, the lead was dismissed.

In the days following Mulligan's murder, fear was palpable around the city. Five more killings perpetrated by a .25-caliber gun rocked Boston neighborhoods, and residents panicked, fearing a serial killer was on the loose.

A double homicide stirred particular horror: On September 29, two African American sisters—Celine Kirk, seventeen, and Tracy Brown, twenty-four—were shot point-blank in a basement apartment in the Mattapan section as Brown's infant daughter and toddler son watched. Two-and-a-half-year-old Ma'Trez Brown then dialed the operator and said, "My mommy's on the floor." The call was traced, and police rushed to the apartment.

The women's murders were quickly solved. Police assured the public they were not connected with Mulligan's. A tip had led them to an ex-boyfriend of Celine's, whom they described as "a very dangerous felon." Eighteen-year-old Craig Hood was a school dropout with a long history of violent crimes and a proclivity for beating up girlfriends. When detectives caught up with him, they found his blood-streaked garments, and he confessed to the killings. The bullets Hood had used on the sisters did not match those in the Mulligan case.

Hood told police he'd argued with Celine over a gold chain and shot her once in the head to end the argument; he shot Tracy when she walked in the door. He ultimately pleaded guilty and received two consecutive, fifteen-year sentences, one for each murder.

Meanwhile, the Mulligan murder investigators were following a promising lead. A "chocolate brown" VW Rabbit holding two men and a woman had been spotted driving away from the vicinity of Walgreens "moments after ... Mulligan was slain." The car had "tinted windows, custom wheel rims, and a vinyl cover over part of the hood and grille." Police began scouring the city for the VW with orders to detain its passengers as "'persons of interest." They drew up a flyer depicting the vehicle and asked for the public's help.

On September 28 police found the VW Rabbit they were looking for parked in a driveway on Stratton Street in Dorchester. It was maroon, not brown, but the car was positively identified by the man who'd reported seeing it. Detectives traced the VW to eighteen-year-old Terry Patterson and began watching the vehicle. On October 3 they picked Patterson up for questioning. The following day they arrested him for Mulligan's murder.

Police would not disclose the details of why Patterson had been apprehended. They attributed the motive to "robbery, pure and simple." "John Mulligan was an innocent victim," said Boston's D.A. Ralph Martin II. Patterson pleaded not guilty and was held without bail.

The *Globe*'s reporting on Patterson's arrest contained a bombshell. Relatives of the murdered sisters Celine Kirk and Tracy Brown said the women knew Patterson. He was "a close friend of [their] cousin, Sean Ellis."

My heart stopped. The murdered sisters were Sean's family.

Reading about little Ma'Trez Brown witnessing his mother's and aunt's murders had left me limp. Learning now that I was just two degrees of separation from the carnage of those slayings gave me pause. This Boston world of Sean's on the flip side of METCO busing held unimaginable cruelties. Did I really want to immerse myself in this milieu, with all its anguish? I had only to close my notebook and shut off my computer and it would vanish, at least for me.

Memories of another small boy resurfaced: Sean Ellis, playing on our backyard jungle gym; Sean Ellis, licking popsicles with Mark; Sean Ellis, the smiling, once-gangly boy whose melancholy adult photo was now pinned to my bulletin board—the man whose spirit looked crushed. The man who said he was innocent. I read on.

Celine Kirk had told her family that she and Sean were together at the Roslindale Walgreens around the time of Mulligan's murder. Police confirmed this, telling relatives, "Kirk and Ellis appeared on a store videotape." At least one family member suspected Celine and Tracy were silenced because "they might have been able to implicate Patterson in Mulligan's death."

Other relatives, requesting anonymity, compounded the dark suspicions, saying Patterson hung out with Hood. But the police rejected any connection between Hood and Patterson, and they continued to deny any link between the sisters' killings and Mulligan's.

The front-page coverage of Patterson's arraignment was headlined "Slay suspect said to blame friend." Police sources told the *Globe* he "blamed Sean K. Ellis" for Mulligan's murder. Sean and his cousin Celine had been passengers in Patterson's car that morning. Yet Sean reportedly had been questioned and released after denying involvement in the crime.

Still not disclosing any evidence, officials charged Patterson with murder one and robbery of Mulligan's 9 mm Glock service pistol. The .25-caliber gun that killed the detective was still missing, and the homicide investigation continued.

On October 6, four hundred friends and relatives of Celine Kirk and Tracy Brown gathered in Roxbury for their joint funeral. The women were laid to rest next to each other in Roslindale's Oak Lawn Cemetery.

A few hours later detectives pulled up outside a Dorchester home holding a gathering of Celine and Tracy's mourners. They summoned Sean outside and arrested him for Mulligan's murder. Being with Patterson at Walgreens had made him a codefendant.

Police Commissioner Bill Bratton announced Sean's arrest at a jubilant midnight press conference. Police said it "basically closed" the Mulligan investigation—this despite earlier reports that "three men may have been in the [VW Rabbit]" and that an unidentified twenty-year-old friend of Sean and Patterson's who was "suspected of involvement" was being sought for questioning. That lead had apparently been dropped.

The police theory was that Patterson and Sean "happened upon Mulligan" and together decided to rob him of his gun for a trophy. Detectives believed Patterson was the triggerman: He "opened the passenger's side door, got in and shot Mulligan five times in the face." They called it a random crime of opportunity.

The evidence against the pair consisted of the witness sighting of Patterson's VW Rabbit near Walgreens between 3:00 and 4:00 a.m., Patterson's fingerprints on the door of Mulligan's SUV, and a Walgreens shopper's photo ID of Sean as the man she saw peering into the SUV's windows while the detective slept.

Sean was charged with participating in a joint venture with Patterson to rob and murder Mulligan. He pleaded not guilty. Defense attorney Norman Zalkind appeared on his behalf and asked the judge for his release on $10,000 bail, pointing out that Sean had no prior convictions. Though he'd had six arrests, five had resulted in acquittals or dismissed charges; the only case still open was a kidnapping charge stemming from a recent dispute with a cousin.

The judge denied bail for Sean and ordered grand jury deliberations to begin.

The following day, October 7, acting on a tip, police cadets swarmed a vacant lot near Sean's mother's Dorchester house. They pushed aside fallen leaves to expose Mulligan's missing 9 mm Glock pistol and a .25-caliber pearl-handled Raven—the murder weapon, police said.

This was fodder for the grand jury, as was further gun evidence: A teenage friend of Sean's, having been granted immunity from prosecution in return for his cooperation, told the police he hid the weapons in the lot. Another immunity deal was reportedly in the works, this time for Sean's girlfriend. Police said she, too, handled the guns, as evidenced by her fingerprint on one of the clips.

On October 27, the grand jury handed down indictments for Sean and Patterson for armed robbery, unlawful possession of a firearm, and first-degree murder "committed with extreme ferocity." They were to be tried separately.

Public doubts lingered, however, and the *Globe* chronicled "significant questions" remaining in the case: If it was "robbery pure and simple," why five shots to the face, execution-style? Could teens really be the culprits? Knowledgeable sources found it "difficult to comprehend two 19-year-olds [sic] deciding to kill a detective they happened upon ... for either kicks or a pistol."

Did the triggerman fire from inside the vehicle, as the police first theorized, or through the driver's window, open just a few inches, as some police were now saying? Finally, was Mulligan's murder connected to the slayings three days later of Sean's two cousins, given that one had been in Patterson's car at Walgreens? Authorities continued to deny the link, calling the sisters' murders perhaps "the cruelest of ironies."

"All of the questions surrounding Mulligan's murder may never be answered.... It wouldn't be humanly possible to prove the case to a mathematical certainty," a veteran prosecutor told reporters.

Sean's attorney had a different take. "At first blush, there appear to be a lot of doubts that are developing in this case. It will be my job to bring out those doubts," Zalkind said.

I wanted to believe Sean had been swept up in a classic wrong-place-wrong-time scenario at the Roslindale Walgreens. It seemed doubtful that his first violent crime would be to assassinate a cop. My heart sank when I dug up several blistering articles about him, Patterson, and the unidentified twenty-year-old man who'd initially been sought by the police.

All three were described as running with a "fast and violent crowd ... a sort of neighborhood 'posse' that sometimes sold crack cocaine and often carried weapons ... an informal alliance in which members pledged to watch each other's backs." Their turf was Hansborough Street, near Dorchester's Franklin Field housing project.

I pulled out my Massachusetts street atlas and looked up Hansborough

Street, Boston. It was a short side street connecting the main thorough-fares of Blue Hill Avenue and Harvard Street. Across Blue Hill and slightly north was Floyd Street, where Sean lived during his teenage years. Stratton Street, where Patterson's VW Rabbit was found, was parallel to Floyd and one street north.

I recognized the area. My father and I traversed Blue Hill Avenue many times in the 1960s on drives from our home on Boston's South Shore to the Chestnut Hill campus of Boston College, where I was a scholarship student forty years after Dad. (Dad's car was one of the few places he deemed "safe" from overwhelming panic attacks.) A star shortstop, he'd received a scholarship that covered his tuition, and he'd graduated in BC's Class of 1927. He'd commuted there by streetcar from Dorchester.

I was struck by the shared terrain between my family and Sean's, albeit two generations apart. Dad grew up on Samoset Street, just a mile and a half from Floyd Street, where Jackie Ellis raised her children as a single mom. My grandmother Alice Finnegan raised her children alone too. At age thirty, pregnant with her third son, she was widowed when her young husband, Frank May Finnegan, hemorrhaged following surgery. Dad, the eldest, was six years old. Alice found work as a bookkeeper and kept the family afloat.

In those days Dorchester was an Irish enclave. Life revolved around the Catholic Church, and people pinned their address to the parish. The Finnegans hailed from St. Mark's. Education was another family mainstay. Both Dad and his younger brother Frannie (the baby who never knew his father) attended Boston Latin, the storied public exam school, before going on to BC. Frannie then went into the seminary, and his assignment as a parish priest at Dorchester's St. Mark's was a source of special pride and status for the family.

Dad knew every corner of Dorchester, but on our rides to BC in the '60s he wouldn't dream of stopping for coffee. God forbid we'd have car trouble. For, after the district "went Black" (as white people called the urban population shift then occurring), the crime rate soared, and Dorchester became hostile, dangerous territory.

A flurry of *Boston Globe* articles after Sean's arrest focused on the crime and fear that was still pervasive in sections of Dorchester in 1993. Sean's neighborhood was described as an "urban war zone" where rampant violence kept residents indoors, making ordinary pleasures like sitting on the front stoop in the heat or trick-or-treating at Halloween unthinkable. "There's always a chance of being shot. The very fabric of what makes a neighborhood a neighborhood has broken down," I read. Teenagers traveled in packs and dealt drugs. They carried knives and guns for protection and used them to defend turfs and settle even minor disputes.

"You think it's easy being a young black[1] male in America?" asked one Dorchester teen. "Part-time jobs are scarce, and the easy money is in drugs. ...It ain't smart, but it is what it is, and you wind up dead or in jail."

Dead or in jail. The youth's bleak assessment of what life held, and his resignation to it, pierced me to the core. This was Sean's world?

Terry Patterson's family lived in nearby Hyde Park, and he'd graduated from West Roxbury High School, but he spent his days hanging out in Sean's neighborhood. By 1993 he'd amassed a considerable police record. His first arrest, for receiving stolen property, had been at age sixteen. By the time of Mulligan's murder he'd racked up fifteen more arrests for escalating crimes including drug possession, possession of a firearm (twice), assault on a police officer, assault with a dangerous weapon, and robbing and kidnapping a man. He'd fathered a child and was the object of a restraining order by the mother.

Sean, on the other hand, had no previous convictions, yet he was lumped in with Patterson—even put on a par with his cousins' killer, Craig Hood, who had an established record of violent crime.

I began noticing a guilty-until-proven-innocent tone in Sean's mentions. The worst example was when columnist Mike Barnicle categorized Sean with Hood as part of "an army of sociopaths" then running rampant in Boston's minority neighborhoods:

"The case of the dead detective momentarily exposes the public to a

---

1 Writing "black" without an initial capital was the convention prior to 2020. I have used this form only in direct quotations from written sources.

few of these beasts.... But even with Ellis in prison, the streets this 19-year-old infects remain in danger.... Black predators like these young men are stalking our city neighborhoods ... teenagers who shoot, loot, rape, maim and terrorize so many of their own people and, once in a while, a white person, too."

"Black predators"? I thought, indignant. "Rape, maim and terrorize"? *Globe* reporter John Ellement had told me Sean's infractions were "small stuff."

I felt better after reading an interview with Sean's mother. "I can't visualize it, even in his deepest anger, that my son would take somebody's life," Jackie Ellis told the *Globe*. She acknowledged Sean was no angel but insisted, "He's no killer." She said several of his arrests were made when she called the police herself. One such incident was in 1992 when, in the heat of an argument with her and her boyfriend, Sean angrily walked out of the house with their young child. Jackie had the police arrest him for kidnapping.

She downplayed a second, recent kidnapping charge, Sean's still-open case. A cousin stole a gun from Sean's room, she explained, and Sean took him to a nearby housing project to retrieve it. That was all. She adamantly denied Sean wielded a knife, as police claimed. She was there. It did not happen that way.

Jackie described Sean's arrest for Mulligan's murder following his cousins' burials. "I was just about to serve him dinner when the minister came up and told us that the police were waiting for Sean.... Sean told me, 'Momma, I just didn't do it.' He was just shaking. That was the first time I ever seen my boy really scared."

CHAPTER 5

Investigative Turmoil

Montreal was experiencing cool and pleasant July weather in 1996, and our backyard garden was abloom, yet I was oblivious, my nose firmly planted in Mulligan-case events of three years prior. As I continued my dive into the *Boston Globe*'s reportage, I learned that a month after Sean was booked, a startling turn in the investigation shattered the slam-dunk aura that characterized his and Patterson's indictments.

In November 1993 two detectives on the Mulligan task force were accused of mishandling crucial evidence and a key eyewitness during the investigation. They were Kenneth Acerra and his longtime partner, Walter Robinson. Their accuser: Assistant D.A. Phyllis Broker, the chief prosecutor in the case. Her allegations made the *Globe*'s front page.

The first instance of wrongdoing Broker suspected concerned Mulligan's personal cell phone. It had not been found in his Ford Explorer after his murder and, like his gun, was deemed stolen. But a full week after the murder, Acerra, who was Mulligan's close friend and station-house colleague, discovered the cell phone in the SUV's center console. Police said the crime scene technicians missed it when they inspected the vehicle the morning of the murder.

Broker found this hard to swallow. How could Mulligan's cell phone, a critical piece of evidence, have been overlooked in such a prominent place? Suspecting that Acerra removed the phone and then put it back, Broker yanked him from the Mulligan task force and demanded that he submit to questioning.

Acerra balked and went to his detectives union, whose president counseled him not to cooperate with prosecutors. The official wrote a letter to District Attorney Ralph Martin II denying any wrongdoing by Acerra and demanding his reinstatement to the task force.

Leaked to the press, the union president's letter revealed a second suspicion Broker had about Acerra—that he and Robinson mishandled the photo array procedure in which a Walgreens shopper identified Sean. The woman had first selected a different man. She ID'd Sean only after Acerra and Robinson brought her back into the homicide unit for a second look at the photos.

"Selected a different man"? A "second look"? My jaw dropped.

When word reached Broker that this important witness had been granted a second photo viewing, she had Acerra and Robinson questioned by another detective about the session, on tape and under oath. This further outraged the union president, who demanded Broker's removal as chief prosecutor. But the DA refused to fire her.

A compromise broke the impasse. According to the *Globe*, Broker was called in to meet with Police Commissioner Bill Bratton, who told her she could remain on the Mulligan case on one condition: She must stop all questioning of Acerra and Robinson.

Broker acquiesced and stayed on the job.

Accusations of police misconduct during a murder probe—made by the chief prosecutor, no less—would be concerning at any time. But in the Mulligan case the accusations were earthshaking, given the backdrop. The Boston Police Department (BPD) was still reeling from a sensational murder case in which police had framed an innocent Black man. The misconduct stained the department, and the memory of it haunted the Mulligan investigation from the start.

In 1989 Charles Stuart and his pregnant wife, Carol DiMaiti Stuart, both white, were driving through Boston's predominantly Black Mission Hill section when Charles put in an urgent 911 call. He said they'd been shot and robbed by a Black assailant, and Carol was dead in the passenger seat. He was wounded in the abdomen and losing blood.

Homicide detectives rushed to the scene and began blitzing the neighborhood, going door to door and strong-arming Black residents for information. They planted drugs on some citizens and threatened their arrest unless and until they coughed up names. The police tactics churned up a local man with a minor police record, and he was charged with Carol's murder.

In truth, Charles Stuart staged the carjacking. Wanting out of his marriage, he shot Carol and grazed himself to divert suspicion. He chose Mission Hill to capitalize on Boston's longstanding, embedded racial prejudices. It worked—until Charles's brother, who was part of the robbery scam but unaware of Charles's murderous intent, went to the police. Charles then jumped to his death from Boston's Mystic-Tobin Bridge.

Charles's leap exposed not only the true murderer, but also Boston detectives' willingness to accept uncritically a white man's tale of a Black murderer. The public was enraged over the police bullying and mistreatment of innocent Black citizens, and a blue-ribbon panel, the St. Clair Commission, was convened to examine not just this case but the entire department.

After eighteen months of review, the St. Clair Commission recommended a complete overhaul of the BPD, including reining in its homicide unit, which the *Globe* described as "rogue." Bratton was hired to implement the reforms and soon rose to commissioner.

This all came to a head in 1992. So, when September 1993 brought the brutal assassination of the white Detective John Mulligan in a heavily Black neighborhood, Boston's police commissioner and district attorney came under enormous pressure to ensure integrity in the investigation. Acknowledging the BPD's bad reputation, Bratton and Martin pledged to run an impeccable, transparent probe. They held daily joint press conferences to report on progress.

Broker's allegations that Mulligan task force detectives Acerra and Robinson mishandled key witnesses and evidence was a major, highly visible setback.

Reading of the BPD's history of misconduct and Bratton's repair efforts, I wondered how much cleanup of Boston's "rogue" homicide unit there had been by 1993, when its detectives pounced on Sean.

Terry Patterson's defense attorney, Nancy Hurley, now lodged her own charge of police misconduct in the Mulligan homicide investigation. She said task force detectives John Brazil and Dennis Harris falsified their report of Patterson's questioning session. In a letter to Broker that leaked to the press, Hurley disputed the men's claim that Patterson was asked if Sean was the shooter and "nodded his head in an affirmative manner."

Hurley was there for the entire interview in homicide. "Patterson was not asked that question, and he did not nod his head," she said. The session was not tape-recorded, so it was the defense attorney's word against the detectives'.

At this point the *Globe*'s coverage stopped for a time. Months passed as Sean sat in prison awaiting trial. Then, in October 1994, a stunning news report brought the Mulligan case back into the spotlight: Two of Sean's friends had been murdered in separate incidents on Dorchester streets. Both were expected to testify in the Mulligan murder trials.

On a mild October afternoon, eighteen-year-old Curt Headen was washing his new Volkswagen in front of his mother's triple-decker home when two gunmen walked up and began firing. Hit in the head, neck, and shoulder, Headen died instantly. His assailants ran off and were not apprehended.

Headen had been poised to testify that he hid Mulligan's stolen pistol and the murder weapon in the Dorchester vacant lot.

Headen's young life was reportedly pockmarked by violence. When he was nine, his father, a Metropolitan District Commission police officer, shot himself with his service weapon, ending his life at age thirty-two. Six years after that, fifteen-year-old Curt, having amassed a considerable arrest record, engaged in a spectacular shootout with the Boston police anti-gang unit, firing six shots at an officer.

The night of Headen's murder, Detective Brazil told reporters, "We're absolutely satisfied his homicide is totally unrelated to the Mulligan case." Characterizing Headen as a member of Patterson and Sean's "gang," Brazil attributed his murder to an ongoing dispute with a rival gang.

Embedded in the reporting of Headen's murder was the revelation that his and Sean's close friend Kevin Chisholm, age eighteen, had been killed the previous July—shot twice in the head on Dorchester's Blue Hill Avenue. Chisholm allegedly had information about the gun hiding in the Mulligan case and was also cooperating with the police.

I searched the archives but found no previous report of Chisholm's murder. Evidently the shooting death of yet another Black teen in Dorchester was too insignificant to crack the news cycle in summer 1994. It was a scathing commentary on the cheapness of life in Boston's Black neighborhoods.

The death toll of Mulligan trial witnesses now stood at three, starting with Celine Kirk's murder three days after Mulligan's. Noting this fact, the *Globe* recapped the thickening stew of irregularities in the case:

An eyewitness "fail[ed] to identify Ellis ... until she conferred with police"; inquiries into Mulligan's financial dealings "evaporated when Ellis and Patterson were arrested." And now, "The murder of another potential witness adds a new wrinkle to a high-profile investigation that has sparked speculation, triggered disputes between police and prosecution, and left numerous questions unanswered."

CHAPTER 6

Convictions

The *Globe*'s coverage now jumped to the four 1995 Mulligan murder trials. Suffolk Superior Court Judge James D. McDaniel Jr. presided over each, and Assistant District Attorney Phyllis Broker argued the Commonwealth's case. It was excruciating to picture Sean enduring three trials in one year—and to know the result.

Sean was tried ahead of Terry Patterson, in January. A month earlier, Sean's lawyers filed a motion to suppress two key pieces of the Commonwealth's evidence: the voluntary statement Sean gave police the week before his arrest, and the photo ID of Sean made by the female Walgreens shopper. A three-day hearing before Judge Robert Banks was held to consider the motion.

The *Globe* reported that Sean first came to police attention at the scene of his cousins Celine Kirk's and Tracy Brown's double homicide three days after John Mulligan's murder. The women's relatives told Detective John Brazil that Sean had recently moved into Tracy's apartment and that Celine frequently stayed there. Detectives picked Sean up for questioning the next evening.

Sergeant Detective William Mahoney, who was Sean's chief interrogator on September 30, told Judge Banks that Sean was initially a suspect in his cousins' murders, but detectives soon dropped that notion. At the three-hour mark, the subject turned to Mulligan's murder at Walgreens four days earlier.

Sean told them he was at the drugstore at 3:00 a.m. that Sunday with his cousin Celine, buying diapers. He said his friend Terry Patterson drove them there and that after his errand he made a phone call outside the store and then went home to bed. He denied any role in Mulligan's murder and maintained this stance during three further hours of questioning.

Banks ruled Sean's voluntary statement admissible, opining, "It could be viewed as exculpatory," i.e., favorable to Sean. I presumed this was because Sean spoke freely to detectives. He'd placed himself at the Walgreens homicide scene—something a naïve kid would do. A kid who knew he was innocent.

The Walgreens shopper who identified Sean from police photos was now revealed as Rosa Sanchez, age nineteen. She shopped at Walgreens just before Mulligan's murder and some hours later phoned the police to say she had information.

Sanchez told the judge she saw Sean crouching beside Mulligan's SUV, peering into its windows, at 3:00 a.m. while the detective slept. Her photo identification of Sean, made at the homicide unit on October 5, was the only evidence linking him to the murder scene. But, just as the *Globe* reported earlier, Sanchez initially identified another man.

After making her first selection, Sanchez left the unit with Detectives Kenneth Acerra and Walter Robinson and spoke with them privately outside, in Acerra's car. Moments later she came back into homicide saying she'd changed her mind. Given another look at the same photo array, this time she immediately pointed to Sean's photo.

Why Sanchez changed her mind was not reported; the *Globe* gave only the bottom line: Sanchez swore under oath she "never saw a photograph of Ellis before being shown one in the homicide unit on October 5." And Broker testified, "No one at any time directed Rosa Sanchez to any photograph."

Sean's lawyers maintained that Sanchez was coached. Attorney Norman Zalkind told Banks, "Sanchez picked [Sean's photo] at the direction of Detective Kenneth Acerra, who ... had a long-term relationship with Sanchez's aunt."

A family connection between an investigating detective and the star witness in the case? This was big news, and the *Globe* picked it up.

Banks ruled the young woman's photo ID admissible, stating there was "no evidence before the court that any of the officers involved suggested or directed Rosa Sanchez to pick out Sean Ellis."

Sean's first trial ran from January 5 to 12, 1995. Broker opened by calling Sean and Patterson "jointly responsible" for Mulligan's death. She admitted she didn't know which man pulled the trigger but said even if Patterson were the shooter, under the legal theory of joint venture Sean was equally responsible if he helped. According to the *Globe*, proving joint venture was a challenge. Prosecutors would have to demonstrate that Sean shared a mindset with Patterson. Mere presence at the crime scene was not enough.

Broker outlined her case theory: Patterson drove Sean and Celine to Walgreens, where Sean noticed Mulligan sleeping in his SUV and decided on the spot to steal his gun. After Sean's errand, Patterson drove his VW Rabbit to a nearby residential street and parked. Leaving Celine in the car, he and Sean walked back to Walgreens through some woods, shot Mulligan, stole his gun, ran back to Patterson's waiting car, and sped off. Afterward Sean kept Mulligan's pistol and the murder weapon.

The prosecution called four key witnesses:

Rosa Sanchez gave her story of stopping at the Roslindale Walgreens at 3:00 a.m.—to buy a bar of soap, she said—and seeing a slim, young Black man looking in the window of Mulligan's SUV. Asked who the man was, she pointed to Sean at the defendant's table.

Under Zalkind's cross-examination, Sanchez acknowledged that investigating Detective Acerra lived with her Aunt Lucy—in the same West Roxbury condominium complex as Mulligan. She said she "lied to police" when she pointed to another man's photo, not Sean's, during her first photo-viewing session.

Victor Brown lived on a residential street near Walgreens in the last house before the street dead-ended at American Legion Highway. Brown described being awakened after 3:00 a.m. that Sunday by a noisy VW Rabbit parking in front of his house. From his second-story window, he saw two Black men standing on the sidewalk next to the car. One was tall and thin and the other "somewhat shorter." The pair set off on a grassy footpath leading to American Legion Highway and headed "in the direction of the mall." Some minutes later the sound of slamming car doors brought Brown back to his window, and he saw the VW Rabbit drive off.

Brown was unable to identify either man from police photos, but he later positively identified Patterson's car in the Stratton Street driveway in Dorchester where police found it parked.

Two witnesses testified that Sean had possession of the murder weapon and Mulligan's stolen pistol after the slaying. **David Murray,** Sean's uncle, described multiple conversations he had with Sean in the week following the murder. Each time Sean denied involvement in the crime. Murray said Sean blamed Patterson for the murder and told him Patterson tossed him the guns to hide.

Sean's girlfriend, **Latia "Tia" Walker**, said that on Wednesday, September 30, four days after the murder, Sean brought two guns to her

Dorchester home and hid them. Broker produced the two weapons police recovered from the Dorchester vacant lot near her home; Walker agreed they were the guns.

Zalkind and his law partner, David Duncan, did not call any defense witnesses. Jurors were left to decide whether the evidence presented by prosecutors proved Sean guilty of joint venture beyond a reasonable doubt.

In his opening and closing statements, Zalkind told the panel Patterson alone killed Mulligan. Although Sean drove with Patterson to Walgreens that morning, it was simply to buy diapers. Rosa Sanchez was an unreliable witness who was under Acerra's thumb: "She's putty. She'll say anything."

Acknowledging that police had "powerful evidence that [Sean] had the two guns shortly after Mulligan was killed," Zalkind stressed that Sean handled the guns only after the crime. Unlike Patterson, no physical evidence linked Sean to the murder scene. If Sean were involved in the slaying, Zalkind said, his fingerprints would have been "all over that car."

Zalkind's bottom line: "He had the guns, but that's not murder."

The jury deliberated for eight days. Although jurors asked Judge McDaniel several times for clarification on the legal definition of joint venture, they were not able to agree unanimously on that point. They found Sean guilty on two counts of illegal gun possession but deadlocked over the murder and robbery charges.

Later, nine jurors told reporters they'd voted to acquit. Several had problems with Rosa Sanchez's credibility. Others were swayed by Sean's story, as told by his uncle, that Patterson shot Mulligan and afterward gave Sean the guns.

D.A. Ralph Martin II said prosecutors would retry Sean. "[Detective Mulligan] was executed. We intend to prove that to the next jury."

In late January Broker was back in the same Suffolk County courtroom to prosecute Patterson for Mulligan's murder. Patterson was represented by Nancy Hurley.

Broker again called Victor Brown to testify about seeing the VW Rabbit outside his house and watching two Black men walk onto the grassy footpath leading out to American Legion Highway.

Rosa Sanchez's husband, Ivan Sanchez, testified that as he waited in the Walgreens parking lot while Rosa shopped, he saw two men walk out of the woods next to the mall.

Boston police fingerprint expert Robert Foilb testified that three of Terry Patterson's left-hand prints were found on the SUV's driver's door, along with a left-hand pinkie print that was, by inference, Patterson's. "The prints were left by someone closing a door," Foilb said.

Under Hurley's cross-examination, Foilb admitted that fingerprints other than Patterson's were taken from Mulligan's driver's side door and that prints from seventeen other individuals were found on the vehicle's passenger-side and rear-hatch doors.

Hurley called several defense witnesses. Two Walgreens shoppers, Joanne Samuel and Eugene Layne, spoke to police the day after the murder. They testified that between 2:15 and 2:40 a.m. they saw a white woman with "stringy blonde or brown hair" sitting in Mulligan's passenger seat, talking with him and "moving her head animatedly." The woman's identity was not known.

A taxi driver and Walgreens regular testified he waved to Mulligan on his way into the store around the time of the 911 call without realizing the detective was dead. This introduced the possibility that Mulligan was already dead—not sleeping—when witnesses saw him reclining in his SUV. The cabbie slipped away without being interviewed in the commotion following the 911 call, raising questions about the thoroughness of the police investigation.

It took jurors just three hours on February 1 to find Patterson guilty of first-degree murder and armed robbery. Jurors later said Patterson's fingerprints on Mulligan's driver's side door were overwhelming evidence of his guilt. Patterson received the mandatory sentence of life in prison without the possibility of parole and was transported to Walpole State Prison.

Buoyed by Patterson's swift conviction, Broker aimed for a matching verdict in Sean's second trial, which ran from March 24 through 29. Victor Brown, Rosa Sanchez, and Sean's uncle David Murray again testified for the prosecution. The defense again rested without putting on a case.

As in the first trial, jurors were confused by the legal distinctions. Twice they asked McDaniel to reread the definitions of first- and second-degree murder and joint venture. Ultimately they declared themselves "hopelessly deadlocked." It was mistrial number two.

Prosecutors vowed to fight on, and Sean's third trial was scheduled for June 5.

In May Zalkind and Duncan filed a motion to dismiss charges against Sean on the grounds that a retrial constituted double jeopardy. Had McDaniel done a better job of instructing the first two juries on joint venture, they argued, neither trial might have ended in deadlock.

McDaniel denied the defense motion and moved Sean's trial to September 6.

All sixteen jurors for Sean's third trial were selected on September 7, with enough time left over to bus them out to the Walgreens murder scene. Prosecutors repeated their opening arguments, and for the third time Sean's lawyers did not call witnesses. Five days later jury deliberations began.

The very next morning the third jury declared Sean guilty.

Reporter John Ellement described the courtroom scene, writing that until now, Sean had remained "virtually immobile, calm, almost stoic." But upon hearing the guilty verdicts, he "appeared shaken."

"As he stood to be sentenced by McDaniel, flanked by his attorneys, Ellis' demeanor changed slightly. He breathed heavily, his eyes filled with tears, and his tall, thin body wavered as if fighting a strong breeze in the courtroom only he could feel.

"He turned toward [his girlfriend Tia] Walker and mouthed the words, 'I love you,' after the sentence was imposed."

CHAPTER 7

On the Rooftop

1996

At cocktail hour on Labor Day 1996, Rich and I sat on our Montreal roof deck enjoying a cold beer and a reunion with our three kids. For the first time in four years we were all about to live in the same city. Mark, twenty-two, had just arrived in Montreal after a three-day drive across Canada in a U-Haul loaded with his belongings. He'd decided to transfer from the University of Alberta to McGill.

It had been months since we'd seen him, and we exclaimed over how skinny and tanned he was after a summer of planting trees in northern

British Columbia. Lumber companies in Canada were required by the government to replace the trees they logged. Paid eight cents per tree, college kids typically earned thousands of dollars working on summer tree-planting crews. It was difficult work in harsh conditions and a Canadian coming-of-age experience.

Janet had put aside her science textbooks for the evening; Alison was home from summer camp in Maine, enthusiastic about starting high school.

All summer long I'd shared the results of my *Boston Globe* research into the Mulligan case with Rich and Janet. Now, as Rich threw steaks on the grill, Mark wanted an update. He'd been shattered the previous September when I had phoned him at his Alberta dorm to tell him of Sean's conviction.

First I had something to show him. "I was rummaging around for pictures of you and Sean from school, and look what I found." I handed him a sheet of paper bearing a short paragraph he'd typed in fourth grade on my old college Olivetti:

> *I am going to Sean's birthday party today. It will be fun. I bought him a solar calculator. The card is a funny sealed one. It will amuse him crazy! It is the first time I will go into his apartment building and apartment. I will meet Sean's friends also. I bet everybody is going to bring him sensational gifts because everybody likes him a lot.*

Mark's note brought smiles all around, but smiles tinged with sadness, given where Sean was now.

Alison didn't remember him; she was a toddler when we lived in Needham. I filled her in on some sad background. "Sean's family had a terrible tragedy back in the '80s. Sean's older brother, Joseph, was also bused to the Needham schools. But at the end of sixth grade, he drowned at a classmate's pool party."

Janet chimed in. "All the kids jumped into the water, but Joseph sank to the bottom and stayed. His friends thought he was joking because that was his way. I wasn't there, but I heard that the kids kept saying, 'Come on

Joe, cut it out!' And when they realized he couldn't swim, it was too late. We cried and cried about Joe. We just couldn't stop. It was the first death any of us had known."

I felt a sudden pang. I'd not reached out to Jackie Ellis after Joseph drowned that hot June day. I hadn't even sent her a sympathy card. Worse, doing so hadn't crossed my mind. Shame washed over me.

Mark broke my reverie. "The thing I don't get about the murder is, why would Sean buy diapers in the store if he was going to kill the cop outside right afterward? It doesn't make sense."

I agreed. "A lot of things don't add up in my mind, especially the idea of random teens committing this gruesome murder." I filled Mark in on Mulligan's heavy-handed policing style, his checkered work history, and the many enemies he'd made. "Because of all that, investigators assumed his murder was a revenge killing. They began digging deep into his cases and his personal life, looking for someone with a grudge. First they suspected his girlfriend, but they quickly ruled her out."

"Wasn't money another motive they looked at?" Rich asked.

I nodded and explained that Mulligan died in hock, both to banks and to friends, having overextended himself on real estate investments and fancy cars. "He always needed money, and so he'd work a hundred hours a week for the overtime pay, plus private-security details, like at Walgreens."

"Get this," I added. "After the police arrested Sean and Patterson, they dropped their theory of a passenger-seat killer. Now they said the shooter stood outside the SUV and fired through a small opening in the driver's side window."

"Ah, I get it," Mark said. "A random kid wouldn't get into Mulligan's car."

As Rich turned the steaks he said, "It's not far-fetched to think Sean got framed by corrupt cops. Boston police had a reputation for doing whatever it took to get a conviction."

I picked up the reputation thread and told the kids about the sensational Carol DiMaiti Stuart carjacking murder and how Boston police framed an innocent Black man. When I got to Charles Stuart's jump off the Mystic-Tobin Bridge, Alison visibly startled. "Whoa! I didn't see that coming!"

"Anyway, the police misconduct in that case hung over the Mulligan investigation, and it was a big deal when the chief prosecutor accused two Mulligan task force detectives of mishandling evidence and witnesses."

Seeing Mark's blank look, I filled him in on Mulligan's missing cell phone, miraculously found a week later in his SUV by his friend Detective Acerra, and this same Acerra and his partner, Detective Robinson, engineering a second look at the photos for the only witness to identify Sean. "And this witness identified another guy in the photos her first time through."

"ID'd another guy first?" Mark shook his head in disbelief. "That doesn't smell good."

"Not only that: She was the teenage niece of Acerra's domestic partner."

We were all silent for a moment. It was tough to picture Sean languishing in prison for life if he didn't belong there.

Our steaks were ready. As we sat down at the table, I summed up Sean's defense. "Sean's lawyers said Patterson alone shot Mulligan, and Sean had nothing to do with it. But they didn't contest that he took the guns from Patterson afterward, to hide. 'That may be a crime,' they said, 'but it's not murder.' So at his first trial, Sean got convicted of gun possession but only that."

"It was nuts of Sean to handle the guns," Mark said, shaking his head.

I didn't disagree but said, "Who knows what pressures there were on Sean to help a friend. The newspaper said he hung with a rough crowd mixed up with drugs and guns. I can't imagine Sean was that hard-core though."

"Oh, Mom, get real!" Janet scoffed. "Those guys were bad news."

"Well, Sean's not in prison for his lifestyle. He's doing life without parole for killing a policeman. And he says he's innocent." That was my bottom line.

"What happens to Sean next?" Mark asked.

"His lawyers are planning to submit a retrial motion. We'll just have to wait and see," I answered.

CHAPTER 8

Dirty Cops!

I began checking the internet regularly for news of the retrial motion Norman Zalkind had promised. Nothing. Then one day, instead of typing "John Mulligan" or "Sean Ellis" into the *Boston Globe* search engine, I entered "Kenneth Acerra." I'd been thinking about the detective's sketchy behavior in the case.

Bingo. Up came a list of more than a dozen articles, all published within the past six months. The *Globe*'s Spotlight Team of investigative reporters had uncovered an ongoing scheme of drug-dealer robberies committed by three detectives from Area E-5: Kenneth Acerra, Walter Robinson, and John Brazil.

I sat back. Area E-5 was Mulligan's station house. The men were his friends. They were prominent investigators of his murder. And they were dirty! My pulse quickened at the potential implications for Sean.

The exposé had hit the news five months after Sean's September 1995 conviction. Living in Canada, I'd missed it. I printed every report and devoured them all.

The first article in the Spotlight series, published February 10, 1996, described an illicit drug bust by Acerra and Robinson four years prior. It read like pulp fiction: "Corruption probe shakes up Boston police detective unit: The case of the disappearing money":

"Tearing apart a West Roxbury apartment in search of drugs, a Boston police detective discovered a strongbox filled with cash. 'I like this,' Kenneth Acerra exclaimed, an eyewitness recalled. He stuffed his coat with bundles of money and shared his bounty with his partner, Detective Walter F. Robinson Jr., tossing him thousand-dollar stacks . . ."

Three suspects were arrested at the scene of the May 1992 search and charged with cocaine trafficking. A prosecutor told the judge that police had recovered $8,000 cash. But Acerra and Robinson never turned in a dime from the raid to the department. The money "vanished as evidence and never appeared again in police reports, court documents or numerous criminal proceedings."

An eyewitness said $8,000 dollars was probably far less than what Acerra and Robinson actually grabbed. The strongbox contained at least fifteen stacks of bound bills, each totaling $1,000.

Soon after the Spotlight Team's first article broke, Acerra was suspended from duty, and Robinson resigned from the force. There was no mention of Brazil's fate. A Boston Police Department internal inquiry was said to be underway, led by the city's new police commissioner, Paul Evans. (Bill Bratton had left Boston in January 1994 to take the top cop job in New York City.)

Reading on, I learned the 1992 West Roxbury robbery was not Acerra,

Robinson, and Brazil's first. The Spotlight Team found that to gain entry to apartments and rob dealers, the trio had falsified search warrant applications for years. They cited bogus informants. They lied about their surveillance activities. They often repeated the same five or six paragraphs on every application, citing "Juan Doe" as their target.

Halfway through the news reports on the scurrilous cops, one article gave me a jolt. Published February 18, 1996, under the headline "1993 charge revived in police probe," it made the front page like many of the others, but this reporting had a new twist: It tied John Mulligan to Robinson in drug-dealer robberies.

Sources told the *Globe* that soon after Mulligan's murder, the Boston Police Department Anti-Corruption Unit began looking anew into credible charges made by a business owner that Mulligan and Robinson together robbed two dealers in Boston's Brighton section in 1991, taking $4,000 from one at gunpoint.

If the allegations were true, it looked like Mulligan was involved in his station-house buddies' corrupt scheme.

The Area E-5 corruption scandal began undoing Acerra's, Robinson's, and Brazil's police work. In one high-profile murder case investigated by Brazil, the defendant petitioned for access to the detective's personnel file, claiming several statements Brazil attributed to him were false.

I recalled Patterson's defense attorney accusing Brazil of lying on his report by stating that Patterson blamed Sean.

The final article in the batch, printed in May 1996, reported that a federal grand jury was now considering indictments against Acerra, Robinson, and Brazil. This brought me up to real time. Bursting to share all this news with someone who'd appreciate its significance, I dialed Mark's student apartment near McGill. "Will Sean get another trial because of this?" he asked right away.

"I imagine things will start moving for him now," I said. "If three Mulligan task force detectives were criminals, it raises questions about the integrity of the investigation. And if Mulligan was robbing dealers with one of them? That could turn the case upside down!"

There was nothing to do now but watch the internet and wait for any spillover effect on Sean.

Months went by with no news on the scandal, and 1996 rolled into 1997. Meanwhile, the grand jury's deliberations remained airtight, apart from a juicy leak in winter 1997 about a robbery allegedly committed by Acerra and Robinson: When the partners learned that a well-known drug dealer had just been locked up for assaulting his girlfriend, they wrote a midnight warrant claiming they'd been watching his Jamaica Plain apartment for the last five days and immediately burst in and stole more than $20,000 in cash, a stash of marijuana, and a half-dozen guns.

Finally, on March 11, 1997, the *Globe's* front-page headline read, "2 City detectives indicted in thefts." Acerra and Robinson stood accused of stealing more than $250,000 in cash, drugs, and guns. Twenty-one counts were lodged against Acerra and twenty against Robinson for extortion, theft, conspiracy, civil rights violations, and filing false income tax returns between 1990 and 1994. Each extortion count carried a maximum penalty of twenty years in prison and a $25,000 fine.

Brazil had flipped on Acerra and Robinson. He went free and remained on the Boston force.

The alleged criminality of the Area E-5 detectives hit Boston like a tsunami. The newspaper was filled with shocked reactions from officials and citizens alike; Police Commissioner Evans deemed it as serious a corruption case as any in the department's history.

Because of Acerra's and Robinson's prominent roles in the Mulligan murder case, the *Globe's* Pulitzer Prize-winning columnist, Eileen McNamara, immediately questioned whether Sean had received justice. In a column titled "Indicted cops taint Ellis trials" she wrote,

"It took the Commonwealth of Massachusetts three trials to send Sean Ellis to state prison in Walpole. It should take one more court appearance to send him home to await a new trial in the murder of Boston Police Detective John J. Mulligan.... The Mulligan case has stunk from the very beginning ... and the odor of corruption that hung over the cop who was killed and over the cops who investigated his killing has to make one ask whether this case really was just a random act of violence ...

"Is it such a leap to suspect that cops accused of falsifying search warrants, fabricating confidential informants and shaking down drug dealers might also have railroaded [Sean Ellis] for the murder of ... a fellow Area E detective whose own reputation was almost as shady as their own? ...

"Sean Ellis was not the boy next door. His arrest in this case was not his first. But even young black men with rap sheets have constitutional rights in the United States."

In the four years since Mulligan's murder, McNamara was the only opinion writer at the *Globe* to have taken an interest in Sean. That she'd lent her influential voice to his cause was thrilling. It gave me heart.

Acerra's and Robinson's separate trials were scheduled for January 1998. It meant another year of waiting.

More months rolled by; January 1998 came and went. Finally, in early March, news broke that the detectives had cut deals. In return for pleading guilty to fourteen counts of criminal conduct, Acerra and Robinson were each sentenced to three years in federal prison and $100,000 payment to their victims as restitution.

Seven months later, with the two detectives now incarcerated, attorneys Norman Zalkind and David Duncan filed a retrial motion for Sean. The October 1, 1998, *Boston Globe* carried the announcement: "Detectives' conviction sparks move for new trial in slaying of officer." They based their motion on Acerra's, Robinson's, and Brazil's patterns of lying. Zalkind and Duncan also renewed their bid to suppress Rosa Sanchez's photo identification of Sean because Acerra and Robinson had arranged it. Getting rid of the Sanchez ID "would effectively end the case against Ellis," wrote reporter John Ellement, back on the beat.

I emailed Mark the news. He'd graduated from McGill in June and now lived and worked in Manhattan, sharing a small East Village apartment with several roommates and writing software for the technology arm of the New York Stock Exchange. For the past three years, along with me, he'd awaited Sean's next legal move.

Three weeks later Mark and I were at Walpole State Prison, reconnecting with the adult Sean.

Following our visit, Mark and I drove to my husband Rich's parents' suburban home north of Boston. Over a dinner of fresh cod in the Murphys' cozy, candle-lit dining room, the two of us, still shaken, tried to convey Walpole's atmosphere of dank alcoves, heavy doors, and menacing voices. My in-laws were wide-eyed. Such a contrast with their well-ordered world. They'd never met Sean but were sympathetic.

"It's unsurprising that a Black kid with few resources got screwed over by the Boston police," my father-in-law said. Rich's mother kept repeating, "Such a shame he dropped out of METCO."

That night, tossing in bed on my mother-in-law's crisp white sheets, I thought, "Where does my responsibility to Sean begin and end?" I'd felt Sean's radiant energy and soft sadness through Walpole's plexiglass. Nothing about him said murderer. Yet there he sat, trapped and wearing prison garb, his existence since his 1993 arrest. It had taken all my bravado to act the cheerful supporter amid the gloom.

Before this I'd felt deeply sad about Sean. Now I felt devastated. What if his conviction was a gross miscarriage of justice? Beyond trying to publish articles pushing his retrial, could I do more for him? I was a freelance writer. I spent my days digging for information. Maybe if I dug deeper into his case I'd turn up information his lawyers could use to free him.

"Divine intervention," Sean had said as I sat across from him at Walpole. The notion reignited all night like a trick birthday candle. Perhaps the hand of God did bring Sean back into my life.

Could I just walk away?

By dawn I had my answer. Having learned of Sean's conviction and the murky circumstances behind it, I could never go back to not knowing. And if Sean were truly innocent and I did nothing, the thought of him languishing in prison would haunt me for the rest of my life.

I was in.

PART 2

Motion

CHAPTER 9

Visiting Jackie

1998

The Sunday after Mark's and my Walpole prison visit, I dropped him off at Boston's South Station for his return trip to New York City and headed north of the city to visit Sean's mother. Jackie Ellis had moved away from the tough Dorchester neighborhood where Sean grew up. The last time I'd seen her was over a dozen years ago, at a book fair at the kids' Needham elementary school. I remembered her as attractive and always smiling. It was time to get reacquainted.

Jackie was leaning on a cane in the doorway of her brick apartment building, waiting for me. She was still pretty, her jet-black hair styled in a short bouffant and her mahogany skin set off by a robin's-egg-blue jogging suit. She looked to be in her early fifties, like me.

She hugged me tightly. "I want to thank you for your interest in Sean. No one else from Needham has been in touch."

Next to her stood a smiling young girl in a white sundress, her head encircled with shiny cornrows, their ends swinging free. Purple toenails peeked out from her fluorescent sandals.

"This is Shar'Day, my youngest," Jackie said.

"Hello, Shar'Day. How old are you?"

"Nine," the youngster replied, her dimples flashing. I knew she'd been baptized that morning, but Jackie had still encouraged me to visit. Now, holding up a gold chain with a tiny cross, Shar'Day said, "I got this necklace from my mother, and an Adventure Bible and twenty-five dollars from my aunt."

As we climbed the stairs to her apartment, Jackie gushed about the morning celebration. "One relative came all the way up from Memphis." Opening the door, she limped over to a small card table set up in the foyer. It was covered with a light blue tablecloth and graced with a bouquet of fall leaves. Two folding chairs were set beside it. "I have a bad knee," she explained, easing herself into one of the chairs and motioning me to sit in the other. Like Sean, Jackie stuttered slightly.

"Mark and I had a good visit with Sean yesterday," I said. Then I asked her about Sean's transferring out of Needham High.

"After Joseph's accident, things started going downhill for Sean out there in Needham," she said. "He missed his brother."

This was my cue. "I realize now that I never expressed my sympathy to you. I feel terrible about it. I want to say how very, very sorry I was, and am."

Jackie gave a wan smile. "Shar'Day is taking swimming lessons," was her reply.

I pulled out a copy of the 1995 *Boston Globe* op-ed article I'd written about Sean. "I never saw this," Jackie said. As she read it, I glanced around the tidy apartment. Cardboard Halloween pumpkins and goblins were taped on the windows. A cluster of healthy-looking houseplants evinced a green thumb. A crucifix was prominent on one wall.

"I'd like to help some more," I said when Jackie finished reading. "Possibly I could generate favorable publicity for Sean that would help get him a new trial."

She nodded and then, with a glance at Shar'Day sitting before the TV, began talking in hushed tones. "My brother David said Sean told him he was in the store buying diapers, and when he came out, 'the incident was over.' What I don't understand is nobody heard anything. The detective's Ford Explorer was parked right outside the store's entrance. So, with the proximity of his vehicle to the cash registers, why didn't anybody in the store hear shots?"

"It is puzzling," I said.

"The niece of a detective said she saw a thin Black man next to the vehicle, but it was a tainted ID process." I told her I'd read all about Rosa Sanchez in the newspaper and found it outrageous that her ID was admitted as evidence.

"All the witnesses' descriptions of clothing were different," Jackie said, her voice shaking with fury. "Totally different! And Mulligan was crooked. The rumor was, they found him with a jum of crack in his sock and his pants pulled down to his ankles."

Jum of crack? (I later learned it was local slang for a rock of crack cocaine.)

Pants to his ankles?

The real shocker came next: "David said Sean told him that when he came out of the store, Terry ran up to him yelling 'Come on! Come on!' And his hands were bloody. David said Sean was confused, and he ran after Terry to the car."

Terry had bloody hands? The revelation was astounding. I'd not read anything about this in the *Globe*. It aligned with Sean's lawyers' defense— and it confirmed what I hoped: Patterson acted alone, and Sean wasn't involved.

Jackie went on. "According to David, Sean was upset and told him over and over, 'I didn't do it, and I know the cops will try to pin it on me because I was at the store.'" She sighed and looked exhausted.

I decided to broach an uncomfortable topic. "What about Sean's prior arrests?"

"Sean's police record was minimal," Jackie said, her chin jutting out defensively. "It was mostly domestic incidents where I called the police myself, to teach him lessons."

I'd read this in the newspaper, and it stunned me again. In what world would a mother do that?

Jackie continued. "His case rested on that witness, Rosa Sanchez, and she had ties to those corrupt cops." Her voice rose. "Sean was definitely guilty of running with the wrong crowd. They said he was guilty of hiding the guns. But I know he's not guilty of planning to kill with Patterson!"

Pointing to a metal shelf holding several three-ring notebooks and large envelopes, she regained her composure. "These envelopes contain legal documentation, and the notebooks contain newspaper articles about the case from both the *Boston Herald* and the *Boston Globe*." She opened one notebook, and I saw row upon row of neat handwriting marked by yellow highlighter. "I keep detailed notes of every conversation I have with anyone about Sean's case. I have to keep up with every possible angle we could use to get him another day in court. Leading the charge is a new and difficult role for me. I'm camera shy, for one, and I have this stutter.

"Sean takes after me with the stutter. His was really thick in those days—the kids called him 'Stutter.' I sent him to the New England Deaconess Hospital clinic for therapy."

Jackie's eyelids drooped as she recalled this earlier time.

"Do you see Sean much?"

She shook her head. "Without a car, I can't get out to Walpole very often."

"How do you keep going, Jackie?"

"My faith—faith in Sean's innocence and in God."

"Tell me about Sean's cousin Celine," I said. "Her murder and Tracy's were so tragic."

Jackie motioned to a framed school photo of a teenage girl. "Celine was so beautiful. She wanted to be a cop. My poor, poor sister, losing both those beautiful daughters."

Next to Celine's picture were smiling school photos of two other teen-age girls. Gesturing toward them, Jackie spoke of her own problems. "Two of my daughters got into drugs. One now seems beyond reach." Then she brightened. "But the other now works in a law office in Boston and is a whiz at computers. The lawyers say she's their right arm."

Beside the photographs was a plaque of commendation from the city of Boston. As I read it, Jackie explained, "Sean and I worked with the Boston police to set up crime-prevention patrols at the Archdale project. I raised all five of my children to respect the law."

We stood to say goodbye, and Jackie's eyes filled with tears. She cried out, "I pray that God lets me live long enough to see that boy walk out of prison. He can take me then, but not till then."

My own eyes welled up. "I'll help you in any way I can, Jackie."

CHAPTER 10

The Walgreens Witnesses

1998   TESTIMONY, ELLIS TRIALS 1 AND 2, 1995

I burned to know the testimony that convinced jurors to convict Sean, so I was grateful when Sean's lawyers granted my request to read the transcripts. Norman Zalkind and David Duncan's law office was in Boston's historic North End, the city's Little Italy. The navy-blue awning over their glass doorway looked swanky, but once inside I noted the well-worn carpet, the listing flight of steps, and the hollow, ill-fitting office door.

"I'll set you up in the library," the receptionist said, leading me down a hallway past a galley kitchen smelling of burnt coffee. The small library was lined with law books and boxed case files. As I settled into a chair at one of the two long worktables, I noticed a slight, youthful-looking man with glasses and wispy blond hair sitting in the corner, pecking away at a computer keyboard. Was it Duncan? Introducing myself, I learned that it was.

Duncan delivered some disappointing news: "Only the first two trial transcripts are available. Sean's third trial hasn't been transcribed. We've filed requests and objections, to no avail."

Dismayed, I asked, "Was there significant new evidence in the third trial?"

"No," Duncan said, "even less evidence. Sean's uncle, David Murray, didn't testify. Prosecutors didn't call him because jurors in the first two trials later said they found Sean's denials to him compelling. Murray was the only witness to get Sean's story out, so it definitely hurt that the third jury didn't hear it."

Sean's uncle had been a prosecution witness. Zalkind and Duncan didn't call him because they did not mount a defense. "Why no case?" I'd asked Jackie, and she'd said the attorneys believed there was insufficient evidence to convict Sean of joint venture. The burden of proof was on prosecutors.

A law assistant came in bearing file boxes marked "Ellis." They contained the transcripts of Sean's pretrial suppression hearing and his first two trials. The volume of paper was daunting, but I was unfazed, my excitement palpable at the chance to understand the Commonwealth's case against Sean.

I would spend the next few days in this small library absorbing testimony and jotting notes. Often I flipped back and forth among proceedings to compare the repeated testimonies of important witnesses. Rosa Sanchez had been much in the press, but the transcripts revealed other witnesses who were not covered in the media. More shoppers appeared, as did Walgreens employees and a passing deliveryman. Task force detectives were identified by name.

As I read the courtroom dialogue, I envisioned the players interacting on a movie screen. The ebb and flow of questions and answers fleshed out the story that had been merely outlined in the *Globe*. A picture of the murder night and investigation began to take shape.

Finding Mulligan murdered

Both jury panels were bused to the Walgreens crime site to gain an appreciation of the setting and the relative distances among landmarks. Jurors were also shown crime scene photos of the position of John Mulligan's Ford Explorer.

The SUV was parallel parked immediately in front of Walgreens in the fire lane (the no-parking zone in front of the store). Its position was to the left of the store's glass entryway and directly in front of two pay phones mounted on the building's exterior. The SUV's nose faced the store's entrance.

BOSTON POLICE CRIME SCENE PHOTO OF 9/26/93 SHOWING DET. MULLIGAN'S VEHICLE PARKED OUTSIDE THE ROSLINDALE, MASS. WALGREENS IMMEDIATELY AFTER HIS MURDER. (PHOTO LATER ACCESSED BY THE AUTHOR).

Walgreens night clerk: Twenty-six-year-old cashier and stock boy **Stephen Bannister** found Mulligan dead. Bannister regularly worked the Walgreens midnight-to-dawn shift. He'd known the detective for some time. Business was slow that Saturday night into Sunday morning, and by Bannister's 3:30 a.m. "lunch break" he'd rung up only two customers.

As he left the store to drive to the nearby Dunkin' Donuts in Roslindale Square, Bannister walked past Mulligan's Ford Explorer in the fire lane. Mulligan was reclining in the driver's seat, apparently "reading something." Bannister didn't disturb him.

Fifteen minutes later, Bannister returned to Walgreens. When he approached Mulligan's SUV to deliver his usual cup of tea, he saw the detective's face covered in blood. "I tried to wake him up, and he just wouldn't wake up," Bannister said. He ran into Walgreens yelling for his manager to call the police.

In his cross-examination of Bannister, Duncan exposed the first of several time inconsistencies I would find in the case.

"You left [Walgreens] about 3:30, is that correct?" Duncan asked.

Bannister said, "I really don't know, because the clocks didn't add up right. The clock in the office was different than the clock outside . . . [The outside clock] said about quarter past four, four o'clock."

First officer on the scene: At 3:56 a.m., Boston police officer **Stephen Kelly**'s walkie-talkie began crackling with commands to get to the Walgreens on American Legion Highway. With lights flashing and siren blaring, he arrived at the strip mall within seconds and drove diagonally across the parking lot toward "a gentleman on the sidewalk . . . waving his arms frantically." Mulligan's vehicle was parked to the left of the store's glass doors, "no more than 12 inches" from the sidewalk, directly across from two pay phones mounted on the store's exterior wall. It had just begun to drizzle.

Kelly said Mulligan looked ashen, with blood and brain matter on his face. The detective was reclining in the driver's seat, with his left hand behind his head. His body was "pointed slightly to the right . . . towards the passenger side . . . kitty-cornered in the seat." The driver's window was open about two or three inches.

Because of Mulligan's position, Kelly first went to the passenger door and tried to open it. He found it locked. "I immediately went to the driver's-side door and opened that as carefully as I could in order that the detective would not fall out." Mulligan's holster, clipped to the right side of his belt, was unsnapped and empty.

Kelly called for an ambulance and police backup.

Medical responders: At 4:01 a.m. the EMTs arrived. They observed "a small round hole in the center of the forehead, just above the bridge of his nose." After that they saw three more wounds in Mulligan's face: a small round hole in his left eyebrow, another just above the center-forehead puncture, and another "on the right side of the forehead in the temple area." Mulligan was bleeding from his right ear and mouth. Dark soot particles—gunpowder residue—were embedded in his skin. The medics said the wounds were made "front to back from a gun held within two inches of his face."

They loaded Mulligan into the ambulance and, with siren wailing, roared off to Boston's Brigham and Women's Hospital. At 4:15 a.m. the ambulance arrived there bearing the five-foot-eleven, two-hundred-ten pound, fifty-two-year-old detective.

Medical examiner: The paramedics missed one of Mulligan's wounds, and the Suffolk County medical examiner set the record straight: A fifth gunshot "entered the body through the left nostril." The official confirmed that any one of the five shots by itself could have killed the detective.

Boston police: Detective Kenneth Dorch arrived at the Roslindale Walgreens at 4:25 a.m. accompanied by his squad supervisor, **Sergeant Detective Thomas O'Leary**, and **Detective Richard Ross**. O'Leary took control of the crime scene, and the area was roped off and secured. O'Leary sent Dorch to the hospital to recover Mulligan's clothing and personal effects. These included the detective's orange rain poncho, navy-blue police uniform, gun holster, belt, and $147 from his shirt pocket.

It misted on and off as police sharpshooters took up posts on the drugstore's roof and police photographers and crime lab technicians set about their tasks.

Walgreens employees

Night manager: The drugstore's night manager, **Joseph Alphonse**, confirmed Bannister's break departure time of 3:30. He said he saw Mulligan three times that morning: just after midnight, when the detective checked in; about an hour later, when Mulligan came inside to get a purchase refund; and at 2:00 a.m., when he went outside to check on the detective and saw him in the SUV, "alert."

Alphonse's 911 phone call was clocked in at 3:49 a.m.

After giving this initial account, Alphonse was recalled to testify about the store's cash register clocks. His testimony revealed further time problems. He said the cash registers were uniformly off by "several minutes" that morning. He noticed this when he compared the registers with the wall clock. Alphonse could not recall whether the registers were fast or slow. "Several minutes off" was all he could remember.

Duncan pushed hard: "And they could have been twenty minutes off?"

"That is correct."

"Two minutes off?"

"It was a little longer than that. I don't think it was that."

Asked to describe the store's video surveillance system, Alphonse said four cameras were located in a ceiling dome, all of them clearly marked "Security Camera." None was recording that morning.

That was a surprise.

Duncan asked whether there was any way a person entering the store could tell whether the cameras were on or off. Alphonse said no.

I broke to refill my coffee cup and reflect. So the cash register clocks were imprecise, and the video cameras weren't working. It meant the times on people's receipts were wrong. It also meant there was no videotaped record of shoppers. That seemed big—and perplexing. I distinctly recalled reading in the newspaper that police told Celine Kirk's family they "had her and Sean on videotape at Walgreens." What gave?

I resumed reading.

Night clerk: Prosecutor Phyllis Broker recalled clerk **Stephen Bannister** and questioned him about a disturbance in the store that occurred about twenty minutes before he left on break.

"There was a—a kid came in through the out door…" Bannister began.

"Came in through what?" interrupted Judge McDaniel.

"Through the door … leading outside," Bannister said. "He came in through that door."

"He came in through the exit door?" the judge asked.

"Yes, through the exit door…. He wanted to know where the diapers were. And I directed him to the aisle. Then he went down the aisle, destroyed the aisle … [He] was throwing around diapers … throwing them off the top shelf with his arm and his hands." The kid then paid for a box of diapers and left the store.

Bannister could not describe the man, but Broker noted he'd previously said the customer was an African American male in his late teens or early twenties, about five feet, six inches tall with a slim build, wearing a dark T-shirt.

Questioned by Duncan, Bannister admitted he didn't initially tell the police about the diaper-throwing incident. In fact, he'd said there were no problems in the store that morning. It was only when Broker prepared him for trial that he recalled the incident.

Evidently Broker meant for jurors to conclude this man was Sean. But Sean was six feet one, more than half a foot taller than five feet six. I knew eyewitness descriptions were notoriously unreliable. Plus, Bannister's memory was over a year old.

Walgreens shoppers

Two couples, **Rosa and Ivan Sanchez**, and **Evony Chung and Joseph Saunders**, testified that they shopped at Walgreens between 3:00 and 3:30 that morning. All four saw young Black men in the parking lot.

Rosa Sanchez, nineteen, and her husband, Ivan, twenty-one, pulled into the Walgreens lot just after 3:00 a.m., having watched TV that Saturday night at Rosa's sister's house on nearby Tampa Street. On their way back home to their Humboldt Avenue, Roxbury, apartment, where they lived with Ivan's mother, they stopped at the drugstore to buy soap.

Ivan parked his car in the marked spaces in front of Walgreens. He got out to check his engine, which had begun overheating. Meanwhile, Rosa walked toward the store. She passed close enough to Mulligan's SUV to brush its front fender. She saw Mulligan in the driver's seat, "leaning like, on a hat, sleeping." She recognized him as "the cop that does the [Walgreens] detail."

Just then she noticed a young Black man crouching behind Mulligan's driver's side window, peering in. He was "thin ... black with dark skin" and wore "a black stocking cap." (In the second trial Rosa added a Buffalo Bills logo to the stocking cap.) He wore a "green sweatshirt ... a big hoodie sweatshirt," navy pants, and black sneakers. (In trial two Rosa described the man's hoodie as "greenish-blue.")

Asked by Broker if she saw this man in the courtroom, Rosa pointed to Sean, sitting at the defendant's table.

Rosa said she and the man briefly made eye contact, and then he looked down. She felt alarmed but nonetheless went into Walgreens and shopped for the next "twenty or twenty-five minutes." Asked by Zalkind why it took her that long to buy a bar of soap, Rosa said she browsed greeting cards first.

The bizarreness of Rosa's errand hit me. One bar of soap. That's why she kept her husband waiting in his car for twenty-five minutes. At 3:00 a.m.

Rosa said that when she exited the store, the thin, dark-skinned African American man whom she'd seen peering into Mulligan's Explorer earlier was now standing at the pay phones. Mulligan's SUV was still parked in the fire lane, next to the phones.

Beside the man at the phones was a second African American man who was "shorter, stockier ... kind of chubby" and dressed all in black: sweatshirt, pants, Adidas sneakers with stripes, and a cap. The taller man held the phone to his chest, and the two were talking. They both looked to be in their early twenties.

Ivan Sanchez confirmed that he and Rosa left his sister-in-law's house at 3:00 a.m. He said it took them "about two or three minutes" to get to the strip mall. After checking his overheating engine, he moved his car from its initial parking spot (which was about six spaces into the lot) and parked it in the Walgreens fire lane to the right of the protruding glass entranceway.

As Ivan looped around to make this maneuver, he noticed two African American men coming out of the woods next to Walgreens. They walked to the pay phones mounted on the brick wall to the left of the store's entrance and stood there talking.

I noticed that Ivan described the two men differently than his wife had. Instead of the "green" or "greenish-blue" hoodie Rosa Sanchez put on the thin man, Ivan's "skinny" man was dressed all in black, with a black hoodie "like, up to his ears." His most noticeable feature was "a flat nose." And, unlike the black hoodie Rosa described on her shorter man, Ivan's "shorter, chubbier" man wore a greenish-blue hoodie. "He had a big belly," Ivan added for emphasis.

Ivan said both men wore "dark baseball caps."

Duncan pressed the witness on the headgear. Did he mean "a baseball cap with a little brim on the front?" Ivan said yes.

Reading this, I paused. Rosa had specifically said "stocking cap." I took this to mean a knit skullcap.

Ivan estimated that Rosa spent about fifteen or twenty minutes inside Walgreens. He affirmed that he sat waiting in the Walgreens fire lane for "about fourteen minutes," with the front of his car facing Mulligan's Explorer, and that the two men remained at the telephone bank this whole time.

When Ivan saw Rosa exit Walgreens, he beeped his horn to indicate his car's new location. She saw him and got in. As the Sanchezes drove away, the two men were still at the pay phones. Mulligan still appeared to be asleep.

Duncan asked Ivan, "Now, didn't you tell your wife when she came out [of Walgreens] that the [taller] guy that was on the telephone was not one of the men that you saw coming out of the woods?"

Broker immediately objected to the question, and Duncan requested a sidebar conference with McDaniel. After the conference, there were no further questions about what Ivan told Rosa about the taller, "skinny" man with the "flat nose."

Duncan also questioned Ivan about a private showing of photos that three police officers gave him in his Humboldt Avenue apartment on October 3. Rosa was not at home. Ivan said, "I told them I didn't know what the person [at Walgreens] looked like, but all I had seen was the nose, and I could just pick out someone that had the same nose."

Shown the two arrays, Ivan did choose a photo, rating his certainty a seven on a scale of ten. The man he selected was neither Sean Ellis nor Terry Patterson. The officers did not ask Ivan to sign the back of the photo, as is customary when making an identification.

In court, Duncan produced the photo Ivan had chosen and showed it to him. He did not remember it.

Evony Chung, thirty-one, identified herself as a travel counselor for senior citizens. She drove into the Walgreens lot with her friend Joseph Saunders in the wee hours that Sunday morning after they'd seen *The Bodyguard* playing at the nearby Dedham Showcase Cinema.

During her initial questioning Chung told the police she and Saunders arrived at the mall close to 3:40 a.m. I noticed that in the second trial she moved their arrival time back to 3:10 a.m. Saunders parked in the lot in front of Walgreens and waited in the car while Chung shopped.

Chung said that as she walked toward the store, two young Black men in their early twenties walked near her. She instinctively tucked her gold chains into her blouse. As the men got closer they split and brushed past her, one on either side, and headed toward the phones.

Chung's descriptions of the men were similar to Rosa Sanchez's, although not identical: She said the taller man was slim and wore a blue or gray hoodie jacket. The second man was shorter and stocky and dressed all in black, including a black hat.

By now I was growing perplexed by all the different descriptions of outer garments and hats worn by young Black men around Walgreens between 3:00 and 4:00 that morning. How many different men were there?

Chung spent five to ten minutes inside Walgreens. She saw Mulligan asleep, both as she entered the store and exited. Twelve days after the murder police showed her the photo arrays containing Sean's and Patterson's images. Chung did not recognize anyone.

Joseph Saunders, thirty-four, said he noticed several cars in the Walgreens parking lot that morning, as well as a number of young Black men. He said the lot was well-lit. While waiting for Chung to shop, he looked in his rearview mirror and saw "a tall, slim black guy" walking toward him. Saunders guessed he was about twenty-two and stood about "five feet ten and a half inches tall." He was wearing "some kind of white shirt" and a jacket whose color Saunders couldn't recall.

I made a note. White shirt and a jacket—not a hoodie.

The man walked to the telephones, all the while "looking at different cars in the area, scanning around in the area.…"A second black man came walking from the rear and joined the man at the phones. He was about the same age and had "a stocky build—muscular." Saunders described his height as "below-average … about 5'5"." He was not asked about the man's attire.

The two men were still talking at the phones when Chung came out of Walgreens with her purchase. The couple drove off. Shown the police photos some days later, Saunders was not able to identify the men.

My main thought after reading the Walgreens customers' testimony: "What were all those people doing shopping at a strip mall at 3:00 in the morning?"

Car sightings

Deliveryman **Albert "Art" DeSalvo**, thirty-two, customarily dropped off newspapers to retail outlets between 3:00 a.m. and 6:30 a.m. He testified that on the morning of Mulligan's murder, sometime around 3:15 a.m., his car was nearly hit by a small brown car "with tinted windows" at the inter-section of American Legion Highway and Hyde Park Avenue. DeSalvo was heading toward the mall, and the brown car was heading in the opposite direction. It buzzed through the red light at about twenty or twenty-five miles per hour. DeSalvo watched in his rear-view mirror as the car turned into a side street behind him and disappeared from view.

Though conditions were misty and the car's windows were tinted, De-Salvo said he could see that the driver was a dark-skinned Black or Hispanic man wearing a dark-colored knit hat. He saw two passengers, a man in front and a woman in back.

Duncan elicited in his cross-examination that DeSalvo initially told the police he couldn't tell the sex of anyone but the driver. He'd also said that the driver's hat was beige and that the time of his near-collision was 3:30 a.m. Now he said the driver's hat was black and the time was 3:15.

Walgreens neighbor **Victor Brown** was a cable TV installer who lived on a dead-end street in a residential neighborhood close to Walgreens, separat-ed from the strip mall by a stand of trees and bushes.

At "3:20 a.m. exactly," Brown was awakened by a noisy car backing into his street and parking. From his bedroom window he saw that it was a brown VW Rabbit and that two African American men were standing on the sidewalk next to it. One was tall, and the other was "somewhat shorter" and "stockier." The taller man had short hair and wore "a windbreaker ... with a white hood over the collar, down." The shorter man wore a long-sleeved shirt and dark pants. "No hats."

I jotted notes: white-hooded windbreaker—yet another description of the taller man's outerwear. No hats on either man.

Brown said the men talked on the sidewalk for a moment and then disappeared into the overgrown tangle behind his house. They made "quite a racket, stepping on branches and twigs." He heard them laughing.

A city streetlight illuminated the area in front of Brown's house, and a powerful security light on a building across the street cast a pinkish glow. Brown agreed that the pink light made the VW Rabbit appear brown, whereas the recovered vehicle was maroon.

A few moments later the men emerged from the woods, stepped onto a grassy footpath, and headed out "in the direction of the mall." Brown estimated it would take about four minutes to reach the stores. He said he watched them until their silhouettes vanished.

With the men now gone, Brown went outside to check the car. He was surprised to find a young woman "slumped over" in the back seat, her head on the headrest of the front passenger seat. Next to her was a cooler. The car smelled of alcohol. The woman looked up, and Brown spoke with her briefly before heading back inside.

About fifteen minutes later Brown heard car doors slam and rushed to his second-story window in time to see the VW Rabbit speeding off.

"How many car doors did you hear slam?" Broker asked.

"More than one," Brown said.

Based on the information Brown gave police, detectives created a flyer depicting the VW Rabbit.

During his cross-examination, Zalkind asked Brown, "When you saw these two men, you thought they were about the same size. One was a little taller than the other; is that right?"

Brown agreed.

"Mr. Brown . . . do you remember being asked [by police], 'Was [the second man] about the same size as the first one?' And you said, 'Yes, maybe not as tall'?"

Again, Brown agreed.

Zalkind pressed him about the time he heard the car arrive outside his house. Brown said he first told the police it was 3:30 but later adjusted the time to 3:20 to account for his wife's habit of setting the clock ahead by ten minutes. He said he made this correction after a detective called him to ask if his clock might be fast.

Zalkind pointed out that in October 1993, when appearing before the grand jury, Brown put the VW's arrival time at "3:30 a.m." without qualification. The defense attorney then jumped to the car's departure from Brown's area. "You said you heard at least two doors close?"

"That's right," Brown said.

"It could have been three doors close?"

"More than one door. At least two. It could have been three."

I made careful note of this part of Brown's testimony.

Another Walgreens neighbor, **Gerald O'Connor,** lived half a mile from Walgreens on Huntington Avenue, Hyde Park. He called the police two days after the murder to say he'd seen their flyer and recognized the car. For the past seven or eight months, the VW Rabbit had been parked outside 280 Huntington. The street was one-way, and the VW's owner drove the wrong way down Huntington so often that O'Connor, annoyed, wrote down its license plate: 195 GFR.

A subsequent tip (whose source remained anonymous) sent detectives to Stratton Street in Dorchester, where detectives found the VW Rabbit parked in a driveway. The 195 GFR license plate was now affixed to an adjacent vehicle.

Brown and O'Connor were ferried over to Stratton Street separately. Each positively identified the car. Its VIN led the police to Terry Patterson.

CHAPTER 11

Where Was Sean?

Sean never testified in any of his 1995 trials. When I saw David Duncan filling his coffee mug in the law office's kitchen, I asked him why. He said, "We couldn't possibly put Sean on the stand. Prosecutors kill kids like him."

I dug back into the transcripts, hoping to find descriptions of Sean's actions between the weekend of the murder and his arrest. The testimony I found came from three sources: Sean's friends, his Uncle David, and Boston homicide detectives who described Sean's answers in his September 30 interrogation. Norman Zalkind's closing argument, while not evidence, also shed light on Sean's thinking and actions. I considered the source for each point of view as I pieced together a picture.

Robert "Rob" Matthews and **Lewis "Lew" Richardson** were Dorchester friends of Sean's. Matthews was Terry Patterson's cousin. They each testified that on the Saturday night before the murder, they, Sean, and "a few other guys" spent several hours drinking beer under a tree in a vacant lot across from 40 Hansborough Street. It was their usual hangout.

Matthews confirmed that the Stratton Street driveway where police found Patterson's VW Rabbit belonged to his family. Richardson said the cooler on the VW's back seat was his.

That was the sum and substance of what they had to say.

Sergeant Detective William Mahoney testified twice about Sean's September 30, 1993, questioning session: at the December 1994 pretrial hearing to suppress evidence and a month later at Sean's first trial.

Mahoney said Detective John Brazil kicked off the session at approximately 7:45 p.m. by reading Sean his Miranda rights. Brazil told Sean the questions would be about his cousins' murders; Sean waived his right to an attorney, indicating he would speak voluntarily.

Brazil then left, and Mahoney took the lead. He was the only detective to remain in the room the whole time. Brazil, Dennis Harris, and Kenneth Dorch rotated in and out, "but the brunt of [the questioning] ... was done by myself and Detective Harris," Mahoney said.

For the first three hours the men quizzed Sean about Celine Kirk's and Tracy Brown's murders in Tracy's apartment. Sean was distraught and "cried on and off" about his cousins. His stutter was pronounced. His answers were appropriate to the questions. He was alert and not under the influence of alcohol or drugs. At the three-hour mark, Brazil returned to the room and switched the subject to John Mulligan's murder.

The hearing judge asked Mahoney if he was surprised at the abrupt change of topic, and Mahoney admitted that he was. "I was intending to question him about the death of his cousins.... My squad was in charge of [Celine's and Tracy's] homicide and not the Mulligan homicide."

Judge: "But at some point you started to question him about the Mulligan homicide?"

Mahoney: "That's correct..."

Judge: "And what was the reason that you suddenly questioned him about the Mulligan homicide?"

In this proceeding Mahoney's response was cryptic: "He was asked several questions by Detective Brazil, and his responses were such that it directed us into beginning to ask him questions about the Mulligan homicide."

At the January 1995 trial, Mahoney related more details about Brazil and Sean's exchange:

Mahoney: "Detective Brazil stated to [Sean], 'You know why you're here. You're here because of the murder of Detective John Mulligan, the police officer up at Walgreens.'"

Sean's response was, "I didn't kill the police officer up at Walgreens."

Mahoney continued:

"[Brazil asked] 'Then what were you doing at the mall that night?'

[Sean said] 'I had to buy something.'

'At that hour of the night?'

'Yes.'

'What did you have to buy?'

'I had to buy some Pampers.'

'Enough fooling around, Sean. You know why you're here. I suppose now you're going to tell us that you didn't use the phone up there, either.'

'I did. I had to call a girl.'

'At what time was that, Sean?'

'About 2:45 or 3 o'clock in the morning.'"

At this point, Mahoney said, Brazil left the room and did not return. Harris took his place beside Mahoney. He asked Sean to "recount his actions during that day," Saturday, September 25. Sean said he was "hanging out with his friends, just chilling, up around Hansborough Street." He was there most of the day and evening. He decided to go home about 2:00 or 2:30 a.m. Before leaving, he phoned his cousin Tracy and asked if she needed anything. She said diapers.

Mahoney went on:

"So, he got on his bike to ride to Walgreens. On the way, he saw Terry Patterson, who offered him a ride home [to Tracy Brown's apartment]. His cousin Celine Kirk was in Patterson's car. [Celine was spending the weekend at Tracy's]. Sean said he put down his bike in the back yard of a Hansborough Street friend… and then he, Patterson, and Celine drove up to Walgreens…

"In some detail, he stated that Patterson drove up in front of the store; and he parked between the lines. He said he got out of the car and walked up to the store … [passing] a red truck that was parked in front of the store. He stated that he looked inside the truck but he didn't see anybody. He stated he then went into the store, purchased the Pampers, was only in there a short time and came back out. And that was when he used the phone that was to the right of the doorway as you exit the store."

Sean told detectives he phoned a girl named Harriet Griffith. "He said it was around 3:00 a.m.… that she had beeped him. She asked him where he was, and he said, 'I'll call you back when I get home'… or something to that effect. He said he then got back into the car, and he and Patterson and Celine Kirk went back to [Tracy's apartment]. He stated that Tracy had put out plates, food for them. They all sat around and ate. Patterson left, and then the rest of them went to bed."

Mahoney said Sean was treated respectfully during the interview. No one shouted at him. They offered him coffee, soft drinks, and cigarettes, which he refused. Twice they asked him to speak on tape, but he declined, saying, "Everything you need to know you've got in those notebooks." It was not until later that Sean said he wanted to end the interview. At no point did he ask for a lawyer.

Under Zalkind's cross-examination, Mahoney agreed that throughout the interview Sean denied having anything to do with Mulligan's murder. He said Sean told them he wore a dark T-shirt and Boss blue jeans that morning.

I made notes: Bannister's diaper-thrower wore a dark T-shirt.

The day after Sean's interrogation, detectives retrieved Sean's purchased box of diapers (they were actually Luvs, not Pampers) from his cousin Tracy's apartment, along with its timed and dated Walgreens receipt.

At Sean's second trial in March 1995, **Detective John Brazil** and **Detective Dennis Harris** described Sean's September 30 interrogation. They repeated Mahoney's trial-one testimony practically word for word.

Pressed by Zalkind, Brazil admitted that Sean's relatives had arrived at the police station that night.

"You didn't let his mother come in to see him, did you?" challenged Zalkind.

"I don't believe it was asked," Brazil retorted.

On redirect, Broker pointed out that Sean, then nineteen, was technically an adult, and the presence of a parent or guardian was not required.

Latia "Tia" Walker was Sean's girlfriend in 1993. She and her baby boy (not Sean's child) lived in her mother's home in Dorchester. In answer to Broker's questions about background, she said she saw Sean regularly but knew Patterson only "distantly." Earlier that September, Sean had begun living with his cousin Tracy, but sometimes he stayed overnight in Dorchester with either his mother or her.

In both trials Tia testified identically about Sean's whereabouts and actions in the days following the murder. She did not see Sean the weekend of Mulligan's murder. He stayed over with her the following Wednesday night, September 29; the next morning they took a taxi together to Tracy's apartment. The jury wasn't told that this apartment was the site of Tracy's and Celine's double homicide approximately twelve hours earlier.

She said she waited in the hallway while Sean went into the apartment. She heard him cry out. Moments later he came out carrying a bag. They went back to her house, and Sean pulled out of the bag fresh underwear, a clean shirt, and two guns with their ammunition clips. She said he hid the weapons under her bedroom nightstand.

The next day, October 1, Sean's friends Curt Headen and Kevin Chisholm came to Tia's bedroom. She said she showed them the guns, and Headen wiped them with a sock and took them away. She thought he hid them in a nearby field.

Broker produced the two weapons that police recovered in Dorchester. Tia identified them as the guns Sean took from his bag.

The jury wasn't told that Headen and Chisholm were subsequently murdered.

Following Tia's testimony, **Sergeant Robert Foilb** from the Boston Police Department's fingerprint unit testified that a print matching Tia's was found on the ammunition clip of one of the guns. He said no traces of Sean's prints were found on Mulligan's SUV, either inside or outside.

In trials one and two, **David Murray**, Jackie Ellis' brother, testified about several conversations he had with Sean in the week after the murder. Comparing both of Murray's testimonies yielded the following picture:

According to Murray, on Saturday, October 2, Jackie phoned him saying Sean was distraught and crying but wouldn't confide in her. "Come out and try to talk with [him], try to find out what's going on," she pleaded.

I added this date to the timeline I'd begun keeping: Sean's uncle began speaking with him the day after police released him from questioning.

Finding Sean shut in his room, Murray persuaded his nephew to go with him to a nearby McDonald's: "I asked Sean what was his involvement ... I asked him to be honest with me as far as what had happened up at Walgreens.... 'Nothing,' he said."

After some minutes passed, Sean opened up: "He said, 'I didn't do it.' That was the first thing out of his mouth.... He [told] me he was in Walgreens that morning...he was there buying Pampers...he didn't say what time.... He told me upon leaving Walgreens he went out the door. And Terry Patterson was yelling at him, 'Come on, come on.' And Sean replied, 'What's going on? What's wrong?' And Patterson started running.

"Sean told me he ran after Patterson. They ran across the parking lot, and they got into the car by the bushes. Upon getting into the car, Terry threw him two guns. And [Sean said] 'What's wrong, what's wrong?' And Terry said, 'I shot someone, I shot someone.'"

I paused for a moment. What did Murray mean, "across the parking lot" and "by the bushes"? This must be how Sean described his run from Walgreens through the woods to Victor Brown's street a short distance away. The bottom line: Patterson's car was now parked in a new place.

Broker asked Murray what time this was. Murray could not recall. But after refreshing his memory by reading the transcript of his October 1993 grand jury testimony, he responded, "Sean told me that it happened around quarter to 4, 4 o'clock…"

Murray continued: "Sean … told me after he got into the car … Patterson was wiping the blood off his hands, on the steering wheel and his clothing."

I exhaled a soft "whoa." Blood. Here it was, in sworn testimony, just as Jackie said. I still couldn't believe the *Globe* never reported this testimony, so damning to Patterson. No wonder the first two juries found Murray's testimony about Sean's denials compelling.

Sean's uncle said he returned to Jackie's house the next morning, and he and Sean resumed discussing what went down at Walgreens. "He said he didn't do it, he didn't do it … [and] when he got to the part about Patterson wiping the blood off of him[self] … that's when he started crying.…

"I said, 'Sean, you know there's a thing called joint venture, and … if a felony is committed by … two persons … both persons could be charged with the same crime. Again, he kept saying, 'I didn't do it, Uncle David.'"

Murray continued describing the scene:

At this point, Jackie began knocking on Sean's bedroom door. Sean begged her, "Ma, leave us alone, leave us alone." Murray said he urged Sean to tell his story to Detective John Brazil, but Sean resisted.

Jackie then said she wanted to phone a lawyer she'd once worked for. Murray didn't like the idea and again pleaded with Sean to talk to Brazil. This time Sean said yes. So they went to Murray's house and phoned the detective.

Broker did not question Murray about what they and Brazil said.

I thought about this. Why did Murray urge his nephew to speak with Brazil instead of calling a lawyer? It seemed odd. If my son or nephew were at risk of being accused of a crime, getting legal help would be my first move. Then it got odder.

Broker asked Murray about his subsequent conversation with Sean. "It was about the guns," Murray said. "I asked him, had he picked up the guns? He told me his prints might be on the guns. Sean was worried about Patterson fingering him as the triggerman."

"What did Sean Ellis tell you about where those guns were?" Broker asked.

"That they were buried…in plastic bags. He didn't tell me where.…He said they were buried in…separate bags in a field. That was it."

"Mr. Murray, did Sean Ellis tell you that he had a good hide at 4 Oakcrest Street [Tracy Brown's address]?

"Yes," Murray said.

Zalkind began his cross examination by clearing up Murray's frequent allusions to Detective Brazil: "Now, all the time you talked to Sean Ellis, you were also talking to the police, is that right?"

"Yes, I was," Murray admitted.

This was a bombshell: Sean's uncle was actually informing on his nephew to Brazil? I'd not put this together. Who would imagine it?

Zalkind continued: "Now, do you remember when the prosecutor asked you about [how], once Patterson was arrested, [Sean] was worried that Patterson would finger him?… And, at that same time … he said to you, 'Uncle, I swear to you, I did not do it?'"

"That's correct," Murray responded to each question.

"And you knew there was a reward for finding whoever did this, is that right?"

"That's right."

"But you knew you couldn't get this reward, because he didn't confess anything to you?"

"I object in that form," Broker said, and Judge McDaniel sustained the objection.

In the second trial, Zalkind again bore in on Murray's role as a police informant looking for payment for information leading to the arrest of Mulligan's killer. "By the way, Mr. Murray, when you were first talking to Sean, you thought you might get a reward, is that correct?"

"At first, no."

"At some point, the police had talked to you about getting a reward?"

"Afterwards, yes," Murray admitted.

"And, at some point just recently, the police have seen you, and they've indicated to you you're not going to be able to get a reward?"

Broker objected to the question. Her objection was sustained.

In his closing address to jurors in trial one, Norman Zalkind enlarged the time frame for Mulligan's murder to "sometime between 2:00 in the morning and a little before 3:49," the time of the 911 call. He pointed out, "Nobody really puts their head into that car, into that window, and confirms that [Mulligan was alive] except [Walgreens manager] Alphonse, sometime between 1:30 and 2:00."

He called Walgreens neighbor Victor Brown "credible," but warned jurors, "he may not be totally accurate on everything.... Certainly, two guys woke him up around 3:30 that morning ... he's trying his best to tell the truth of what he saw ... and he doesn't identify Sean Ellis as one of those people. He makes no identification... but he tells us something else that's a little bit interesting, and you should think about it. He says that there may be two or three [car] doors that close. So, when somebody was coming back into that car, were there two people, or were there three people? Was there somebody that was actually at Walgreens already and that came back with Terry Patterson and somebody else? ... I want you to think about this."

Ticking off the different jacket colors witnesses described, Zalkind again questioned the number of men at Walgreens. "Is it really two men? Is that the magic number, two men?"

He disputed Rosa's and Ivan Sanchez's separate sightings of a tall, thin man, saying it was impossible for one man—Sean—to be in two places at the same time: peering into Mulligan's SUV and walking out of the trees into the parking lot. "This all happens in one minute," he reminded jurors.

Zalkind dismissed Rosa Sanchez's expressed fear of the man positioned next to the SUV, saying this didn't jibe with her nonchalantly browsing for greeting cards moments later. "She says that the person is crouching down. She sees nothing in his hands.... She doesn't see any box or anything.... What did he do with the Pampers if it was Sean Ellis?" She also said the man had no facial hair. "Well, Sean Ellis has a mustache."

Sean had a mustache? I made a note. Not one Walgreens witness had described this.

Zalkind emphasized that Sean spoke voluntarily with detectives and signed away his right to an attorney. "He doesn't see his relatives. He's a stutterer. He's a kid. And he's in there talking [to the police]... for hours ... conversational, no resisting, no evasion. And Sean Ellis told [them] he was at Walgreens... used the phone... [but he] consistently denies being involved in the shooting of Officer Mulligan....

"He wants to help Terry Patterson, and he knows possessing firearms is a serious crime. And you have to decide that separate issue in this case, the possession of the firearms. If he's guilty of it, you've got to, of course, convict him of the possession of those firearms. And he is admitting that he got the firearms after this horrible act occurred.... We know he's trying to hide the police officer's gun that Patterson took. And we know in this community his girlfriend is hiding it and... that people are passing these guns around. And he doesn't want to hurt [Patterson]. He doesn't want to tell the police about his friend. But ... he's not afraid to talk to the police, because he knows he didn't kill a police officer. He knows he didn't rob anybody.

"But he talks to his uncle, and he trusts his uncle, even though his uncle is secretly working with the police and, at that time, looking for a reward. And his uncle is pushing him. Time and time again, he's pushing him and starting to talk about things like joint venture. And what does

Sean Ellis tell to this most trusted human being, the person the family brings in that he can trust? 'I didn't do anything. I didn't kill the police officer. I didn't do it.'

"But he gives his uncle some details ... [that] Terry says, 'Come, come.' He doesn't even know what it's about. And he follows Terry. And he gets to the car, and he's handed these firearms....

"Now, Terry Patterson's prints were on [Mulligan's driver-side] door ... and that's consistent with what Sean Ellis tells his uncle, that Terry shot the police officer, at least [Terry] said he did. Sean didn't say he saw him do it. But where are Sean Ellis' fingerprints? ... If you were robbing that car, you'd be all over that car. You have to get in the car. You have to be looking in the car. You'd have to be touching the car. And that's why they got Terry's prints. But ... they don't have Sean's prints."

As for joint venture, Zalkind counseled jurors, "A knowing spectator is not a joint venturer. Mere presence is not a joint venturer. If he took these firearms after the crime, that is not a joint venturer. They have to prove you have the mental state, that you joined in the venture."

He listed areas of reasonable doubt. "Could it have been Sean Ellis that left from the Brown residence? ... First of all, they haven't proven it. But, even if you believe they did prove it to you, what did he do? ... Where is the trail of evidence? ... [I]f the links aren't there, you have to acquit.

"Now, has there been doubts raised? Has there been doubts raised through Rosa Sanchez ... this young, probably troubled woman who just will make up anything at any time? Two [men] coming, and one crouching, and then one coming, and all these different stories.

"And [Joseph] Saunders seeing other people, the numbers changing, does that give you a doubt? ... Does [sic] the descriptions give you a doubt? When you really come down to it, are you able to convict a man on this evidence?"

Reading over Zalkind's impassioned defense, I felt he'd done a good job for Sean. Had I been on the jury, I would have voted to acquit.

CHAPTER 12

No Violin

1998

After my law office reading, as I drove back to Montreal through the red and gold New Hampshire hills, thoughts of David Murray's testimony swirled in my mind. "Terry's hands were bloody." Would Sean have shared this damning detail with his uncle if he were truly in a murderous joint venture with Terry Patterson? Would he have cried and been distraught in the days after the murder, as Murray said?

I reflected on how much ground I'd covered during my Boston stay. I'd reconnected with Sean and Jackie and met the adorable Shar'Day. I'd committed to helping their family. I'd introduced myself to David Duncan. By reading the testimony from Sean's first two trials, I'd developed baseline knowledge of the case.

I was gripped by the eerie sensation of having crossed from two dimensions to three. Until now I'd only read words on paper about Sean and his case. The past several days had catapulted me into the real-time world of the actual players. It felt otherworldly, like starting out in the audience of a play and suddenly jumping onstage and joining the actors.

The feeling intensified when Sean's now-girlfriend, Pam Boykin, phoned me the day after I arrived home. "Thank you for visiting Sean," she said. "I love him with all my heart."

I had so many questions about Sean's life in Dorchester, and here I was, on the phone with the person who was now perhaps closest to him. I was curious. Why would this young woman devote herself to a man sentenced to life without parole? "Tell me about yourself, Pam," I said.

She said she worked at a real estate company in Boston's Faneuil Hall Marketplace and lived alone in Dorchester near the Ashmont T station. I saw the chance to make a connection. "Ashmont—that's where my father grew up," I said. "He lived on Samoset Street, by St. Mark's church."

"That's near my street!"

"How do you think Sean is doing?"

"Well, he doesn't sleep well."

"Yes, he mentioned that."

"After breakfast, he exercises and then goes to the library. He works in the kitchen from 1:00 till 6:30, but it's hard for him to be on his feet that long. His knees bother him. After work he goes back to the library to read law books and research his case."

"Were you dating Sean in 1993?"

"Yes, we'd just begun seeing each other before the incident."

"What about Tia Walker?"

Pam's tone grew testy. "The newspaper described her as his girlfriend, but it wasn't that way. Sean had broken up with Tia before he started going with me. But she wanted to get Sean back. She was obsessed with Sean, crazy. She wanted him all to herself. She was always in the courtroom. She was at Sean's sentencing."

Pam was animated now. "Tia told the cops she got the guns from Sean. Why did she do this? Because the cops threatened to take her child away, I guess because of her knowledge of Sean's involvement at Walgreens. So she was forced to say it."

I stared at my phone receiver. Tia testified about the guns because the cops threatened her?

I remembered reading that after hearing his verdict, Sean turned to Tia in the courtroom and mouthed the words "I love you!"

Learning about this case was like peeling an onion, layer by layer.

"How did the whole ordeal with the trials affect you, Pam?"

Her answer surprised me. "Oh, I couldn't take all that. I went down to Alabama, to my parents' house in Mobile. But I kept in touch with Sean." Her voice dipped low. "Afterward, I felt like I'd lost my best friend."

As gently as I could, I asked, "Was Sean violent, like the newspaper reported? Was he running with a gang?"

Pam laughed and fairly shouted, "No! They weren't into bad things. I wasn't interested in anyone like that, anyone violent or in a gang. Plus, my father would never have allowed me to be with a guy like that. He'd kill me. I was brought up strict. Sean didn't even like to argue. He wouldn't argue with me. If I'd start something, he'd say, 'OK, girl, when you get a better attitude, call me back and we'll talk then.'"

"Didn't he get into some trouble though?" I said, thinking of his half-dozen arrests.

Pam's voice turned steely. "Sean had no convictions."

She changed the subject. "I really admire Sean. He has endured so much, losing Tracy and Celine and then his two best friends."

"And his brother, Joseph," I reminded her.

"Yeah, Sean sure took it hard about Joe," Pam agreed. "His mother told me they were really, really close. Sean had a favorite bike in those days, and he'd end up riding over to Joe's grave and just sitting on top of it for the rest of the day. He did that on many, many days."

Swallowing hard, I asked her about her prison visits.

"I just go whenever I can," she said. "I take the train, and then a cab from the train station to the prison. And when I'm short of cab fare, I walk."

"Walk?" I pictured the forlorn road leading to the prison. "It has to be four miles, Pam."

"Some of the guards at Walpole have taken to Sean," she said, her mood brighter. "One woman guard who used to be mean is now nice to him. She says, 'Hang in, you'll be outta here.'"

As our conversation ended, Pam said, "What bothers me most is, how can Sean be held accountable for the actions of another? That is central to this case!"

A week later I received a letter from Jackie.

> Hi, Elaine. I am writing this letter to let you know how much I appreciated your visit. You know, at one time I felt that no one cared about what happened to Sean but me. And it feels good to know I am not alone. I know Sean's fiancée [Pam] cares, and believe me she has been very supportive. But she doesn't relate as another mother would. ... It felt good talking to another parent who genuinely cared ...
>
> Elaine, your visit has really empowered me to continue on in my battle to see that my son gets a fair and justified trial. Right now I'm struggling to keep my head above water. I'm worried about Sean, and I have an older sister, the mother of my two dead nieces, who is battling cancer. She's the only one I'm close to out of 11 surviving siblings ...
>
> I hope our re-acquaintance is the beginning of a long relationship. I have to close my letter now. I will keep in touch. May God bless and keep you. Love, Jackie

I wrote back right away to thank Jackie and tell her how I sympathized with her as a mother. By now I'd written two articles about Sean to pitch to the *Boston Globe*. My intent was to humanize him, to counteract the negative press back in 1993. I tucked drafts of my articles into the envelope and asked Jackie for her comments and closed with words of encouragement: "Everyone I tell about this case is amazed by what they hear.... Keep in touch, Jackie, and keep your spirits up."

A letter postmarked Walpole State Prison arrived next.

> *To a Special Person and Dear Friend. Hello Mrs. Murphy,*
>
> *How are you doing? I hope that as this letter travels the distance between us that it finds you and your family in the best of health, as well as spirits. As for myself, I am trying to maintain my health and sanity, all while striving to overcome the hardships evolving around my life. It is a wonder that my pleasant memories have not been completely void [sic].*
>
> *I did enjoy the visit, and the break-dancing Mark spoke of....I didn't know what I was doing back then, I had big feet and two left ones at that.*
>
> *Actually Mrs. Murphy, you are an answer to my prayers. When my attorneys filed the motion for a new trial, I was told that the media may try to make contact with me for a statement. If they did, I should say "no comment." I understood the advice due to the ability of the media to utilize the "forked tongue." However, I was crushed, because I have been wronged, and this is not fair.*
>
> *The assistant district attorney knows about those [corrupt] officers and the scenario with the Rosa girl, but it is as if a blind eye was turned on the situation. Things are just so wrong, and it's against human nature to sit and watch yourself be wronged. That's exactly what I'm required to do, 'don't say anything because it may be taken the wrong way.' Just sitting is hard.*

It is a blessing to have you back in my life. It is a blessing that
you have the ambition you have and offer. Thank you very much.

With Sincere Love, Yours Truly,
Sean K. Ellis

"Strike the snitching reference," Pam commanded on the phone, her voice agitated. "Sean wants you to."

"Snitching reference?" What did Pam mean?

"Sean read your article. Mrs. Ellis sent it to him. And a couple of sentences you wrote make it sound like Sean said Terry committed the murder. And he's very, very upset. He does not want Terry's name mentioned at all. 'That's making it sound like I'm a snitch!' he said."

I couldn't imagine what I'd done. Nervously, I retrieved my draft, and Pam guided me to the offending passage:

According to Sean, he went into the drugstore by himself to buy
diapers (a purchase police confirmed), and when he came out, the
murder had occurred and a bloodied Patterson was shouting,
'Come on, Sean, come on. I've shot someone.' Sean jumped into the
car with his companion and they sped away from the scene. He also
held onto the guns Patterson tossed him and hid them for a time.

Pam said, "Sean still doesn't know what really happened at Walgreens. He never saw what happened. He never heard what happened. So how could he know? He was totally confused during that period. And he's still confused."

Now I was confused. Hadn't I simply restated his uncle's trial testimony? But Pam was on a mission. "You need to strike out anything that sounds like snitching."

I took a closer look at my paragraph. Suddenly I saw the problem. "Oh! By writing, 'According to Sean,' I put his Uncle David's testimony about what happened at Walgreens into Sean's mouth, but Sean didn't say those words, David did. Tell Sean I will clarify this."

Jackie called the next day, apologetic. "There was talk at one time about Terry getting a gang against Sean in prison." And then, slowly and firmly, she said, "Even if Sean knew something he could snitch about, as a matter of principle he would not snitch."

When we hung up, I digested all this soberly. Sean's world was complicated; I didn't know how to navigate it. I'd better tread carefully.

The following week I got a phone call from the assistant metro editor of the *Boston Globe*, Steve Kurkjian. He wanted to discuss the two articles about Sean I'd pitched. He said the Mulligan case was of interest to them —that his colleague John Ellement "feels maybe bad evidence was used against the guy." But he politely rejected my articles, explaining that the *Globe* wasn't interested in printing things of a personal nature about Sean, only new evidence if it surfaced. "We're not ready to play the violin," was how Kurkjian put it. "Keep us informed."

In early December, on a phone call with Jackie, I had a light-bulb moment. I asked, "Would you like to join me after Christmas to research the case at the law office? We could read the transcripts together and list all the issues that don't add up."

"I'd love to!" Jackie said.

CHAPTER 13

Digging Deeper

Three days after Christmas 1998 I was sitting in a booth at Pizzeria Uno in Boston's Faneuil Hall Marketplace with Sean's girlfriend, Pam Boykin. She'd just returned to the city after spending the holiday with her family in Alabama, and I'd just pulled in from Montreal, having hit the highway at dawn. I'd engineered this lunch date, curious to meet her.

Pam was twenty-four, attractive, and stylishly dressed, with rows of necklaces atop the ruffles on her blouse. A slim, athletic five feet six, she wore her dark, curly hair pinned up. At first she was stiff, but she warmed as I reminisced about Sean as an endearing little boy.

"I believe the cops are behind the rumors," she confided.

"Behind what rumors?" I asked.

"The rumor that Celine was the woman in Mulligan's car, giving him oral sex."

My mind raced. I remembered Jackie's claim that when Mulligan was found, his pants were down around his ankles. Yet the mystery woman seen by witnesses was white.

As we finished our lunch, Pam brought up what to her was an agonizing point: "Detective Brazil took Sean in to question him about the murder of his cousins. Sean was crying. And suddenly they started asking questions about Mulligan. So how did Brazil know to switch the questioning over to Mulligan's murder?" Pam's fists were clenched. Her eyes flashed.

After lunch Pam walked back to work, and I headed toward Norman Zalkind and David Duncan's office near the waterfront. Pam's question about Brazil lingered on my mind.

Settling into the lawyers' conference room, I pulled out Sean's trial transcript and homed in on Brazil's change-of-subject question: "You know why you're here. You're here because of the murder of Detective John Mulligan, the police officer up at Walgreens."

What made Brazil connect Sean with Walgreens and Mulligan?

I pondered the timing. Celine and Tracy had been killed twenty-four hours earlier. Brazil was in charge of that crime scene. Celine had told family members she and Sean were together at Walgreens the morning of Mulligan's murder. With the detective's murder so fresh in the news, relatives must have told this to Brazil. It was the only explanation I could think of.

I turned my attention to the transcript of the December 1994 pretrial hearing to suppress evidence, focusing on Rosa Sanchez's photo ID of Sean. The *Globe* hadn't reported many details about the hearing. I needed to learn more about her back-to-back photo-viewing sessions, held nine days after the murder.

Detective Richard Ross presided over both photo showings. He testified that Rosa Sanchez arrived at the South Boston homicide unit at around 9:00 p.m. on October 5, accompanied by her husband, Ivan Sanchez. They were driven there by Detectives Kenneth Acerra and Walter Robinson in Acerra's personal car. Acerra and Robinson stayed in the viewing room with the Sanchezes for the entire first session, joining Ross and Sergeant Detective Thomas O'Leary, the lead investigator.

Ross showed Rosa two photo arrays, each consisting of eight photos, four on top and four below. The first array included a photo of Patterson, the second a photo of Sean. When Ross asked her if she recognized anyone in the first array, she burst out crying and said one of the photos was of a man who'd been stalking her. To calm her, Ross covered this photo with paper.

After viewing both arrays for several more moments, Rosa pointed to a photo—neither Sean nor Patterson—and said, "This looks like the man." She immediately left the building with her husband, Acerra, and Robinson. She was crying.

The couple sat with the detectives in Acerra's car. After about five minutes Acerra and Robinson escorted the pair back into homicide, saying Rosa had "changed her mind." Ross showed a now-composed Rosa the two unchanged photo arrays. This time, "It only took the teenager a split-second to identify Ellis as the man she saw in the parking lot where Mulligan was killed."

Judge Robert Banks wanted to know about the conversation in Acerra's car between sessions. Rosa testified that as she climbed into the back seat, she whispered to Ivan that she'd seen the Walgreens man in the photos but purposely didn't identify him. She said Ivan then told this to Robinson, and Robinson insisted she go back in and identify the correct man.

Acerra testified differently. As he recalled, when Robinson saw Rosa crying, he asked her directly, "What's the matter? Did you see him in the picture? Why are you crying?" And Rosa told Robinson, "My mother said not to get involved. I'm scared. They killed a policeman. Why wouldn't they kill me?"

I mulled this over. Rosa's account and her "Uncle Kenny" Acerra's didn't match. Sean's lawyers believed Acerra coached Rosa. Nonetheless, Banks ruled her ID admissible. Of course all this transpired before Acerra's criminal activities came to public light.

"Uncle Kenny's" now-admitted pattern of lying made me deeply skeptical of Rosa Sanchez's second-thought ID.

Next I pulled the police account of Terry Patterson's questioning session a week after the murder. I was eager to read what Patterson told detectives. I kept in mind that the report was cowritten by John Brazil and that its accuracy had been contested by Patterson's attorney.

Patterson admitted he drove to Walgreens the morning of September 26. He said he was with Sean Ellis and Celine Kirk, doing an errand. He denied any role in Mulligan's murder.

Asked to described the events of the previous Saturday night, Patterson said that from 6:00 p.m. until just after 11:00, he hung out on Hansborough Street, Dorchester, drinking beers with his friends Lew, Ant, Sean, and Robert. Sean wanted to go to sleep in the back seat of his VW, but he talked him out of it.

"Did anyone have a bike?" the detectives asked.

"Sean had a bike, but he put it up," Patterson said. He didn't know where.

He later drove Sean to Walgreens to get diapers. Sean sat in the passenger seat. They "pulled into Walgreens' parking lot . . . and parked next to the curb." In front of them was a small red car, and in front of that, by the store's doors, a "red truck."

Sean got out and walked to the pay phone. He patted his pockets for change and then picked up the receiver and placed it to his ear. Patterson didn't know who he called.

"Did you see Sean Ellis go near the red truck?" police asked.

"I don't know, man," Patterson said, explaining he was drowsy and "just listening to music." Sean went into the store, and the next thing Patterson remembered, Sean woke him up, saying, "Let's go! I want to go home!"

"Did Sean buy anything?"

"I don't know. He threw something in the back seat."

Patterson said he drove out of the Walgreens lot, took Sean to his cousin's house, dropped him off, and went home.

"Did you go into Sean's cousin's house and have something to eat?" the detectives asked.

Patterson didn't recall eating; he believed he went straight home.

"Is it possible you parked anywhere else while in the vicinity of Walgreens?"

Patterson was positive he had not. He told the detectives to check the video of the parking lot: "They must have one . . . [and] you'll see my car and exactly where it was parked."

"Were there any females in the vehicle?"

"No."

At this point Patterson's attorney, Nancy Hurley, asked to confer with him in private. Fifteen minutes later she told the detectives her client wanted to make "a slight change."

"Celine was with us," Patterson admitted.

The detectives asked him to go through his story again. This time Patterson enlarged his account: When Sean came out of Walgreens and got into the car, "he wanted to do a blunt." So Patterson drove around the corner to a dead-end street where he "used to bring girls parking" and backed in at its end. "Come on. Come on," Sean said. They left Celine in the back seat and walked into the woods.

"Where were you and Sean going?" Detective Dennis Harris asked.

"Sean wanted to go back to the store to get a cigar so we could do a blunt."

Patterson said he "had to take a piss and a shit but had no napkins." They were standing beside a dumpster, and Sean asked him, "Ain't that the store?"

Patterson said he did not leave the woods and never walked into the parking lot.

Harris asked, "If the camera recorded your vehicle in the parking lot, don't you think it recorded you and your friend walking out of the woods into the parking lot? Terry, what is the truth?...You have to be concerned only about yourself.... Don't tell only 90 percent of the story." He asked Patterson again what happened in the parking lot.

"Nothing," was Patterson's answer.

Harris pressed: "Did Sean ask you to do something stupid? ... Terry, what happened in the parking lot? Are you the triggerman?"

"No," Patterson said.

Harris tried again. "Did you get involved in something stupid? Terry, are you the triggerman? Or is Sean?"

Now came the part of the report Patterson's attorney complained about—the part she said detectives invented: Brazil and Harris wrote, "In response to this question, Patterson started nodding his head up and down, indicative of a positive response, then stood up, rolled his eyes toward the ceiling..."

Harris and Brazil also questioned Patterson about finding Sean's two cousins murdered on Wednesday, September 29. Patterson said he spent that entire day with Sean. He, Sean, and Rob Matthews rode around in Matthews's Chevy and ended up at the Sears at Burlington Mall, where Matthews worked. A friend let them take rides on his motorcycle. Afterward they drove to Tracy's apartment to drop Sean home and saw police "all over the area." Instead of stopping, they moved on to Patterson's girlfriend's house nearby.

On the way Sean tried to reach Tracy on Matthews's car phone but got no answer. Sean tried her number again from Patterson's girlfriend's house; again, no one picked up. From there Sean called a taxi to take him back to his cousin's apartment.

The next morning Sean called Patterson to say his cousins had been murdered.

To my surprise, Pam appeared in the doorway, having cut out of work early. I filled her in on Patterson's statement. "He said they stopped on Brown's street next to Walgreens 'to do a blunt.'" I paused, embarrassed and feeling my age. "Pam, what's a blunt?"

"It's when you put a joint into a cigar and smoke it."

Suddenly I understood. The teens had parked on Victor Brown's secluded, dead-end street to get high.

One other detail in Patterson's statement perplexed me. I told Pam about it. "Patterson said he was sure the Walgreens parking lot was being surveilled by video cameras. He told Brazil and Harris to go there and check the tapes. So if that's what he thought, it's hard to imagine him standing next to Mulligan's car, or forcing his way inside, and shooting him."

Pam shrugged. Nothing about Patterson elicited her sympathy.

She was eager to research how Rosa and Ivan Sanchez came forward to the police. Digging through the transcripts of the suppression hearing and trials, we found the subject had been addressed three times—and the accounts varied.

Rosa didn't remember who phoned the police: "I think my mother-in-law ... called my husband's brother-in-law. He's a cop ... Elvis Garcia." Ivan was equally vague: "Somebody in the family" called, definitely not him or Rosa. But at the hearing, Officer Garcia testified that Rosa herself telephoned him at "about four o'clock" that Sunday afternoon:

"She was telling me something she had saw, and she was like hesitant as to what she had saw. She started to tell me she seen something, and ... she started explaining what she saw. Then I was like, 'What are you talking about?' She said, 'Well, I was at the store during this incident.'"

Garcia, who was stationed at Area E-5, knew the "incident" was Mulligan's shooting. "She was giving it to me in bits and pieces, because she was kind of hesitant as to exactly what to say. She ... told me she seen two gentlemen, two black gentlemen. One was like behind the car and one was by the phone."

Garcia referred Rosa to another officer. He didn't remember who.

"It was Brazil," Pam said, fire in her eyes.

Garcia took no notes of his conversation with Rosa. He did not write up an incident report documenting Rosa's phone call until nearly 14 months later, on November 19, 1994, after being "requested to do so."

I was astounded. "They had Garcia backfill the paperwork just before the hearing—fourteen months after Rosa's call!"

Pam scowled. "Their most important tip, and they didn't write it down? The whole thing sounds suspicious to me."

After Rosa's phone call, Brazil tapped Acerra to help him go to Roxbury to interview her. We looked for Acerra's testimony and found he'd been called to the stand only twice, at the pretrial hearing and at Sean's second trial.

Acerra was first asked where he was when he learned of Mulligan's murder. He said "at home": "I just finished doing my tour of duty.... And, at about I believe four or five o'clock in the morning, I received a telephone call." He went downstairs in the condo complex to meet other detectives in front of Mulligan's unit. He had his own key, so he let everyone in.

"Acerra kept a key to Mulligan's condo?" Pam said, eyebrows raised.

"Yes. They were that chummy," I replied. I'd read that Acerra purchased one of Mulligan's investment units in the complex during the financial downturn, to help him out.

The prosecutor asked Acerra to describe all his actions that day. He said he was assigned to look through Mulligan's condo and "later in the day" reported back to the Area E-5 station house. There he found Brazil, his former station-house colleague who'd transferred to homicide the previous year. Brazil told him about the phone tip Garcia received and said, "Come on, Kenny, I think there's somebody named Rosa Sanchez, and ... there might be a language barrier."

Acerra, Brazil, and their station supervisor, Sergeant Lenny Marquardt, went to the Sanchezes' apartment on Humboldt Avenue in Roxbury. They arrived between 4:00 and 6:00 p.m. and quickly concluded that Rosa Sanchez and her husband had "information of significance" about Mulligan's killing.

Acerra said he did not know in advance he'd be interviewing his girlfriend's niece because he did not recognize Rosa's married name. It was only when he arrived at the apartment that he saw she was Rosa Delvalle.

"I think [Rosa and I] were a little shocked to see each other," Acerra said. "I didn't expect her, and she didn't expect me."

Asked if he told his department that he knew Rosa, Acerra dodged. "I might have ... I [explained] it so many times that I would have to say yes."

He said he knew Ivan Sanchez "from police work." He was friends with Rosa Sanchez's mother and knew that Rosa and Ivan were a couple. Asked if he knew when they got married, he said "around September 1993."

This tidbit jumped off the page. I recalled Ivan testifying that he and Rosa had been married for some time. A check of Sean's first-trial transcript confirmed it: married in October 1991.

Acerra said he was "not close" to Rosa, although he'd known her for about six or seven years and saw her at family functions: funerals, Christmastime, birthdays, a barbecue. He also knew Rosa had not lived with her mother "for about four years."

Pam and I chewed this over. It was obvious that Rosa and Acerra were deeply connected.

After the Sanchezes' police interview on Humboldt Avenue, the couple were asked to give taped statements. They balked at riding to the station house in a police cruiser or unmarked car but agreed to go in Acerra's personal vehicle. So Acerra left and came back "before six o'clock" to pick them up. This time he was accompanied by his partner, Walter Robinson.

"[Rosa] was scared. She was afraid. She didn't even want to come," Acerra said. But their "friendly relationship" helped convince her to cooperate.

At the station house, Acerra, Brazil, and a third detective interviewed and taped Ivan. Rosa went off with other detectives to give her statement.

Nine days later, on October 5, Rosa identified Sean's photo. Acerra and Robinson drove her and Ivan to the homicide unit that evening. Asked about the conversation in the car, Acerra said neither he nor Robinson conversed with the couple about why they were going to homicide. "Just small talk." The two detectives proceeded to sit at the conference table with Rosa during her first viewing session.

Acerra said he had no part in making up the photo arrays. He did not see them prior to the showing, nor did he see any photographs within them. He had no idea that Sean Ellis' photo was in the arrays. He also didn't know if the arrays included Terry Patterson's photo.

We took stock of this. Patterson had been arrested the previous day—booked by Acerra.

Asked, Acerra said he'd never seen Sean Ellis in person; he did not direct Rosa's attention to any photograph; he did not coach her to make her identification of Sean.

Questioned by Zalkind, Acerra agreed he was an active member of the Mulligan task force, went to all the briefings, read the daily *Boston Globe* and *Boston Herald* reports on the case, and had been present in the homicide unit the night Sean was questioned.

Zalkind asked Acerra if he was "at all interested" in whether Rosa Sanchez was going to make a positive ID, given that he was investigating the case.

Acerra said his job was not to "participate...just to be there to comfort her, to be with her. That was all."

"And you weren't interested in what she was going to do?"

"I would have been interested in the outcome, yes..."

"And this was also a close personal friend of yours that had died?"

"As close as anyone would ever get to John Mulligan. I don't know how close that is to be considered."

I considered the strangeness of Acerra's response and also the pressure he and Robinson probably put on Rosa Sanchez. Patterson and Sean were the only suspects police had, but no one had identified them from photos. In my mind, they needed Acerra's girlfriend's niece, Rosa, to do it.

Pam and I talked over the perplexing issue of Sanchez's stalker. The man in the photo that so unnerved her during her first photo-viewing session was not in fact her stalker. His name was Alfred Glover, and he'd been incarcerated at the time of Rosa's stalking incidents. I said, "After thinking she saw the guy who'd stalked her—though he wasn't that guy—and bursting into tears, Rosa pulled herself together and identified a man. And he wasn't Patterson, and he wasn't Sean. Then, at trial, she admitted she lied to the police and fingered this guy on purpose."

Pam was a step ahead of me. "Did you know that man Rosa identified was the same guy Ivan picked when they showed him the photos at home?"

I didn't know. People's first responses were generally correct. "Who was that man?"

Pam didn't know.

Acerra said that after Rosa identified Sean from the photos she was fearful, and prosecutors deemed it necessary to move her and Ivan to a place where she'd "be safe." He said he was assigned to help the couple find an apartment. After Rosa found a place on her own in suburban Norwood, he wrote a personal check for the deposit, having been told he'd be reimbursed by the Commonwealth. A copy of Acerra's check was in the file.

I was filled with disgust. The corrupt Kenneth Acerra—the man Rosa called "Uncle Kenny"—had shepherded his young friend from her first police interview to her "correct" photo ID and subsequent relocation (for safety or reward?) to a better life.

As Pam and I were packing up to leave, we came across a defense motion for further discovery dated September 14, 1994. Zalkind and Duncan had requested "any information or evidence in the possession of the Commonwealth regarding...

- any personal or business relationship between Detective John Mulligan and either Detective Robinson or Detective Kenneth Acerra, and
- either Detective Robinson or Detective Acerra having been untruthful in any other investigation or prosecution of which the Commonwealth is aware, including but not limited to such information in Boston Police Department personnel or internal affairs records."

To support their query about a "personal or business relationship," the lawyers attached a letter Acerra sent to his department on October 3, 1993—seven days after Mulligan's murder—stating that in 1992 he and Mulligan purchased four Panasonic cell phones together. One phone was registered to Acerra, two to Mulligan, and one to Brazil.

The import of this hit me: "Acerra, Mulligan, and Brazil shared a network of private cell phones, probably to support their nefarious 'business' activities. And Zalkind and Duncan suspected they were in cahoots, even before the *Globe* outed them!"

That Mulligan was in the mix fit the *Globe*'s scoop about him and Robinson being investigated for allegedly robbing dealers together. The phones were concrete evidence tying Mulligan to the crooked crew.

As for the detectives' prior untruthfulness, Zalkind and Duncan attached news articles reporting on Robinson's perjury and evidence-doctoring in a recent criminal case against a fellow Area E-5 officer, Adelberto Lio. Lio, a bodybuilder, was suspected of dealing steroids. Detectives set up a sting to prove it, and Robinson participated. In the resulting fracas, he took a shot at Lio, grazing his head and nearly killing him.

In a 1992 hearing into the incident, Robinson lied under oath about his actions and altered a police photo to support his lies. When Robinson was found out, the D.A. had to drop charges against Lio. Robinson went unpunished, but the case hit the press and became a stain on the department.

Pam hadn't heard the Lio story, so I filled her in. The take-home message for Sean crystalized. "Here you have Robinson, just publicly exposed as a perjurer, yet they put him on the Mulligan task force—supposedly made up of Boston's finest!"

The corruption sickened us.

Broker had opposed Zalkind and Duncan's discovery motion. Her written opposition was in the file. She criticized the defense for engaging in "speculation, based on rumor and innuendo" and called their request "a fishing expedition for information which is neither relevant nor material to the instant case."

Two months later the hearing judge (not McDaniel) agreed with Broker, writing, "[T]he defendant has failed to demonstrate the relevance and/or materiality of the sought-after materials to the trial of his case."

The defense motion for further discovery was denied.

CHAPTER 14

Two
Mothers

On the day before New Year's Eve 1998, Jackie Ellis was waiting for me inside her building's glass entryway with Shar'Day beside her bundled up against the cold and carrying a sack of dolls and art supplies. They climbed up into my Jeep Grand Cherokee—a feat for Jackie, given her bum knee—and sank into its plump cushions. "Oooh," Shar'Day cooed from the back, setting her dolls beside her. "This is nice."

Jackie and I had decided on goals for our research in Norman Zalkind and David Duncan's law office. She wanted to look at the differing descriptions of Sean made by the Walgreens witnesses. She also planned to revisit the testimony of witnesses who'd had their criminal cases disposed of favorably, for she suspected *quid pro quos*. I wanted to reread David Murray's testimony and reexamine the testimony about two men going in and out of the woods next to Walgreens, the men prosecutor Phyllis Broker said were Sean and Patterson.

On our ride into Boston I probed Jackie about Sean's initial status as a suspect in Celine's and Tracy's murders. "He was clearly a cousin in grief," I said.

"He loved those girls," Jackie said. "He and Celine were like brother and sister, all their lives. They were so close, some people mistook them for boyfriend and girlfriend."

"Didn't you and a relative try to get into homicide the night Sean was questioned, to be with him?"

"Right. My brother David and me. We kept asking to see Sean. We were frantic, begging, but they wouldn't let us in."

"Brazil?"

"Yes, Brazil. And all the while they were telling Sean, 'Your family doesn't care about you, nobody cares about you.' Sean was never even told we were outside."

"Pam and I are convinced Acerra lied about not knowing that Rosa Sanchez was the witness he and Brazil were going to interview."

"Maybe they gave Rosa a favor in return for her testimony, like they did the others," Jackie said.

"Well, she and Ivan got moved from a rough part of the city to a garden apartment in the suburbs. That could be the favor." My thoughts exactly.

At the law office, Shar'Day took a seat at the far end of the table and arranged her dolls, workbooks, and crayons. Jackie and I attacked the box of discovery materials. I spied Sean's arrest papers, dated October 6, 1993. The detective who booked, searched, and informed him of his rights? Walter Robinson.

I recalled that Kenneth Acerra was the detective who booked Terry

Patterson. Funny. Of all the investigators on the Mulligan task force, those two Area E-5 buddies of Mulligan's were always in the center of the action.

"Tell me about Sean's arrest," I asked Jackie.

"They came after the service for the girls. I begged Brazil, 'Please don't cuff Sean in front of his little sister.' And to his credit, he didn't. He walked Sean outside without cuffs."

I made no response. I refused to cut Brazil any slack.

Jackie and I delved into the various witnesses' descriptions of the tall, slim Black man they saw outside Walgreens, the man Broker said was Sean. We saw lots of problems.

Recollections of the man's outer garment were all over the map:

- Rosa Sanchez said he wore a greenish-blue oversized hoodie.
- Ivan Sanchez said his hoodie was black.
- Evony Chung called the hoodie bluish-gray.
- Joseph Saunders saw "some kind of white shirt" on his tall guy in the parking lot.
- Victor Brown's taller man wore "a windbreaker … with a white hood over the collar, down."

There was a puzzling lack of agreement over hats:

- Rosa Sanchez said the thin man wore a stocking cap with a Buffalo Bills logo.
- Ivan Sanchez said he wore a black baseball cap.
- Victor Brown specified he wore "no hat."
- Evony Chung did not mention a hat.
- Joseph Saunders did not describe a hat on his parking lot man.

Descriptions of this man's heights also varied. None quite reached Sean's height of six feet one:

- Ivan said the man was about five feet, eight inches tall.
- Saunders's man was a curiously specific five feet, ten and a half inches tall.
- Brown estimated his height at five feet ten, "somewhat taller" than his companion.

Jackie sighed. "No two descriptions match each other," she said, her voice flat. It couldn't be easy for her to see all this uncertainty about the man Broker insisted was her son—the son now in prison for life.

I reminded her that all these different descriptions had prompted Zalkind to ask jurors to consider whether two men or three were outside Walgreens that morning and, specifically, whether a third man—"somebody that was actually at Walgreens already"—had run back to the VW Rabbit with Patterson.

My money was on three.

Jackie turned her attention to the witnesses with prior criminal cases. There were two: Saunders and Ivan Sanchez. In Sean's first trial, Zalkind asked Saunders about his pending criminal case for larceny over $250 and conspiracy: "And you're hoping that the police are going to help you out here?" Saunders denied it.

Ivan Sanchez admitted he'd been convicted in 1991 on charges of "assault and battery on a police officer" and "larceny of a motor vehicle" and given a six-month suspended sentence. In 1994 those charges "were dismissed at the request of the Commonwealth."

"Did the district attorney's office ... help you in doing that?" Ivan was asked. He said no.

This provoked Jackie's ire: "All Ivan's charges were dismissed in 1994, after the murder and before Sean's trial!"

"At the request of the Commonwealth," I pointed out.

By the second trial, Joseph Saunders had been convicted of larceny and conspiracy and was on probation. Duncan again went over Ivan Sanchez's dismissed charges of assault and larceny. Then he brought up another charge, "operating after a suspended license and violating a red light." It had been dismissed on October 22, 1993.

This was two weeks after Rosa Sanchez made her photo ID of Sean.

"Did police or prosecutors help you in getting that case dismissed?" Duncan asked. As before, Ivan said no.

"All those cases were dealt with mighty leniently," Jackie said. "And the timing looks suspicious." She sounded grim.

I suggested we turn to the portions of testimony about the two men in the woods. It troubled me. Broker had framed Brown's and Ivan Sanchez's separate sightings as two halves making a whole: two Black companions, one tall and thin, the other shorter and stockier, entered the woods on Brown's side and came out on the Walgreens side. Although no positive IDs of the men were made, Broker said they were Sean and Patterson coming back to Walgreens to kill.

Jackie and I pulled out Brown's and Sanchez's accounts. "Let's piece together both sightings," I suggested. I began sketching out a timeline to reflect each man's testimony. Right away we saw timing problems. Big problems.

I walked through Brown's account aloud. "He said the two men parked the VW on his street at 3:20. That was his adjusted time."

"Well, first he said 3:30," Jackie said. "Then the cops got him to change the time. I'm suspicious about that."

"I think we have to use 3:20 here, because that was his testimony," I said. Jackie nodded.

"Anyway, the men got out and talked on the sidewalk for a minute. They fooled around in the woods for a few more minutes. Then they set off on the path toward the stores—a four-minute walk. So adding up all the minutes, Brown's two guys would reach Walgreens just before 3:30."

Jackie looked up from her reading. "Ivan saw his two guys just after 3:00! That's when he moved his car next to the Walgreens doors."

We stared at each other. There was a half-hour discrepancy between the two accounts. Not only that, but the in-and-out times of Sanchez's and Brown's men were upside down.

None of it fit Broker's narrative.

"It sounds to me like two different pairs of men," Jackie said. She pointed to another discrepancy: "Rosa said that at 3:00 Sean was already there, crouching by the SUV."

"Exactly! Zalkind underlined that in his closing argument. He said Sean couldn't be in two places at once, right next to Mulligan's car and walking out of the woods with a companion."

Jackie noticed something else: "The tall guy at the phone that Ivan described doesn't match Sean at all. Sean doesn't have 'very dark skin.' I'd call his skin medium brown. It's not as dark as mine. And Sean doesn't have a 'sticking out, flat nose … a wide … wide nose,' like Ivan said."

I reread Ivan Sanchez's testimony and came upon a new nugget. In trial two, when Duncan asked him to describe the two men, Sanchez said they came out of the woods and went "directly to the phones."

Duncan challenged this: "Now, didn't you tell your wife when she came out [of Walgreens] that the guy that was on the telephone was not one of the guys you saw coming out of the woods?"

Broker objected to the question, and the judge called her and Duncan to the bench for a sidebar conference. Their discussion had been transcribed, which was unusual. I read the back-and-forth eagerly.

Judge McDaniel asked Duncan where he was going with his inquiry. Duncan said, "Ivan and Rosa are in the car together … [and] Ivan told her the guy on the phone was not one of the two guys who came out of the woods."

Broker: "It's not his statement. It's hearsay."

Duncan: "I'm impeaching him now … he [is now saying] that two guys came out of the woods, and one of them was on the phone. According to Rosa, he gave a very different statement, that [the] guy on the phone was not one of those two guys…. He said, 'I saw two guys come out of the woods, but that tall guy is not one of them.'"

Broker: "It's hearsay."

Duncan was overruled, but he succeeded in preserving for the record, "On Sept. 26, Rosa Sanchez made this statement to police, and this contradicts Ivan's statement today."

This was vital information, and it had gotten buried. Energized, I dug for the transcripts of Rosa and Ivan Sanchez's police interviews, conducted the afternoon after the murder. Reading Ivan's transcript, I was disappointed. Though he gave the police detailed descriptions of two men he saw walk out of the woods and go to the payphones, he made no mention of a third man. Yet scanning Rosa's interview, I found she told her police interviewers exactly what Duncan recounted to the judge— that Ivan said a pair of men scared him, and he pointed to two men at the phones and said the shorter man was one—but not the thinner man next to him.

Detective Dennis Harris pressed Rosa to describe in detail what she saw as she left Walgreens. She said, "I seen the same guy that was crouched, you know, bent down by the cop's car. There was another guy on the phone . . .

Harris interrupted her: "[T]he guy . . . wearing the green hoodie who was initially crouched down? . . . now you say he's at the phone bank?"

Rosa: "Yes."

Harris: "Would you say that there's two guys there now? Is that correct?"

Rosa agreed. Harris asked her to describe the second man.

Rosa: "He was short. He had like a belly, real fat. He looked fat and he was wearing black pants, black sneakers with white stripes like Adidas ones and had a cap [on]. Black cap. No writing on it."

Rosa went on to say that as she got into Ivan's car, he told her he'd been spooked by "two guys coming out from the bushes": "I asked him if it was the two guys that was on the phone. He said, 'Only the short one.' . . . And I told him that I seen the tall one next to the car . . ."

Harris: "So what we have is, you saw the tall guy . . . at the phone bank now . . . the one with the green hooded sweatshirt . . . the same individual that you saw crouched by Detective Mulligan's vehicle? And the second time you see him, he's on the phone, correct?"

Rosa: "Yes."

Harris: ". . . And your husband tells you that the [other] individual on the phone, the heavy, shorter individual . . . is one of two guys that scared him?"

Rosa: "Yes."

Harris: "But there's an individual missing?"

Rosa: "Yes."

Harris: "According to both of you now, right?"

Rosa: "Yeah."

"'An individual missing,'" I read aloud to Jackie. "This is key! There were three men, not two, outside Walgreens: the two guys who scared Ivan when they came out of the woods, plus the thin guy Rosa later claimed was Sean. Three!"

My thoughts spun. Who were the two men coming from the woods? Was Terry Patterson the short man? I'd seen pictures of Patterson, and he didn't appear "real fat" with a "belly" as Rosa described. And who was the now-missing third man? Why didn't the police follow that lead?

Another realization hit me. When Walgreens clerk Stephen Bannister testified about leaving the store at 3:30 a.m., he said nothing about men at the telephones. Prosecutors surely would have asked him to describe the men if he saw them.

Bottom line: No men were at the phone bank at 3:30 a.m.

Pondering all this, I noticed something odd on the cover pages of Ivan and Rosa's separate interviews. Police had made handwritten notes of the starting and ending times on each, and the couple's times didn't line up. Ivan's session began at 4:00 p.m. and ended at 7:27 p.m., for a total of three and a half hours; Rosa's session didn't begin until 8:15 p.m. and ended a half hour later.

Not only was this discrepancy weird, but Boston officer Elvis Garcia said Rosa phoned him at 4:00 that afternoon with her tip. And Brazil, Marquardt, and Acerra didn't arrive at the Sanchezes' Humboldt Avenue apartment to conduct their initial interview until sometime after that.

How could Ivan be at the Area E-5 station, giving his statement, at 4:00 p.m.?

It was past time for lunch. Shar'Day, who'd played uncomplainingly all this time, put down her dolls for a nap, and the three of us walked to a tiny North End sandwich shop. Over roast beef subs and a hot dog for Shar'Day, we talked about everyday life. Jackie spoke of how important her church was to her, how much she enjoyed her gospel music tapes, and how wonderful it was to be rearing this youngest daughter away from her former Dorchester neighborhood with all its pressures.

I confided that, for Rich and me, bringing up sixteen-year-old Alison was a growing challenge. The pressures we faced in Montreal were, strangely, polar opposites of the deprivation and insecurity that had stalked Jackie's family in Dorchester. We were struggling to hold course in an environment of extravagance and coddling.

When we moved to Montreal in 1992, we were confronted by the Province of Quebec's mandate that children of immigrants be instructed entirely in French, even those from English-speaking countries. We dodged that requirement by choosing a private school for Alison with a fifty-fifty blend of French and English. But along with the language mix, the fancy school served up mega-wealthy peers and a permissive culture.

"All my friends go out on school nights," Alison would shout during our now-frequent family tempests. Where did these friends go? To the library? No, to clubs. Nightclubs.

"Nobody but me has a curfew!" she would scream. "On weekends, nobody even goes out till 10:00 or 11:00, so you have to stay out late!" Rich joked that the battles with our daughter kept the two of us united against a common enemy.

"The wealth culture around us is a problem," I told Jackie, describing the upper-crust Montreal lifestyle we found so alien. "Alison's school chums use their parents' credit cards to buy designer clothes and eat out together in restaurants. Her best friend's parents recently threw her a Sweet Sixteen party in the ballroom of a downtown Montreal hotel. Her birthday present? A silver Jeep."

Jackie looked astonished. I wanted her to be clear about my means and my values, so my words were deliberate: "This is all so far from how Rich and I were raised that we can't bend our minds around it. For Alison's sixteenth birthday last spring I cooked dinner for her and a few friends and capped it off with our usual homemade cake. Her gift was a jacket. So she feels like a church mouse next to her classmates."

Rich and I each came of age in families that were financially strapped. My dad's nervous breakdown immediately halted his regular salary. We had to sell our center-entrance Colonial in suburban Boston for the cash and move to a bare-bones summer cottage we owned in Scituate, Massachusetts. The thin insulation my parents added to its walls couldn't keep the winter wind from whistling through, and in big storms the house shook. Ours was one of the few winterized dwellings in a deserted, dark area of boarded-up summer cottages.

In my senior year of high school, I rotated two skirts and two sweaters bought from my summer earnings as a salesgirl. My family's idea of a vacation was to drive to Rhode Island to visit a saint's grave.

Rich, like me, was a scholarship student in college. His dad was a self-employed sales representative who'd dropped out of school in eighth grade because of family hardship in the Great Depression. As a teen, Rich earned every dollar of his spending money by mowing lawns and working as a caddie. He never once had a family vacation. At least I had the ocean; the only swims Rich had were by dint of friends' invitations to lake houses.

We each began our careers as schoolteachers. That's how we still viewed ourselves: sensible, unshowy, maybe bookish. Working to survive and possibly contribute to society, not accumulate riches. These days we were comfortable on Rich's academic salary, supplemented by my freelance earnings, but hardly wealthy. Our income matched our expenses, so life was good. But I never forgot our early-married days, when month's end would find me walking through the supermarket pushing toddlers with two dollars in my pocket. "Waffles for dinner!" I would declare, much to the kids' delight.

The Montreal teenage Alison blew off those family stories. She thought Rich and I were from Mars.

As Jackie, Shar'Day, and I stood up to leave, I threw out a final anecdote I hoped would make Jackie smile. "Last week we had a big argument with Alison over spending. We told her there was no chance our family could go to the Caribbean for February vacation, as many of her schoolmates did. She was moping around about this, because she wanted a tan like the other girls. So she screamed at Rich and me, 'You two are a couple of losers! You should have gone into retail!'"

Hearing this, Jackie let out a whoop. I laughed too, explaining between breaths, "Alison's best friend's father owns a clothing line."

Back in Zalkind's office, we pulled out David Murray's testimony. "Your brother's story was crucial in trials one and two," I said to Jackie. "Some jurors told reporters his testimony was why they voted to acquit. David painted Sean as a scared, confused teenager, crying over the dilemma he was in and terrified of being fingered by Patterson. The third jury never heard that description, so Sean remained in the shadows. And because he went to Walgreens with Patterson, and drove off with him, and helped him hide the guns, the jury convicted him."

In the box of discovery materials I found several pages of handwritten notes signed by Detective Mahoney documenting two meetings he had with Murray, whom he described as a confidential informant. Brazil was present at one meeting.

Mahoney summarized Murray's story about Sean leaving the Hansborough Street gathering and catching a ride to Walgreens with Patterson. His notes then recorded details about Sean's experience after he shopped:

"...Sean said...[he] went and got Pampers, and when he came out [Patterson's] car wasn't there. When he arrived at Walgreens, the car was parked out front. When he came out of the store, the car had been moved...

"WHERE'S THE CAR?...[I]t was no longer between the lines."

Mahoney had written WHERE'S THE CAR in uppercase letters. Suddenly I saw the scene clearly. When Sean came out of Walgreens, Patterson's VW Rabbit was gone from its parking spot in the fire lane next to the sidewalk. Though it was a no-parking zone, Patterson had evidently parked there. Now his car was gone.

Sean was confused. "Where's the car?" he thought.

"Jackie," I gasped, gripping her arm and showing her the notes. "The VW was moved while Sean was inside shopping. That means he wasn't in it when Patterson drove to Victor Brown's street!"

"I think so," she said softly.

We cross-checked Mahoney's notes with Murray's trial testimony. Sure enough, in Sean's first trial Murray said Sean told him, "When he went into Walgreens the car was in front of Walgreens, and when he came out of Walgreens the car wasn't there."

In the second trial Broker asked Murray, "Did Sean tell you they backed into a dead-end at Mr. Brown's house?"

"No," Murray said.

"Did he tell you anything else about the car in that Sunday conversation?"

Murray held to his earlier testimony: "[Sean] said...when he came out of Walgreens, the car wasn't there." Asked where the car was, Murray said, "Across the parking lot." As before, I concluded this was Sean's cryptic description to his uncle of the car's new location on Brown's street, a quick run across the Walgreens woods.

I turned to Jackie. "Phyllis Broker was so locked into her case theory, the notion that Sean wasn't in the VW Rabbit when Patterson moved it to Victor Brown's street didn't occur to her."

The Jeep was quiet as Jackie and I drove out of Boston in the brisk night air. Shar'Day dozed in back, surrounded by her dolls. I felt jubilant. We'd found areas of serious doubt about Sean's participation with Patterson. But we still didn't have the third-trial transcript, the only trial that counted.

I was puzzled over the David Murray angle. Why did the uncle report Sean's words and actions to the police? Was it the reward money as Norman Zalkind said? And when Sean insisted he was innocent, did Murray then finger Patterson to get the money? How reliable a narrator was Murray? I had no way of telling.

I was developing a healthy skepticism of every assumption.

Picturing Sean sitting in prison for the past five years, I grew angry. Prosecutors surely knew that Ivan Sanchez said the thin guy at the phones didn't walk out of the woods. Yet Broker insisted it was Sean, coming back with Patterson, intent on murder. She'd fought to persuade the judge not to allow jurors to hear Ivan's exculpatory observation.

Broker's hearsay objection might have legal merit, and I knew this was what lawyers were trained to do. But to me it was repugnant, morally. The semesters I'd spent with the Jesuits at Boston College, studying theology and philosophy, had sharpened my moral code. Even if the rules of evidence say otherwise, to me the omission of an important truth is the equivalent of lying—and here the stakes couldn't be higher. A young man's life hung in the balance.

If jurors had heard that Sean was not one of Broker's two "killer" woodsmen, would he be home now? It was enough to break your heart. And it taught me a valuable lesson:

The rules governing trials can keep the truth from coming out.

CHAPTER 15

Happy New Year

The following morning, New Year's Eve, David Murray stood waiting for me at the entrance to Linda Mae's diner in Dorchester. Sean's uncle was short, square, and powerful looking. He was dressed entirely in black—turtleneck, trousers, and leather jacket. Jackie Ellis had connected us.

As we slid into a booth in the dark restaurant, I took out a copy of my 1995 *Globe* op-ed about Sean. I wanted Murray to see I had a history with his nephew. He glanced at the article and nodded.

After the waitress took our breakfast orders, Murray began speaking in a staccato stammer much like Jackie's and Sean's. "This is how it worked. The four boys, they had the neighborhood, see? Sean and Terry Patterson and Curt Headen and Kevin Chisholm. They dealt drugs together. It was their area, sanctioned by the cops."

The drugs didn't surprise me. "The cops?"

"It worked like this. The police would conduct drug raids and afterwards turn in only a small portion of the confiscated drugs. And see, they'd sell the remainder back on the street through selected drug dealers. The dealers paid the police for the privilege. The cops also got a cut of the profits."

As I digested this, Murray added, "Sean had only one foot in it though. My sister had a strong hold on him. She kept him under a tight rein. Those other guys, they were in it much deeper. They had the corner—Patterson, Curt, and Kevin. But Sean, he walked the line."

The waitress delivered our coffee. Murray leaned over his steaming mug and said in an ominous, low tone, "I think Mulligan was supplying Patterson."

My eyes opened wider. I knew John Mulligan had a bad reputation, but this was news. Terry Patterson and Mulligan dealt together? No connection between the two had ever been made, either by prosecutors or defense lawyers.

Murray continued: "Those other two murders, Headen's and Chisholm's? They're connected." He shook his head and looked pained.

"Connected with Mulligan's?"

"Yes. I strongly believe that."

"But weren't Headen and Chisholm killed by rival gang members?"

"Those murders are connected," Murray repeated, as if he hadn't heard me.

"Celine's and Tracy's too?"

"No. The murders of Kirk and Brown, they weren't the same thing. But those other two murders, they're connected to this case. I've wanted to get to the bottom of that, but if I was to look into it, really probe I mean, I'd have to go back on the street. And I really don't want to do that. I really can't."

Murray had done time for armed robbery. His life now was on a different track. Jackie said he had a wife, two kids, a nice house, and a brand-new minivan. He was a counselor at a men's homeless shelter. Who could blame him for not wanting to rekindle old contacts?

"Let me tell you about those poor girls. Oh, what a waste. What a waste." He took a deep breath and steeled himself before continuing.

"Celine and Tracy's mother—my sister Jean—was overcome with grief. So I went to Tracy's apartment on Oakcrest. Detective Brazil took me there. And when I looked in the door I saw the ring on Celine's finger. She had this big ring she always wore. And that's all I saw—just the ring on her bloody finger on the floor. And then I knew." His face was anguished. "I think the 911 call was made by Sean."

"Sean?" I blurted out.

"Yes. I think Sean was the first one on the scene. I think what happened was, he tried to get in the apartment door—he was living there then—and he couldn't open the door because the body was lying in front of it. So he pushed it open harder, and when he saw Celine lying there he freaked. He must have reached in for the phone and dialed 911 and then handed the phone to Tracy's son, Ma'Trez. And then he took off.

"Sean and I talked about the girls' murders," he continued. "We were outraged, sickened. And we went on the street looking for information. We went all through the Franklin Field project, person to person. Within two hours we learned from Celine's friend Nikki that the murderer was Craig Hood."

"How did Nikki know?"

"At the time of the murder, she and Celine were on the phone. Hood came in and began arguing with Celine about a gold chain. Nikki heard it all. It was a terrible fight, she said, and then she heard shots."

Murray leaned back and said matter-of-factly, "So Sean and I got a gun, and we went looking for Hood."

"A gun?" I was aghast. "You were going to shoot him?"

"Yes. We went together to Brockton to find Hood. Nikki said he lived there. We wanted to kill him, but we couldn't find him. If we had, we would have killed him. I know it.

"So I tipped off the police about Craig Hood. I told Brazil, and the police found him. They picked him up on outstanding warrants and questioned him about Celine's and Tracy's murders. And that was it. My tip led to Hood's arrest."

We turned to the Walgreens videotape, and Murray got angry. "This thing about the Walgreens video system 'not working'? Well, Detective Mahoney told me, 'We have Sean and Celine on videotape.' And suddenly the tape doesn't exist? I don't believe it."

"I've been suspicious about that," I said. "So, you think there was a video-tape, and it was suppressed?

"Yes."

"Do you know if there was a third guy at Walgreens with Terry and Sean?"

He looked surprised. "No. No, I never heard that."

Our coffee mugs were empty. I said, "It would be amazing for Sean if we could show that the Walgreens videotape was suppressed evidence. It would crack his case wide open. How could we find that out?"

"Well, maybe I could do some digging," he said. He hesitated. "Maybe I can find out something more on Headen and Chisholm's murders too, be-cause, like I say, those murders are connected. But that's a tough one, really tough. And, like I said, I don't wanna go back on the street."

The winter sun was blinding as Murray and I emerged from the restau-rant, and a cold wind blew off the ocean. Flurries were forecast for later in the day. We exchanged email addresses, shook hands, and agreed to stay in touch.

I felt slightly dizzy as I turned my Jeep's heater to high. Sean's uncle had dumped so much new information on me. Chilling information. Mul-ligan supplied Patterson? The Mulligan murder might involve a toxic mix of cops, drugs, and murdered kids?

As my frigid Jeep grew warmer, I had a flash. Of course neither side ever connected Patterson with Mulligan. The authorities couldn't admit Mulligan was dirty. So they had to describe a seamy cop's murder as a "ran-dom crime of opportunity." Everyone knew that was a reach.

As for Patterson's defense, it was a whole lot easier to debunk "random kids shopping" than to defend a kid who knew Mulligan and might have an actual motive, say a beef over business.

A kid who could get into Mulligan's passenger seat.

I was perplexed by Murray's insistence that Headen's and Chisholm's murders were connected with Mulligan's. I'd entertained the idea of Celine's murder being a silencing, given what she knew or might have seen. Murray dismissed that notion. Yet he apparently believed these two drug-dealing kids, supplied, he said, by corrupt cops, were bumped off in some sort of link with Mulligan. Were they silenced? If so, by whom?

It pointed to a very dark place.

I checked the clock on my dashboard. Pam was getting off work at noon, and the two of us were going to drive out to Walpole to pay a New Year's Eve visit to Sean. I had some time to kill, and the *Boston Globe*'s Dorchester headquarters were a short distance away on Morrissey Boulevard. I grabbed my cell phone and called metro editor Steve Kurkjian. He'd said to keep them informed. Besides, it would be nice to give him a face to put with my name to dispel any notion of me as some crazy lady from Montreal.

"Come on over," Kurkjian boomed.

The editor strode into the *Globe*'s glass-and-marble lobby accompanied by reporter John Ellement. Kurkjian was rather short and freckled, with glasses and a mop of gray-tinged, brownish curls. He looked fiftyish. Ellement was tall, with rumpled white hair and a young-looking face. Shaking his hand, I thanked him for his kindness in talking with me after Sean's conviction, when I'd had so many questions.

Kurkjian cut to the chase. "Anything new? Is Sean innocent?"

"I just had breakfast with Sean's uncle," I said. "I'm pretty sure Mulligan was dirty, up to his eyeballs in drugs, just like his friends Acerra and Robinson."

Kurkjian nodded. "Some people say he was the worst of the lot. They say if he wasn't dead, he would have been indicted. So, you think Ellis is innocent?"

"Yes, I do. When I reread the testimony and saw some discovery materials, a bunch of things didn't add up. For one thing, none of the witnesses' descriptions of the tall, thin guy were the same—the guy who supposedly was Sean. And the witnesses' sighting times don't synchronize. The whole framework of the prosecution's theory is shaky."

"How so?"

I reprised Phyllis Broker's case that Sean and Patterson went to Walgreens so Sean could shop and afterward drove off, parked on a side street, and walked back through the woods to kill Mulligan.

The men nodded.

"Two things. First of all, Sean was not in the car when Patterson moved it to the side street. Sean's uncle testified that Sean told him when he came out of Walgreens after shopping, Patterson's car was gone from its spot in the fire lane. This confused Sean. His first reaction was, 'Where's the car?' I saw these words written by hand in the police notes of the uncle's interview. So, I believe Patterson moved the car while Sean was shopping.

"Second, Sean wasn't one of the two guys Broker's witness saw come out of the woods at Walgreens—the men she called killers. This witness was sitting in his car, waiting for his wife to shop, when the men emerged. They scared him, and he told his wife about it when she got back in the car. He pointed at two men at the phone bank and specifically told her only the shorter man came from the woods—presumably Patterson—but not the thin man, presumably Sean.

"Here's the rub: The husband saw a different guy walk out of the woods with the shorter man, but then this man dropped from view. Sean's lawyer wanted to get this testimony in about Sean *not* coming from the woods, as Broker claimed, but she objected to it as hearsay, and the judge agreed. So, jurors never heard any testimony about the existence of a third guy."

Ellement shook his head. "No way! Ellis wouldn't be sitting in prison, doing life, if there was another guy who might be implicated. No way would he cover up for someone to that extent."

"Well, I don't know about covering up for anyone. According to Sean, he shopped, made a phone call, and then went home. No one was seen at the phone bank after the husband and wife drove off at about 3:20 or 3:25. A clerk making a coffee run left Walgreens at 3:30 and did not report seeing anyone outside the store. He said Mulligan was alive at that point but dead fifteen minutes later when he returned with the coffee."

Kurkjian looked perplexed.

"There's other sketchy stuff in this case," I continued, like the 'missing' Walgreens videotape.

The journalists exchanged glances, and Kurkjian said, "The *Globe* had suspicions all along about that tape. We tried hard to track it down, believe me."

"Then there's the woman seen in Mulligan's car who was never identified." I paused and then decided to say it: "I heard a rumor Mulligan was found with his pants down."

"Yeah, yeah." Kurkjian waved his hand dismissively. "We heard that too, and crack in his socks, and all that." The editor ended our conversation by stating the *Globe*'s position: "For us to get back on this story, we'd need new information, and I don't see anything yet to print. But keep in touch with us."

The holiday visiting period at Walpole was from 1:00 to 2:00 p.m. With Pam beside me, the prison check-in procedure—the frisking, the wand, the metal detector—seemed easier. Sean was waiting for us behind the plexiglass barrier, all smiles. He and Pam began cooing and fussing. I moved away and gazed downward to give them privacy.

Sean was making a big deal over Pam's new hairstyle. She'd cut it short but was wearing extensions. "I like women to be natural-looking," he said. "I don't like it." But he couldn't take his eyes off her.

All too soon the hour was up. "Happy New Year," we wished one another fervently.

"This will be the year," Pam said, and Sean nodded solemnly.

As Pam and I walked toward the exit, we passed an inmate sweeping the floor. "Hi," Pam mumbled. She squeezed my arm and hissed, "That's Terry."

I looked back. Patterson was leaning on his broom, watching us nonchalantly. He had curly hair and was on the short side, with a solid, muscular build. I noted he was neither "real fat" nor had a "big belly" as Ivan and Rosa Sanchez described the man they saw at the Walgreens phone bank.

Seeing him gave me a chill. Here was a convicted cop killer who'd allegedly fired five bullets into Mulligan's face. He looked like a pleasant young man.

"He's in the same unit as Sean," Pam said under her breath. "And he's always after Sean for news. Sometimes he's on the phone right next to Sean. He's even talked to me on the phone—or tried to. This year he got on the line and said 'Merry Christmas.' The nerve."

As we walked on, Pam unloaded. "Terry is convicted. Why can't he just tell the truth and say Sean didn't do it?"

I needed to make good time on the drive home to Montreal. In about six hours Rich and I were scheduled to attend a New Year's Eve dinner party. Apologizing, I dropped Pam at the Walpole train station—"It's fine," she insisted—and pressed northward. In New Hampshire it began snowing. As I neared Stowe, Vermont, the darkness was inky, and conditions had degenerated to whiteout.

Visibility was nil, and an intense squall swirled outside my windshield. My hands gripped the steering wheel tightly as I guided my Jeep in icy grooves made by the eighteen-wheeler traveling ahead of me, the snow flying off its roof compounding my difficulty. I was trapped between the truck's red lights and a car close to my own tail, all of us engulfed in blackness. We snaked along the highway in this manner for perhaps half an hour, with an unknown number of other vehicles ahead of us and behind. There was no way to slow down, and no way to stop. "Please God, get me home safely. Get me out of these mountains and off this damn highway." My heart pounded. I hadn't talked to God in a while.

Fear gave way to anger. Why was I even in this treacherous place? What was I thinking? Why was I risking my life when I didn't have to? Was working with Sean more than I could handle?

Conditions eased when I reached Quebec. Traffic was light on the farm roads, and snow wisps danced innocently about. For once the flat landscape leading to Montreal didn't seem boring. I could have kissed the snow-dusted fields.

Safe now, my mind drifted back to what Sean's uncle had told me about the kids, the cops, and drugs. What a world! And it fit Mulligan's reputation. I recalled reading that a Boston drug dealer once testified he paid off Mulligan to let him keep selling.

Easy money from drugs was a temptation for city cops, I knew. But Mulligan ended up murdered, gangland-style. And now I'd learned the street linked his murder to Sean's friends' murders. This heavy case was growing even heavier.

I'd been heartened by Murray's description of Sean as being tightly reined in by Jackie and not 100 percent involved in the neighborhood's drug action. That sounded like Jackie.

From all I'd read and learned so far, the best spin on Sean's presence at Walgreens was exactly what his lawyers claimed: a classic case of wrong place/wrong time/wrong companions. He'd gone to Walgreens just to buy diapers, unconcerned about either witnesses or video cameras. And someone else's dealings with Mulligan had spiraled into bloodshed in that parking lot.

An anxious Rich was pacing in the kitchen. After a hug, a quick change of clothes, and a brush of blush, I hastened into the passenger seat of his Audi, glad to surrender the wheel. As we negotiated the snowy roads out to Montreal's West Island, I told him all I'd learned in Boston.

"The more I find out, the more I think Sean was railroaded," I said as we pulled up to the iron gates of a bona fide mansion, the home of new friends.

Our hosts proudly gave us a tour. Designed by a noted nineteenth-century architect, the manse had thirteen fireplaces, each now lit to usher in the new year. In the immense dining room their extended family was tucking into a lavish buffet at a gargantuan dinner table loaded with wine bottles and food reflecting the family's Greek heritage. The multigenerational group, including great-aunts and a grandmother, could not have been warmer. Brothers, sisters, and cousins all wanted to hear about my visit to a maximum security prison and murmured wishes that Sean might yet be found innocent.

After dinner we retreated to the game room and clustered around a cinema-size TV screen to watch the Times Square ball drop. Around us was every possible means to have fun, from pinball machines to a pool table, jukebox, and dance floor complete with a mirrored disco ball. Seeing my upward gaze, our host flicked a switch and set the ball turning and sparkling.

I smiled weakly and sank back into the cushions. I was dazed from fatigue, from the wine, and from the impossibly full day. But mostly I was dazed by the utter contrast of this setting with what I'd experienced hours earlier. How to reconcile this opulence with sitting across from an ex-convict in a Dorchester diner and hearing the story of a young woman lying in her own blood, identified by a telltale ring? And after that sitting in a visitors' cubicle at Walpole?

It made my head spin, this range of fates: Sean's world in prison so miserable and my world so comfortable. How could they coexist on the same planet, let alone intersect in one twenty-four-hour period in my life?

At midnight the TV revelers exploded into cheers, the disco ball above us twirled and glistened, the great-aunts danced together below it, and everyone kissed and wished one another happiness and good health for 1999.

It was also midnight in Walpole.

How was Sean marking the new year?

CHAPTER 16

The Ruling

1999

As Jackie, Pam, and I waited over the long winter for Judge McDaniel's ruling on Sean's retrial motion, we pooled ideas by phone, fax, and letter. Together we groused about the supposedly nonexistent Walgreens videotape, the dismissal of Ivan Sanchez's criminal cases, and Detectives Acerra and Robinson's dodgy handling of Rosa Sanchez.

Jackie dropped an interesting tidbit. "I met a woman who told me Mulligan was in a detox program with her, either for alcohol or drugs, I don't remember which. She saw his picture in the newspaper after his murder and recognized him. She brought it up when she found out Sean was my son."

One day Pam phoned to say a cousin of hers had recently gone out on the street asking questions about Mulligan. "He came back saying, 'Mulligan was always looking for trouble, harassing Blacks. And he liked young girls.'"

"Think about it," Pam said in another phone call. "All the witnesses who could testify for Sean are dead."

I kept thinking about the Sanchezes seeing a third guy at the pay phones. It aligned with Norman Zalkind's hints of two not being the "magic number" of guys at Walgreens and the witness descriptions that didn't match either Terry Patterson or Sean.

Who was Victor Brown's tall, thin man wearing a windbreaker with a white hood? Who was the Sanchezes' short, fat guy with a "big belly"? Who was Joseph Sanders' man in the white shirt? Any one of them could be the third man.

Two leading possibilities were Curt Headen and Kevin Chisholm. If their murders were indeed connected with Mulligan's, were either of them at Walgreens?

I shared my thoughts with Pam and asked her what Headen and Chisholm looked like. She didn't know about Headen but said Chisholm was stout but not short—almost as tall as Sean. Then she said abruptly, "I hope Sean will be moved to the prison in Shirley, where I can sit next to him and talk about everything."

I wrote to Jackie and asked whether she thought corrupt police were behind Headen's and Chisholm's murders and whether the two had a drug link with Mulligan. By now a fifteen-year-old youth had been convicted of killing Headen, allegedly to prevent him from testifying against a relative.

Jackie replied:

> I kind of agree that Chisholm and Headen were smoked by the
> police through the street punk hit men, but it's only speculation,
> and we don't have any proof. I am aware they were involved

in dealing drugs, and rumors are that their source was Mulligan,
but again I have no proof. There is a lot of unanswered questions
I wished I had answers to but since I've moved out here ... I have
lost contact with the fellas. And even if I knew how to reach them
I don't know if they would do any talking. The only one who I am
sure would have talked is Headen, and he's no longer with us.

In my next conversation with Jackie I asked, "If Headen was the third guy at Walgreens, do you think he could have fired the gun?"

She said, "Based on his past, I'd have to say he's definitely capable of it. Curt was a nice guy, but sometimes he was a wild man. Once he tried to rob a crack house. The cops were called—his uncle among them—and when the police came through the window, Curt saw his uncle and without hesitation opened up on him."

This seemed important to know about Headen.

By now Rich had reached a conclusion: "The street knows exactly what happened in this crime." It would become his mantra.

My thoughts had also solidified. Drugs were the third rail in Mulligan's murder.

I was skeptical about the forensics. Authorities had revised their theory about a passenger-seat killer, ultimately saying the killer fired from outside the vehicle through Mulligan's slightly open driver's window. To me, this seemed not only awkward but also incompatible with Mulligan's wounds. His reclining body was found angled slightly toward the passenger seat, with his head turned away from the driver's window. I'd seen no trial testimony from experts about the angle of entry of bullets to his face or whether a side-window approach was feasible.

It also seemed unlikely that Patterson—or anyone—could shoot Mulligan through the window, then open the driver's door and grab the detective's pistol from the right side of his body without causing Mulligan to fall out.

One evening I lay in bed reading my notes, trying to make sense of prosecutor Phyllis Broker's case theory and the murder timeline. I saw a major problem. Rosa Sanchez supposedly saw Sean crouching just after 3:00 and again twenty-five minutes later standing at the pay phones. Ivan Sanchez's two guys came out of the woods just after 3:00, went to the phones, and loitered there "the whole time" Ivan waited for Rosa in his car. Two men were still standing at the phones when Rosa came out of Walgreens at around 3:25 a.m. Broker said the men were Sean and Terry Patterson.

But Broker also introduced testimony that a "brown" car—supposedly Patterson's VW—drove down American Legion Highway on its way to Victor Brown's street and nearly hit deliveryman Art DeSalvo's car at 3:15. And Patterson's VW arrived at Brown's area at 3:20.

The hitch: Ivan's two men stood at the phones the "whole time" he waited for Rosa. In other words, between 3:00 and 3:25 a.m. these men were still in the parking lot.

The Commonwealth's timeline for Sean and Patterson didn't work.

Janet poked her head into the bedroom. "I think you're being naïve, Mom," she said. "It's well-known that people in prison will say anything to get out. They will look you straight in the eye, and they will lie, and they will be very convincing."

She had my attention.

"Listen, Sean at nineteen was not the sweet, innocent boy you remember," she went on. "Those guys were drug dealers. I'm afraid you're getting sucked in."

"Like I've said, I know Sean hung with a bad crowd. Of course I deplore the drug dealing. But it's not the issue. The issue is whether he helped murder Mulligan. That's why he's doing life without parole. And I see a lot of reasonable doubt."

I reeled off my findings to date, and Janet became contrite. "I hope you don't mind me saying all this. I realize you want to help. And of course I want Sean to receive justice if it's been denied him. I just don't want to see you get tangled up in something that's way beyond your understanding."

"I know," I said, "and you're right. People do lie to get out of prison, and I don't want to be involved in a fool's errand. So challenge me. Keep asking me hard questions."

"Sean had a little skirmish at Walpole," Jackie called to say. An explanatory letter soon arrived from Sean.

> *February 25, 1999*
> *To: A Special Person & Close Friend,*
> *Dear Mrs. Murphy,*
> *I'm locked down 22½ hours a day now. I was at work and this instructor and I had a little incident (he was really speaking down to me, and when I spoke against it he fired me). In any event, it was enough to get me in trouble and locked down. The weird part is, he lied on the disciplinary report to justify firing me. I'm okay though. It's been about a week … I'm waiting to go back to population now …*
> *Mrs. Murphy, I'm starting to feel worn out again so I must close. I'll write again within a week.*

Pam phoned on the first day of March. "The CO [corrections officer] wrote on his report that Sean said, 'Fuck you,' but what he really said was, 'Talk to me like a man.' It was a respect issue. Sean got a ticket, and no one beats a ticket. Now the COs keep searching him."

On March 5 Pam called again. This time she was sobbing. "Sean's motion for a new trial was denied by Judge McDaniel. He said Acerra's and Robinson's corruption in drug cases didn't automatically apply to this murder case. And he said Acerra played just 'a minor role' in the investigation."

"Minor role? Minor role?" I parroted.

"I don't know what to do now," Pam wailed. "I don't know what to do."

To A Close, Sincere Friend & A Very Special Person,
Dear Mrs. Murphy,

    I'm trying to maintain and stay focused.... The denial was
a disappointment, but on the larger scale maybe it was best ...
[as] the trial judge that sat on the case is to retire in June.
It's too bad he had to be seated on the case in the first place.
I truly believe that had he answered my first jury's question
clearly I would be home right now.

Sincerely,
Sean

Jackie poured out her disappointment in her next letter:

I'm still trying to hang in there. I've been a little down in
spirit, but I keep praying for things to turn out okay in the long
run. I stay in phone contact with Sean. I try to be cheerful and
encouraging for him, but things just seem to be happening so slow....

    Shar'Day is doing well. She's working very hard both in
school and at the church. Bringing God back into my life was the
best thing that could happen to me.

    After I lost Joseph, both my parents, and one of my sisters,
I kind of lost faith. Now I see everything just fell into a plan the
Lord set for me. I'm not yet sure what it is, but I'm not going
to lose faith again....

    Well, Elaine, enough crying on your shoulders. Thank you
for being there for me. I feel a closeness because of Sean and
Mark's relationship. I'll hang in there, and you do the same.

At a candlelit dinner on a wintry St. Patrick's Day 1999, I passed platters of
home-cooked corned beef and cabbage to Janet and her new boyfriend,
Devin. Like Janet, Devin was engrossed in postgraduate study in Montreal, in his case preparing for the rigorous Chartered Accountant exams.

The Irish saint's holiday was big in the city, with a large contingent of French-speaking O'Malleys and Flanagans, descendants of Ireland's potato-famine immigrants, marching in an annual parade that rivaled Boston's.

I was otherwise alone for the holiday. Rich was at a scientific conference in Japan, and Alison was spending spring break at her grandparents' home in Florida, a trip I'd shamelessly engineered to gain a week of peace. She'd blossomed into a blonde, blue-eyed beauty with a dazzling smile, but we rarely saw that smile. Her stormy relations with a handsome but petulant new boyfriend were all she could think about. A trip south promising a tan was my attempt to change the subject.

On a rage scale of one to ten, I was a fifteen. Jackie had mailed me Zalkind and Duncan's retrial motion. Any reasonable person would agree with their contention that Acerra's, Robinson's, and Brazil's crimes and "unhesitating willingness to lie under oath...to achieve their personal objectives" snuffed out their credibility as investigators.

The defense attorneys maintained that prosecutors knew of Robinson's prior bad acts, but deliberately withheld this information. They believed his history of falsifying evidence was why Broker had him and Acerra questioned on tape about Rosa Sanchez's photo ID session. Had the defense been allowed to see Robinson's Internal Affairs file, they argued, they could have discredited him during the motion hearing to suppress Rosa Sanchez's photo ID. Indeed, they could have "impeached the entire police investigation of this case."

But their motion for further discovery—the motion Pam and I saw in Sean's case file—was denied. And now, with the denial of Sean's retrial motion, Acerra's, Robinson's, and Brazil's conduct during the Mulligan murder investigation would escape further scrutiny.

As I served the Irish fare, I steamed. Why did Judge McDaniel, the judge in Sean's trial, get to pass judgment on his own case? Didn't all of us, including judges, have a bias for self-preservation? What kind of justice system allowed such an enormous conflict of interest?

I filled Devin in on the basics of the case, emphasizing the roles of the felon detectives. I told him about Sean's uncle's revelation that dirty cops supplied the kids with drugs to sell and his hunch that Mulligan supplied Patterson.

I'd had an insight about the drugs. "I think Mulligan's private security shifts at Walgreens were his illicit 'office hours.' His dealers knew they could find him there most nights after midnight. After all, they couldn't transact business at the police station."

A new theory was percolating in my brain: "In their retrial motion, Sean's lawyers argued that Acerra and Robinson rigged the case using Rosa Sanchez because they wanted to avenge the death of their buddy. But I disagree about motive.

"I think those guys pulled in Rosa to shut down the homicide investigation before all the digging into Mulligan's police work would expose their own crimes. They—and Brazil—must have been panicked that the drug dealers they robbed would tell investigators about them, to cut deals. They had to keep the lid on. So Acerra grabbed his girlfriend's niece and set her up to identify Sean.

"And it worked. Two kids who'd been at Walgreens that night got arrested; the Mulligan investigation stopped; and Acerra, Robinson, and Brazil's drug-robbing enterprise stayed hidden for two and a half more years, until the *Globe*'s investigative reporters found them out."

As the first green shoots of May pushed through snow clumps under my kitchen window, I phoned Jackie.

"Hello?" Jackie's voice was the faintest of whispers.

"Did I wake you, Jackie?" I glanced at my watch.

"No, no. I just got home from the hospital. I had emergency surgery— for a bubble in my colon. It was cancer. And they found a spot on my liver."

PART 3

Appeal

1999–2000

CHAPTER 17

Plunge In

1999

In early June, Jackie gingerly hoisted herself up to my Jeep's passenger seat. Her recent abdominal surgery had left her with a colostomy bag. We were heading to Walpole to visit Sean. "I haven't seen him since last Thanksgiving, when you drove me out," she confided.

Jackie had asked me to help her deal with the lawyers as they crafted Sean's appeal of the denial of his retrial motion. I'd assured her I'd do anything I could. To my mind, this included looking for further leads that could help Sean prove his innocence.

I was eager to dig into Sean's case. In summer my editing work slowed down, and with friends and family members living around Boston, I always had a place to stay. Jackie's cancer added new urgency to the mission. I very much wanted to drive her out to see Sean.

I'd been happy to leave Montreal. Rich and I were battling almost daily with Alison, now a headstrong seventeen. It seemed all she thought about was her roller-coaster romance. Our family rows over her curfew had only intensified, and she continued to defy us and stay out late. Rich and I were beyond concerned. Handcuffing a teenager to the furnace wasn't an option, we agreed. (Gallows humor sustained us through the stress and heartbreak.) Where had our wonderful daughter gone? As a child, though sassy and de-termined, Alison was the very definition of "good egg."

Our most recent blowup was over her desire to return to summer camp in Maine, where she'd gone since third grade. Rich and I thought she should get a summer job in Montreal. When I remained firm, she put her face close to mine and screamed, "I have no respect for you as a human being."

I didn't cry easily, but this provoked sobs. I wept through an emergency meeting with the therapist who was guiding Rich and me through these adolescent storms. "Get away from her," he said. "Get physically away. Don't let Alison do this to you."

An international border was just the thing.

I glanced over at Jackie, her pretty face framed by short bangs. Her struggles put my domestic problems in perspective. "The surgeon removed a tumor the size of a deck of cards from my colon," she said. "It had trav-eled to my liver, but he told me he 'scraped' that organ and got it all." She'd chosen the most aggressive chemotherapy regimen available.

Despite the devastating denial of Sean's retrial motion, we were feel-ing positive about his case. David Duncan was already at work on his ap-peal, to be heard by the Massachusetts Supreme Judicial Court (SJC). If the justices agreed with the defense that Acerra's, Robinson's, and Brazil's now-proven corruption had contaminated the Mulligan homicide inves-tigation, they would reverse the lower court's ruling, and Sean would get a new trial. By now Acerra and Robinson had been in prison for a year;

Brazil had quit the force.

Before this trip I'd written to Sean to tell him I was coming to Boston and to ask for his guidance on who to talk with and what issues to raise. I concluded my letter with three central questions:

> 1. **Third man?** Was there a third man there that night, along
> with you and Terry Patterson? A third guy would help explain some
> of the conflicting descriptions.
>
> 2. **Moved car?** I read that when you first came out of Walgreens
> with the diapers, you looked for Patterson's car but it wasn't there.
> Did you not know it had been moved? If I were a juror, this would
> be a key question.
>
> 3. **Walgreens receipt?** What time was on your Walgreens' diaper
> receipt?
>
> Hang in there, Sean.... Please know that there are others out
> here, like me, Mark, and the many people I've told about your
> case, who are concerned and thinking about you. It will all come
> out OK in the end. Have faith.

Sean answered my letter by giving me leads to follow:

> Stephen Bannister ... [testified] that I came in the store, and that I
> was causing a disturbance (by knocking things off of the shelves)....
> The thing about him [was], he visibly seemed uneasy and on edge.
> He wasn't a good liar, and ... I'm thinking that maybe he could shed
> some light about the videotape, or who really was in the store that
> night. I'm sure he was pressured or coerced into saying what he
> said.... If anybody says they were pressured or coerced by the police
> ... that could prove to be helpful ...
>
> I feel that any investigating should start with the Sanchezes,
> because due to the connection [with Acerra], they would appear to
> be the easiest to coerce.... They're the nucleus of the case, and there's
> so much wrong with them. If they say they were pressured or

coerced, or shown my picture or told which picture was mine, the
court would be obligated to revisit my case.

It's obvious something happened down in that car between
them, and maybe they were too scared to fess up.... The thing is,
now those cops are locked up ... so [the Sanchezes] would have
nothing to worry about ... [Acerra and Robinson] pressured their
own colleague [Brazil] to lie for them, so it would be ludicrous for
anyone to think the Sanchezes weren't pressured ...

There should have been a hearing in my situation, due to the
circumstances.

Sean did not answer any of my questions. I was perturbed. Why did he dodge them? Janet's warning not to be naïve came back to me. On the other hand, Jackie said Sean's phone calls were monitored. Maybe his letters were too? (I later learned they were.)

The Walpole CO at the entrance desk appeared uncertain about my Quebec driver's license. "Have you visited before?" she asked, her brow furrowed. She searched through her file drawer, pulled out a folder, and jotted something down.

They were apparently keeping tabs on me.

Sean was already on his side of the plexiglass when Jackie and I went in. He plunged animatedly into his case, ignoring Jackie's health problems and recent surgery.

"What would you do differently in a new trial?" I asked.

Without hesitation he said, "Use diagrams. When jurors see things and not just hear things, they get a better idea of how the scene was." He wanted jurors to note the conflicting accounts of the parking-lot witnesses: Ivan Sanchez seeing two men in dark clothes come out of the woods and walk to the pay phones; Joseph Saunders seeing a man in a white shirt walk to the phones from a different direction.

Across the visiting room, a Spanish-speaking visitor who'd been arguing with an inmate began crying and wailing without stop. I wanted to ask the woman to be quiet. We had limited time with Sean. Then I thought better of it. The inmate might make Sean's life miserable after we left.

I summoned my courage and brought up Terry Patterson's moved car. I didn't want to broach uncomfortable territory in front of Jackie, given her fragile health, but I needed to know whether Sean was in that car when it was parked on Victor Brown's street. "Terry's car parked by Brown's house seems like a big problem," I began.

Sean cut me off. "I had a conversation with my lawyer about it. There are things he doesn't want to reveal. But he wasn't worried about that. He was more worried about Rosa Sanchez." Sean's voice grew soft, and he mumbled, "After all, it's not my car. It's Terry's car. So how can I be responsible . . ."

I was thinking this sounded weak when Sean, his voice a near-whisper, said, "I wasn't in the car." At least that's what I thought I heard him say. I opened my mouth to ask when he abruptly announced, "I've been considering whether to dismiss my lawyers."

"Why, Sean?" Jackie demanded.

"I'm afraid Duncan lacks passion. When I read the daily Court News, I never see his name on anything. Maybe I need a lawyer who's more schooled in appeals."

Jackie and I heard Sean out but cautioned him to defer judgment. Jackie told him we would soon meet with Duncan. She promised to assess how motivated he seemed and report back. "Until then, do nothing," she said. Sean nodded.

"Your lawyers want to win as much as you do, Sean," I said.

Jackie agreed. "Yes. I believe the loss was a real slap in the face to Zalkind. After two hung juries, the lawyers felt sure the case was either gonna be won or dismissed."

The subject turned to Patterson. Jackie asked, "Is that dude still up your rear?"

I noted that Patterson's name was not spoken aloud between mother and son.

Sean shrugged. "He has a new lawyer. They're trying to appeal based on the fingerprint evidence being inadmissible."

The conversation moved to Jackie's cancer, and Sean became emotional. With voice quavering, he began to quiz his mother about "the goals" of her various treatment options. I slipped out to give them privacy.

While I waited in the reception area for Jackie, I jotted down the key areas Sean said he wanted investigated:

- Why wasn't the Walgreens videotape system functioning that morning? Was it broken? Is there a repair log?
- Were the witnesses really at Walgreens at 3:00, or did they claim this in return for having their criminal charges dropped or lessened?
- Did Evony Chung and Joseph Saunders really see *The Bodyguard*?
- Did Rosa Sanchez really buy soap?
- Does Walgreens have a master cash-register list showing what was sold and when? If so, was soap sold around 3:20 that morning?
- Acerra testified he knew Rosa's husband, Ivan, from "police business." Ivan had several arrests. Did Acerra set the Sanchezes up as witnesses using Garcia—their relative and his colleague at Area E-5?
- Check out all the 1993 arrests on record at the Sanchezes' Humboldt Avenue, Roxbury, address.

"Ah, the Mulligan case. It's a big file," said the clerk at the Old Federal Courthouse in Boston's Post Office Square, the temporary site of Suffolk County Superior Courthouse records while that building was undergoing repairs. He handed me the thick binder holding Sean's case records. The file could not leave the premises or be copied; I had to read it onsite.

It was already late afternoon, so I could only make a start. I had just over an hour until I'd meet Pam for dinner. I'd spent the morning setting up for my Boston summer by procuring a cell phone with a 617 area code. My Canadian cell was near useless, given the hefty foreign long-distance fees.

I spread out the documents on a massive table in the adjoining conference room. The papers were a jumble, and it took me a while to sort them out. Here was Sean's October 1993 arrest warrant for first-degree murder. Next, an affidavit attesting to his indigence. A series of defense motions requesting funds from the Commonwealth of Massachusetts: pathologist, $1,000; news-tracking service, $1,500; investigator, $3,000; ballistics expert, $200; photographs, $1,200; fingerprint and crime-scene expert, $1,500; hair-and-fiber expert, $1,000; ballistics expert (again), $1,000; investigator (again), $3,000.

I wondered what the forensic tests turned up. Evidently nothing implicating Sean.

I saw a February 1994 defense motion to bring Alfred Glover into court—the man whose photo in the police array brought Rosa Sanchez to tears when she mistook him for her stalker. The motion was denied.

The next document I pulled was a February 1994 FBI "Report on Anthony Gonsalves." Reading it nearly stopped my heart.

Gonsalves was described as an ex-boyfriend of Sean's older sister, Johnna, and an informant for the agency's bureau in New Haven, Connecticut. He told his FBI contact that three months after Mulligan's murder, Johnna patched through a phone call to him from Sean in jail. He said Sean asked him for a loan of $25,000 for his bail and promised to repay him with twenty-six to twenty-eight kilos of cocaine as soon as he was free.

Gonsalves said he learned Mulligan had been murdered because he got greedy and "took 3Gs [$3,000] from a drug raid and was asking for too much money to allow Terry Patterson and Sean to continue distributing." He said Sean told him that he and "another individual" were in a car with a gun belonging to Sean's girlfriend. Sean gave the gun to this man, who shot Mulligan. Bottom line, "Terry Patterson and Sean Ellis plotted to kill [Mulligan]...they made it look like a common robbery."

Stricken, I read on: Gonsalves said Johnna told him "the officer was dirty" and for that reason Sean believed the Commonwealth wouldn't go to trial. He told his FBI handler he asked Sean whether he shot Mulligan, but

Sean did not answer him directly: "He said the only thing they had on him was his girlfriend's fingerprints on the clip of the gun that was recovered."

As for Sean's girlfriend, Gonsalves said Sean told him "they'd taken care of her." He said Sean believed he was "doing dead time and had the case beat ... because he could not be identified. No fingerprints of his, and 'it was raining very hard that night...'"

The FBI agent asked Gonsalves why he'd come forward with this information. He replied, "It bothered me because Sean Ellis had said he'd 'taken care of' his girlfriend.... Could I have stopped something?... Had it already transpired, or was it about to happen?"

Typing these notes into my laptop, I felt sick. If true, Gonsalves's claims were devastating.

"Time's up," the Suffolk County clerk said, poking his head into the conference room. "The office is closing."

In a daze, I stuffed the assorted papers back into the binder. Riding down the antiquated courthouse elevator, I felt shattered. Sean and Patterson set out to murder Mulligan? What had I gotten myself into? I'd just arrived in Boston, raring to prove Sean's innocence, and the first thing I came across was Sean "plotted to kill"?

In just a few moments I'd meet up with Pam. Did she and Jackie know about this FBI informer? Should I broach the explosive topic with them? How could I hold it in?

On my walk to Faneuil Hall Marketplace, I mulled over Gonsalves's claims. Prosecutors had not used him as a witness... of course. His account would expose Mulligan as taking drug payoffs. Suddenly it hit me: Gonsalves must be the informer whom reporter John Ellement told me about on the phone, the guy who made drug claims about Mulligan and Sean but was "said to be lying."

Aspects of Gonsalves' story did sound credible though. Tia Walker's print did turn up on a gun clip. Mulligan's supplying drugs to kids was in line with what David Murray said. Mulligan's demanding more money seemed plausible—and a recipe for murder.

I had a dust-settling insight. Gonsalves' scenario of the kids making the murder look like a common robbery could have come straight from the newspaper. Likewise, Tia's print. That information was reported at the time of Sean's October arraignment; Gonsalves' FBI interview didn't occur till the following February.

The very existence of the FBI informer was troubling though.

I decided there was no way I could blurt out my finding to Pam. No way would she believe an FBI informer over Sean. Jackie, too, believed whole-heartedly in Sean's innocence.

A rock band was playing at the entrance to the North Marketplace. Pam was waiting. But when I reached out to kiss her hello, she visibly stiffened. I was confused. Hadn't we become close through those winter phone calls?

We took our seats on the corner restaurant's granite patio, ordered cocktails, and clinked them together in the late afternoon sun, toasting "good work for Sean." I tried to present a cheery smile. It was hard. Gonsalves and his statements flooded my mind. I couldn't carry on with this project if I suspected Sean was a killer.

I noticed tattoos of a heart and Cupid peeking out from under the short sleeve on Pam's left arm. For the first time I saw prominent Gothic letters descending down her right calf: STUTTER, Sean's street name.

I asked Pam about a possible prison transfer that was in the wind for Sean. "Nothing is happening," she said. As she spoke, her eyes remained down, and she drew incessant circles with her straw in her slushy drink, her mood as sour as the daiquiri. I chalked this up to her profound sadness about Sean and her frustration at not being able to touch him for the past six years.

With downcast eyes, Pam sighed deeply. "I tell Sean he's an amazing, strong person to be doing time for another person's crime. I could not stand it myself. I'd think of suicide." We picked our way through our seafood platters.

As Pam talked, I struggled. I was thinking of writing a book about Sean's case, and Pam, Sean, and Jackie were keen on the idea. But what approach would I take? As Sean's friend and advocate? Or as a journalist reporting Sean's story, no matter what the facts revealed?

After dinner Pam caught a Dorchester-bound T, and I headed back to my friend Judy's apartment, all the while asking myself hard questions. What would I do if I found verifiable information implicating Sean? I thought about it all night.

By morning I'd decided I had to be open to any information I might uncover. I would never lie, but at times it might be necessary to remain quiet about what I learned. I wanted to hear everyone's take on events, most of all Sean's.

As a friend to Jackie, I could take her to visit Sean. Guilt or innocence did not come into play with that. Maybe I could help during her chemotherapy treatments. But as someone investigating the case, my first and only loyalty had to be to the truth.

"Can I bring coffee into the conference room?" I asked the courthouse clerk the next morning.

He nodded and shot back in his broad Boston accent, "Just be shoo-ah to use the cowe-stahs on the table." He chortled at his jest, and I smiled back. The idea of being fastidious in the dumpy surroundings was amusing.

I picked up where I'd left off in the case file. The FBI notified the Boston police about Gonsalves' information on February 10, 1994, three days after his New Haven interview. Yet Mulligan task force detectives Thomas O'Leary and Kenneth Dorch did not interview Gonsalves until September 8, 1994. My eyes lingered on the date. Why did Boston police wait seven months to speak with Gonsalves?

The first part of Gonsalves' Boston interview echoed the information he'd told the FBI agent in New Haven, as written up in the agency's report. Then things started getting weird. At the close of the session, O'Leary told Gonsalves they were "basically finished" and that he'd play back the tape to see whether Gonsalves wanted to correct or add anything. After that O'Leary added this exchange to the record:

O'Leary: "Did you ever...tell [the New Haven agent] or any other agent that John Mulligan was running a cocaine distribution ring?"

Gonsalves: "I don't know if Detective Mulligan, you know..."

O'Leary: "And did Sean Ellis ever tell you that John Mulligan was receiving money from their organization to allow them to continue selling cocaine?"

Gonsalves: "No, I had no conversation to that, other than the effect of... Sean telling me that it would not go to trial because the officer was dirty..."

Gonsalves also said Sean never told him the gun belonged to his girlfriend.

This was screwed up. Weren't these the very things Gonsalves had just told the Boston detectives, the same things he told the FBI? Now all that remained of Gonsalves' earlier story was Sean saying his girlfriend's fingerprints were on a gun clip.

Rereading the Boston Police Department transcript, it appeared to me that O'Leary was leading Gonsalves and that his tacked-on conclusion was an elaborate cover-up of Mulligan.

Next I came across a motion submitted by Zalkind and Duncan to subpoena the New Haven FBI agent who interviewed Gonsalves. They said the agent's "notes would substantially differ from the recollections of Gonsalves."

I had to think about this for a moment. Then it struck me. Sean's lawyers were signaling to prosecutors, "If you bring out your informer, we'll bring out the FBI agent he spoke with, and the world will learn what he actually told the FBI about Mulligan's activities." It was brilliant.

The more I thought about Gonsalves' story, the more implausible it seemed. Sean never was granted bail. Zalkind requested bail, but it was denied. Moreover, all of Sean's phone calls were monitored. It was hard to imagine him announcing over the prison telephone that he intended to "do a large cocaine deal right away" to pay Gonsalves back. Or that he'd "given his girlfriend's gun" to Patterson to kill Mulligan.

I'd seen how circumspect Jackie and Sean were at Walpole. They didn't even say the name Patterson aloud. They referred to him in code. Also, Tia was very much alive. And it was not "raining very hard" that morning.

One other thing Gonsalves said didn't jibe: The detectives asked him if Sean had a speech impediment. Gonsalves said Sean "did not have a stutter."

Though reluctant to leave Boston, I had to return home briefly to meet with a client. As I approached Montreal, the Champlain Bridge appeared magically awash in swirling mists born of the high heat and humidity. A half hour after crossing it, I climbed to my non-air-conditioned, third-floor study. Weary, I girded myself for a return to everyday life and continuing battles with our rebellious teen.

My eyes fell on a note written in a bold, familiar hand and clipped to a printout of a feature article I'd written about Sean that I'd hoped to publish in the *Globe*:

> *DEAR MOM,*
> *I READ YOUR ARTICLE ABOUT SEAN.*
> *IT WAS AWESOME.*
> *SEAN IS LUCKY TO HAVE YOU.*
> *KEEP UP THE GOOD WORK.*
>
> *LOVE, ALISON*

CHAPTER 18

Strategy and Sleuthing

"The third-trial transcripts are now done," David Duncan said as he greeted Jackie and me two weeks later. It had taken three and a half years for the Commonwealth of Massachusetts to produce them. "Sean has his copy, and I'm reading mine and making a list of issues for appeal."

Jackie had requested this meeting with Duncan to discuss next steps. I'd returned to Boston for the meeting and planned to spend several weeks down this time.

It was clear Jackie was ill. She was exhausted from the chemotherapy and plagued with mouth sores. I'd transported her across the Mystic-Tobin Bridge like a fragile egg.

The two of us settled into easy chairs in Duncan's office, and the attorney explained the task he now faced. "For an appeal, reasonable doubt issues—evidence issues—have no bearing whatsoever. These can come in at a new trial, for a jury to consider. But the appeals judges review the case for judicial error only. They look at, 'Was the trial properly conducted?' So we have to focus only on the conduct of Sean's trial."

He and Norman Zalkind had settled on three main issues. First, they would again try to get charges dismissed on double jeopardy grounds. Although Sean was not convicted of murder and robbery in his first two trials, the attorneys believed a third trial on these charges was not a "manifest necessity" but rather an error resulting from the judge's inadequate instructions to jurors about joint venture. "If we won on that, Sean would walk out of prison."

Second, they would again move to dismiss Rosa Sanchez's photo ID of Sean because of the highly unorthodox procedure.

Third, they would move to dismiss Sean's conviction on two evidentiary grounds: the defense's inability to confront Rosa Sanchez in court with Alfred Glover—the man she'd misidentified in the photos as her stalker—to show her unreliability as an eyewitness; and their inability to confront witness Evony Chung over her drug charges.

"Drug charges?" I asked.

"Drug charges," Duncan answered. He leaned forward, his manner intense: "Between Sean's second and third trials, Evony was arrested on a 'possession with intent' drug charge. They seized marijuana and took $3,580 from her underwear. And in the third trial she shifted the time of her arrival at Walgreens earlier and described seeing two men in hoodies in the Walgreens lot sometime after 3:00 a.m. Afterward, her drug charges were dropped, and her confiscated money was returned."

Duncan continued: "Evony Chung's new arrival time fit the Commonwealth's timeline better. It dovetailed with Rosa's times and bolstered the Commonwealth's case. She had special treatment by police. And the trial judge did not allow the information about Chung's arrest as evidence, although we tried to get it in."

Jackie and I sat openmouthed. Chung's drug arrest lent credence to my theory of Mulligan holding illicit "office hours" at Walgreens. Was Chung being supplied by Mulligan? Were other witnesses in the parking lot there for drug business, not just cough syrup? Or soap? My mind raced. Who wasn't up to no good in that parking lot at 3:00 a.m.?

Duncan turned to the capriciousness of juries. "It can go any way," he said. "Our defense strategy was to keep things simple, to blame Terry Patterson. This case was extremely complex. We ran the risk of losing the jury if the prosecution's case were simpler and thus more appealing. Perhaps it would be different in the next trial. We could use different issues." He sounded wistful. Maybe this explained his and Zalkind's decision not to mount a defense.

"What about trying again to get the Internal Affairs files on Acerra and Robinson and going after their prior corruption?" I asked.

"We can't get at those materials now. We can only get them if there's a new trial," Duncan said.

I sagged in my chair. "I have an idea about a possible new approach," I began, when Jackie perked up and asked Duncan, "Are you comfortable with Elaine making suggestions and being involved?"

"Absolutely. I welcome any good idea, no matter where it's from, anything that will help. I don't have to be the one generating every idea," Duncan said.

I shared my theory of Mulligan being involved with Acerra, Robinson, and Brazil in ripping off drug dealers—an idea not just from my gut but also supported by the 1996 *Globe* report about him and Robinson being investigated by police Internal Affairs. "After Mulligan's murder, I think the three of them panicked when people started examining Mulligan's police work. They were afraid their own crimes would be exposed. To keep the lid on, they needed to put an end to all that digging. So they brought in Rosa

Sanchez and rigged her photo ID of Sean. Then they said, 'Look no further, we've solved the case.'"

Duncan was interested. "We never linked Mulligan with Acerra and Robinson's criminal activity. We'd have to show they were all linked, to show motivation. Would you be willing to research that?"

"Absolutely!"

Just then Zalkind appeared in the doorway. He paid his respects to Jackie, then said, "The press keeps calling me and asking, 'Is he innocent? Is he innocent?' And I tell them, 'We can't say that. All we're interested in is providing him a proper defense, a good defense, the best defense.'"

"Norman, Elaine has an idea," Duncan said. He recapped my theory.

Zalkind's response echoed his partner's. "We didn't go after Mulligan. He was already dead, and you can't be indicted posthumously. We'd have to find evidence connecting them though. News stories don't impress judges."

"One place to look is Mulligan's search warrants," Duncan said. "The *Globe* reporters nailed Acerra and Robinson by pulling their warrants. The two of them—and also Brazil—had a dismal success rate in finding money and drugs. That's probably the place to start."

As Jackie and I got up to leave, I decided I had to bring up the informer Anthony Gonsalves—carefully. "By the way, in the courthouse files I found an FBI informant who said Mulligan was protecting the kids' drug sales and demanding more money from them. What happened to that guy?"

Duncan looked blank, but after a moment he said, "Oh, right. We had him in here. He was a flake. Not reliable at all. It was basically nothing."

"I noticed the prosecutor never called him."

Duncan looked amused. "Why would they? That wasn't going to help their case."

Jackie and I emerged feeling reassured that Duncan was on top of Sean's appeal. She would report this back to Sean, pronto.

Next we headed across town to Boston Police Department headquarters at the edge of Roxbury. On my previous trip to Boston, following Sean's advice, I'd requested the 1993 incident records for Rosa and Ivan Sanchez's

Humboldt Avenue address. The clerk had said the names of any arrested persons would be redacted because of privacy rules, so I'd nearly canceled my request but pressed ahead, and the reports were now ready. I owed the police department twenty dollars.

The afternoon sun had enveloped Boston in intense heat. Passing Northeastern University's newly expanded campus, I invented a parking spot next to a dusty vacant lot. Leaving Jackie in air-conditioned comfort, I walked through the shimmer toward Boston's new, multimillion-dollar, glass-and-steel cathedral to law and order.

In the cool, hushed lobby, the clerk handed me the reports in exchange for my twenty-dollar bill. As I skimmed the sheaf, my knees went weak. I bolted outside and flung open the Jeep's door. "Jackie, you'll never guess. Rosa Sanchez nearly died from a pill overdose five months before Mulligan's murder!"

"Get out!" Jackie screamed. "An overdose?"

I waved the papers before her eyes. We pored over the report. On April 6, 1993, Ivan Sanchez called 911 from their Humboldt Avenue apartment saying his wife had swallowed an "unknown number of unknown pills." An ambulance rushed Rosa to Brigham and Women's Hospital. The Sanchezes' names remained visible because it was a medical emergency response, not an arrest.

"What do you make of it?" I asked Jackie.

"Maybe she had a drug problem?"

"Well, if she was on drugs, maybe Acerra used that to hook her in. A weakness like that would make her vulnerable. The other possibility is a suicide attempt."

"Maybe Zalkind and Duncan can use this to show Rosa was unstable?"

"I don't know if it's even admissible, but that's what I'm thinking, unstable. One more thing added to the unsteady things Rosa has done."

Shar'Day was scheduled to get out of school in an hour. Using a short cut I recalled from our family's Needham years, when Rich ran a lab at nearby Harvard Medical School, I darted through Frederick Law Olmstead's "emerald necklace" of waterways and parks adorning

Boston. After a quick stop at an Office Depot to fax the Sanchez police report to Duncan, we made it to Shar'Day's school just as the dismissal bell rang.

The three of us then ran errands: first to the bank to cash a check Jackie's church choir had donated to help subsidize her fruit-and-vegetable juicing program to combat cancer, and then to the grocery store. Afterward I decreed a third stop as an essential defense against the heat and humidity: an ice cream shop. Jackie chose butter crunch, I picked chocolate walnut, and after a lengthy deliberation, Shar'Day settled on vanilla. The three of us stood licking our cones in contented silence on the searing, dusty sidewalk as cars and trucks whizzed by.

Rosa Sanchez was a mystery. Was her relocation a reward? I embarked on some geographical snooping and brought Pam with me to find the Sanchezes' former Roxbury address. She knew the area and was as curious as I.

At first we couldn't locate Ivan's mother's Humboldt Avenue apartment house. The street numbers seemed to run out. Then we realized it was the abandoned-looking building on the corner. The main entrance was covered in plywood, but we spied a decrepit door on the side street and noticed curtains fluttering from a second-floor window. "It looks like a crack house," Pam said, startled. It was hard to imagine anyone living there.

The next day I drove alone to the Norwood address where Rosa and Ivan were relocated. Perhaps they still lived there. I found a well-kept suburb of tidy lawns, attractive shrubbery, and American flags flying from front porches. The downtown common boasted a distinctive gazebo of white-painted wood. I imagined summer band concerts there.

I drove past the Motor Vehicle Division where I'd gotten my license at age sixteen and smiled at the memory. Driving a standard-shift Ford Falcon, I'd forgotten to put it back into first gear after making the obligatory stop on a hillside. My driver's ed teacher, who'd been cringing in the back seat, told me afterward the reason I passed was that I'd kept my cool.

I found the Sanchezes' garden apartment building, a modest, two-story, red-and-white brick structure on Washington Street next to a chiropractic office and kitty-corner from a Northrop Grumman factory. Closed venetian blinds at every window gave it an inhospitable air. It was a clear improvement over Humboldt Avenue, however.

I parked and walked to the front door. It was locked. Peering in, I saw split-level-style stairs leading up and down. Two names were inked on yellowing paper stapled to the doorframe. Neither was Sanchez.

At a nearby pay phone I dialed 411 and asked for Ivan or Rosa Sanchez. The operator said, "There's no one by that name registered. The only Sanchez I have for Norwood is unpublished, and it's neither of those names."

The couple had vanished.

I headed for the West Roxbury condominium complex that was once home to Mulligan and Acerra. It, too, was on Washington Street. Checking my street atlas, I was surprised to find that Washington extended for miles, from Norwood all the way into West Roxbury and beyond. It was ironic. The Sanchezes, Mulligan, and Acerra basically lived on the same street.

Highview Park was a prosperous looking, well-maintained cluster of three-story, red-brick buildings, a cut above the tired-looking houses surrounding it. Lovely green pines separated the units from Washington Street, and tasteful landscaping graced the divider islands that carved out parking areas for each cluster. A uniformed worker was picking up litter in the gardens with a pointed stick.

Balconies in the upper units held grills, potted plants, and plastic chairs. Ground-floor units like Mulligan's had patios. I'd read that he often stood outside, like a sentinel. Rosa testified that she saw him there when she visited her aunt.

The Roslindale Walgreens stood in a bleak strip mall set back from American Legion Highway by a vast parking lot. The store was fronted by a covered sidewalk. Its glass, weather-protected entranceway protruded from the building. Two pay phones were still mounted on the store's exterior wall immediately to the left of the doors.

I walked into the drugstore past a prominent sign on a pedestal announcing "Videotaping." It felt creepy being there. I bought a candy bar and checked the date and time on the receipt. They were correct.

Next stop was Tampa Street, around the corner from Walgreens, where Rosa and Ivan Sanchez spent that Saturday night watching TV with her sister. Located about half a mile east of Walgreens, it was a pleasant street of compact houses, some of brick and others clad in vinyl siding. Each had a garden. Climbing roses were popular, I noticed. Rosa's sister's house was brick with a wooden porch in front. All was quiet.

Victor Brown's house on Fieldmont Street was just over three-tenths of a mile from the Walgreens mall. It was the last house on Fieldmont before it dead-ended onto American Legion Highway. The area was well-kept. Brown's side yard was surrounded by a chain-link fence. In back was a dense tangle of trees and bushes.

I looked for the footpath he'd described and was surprised to find it was just a short, grassy swath connecting the end of Fieldmont to the sidewalk along American Legion Highway. To reach the strip mall from Brown's house via this path, you'd immediately spill out onto the sidewalk and walk beside the roadway, exposed. There was no hidden route.

CHAPTER 19

The Man at the Window

"It was a dark and stormy night..." Victor Brown said with a nervous laugh. He'd been easy to find in the phone book. I wanted to hear firsthand what he saw outside his house that morning.

At first Brown had been reluctant to speak with me, but after I explained Mark's friendship with Sean and my interest in the case he'd agreed to meet. Now we were sitting at a high two-seater table having lunch together in a crowded Needham bistro.

Brown was white, wore glasses, and was short and slight. He appeared to be in his forties. His medium-length brown hair was gelled back, and he had a brown beard dappled with white. He was dressed casually in khaki pants and a short-sleeved madras shirt.

At the outset of our conversation he wanted to establish three key things about himself: Though not a native of Boston, he'd lived in the area for thirty-plus years. He was quite interested in true crime. And his brother was a detective on the Baltimore police force.

"My friends who grew up in West Roxbury told me Mulligan was a prick," Brown continued. "He'd steal from kids and was known for getting girls in his car. When he was killed, people thought someone might be getting even with him."

His own case theory: "Ellis was the shooter, and Patterson was the hanger-on. Otherwise, why would Ellis hide the guns in Dorchester, near his home? And it was Ellis' girlfriend who helped."

In answer to my questions, Brown described seeing the VW Rabbit outside his house in pretty much the same words he'd used at the trials. But he fleshed out the details. Because he was "a true-crime devotee," he said, he made it a hobby to identify different makes and models of cars, "like the crime fighters." He'd noted the racing bra on the VW and its custom wheels.

He said cars parking at his dead-end street were a nuisance he'd come to expect. Sometimes it was kids necking, other times kids drinking. A couple of times stolen cars were left there, stripped. So when he heard the noisy VW back in, his reaction was, "What is it this time?"

He described seeing two young Black men standing on the sidewalk next to the car. Then they walked into the woods behind his house and began "making a racket": "'What on earth are they doing?' I thought, because the woods are quite tangled and impossible to negotiate. I heard them try to bushwhack their way through, and then I heard them laughing. That kind of put me at ease."

This caught my attention. I pictured Brown at his open second-story window, looking down. The men's "racket" had reached his ears from the brush behind his house. Terry Patterson told detectives he went into the woods to relieve himself. That, plus the teenagers' loud laughter, didn't match Phyllis Broker's description of men creeping around stealthily, intent on going back to Walgreens to murder Mulligan.

The two men then set off on the footpath next to Brown's house "heading in the direction of the mall." With the men now gone, Brown went outside in his boxers and T-shirt to check the vehicle—to see if it had been abandoned with the ignition popped. When he peered inside, he was taken aback to see a Black teenage girl in the back seat. She didn't move, and he figured she was drunk. Suddenly she lifted her head.

"Are you all right?" he asked.

"Yeah," she answered.

Brown then went back inside. He got a drink of water in his kitchen and went upstairs to use the bathroom. As he finished, he heard car doors closing. "Two doors," he told me. "Quickly. Thump, thump!" He repeated the sound: "Thump, thump!"

Brown's confidence surprised me. At the 1995 trials, he'd been unsure of the number of closing doors. He'd agreed with Norman Zalkind "it could have been three."

Now, nearly nine years later, he was positive it was two.

I'd learned from Rich's neuroscience colleagues that when people remember an incident, they call upon their last "copy" of the memory, not the original event. Each time they recall the incident, they create a new copy, increasing their distance ever further from the original memory. It is one reason eyewitness testimony is so unreliable.

The next morning, after Brown heard about John Mulligan's murder on TV, he called the police and went to the Hyde Park station. He told his story to one detective, repeated it to a second, and gave it a third time to two more detectives: "This time they taped it."

The detectives had him draw a diagram of his house and its physical relationship to Walgreens, and then another diagram and another, each time adding more detail. One detective, "a heavyset Black guy," challenged him: "Mr. Brown, are you in the habit of going out at night in front of your house and confronting people?"

Brown explained that area kids often drank and parked there. He said he sometimes yelled out to them, "Hey, take it someplace else, we've got kids here." He explained he'd even rigged a portable floodlight to scare them off. It had a dangling plug, but that morning he hadn't reached through his window to plug it in.

The detectives wanted to view the area. To avoid the TV-news crews swarming the station house, they arranged to leave singly and follow Brown to his house. They spent half an hour there on Sunday, looking around the wooded area and going house to house, asking neighbors whether they'd heard anything. They had not. The police also searched the footpath, apparently for a gun. One detective went upstairs to Brown's bedroom to get a visual perspective on the street.

The next day Brown was asked to go to the homicide unit in South Boston, where detectives asked him for more detail on the car and showed him brochures depicting various makes and models, paint-color chips, and car accessories.

On Tuesday a detective called him and asked, "Are you sure about the time of 3:30?"—the arrival time for the VW that Brown had reported. Brown said he was sure. The detective persisted: "Do you keep any clocks set ahead?" This jogged Brown's memory. "Yes!" he replied, "my wife does!"

"She still does," Brown commented to me. "It drives me crazy!"

"What did the detective say when you told him that?" I asked.

"Thank you!" Brown said emphatically, imitating the officer's reply.

Soon three detectives came to Brown's house saying they had a car for him to look at. They took him to Stratton Street in Dorchester, where on a narrow driveway Brown saw the same VW Rabbit with the racing bra and custom wheels. In the daylight it looked maroon, not brown.

"How did the police find the car there?" I asked Brown. I knew the driveway belonged to the Matthews family, relatives of Patterson's.

"I think they were tipped off by somebody from inside that Stratton Street house," Brown said. "Those guys living there were up to no good themselves, and I think they tipped off the police because they were in trouble. They had the getaway car in their driveway. The cops basically said, 'We'll let you off if you give us information.'…

"Ironically, I'd encountered Mulligan before," he suddenly said with a wry smile. "People leave shopping carts from the mall all over my area, at the end of the footpath. They bring them as far as they can, then take their stuff out and abandon the carts. The stores pay a bounty for the returned carts. Usually it was a minority guy or a Hispanic who shagged carts for the reward. But then I noticed a white guy working the carts. He drove an old Jeep pulling a flatbed trailer on which he'd put the recovered carts. I'd walk my dog, and I'd see him.

"Just a few days before the shooting, I noticed this same guy, now driving a beautiful Ford Explorer and pulling the trailer. I laughed to myself and thought, 'Hey, there must be good money in this. Maybe I should go into it!' Later, when I read in the paper that Mulligan was so indebted that he was shagging carts for dough, I realized the man I saw was him."

Brown brought up prosecutor Phyllis Broker, calling her "a piece of work": "She wore penny loafers—who wears those anymore? And various out-of-date skirts." He said he was "really surprised at all the emotions that came forth" in being a witness. While Broker was preparing him for his courtroom appearance, "Suddenly I burst out crying. I totally surprised myself. I just couldn't stop."

"Were you afraid because of what you'd seen?"

"No, just jumpy. But the police assured me if they ever learned anything that indicated I should take precautions, they'd immediately let me know."

He said that after he testified, Mulligan's brother, Richard, approached him: "He thanked me 'for all I'd done,' [and] it made me just burst into tears again. All I could say was 'I'm, sorry, I'm sorry.'"

Relating this, Brown choked up. "I don't know where all the emotion comes from," he said, pausing to collect himself. Tears filled his eyes. "This is hard. The emotions, the intensity, it still runs high. And after all these years!"

"There's a lot of responsibility in being a witness," I mumbled, caught off guard by Brown's tears. "And it was a murder case. That has to be intense."

"And the guilt," Brown said.

"Guilt?"

"Yes! Why didn't I turn on that floodlight? Why didn't I yell out to those kids and say, 'Hey, you, I'm calling the cops.'" Brown was crying openly now. "If I'd only put on that floodlight or maybe called the cops."

"I doubt the cops would have responded," I said. "A car parked on your street? A couple of kids, maybe drinking? Would that be a high priority for them?"

"Yeah," he said, composing himself. "And maybe if they did respond, and if a cop had come out, the guys would have shot him, too, on their way back to the car." The thought of avoiding a second tragedy seemed to cheer him.

"Sometimes I'm angry," he said. "Those motherfuckers dragged me into this. They just dropped into my life, came onto my street, and did this thing. And now I have all this self-doubt about what I maybe could have done. It's not fair."

CHAPTER 20

"Plain View Mulligan"

"Mulligan was a bad cop," defense attorney Brendan O'Donovan told me matter-of-factly. Brendan had been Rich's buddy in the Holy Cross College Class of 1966. I'd reached out to him, and he invited me to his office in Boston's financial district. He said he recalled the Mulligan case and considered Norman Zalkind a friend. "Remind me, who was the judge?"

When I told him, he pounded his desk. "I should have known that. I shouldn't have even asked. McDaniel was a horrible human being. He probably denied the motion without even reading it."

"That's just what David Duncan told Sean," I said.

"That's the kind of guy he was. Contemptible. By the way, did you ever ask Sean whether he committed the murder?"

"No, I've not asked it directly. I've spent my few prison visits so far getting reacquainted with him, and I'm always with either his mother or his girlfriend."

"Well, you probably shouldn't ask the question, ever," Brendan advised. "You should sit back, let everything accumulate, and come to your own conclusion."

"I guess that's what I'm doing, letting it all seep in."

"That's exactly what lawyers do. You have to live with a case long enough."

I told him I planned to dig into Mulligan's search warrants. He suggested I scour several courthouses the detective probably used: West Roxbury, Roxbury, and Dorchester. Then he announced, "It's Miller time," and we set off for the corner pub to join his cronies for their regular afternoon "brewski."

Walking into the packed bar was like entering the TV set of of the '80s sitcom *Cheers*, only louder and with men only. Picking through the standing-room-only crowd, Brendan found who he was looking for: "Tom Dowd, meet Elaine Murphy. She's working on the Mulligan murder case." Then he sauntered off.

Dowd's business card identified him as a supervisor at the U.S. Department of Treasury's Bureau of Alcohol, Tobacco, and Firearms. I pumped him on what he knew about the case. Dowd didn't have much, only a street rumor. "I heard it was a crime of the moment, that Mulligan induced some woman to have oral sex with him, and the guy who murdered Mulligan evidently saw this or came upon it and got absolutely enraged and flipped out and killed Mulligan. It wasn't premeditated. That's the word out there."

He asked me to fill him in. So, over mugs of beer I shouted out the case basics. When I got to Rosa Sanchez's two tries at the mug shots, Dowd stopped me. "No way! No way you get a second ID!" he yelled. "You never, ever get a second chance to do a photo ID!"

The Area E-5 station house in West Roxbury, the most suburban of Boston's many neighborhoods, was a rambling, shingled, New England-style building. Its sedate appearance belied its notorious reputation. Just down the road was the West Roxbury Courthouse, the first stop in my quest for Mulligan's search warrants.

I filled out a form requesting the detective's warrants from 1990 to 1993. The clerk found only one, issued in 1990. Perhaps Mulligan's warrants had been pulled during the homicide investigation and not returned? On the other hand, maybe he hadn't written many. The detective had been famous for insisting the evidence he found was "in plain view"—so much so that Boston defense attorneys called him "Plain View Mulligan."

My searches at Dorchester District Court and Roxbury Municipal Court fared better. They yielded twenty-one Mulligan warrants for 1991, plus a note referencing a September 1992 Roxbury warrant that had been removed. But there were no other Mulligan warrants for 1992, and none for 1993. If Mulligan had actively pursued drug dealers, it wasn't reflected in his paperwork.

I did an analysis of his twenty-two warrants from 1990 and 1991:

- In nine instances, Mulligan indicated he expected to find drugs.
- Of these, three warrants were marked "no search executed."
- Of the six drug-related warrants Mulligan did execute, only one search resulted in drugs seized, for a success rate of 17 percent.
- In his 1990 search (in Jamaica Plain), drugs were not indicated in the affidavit, yet Mulligan found "cocaine & paraphernalia," boosting his seized-drug success rate to 20 percent.
- Mulligan never once found cash with drugs, giving him a zero percent success rate in this category.

Mulligan's success rate in finding drugs vis-à-vis the warrants he submitted was exactly as pitiful as the rates the *Globe* had reported for Kenneth Acerra, Walter Robinson, and John Brazil. Moreover, Mulligan failed to execute a third of the warrants on which he cited both informant information and surveillance work showing ongoing drug dealing at the address. Why did he lose interest in those cases? Or did he? There was no way to prove that any of Mulligan's executed or non-executed warrants had turned into robberies. But his no-cash findings and nonexecuted searches had a bad smell.

Mulligan appeared to work solo. There was no mention of Acerra, Robinson, or Brazil joining his searches. Was Mulligan's name noted on those other guys' warrants, pulled by the *Globe*? I doubted this; it would have made the news.

Disappointed, I crafted a memo summarizing my findings, faxed it to Duncan, and phoned Jackie to report. Trying to prove Mulligan was a criminal through his warrants was like grasping Jell-O.

CHAPTER 21

"Fill in Gaps"

Over the long Fourth of July weekend Boston's searing heat wave intensified. I escaped the worst of it by visiting my older sister, Janet, and her architect husband at their New Hampshire lakeside cottage. Boston's baking heat had driven them from their stately town house along the Charles River.

My sister and I had never been close. (Despite the common name, our daughter Janet's namesake was Rich's younger sister, who died at age six following heart surgery.) Beyond the eleven-year age difference between us, an even larger gulf separated our values. My sister and her husband were high-flyers and big drinkers. Nonetheless, our visits, though infrequent, were cordial.

As I stood thigh-high in the cool lake water, I wondered how Jackie and Shar'Day were managing in the hundred-degree heat. It gave me a twinge. I knew Jackie used her small window air conditioner sparingly to save on electricity. I admired her so very much. She was a survivor. Our shared bond of motherhood transcended our racial differences, at least in my mind.

No African Americans had lived in my hometown of Scituate, dubbed "the Irish Riviera." The only brown skin I ever saw, apart from the marching bands imported from Boston for Labor Day parades, was on the small group of Cape Verdeans who lived in Scituate's Greenbush section. And it was made clear they were Portuguese in descent, "not really Black"—a lore that presumably softened their impact on the town. Their kids went to school with us and were well-accepted.

My parents certainly shared these racial prejudices, though they were not loudly articulated. The only time I recall race coming up was when I learned that a popular Cape Verdean boy planned to invite me to the Junior Prom. My father got wind of it and sat me down. "You are not going on a date with that boy," he said in the firmest voice I'd ever heard him use. Dad didn't need to give his reason. This was 1962. He was expressing the natural order of things as he saw it, having adopted the racist worldview widely held by white people in those days. I'd simply acquiesced with a shrug.

At Boston College in the late '60s, the handful of Black students (all men) had foreign accents. They were rumored to be tribal princes from Nigeria. Certainly no African American kids from inner cities trod the paths of BC's Gothic campus, at least none that I remember.

Outside campus the civil rights movement was brewing, but we remained insulated. Motown sound and certain star athletes were our Black cultural references, not the Freedom Riders or the March on Washington. I remember seeing the Birmingham riot on the TV news, and my sympathies were surely with the "Negroes"—human beings created by God who deserved fair treatment and dignity. But the civil unrest seemed distant. It was the South's problem, not ours. There were no seg-regated lunch counters in Boston, no fire hoses turned on anyone. We Northerners were enlightened . . .

That's what I actually believed. I knew Boston had Black districts, but I hadn't a clue about what life there was like for residents, apart from media reports of violence. Nor had I given it much thought.

My dawning awareness of Bostonians' long-held prejudices came when Rich and I were first married. I taught school in Charlestown, a strictly white, working-class section of Boston that was famously wary of outsid-ers, even those like us who had Irish surnames but weren't "townies," i.e., lifelong residents. My teacher's aide, Greta, was a townie. She constantly railed against "the Blacks," whom she said took jobs away from her longshoreman husband because of newly implemented minority-hiring quotas. "Kevin Black," Greta would sneer of our mayor, Kevin White, for his perceived concessions to race.

I weathered Greta's frequent verbal storms, astonished at her vitriol. She was an otherwise admirable woman—diligent and caring and gener-ous toward our students, donating her own kids' outgrown winter jackets to the neediest. Of course, our students were white.

During this era Rich taught high school science by day and attended night classes at Northeastern University, working on his master's degree in microbiology. One day he invited his lab mate, Gil, home for dinner. Gil was Black, and he declined the invitation, "too afraid to come to Charlestown." Rich and I were shocked—and ashamed.

Rich then went on to Rutgers University in New Jersey for his Ph.D. After Janet was born I turned our student bungalow into a family day care home. One of my charges was Thandi, a beautiful five-year-old Black girl whose parents were elegant, rather aloof professors from South Africa. I fashioned a Black Christmas tree angel made of felt for Thandi, which pleased her. We still hang that angel up every year.

I never truly knew a Black adult until I reached my thirties and two of my close colleagues in the Massachusetts Department of Education were Black: Shirley and Blanche. I adored them both.

Shirley's desk was next to mine in a cramped office, but her soft, confident tones when phoning school districts posed no intrusion. She hailed from New Jersey, and because of Rich's and my Rutgers days, I knew the geographical references of her family stories.

Blanche was older, perhaps sixty, and sat in an adjoining office. She had bleach-blonde hair and was always smartly dressed in a beautiful pantsuit with matching high heels, plus her signature layers of costume jewelry. Blanche radiated wisdom. Once, when I expressed surprise at her refusal to wear jeans to our regional center's summer picnic—a departure from our professional attire that made the rest of us as excited as schoolgirls (this was the 1980s)—Blanche admonished me in a suddenly serious tone: "When you're a Black woman, you don't dress down, ever. To be taken seriously, you dress up." I was first astonished, then chagrined, to realize she lived under this burden.

It was during this period that Mark started bringing Sean home from Needham's Mitchell School. That was the extent of my experiences with Black people. After Needham, our Canadian years were as relentlessly white as the snow—until I reconnected with Sean and Jackie.

On Tuesday I picked up Jackie and Shar'Day for a quick trip to the law office. We'd set aside time to read Sean's trial-three transcripts. On the ride into town, Jackie said Pam and Sean were arguing again, this time about her hair extensions. "Sean told her, 'My woman's not going to be fake,' and Pam took the heat. It's blossomed into a regular womanhood-manhood thing."

Though she was smiling, Jackie sounded exasperated. "He called me at 7:00 on Saturday morning, again at noon, and then at the end of the day, to referee their fight. Then Sean's friend—I call him 'Old Dude'—counseled Sean and told him exactly what I'd already said: 'Apologize. Don't insult Pam's appearance.' I said to Sean, 'How come you listen when Old Dude tells you that, but you don't listen to me?'"

"It's the mothers' lament," I laughed. "They never listen to us, only to other people." It held true no matter where the kids were, I thought, picturing Alison, impervious to any advice Rich and I might offer. As if to underscore her independence, she'd moved to the basement suite in our home the minute Janet moved out to share an apartment with Devin.

Jackie and I read the transcripts all morning while Shar'Day played with her dolls. It was distressing to be reminded of the absence of testimony from David Murray. The convicting jury never heard of Sean's heartfelt denials to his uncle or of a bloody Terry Patterson running up to Sean outside Walgreens and then tossing him the guns.

The two of us shared a chuckle over a transcribed bench conference concerning Murray at the start of the trial. Sean's attorney David Duncan asked Judge McDaniel if prosecutors planned to call Murray as a witness, and the judge turned to Phyllis Broker. She hemmed and hawed and finally told McDaniel, "If you ask David Murray what he had for breakfast, he'll say, 'Cheerios, and Sean Ellis didn't kill Officer Mulligan.'"

To my surprise, Ivan Sanchez also didn't testify in trial three. "They supposedly went looking for Ivan but couldn't find him," Jackie explained.

Couldn't find Ivan? How convenient for the Commonwealth's case. It meant there was no description from Ivan of a black hoodie worn by the tall, thin man at the phones—supposedly Sean—in contrast with the greenish-blue hoodie Rosa Sanchez put on this man. No confusing jurors with the pesky time reversal between the two men Ivan saw come out of the woods just after three a.m. and the pair Victor Brown saw go into the woods from his side *twenty-five minutes later.* No testimony from Ivan about watching these men—whom Broker said were Sean and Patterson—still standing at the phone bank until he and Rosa left at 3:25, conflicting with both deliveryman Art DeSalvo's testimony about a "brown" car—supposedly Patterson's—almost colliding with him at 3:15 and Brown's testimony about Patterson driving into his side street at precisely 3:20.

Reading the transcript depressed me. The third jury heard only part of the story.

Some days later I found myself seated in a plush easy chair in the well-appointed, walnut-paneled "Great Library" of a swanky high-rise Boston condominium building. I'd been surprised when the jury foreman from

Sean's third trial agreed to meet. Although jurors' names were not released, I'd spotted his signature on the verdict slip and tracked him down.
Now the two of us were having tea and cookies, an amenity set out for the
building's residents every afternoon.

The foreman appeared to be about sixty. He was a business professor
at a prestigious local university and was short, portly, and growing bald,
his head crowned by a ruffle of gray and brown waves. He wore a suit
and tie.

As we shook hands and took our seats he asked, "What ever happened
to Ellis? Did he get out on appeal? I never followed it up after the trial."

Taken aback, I struggled to keep my voice even. "No, he's still in prison,
serving out his sentence of life without parole. So far, his appeals have
been denied."

"So, you think he may be innocent?" The foreman eyed me over his
china teacup.

"Well, it just may be—"

"Not a chance," he interrupted with a knowing smile. "He's a murderer.
Multiple times."

"Multiple times?"

"Well, anyone close to the case got murdered. The girlfriend, the
friends..."

"Oh," I responded weakly. How could I counter this degree of misinfor-
mation? "Let me tell you about my interest in the case," I said, explaining
my family's relationship with Sean.

"I didn't know Ellis was in METCO."

"Yes, but he dropped out of the program after his older brother
drowned in Needham." I described Joseph's accident and its devastating
effect on Sean, adding, "He had way less of a criminal record than the
Dorchester kids he hung with."

"I never knew anything about criminal records. All that was kept from
the jury."

"Anyway, the week following Sean's conviction, the *Globe* printed a short op-ed I wrote about him from the standpoint of what a shame and waste of potential his story was."

The foreman's eyes lit up. "I bet that didn't go down too well with the Irish South Boston set. Not much sympathy over there."

He was eager to describe his role in the proceedings. "First off, my colleagues couldn't believe I even got picked for the jury. You'll never get chosen, they said. A university professor? But what I think happened was, that Jewish defense lawyer . . ." He groped for a name.

"Norman Zalkind?"

"Yes. Well, I think he looked me over and figured, 'Here's a liberal Jew from Newton, a do-gooder. We'll be safe with him.' What he didn't know was, I'm from Chelsea."

Chelsea was a hardscrabble city on Boston's northern edge, and the foreman pronounced its name with defiance. That and the way he said 'do-gooder' seemed meant to dispel any whiff he was soft on crime.

"I went home that night and told my wife, 'I got picked, and it's some murder case.' I had no idea at the time how much interest there was in it. That's because I only read the *Christian Science Monitor*. So I was in the dark about the case, totally. Later, I was absolutely floored to be selected foreman by the judge."

"Was the panel racially mixed?"

He strained to recall. "Yes, there were two—no, I guess three—Black members, two women and a man. One woman was a public relations person for Gillette, a real up-and-comer, a sharp dresser and very outgoing. The other Black woman was older. She'd been a nurse.

"As soon as we got in the room," he continued, "some people were impatient, one guy in particular. Right away he said, 'He's guilty, guilty as hell. Let's just vote and get this whole thing over with.' And there was some sentiment for this. People were actually all worked up and shouting.

"I had to restrain this man. 'You may be right,' I said, 'but put the thought aside for a little while.' I tried to calm everyone down. 'We'll get to that,' I said, 'but since we may be working here together for a few days,

I think it would be a good idea to get to know each other.' And so we pro-ceeded to introduce ourselves and say what we did for a living. That's why I remember those details about the two Black ladies.

"Anyway, the impatient guy was still grumbling. 'Let's do it quickly,' was his manner. But I insisted we go about things carefully. I said, 'Some of you, maybe all of you, may have reached your conclusion, but before we get to that, let's throw out on the table any questions or areas of concern each of us may have. This will become our agenda. We'll set all our minds to these concerns. Some of us may have better memories than others around this or that point, and we'll be able to help each other.' And they did. And all the issues of concern were brought forward and aired."

"Do you remember what the issues were?"

He searched his memory but could recall only one. "The timeline of the murder night was mostly on people's minds. So we figured out that timeline till we had only about thirty seconds unaccounted for."

This assertion stunned me, given my own lengthy analysis of crucial minutes. Judge McDaniel had prohibited jurors from taking notes—a rul-ing I deplored. How could they be this confident? In my mind, the prosecu-tors' timeline was the weakest part of their case.

"The judge's instructions on this were powerful," he continued. "Two aspects were totally liberating. McDaniel indicated we could 'fill in gaps' using our own logic. I didn't realize you could do this, and it helped me, personally, to jump over that missing gap of time."

Fill in gaps?

"The second point was joint venture, that as long as the two boys were shown to have been together before and during the crime, that was joint venture. It didn't matter which one actually pulled the trigger. And that changed the way I looked at the case."

My radar went up. Terry Patterson and Sean, together *during* the crime? What evidence was there of that? Anyway, didn't Zalkind inform jurors that "mere presence" did *not* constitute joint venture?

"When the jury finished hashing over all the outstanding issues and settled each one to the group's satisfaction, they went for a vote. It was on the second day. And one by one, around the table, each juror said 'Guilty.'

"The only person who paused was the Black nurse. She said she thought Sean was guilty, but she was concerned with human life and felt very unsure about rendering this verdict, lest he be executed. The other jurors reassured her that the death penalty had been repealed in Massachusetts. Given this assurance, the woman voted guilty."

The foreman paused to finish his tea. "Finally it was my turn to vote. I'd carefully remained neutral. The others turned to me. 'So? How about you?' 'Guilty,' I said, and a roar went up."

Telling me this, the foreman seemed satisfied all over again. "The court officer was astonished we'd reached a verdict so soon. And when we filed into the courtroom, the excitement was extreme. The courtroom began absolutely filling with people, far more than had attended the trial. I think most might have been Boston police officers. The tension in the air was amazing, just electric.

"When the verdict was announced, we were swept outside on this current of high emotion. We were told we were heroes, heroes! They said we were courageous, we were wonderful. And we couldn't believe it. We truly had no idea. It was hard to take it all in. I was astounded. I had absolutely no idea we were heroes or anything of the kind, no sense of the incredible interest in this case. As I said, I only read the *Christian Science Monitor.*"

He sat back. "What questions do you have for me?"

"What did you think when you learned that three Mulligan murder investigators, Acerra, Robinson, and Brazil, later admitted guilt for a decade of stealing drugs and drug money and making false statements on warrants?"

This drew a blank. "Were they? Did they? I had no idea."

"Yes. Brazil turned state's evidence, and Acerra and Robinson went to prison. They were the detectives who brought forward Rosa Sanchez, the teenage witness who said she saw Sean crouching by Mulligan's SUV."

"Crouching? I don't remember crouching."

"By Mulligan's Ford Explorer. Rosa Sanchez said she saw Sean looking inside."

He shrugged, the memory of Sanchez's testimony evidently having faded. "You know, I had no notion the cops might have been shady, but others on the panel were surely far savvier than I, more in the know about things like that. Afterward a couple of them said, 'You knew those cops were shady, didn't you?' I didn't know any such thing.

"Another said, 'Of course, you can't believe a thing the Boston cops say,' and I was surprised. So there's no doubt some of the jurors were knowledgeable about the undercurrents going on. We never discussed anything like that during our work though."

I told him Sean's cousins Celine and Tracy were killed by an ex-boy-friend of Celine's in a dispute over a gold chain, not by Sean—that the young man confessed and was doing time. "Also, Sean was in jail awaiting trial when his two male friends were murdered in Dorchester."

The foreman heard me out, then said he bought the prosecution's case that Patterson and Sean moved the car to Victor Brown's house, and he "presumed" the two walked back to kill the cop. "Sean was there with Patterson, and he left with Patterson, and afterward he hid the guns."

"What did the jury make of the discrepancies in witnesses' descriptions of the Black men in the parking lot that morning?" I asked.

"Discrepancies?" He looked puzzled.

"Two witnesses described a thin man around five feet, ten inches tall who wore a white shirt or a white-hooded outer garment. Sean is six foot one. And three other witnesses put him in a hoodie that was alternately greenish-blue, black, and gray. Another witness put him in a dark T-shirt."

The foreman dismissed these inconsistencies with a wave of his hand. "It was night, it was dark, memories aren't perfect," he said. "Those things just weren't a concern to us. We didn't analyze them."

Given that "those things" were of vital concern to me, I persisted, my fortitude against his seeming indifference finally crumbling. He heard me out but didn't waver. "Twelve jurors voted guilty," he said.

"The first jury voted nine to three to acquit," I shot back. He seemed astonished to hear it. "Your panel didn't hear the testimony by Sean's uncle that the first two juries did hear," I added, filling him in on David Murray's account of his conversations with a distraught Sean.

He looked skeptical. "It was a unanimous verdict," he repeated. "Every single person felt Ellis was clearly guilty. You're thinking he's innocent because he stayed in your home, and you want to believe it."

No, I thought. I know what joint venture means. And I have a decent grasp of what reasonable doubt is. What I said aloud was, "Yes, I do want to believe it, and you may be right." I thanked him for his time.

As I turned to leave, he called out, "Why did the defense not put on a case, not call even one witness who would make the jury pause?"

CHAPTER 22

Jeffrey

Pam and I got as far as the first holding room at Walpole when the female CO looked closely at me. "Stop," she barked. "You can't go in there wearing that. No sleeveless tops allowed."

"Why?" I asked, surprised. I glanced down at my black, jewel-necked Gap blouse.

"I don't make the rules, lady. I just enforce them," a male guard bellowed at me from across the room. A nicer young officer quickly asked if I had a sweater in my car. "I have a trench coat," I said.

"Nope, that won't do."

"Have a nice visit," I told Pam, shooing her off. "Don't worry about me. Go, go, go!"

Sitting down on one of the entry room's hard wooden benches and feeling discouraged, I suddenly remembered a blazer I kept in my car as protection against air conditioning. I rushed out and came back wearing it, strutting before the rude guard, who was now shooting the breeze with a colleague.

"A jacket?" he grunted. "Well, you'll be hot. And you have to keep it on."

"I promise," I said in exaggerated fashion, silently adding "asshole."

"You have two minutes," he growled, meaning the time I had to stow my purse and present myself before the sliding metal door.

When the door opened, the nicer guard, now on the other side, greeted me with a smile. "They'll be surprised to see you."

Sean, seated in the first cubicle, beamed and waved. Today he was full of energy, brimming with ideas. "I've found judicial error!" he announced triumphantly. "The Commonwealth's case did not show grounds for intent."

Seeing our puzzled expressions, he elaborated: "'Crouching by a car' does not indicate intent to steal a gun. I wrote Duncan a letter about this, but he replied that it did. I wrote him back saying, 'I beg to differ. There are other reasons to be crouching. Intent is not supported tightly by a chain of evidence.' I referenced several cases for Duncan that illustrate this point—trials where the jury found the defendant not guilty because intent could not be established."

Pam nodded solemnly. I frowned. Sean was spinning wheels.

"Before, I was more passive and let my lawyers do all the work," he continued. "Now I want to be an active participant in my defense. I'm afraid Duncan might think I'm stubborn, but I don't care. I feel compelled to bring these issues forward. And if I have an issue my lawyer does not wish to bring forward, I can do so myself under the law."

In high spirits, he described his personal regimen. In an effort to bulk up, he was pressing 320 pounds and eating three peanut butter and jelly sandwiches for breakfast, three more after lunch, and another three after dinner. He still looked like a beanpole. Pam was impressed with his muscular arms.

He was also working on his mental conditioning. "I try to picture how it will be to get a new trial," he told us. "Everything starts with a thought. It sets things in motion, and then you watch the fruits of that thought occur. Just think. When God created the earth, it all started with a thought, and the whole world resulted."

On the way home Pam and I stopped for lunch at Legal Seafood at South Shore Plaza in the Boston suburb of Braintree. After that we went to Macy's so I could pick up a bathing suit for the beach outing I'd promised Shar'Day for the next day. Driving Pam back to Dorchester, I noticed that my Jeep's thermometer hit ninety-nine degrees. "I'd love to see three digits on that thing," I said, and just like that it blinked to one hundred and stayed.

That evening in my friend Judy's elegant Back Bay condo, I chopped fruit for the next day's outing and brooded. Sean's lawyers weren't dealing with evidentiary issues right now, boxed in as they were by the ground rules for an appeal. But if the appeal was granted, and Sean got a new trial, we'd need compelling evidence to convince the new panel of jurors to acquit.

I felt frustrated. David Murray's testimony about his conversations with Sean portrayed a bloodied Patterson rushing away from Walgreens. Why didn't Sean tell prosecutors what he knew and cut an immunity deal for himself, the way his friends Curt and Kevin and Tia did? Instead he went to prison, and now he was spending hour after hour in the law library, digging into court cases, searching for any technicality that might overturn his conviction. ("Nits on the nuts of gnats," Rich said when I told him.)

My gut told me the rotten core of this murder was the drug corruption of Kenneth Acerra, Walter Robinson, and John Brazil, and likely John Mulligan too. But how to prove it?

Pam's voice on the phone the next morning was shrill. "Have you heard the news? Sean's nephew Jeffrey shot himself playing Russian roulette. He's dead."

"Who? Who's dead?"

"Jeffrey, Mrs. Ellis' grandson, the son of Sean's sister Dee Dee. He's seventeen. He was at his house with some friends and his eleven-year-old brother. They all watched him shoot himself. I have to go." She hung up.

I'd been putting picnic supplies into an insulated bag. Should I stop? The radio on the kitchen counter kept issuing bulletins about the tragic loss of the small airplane John F. Kennedy Jr. had been piloting over the waters off Cape Cod.

My phone rang again. It was Jackie, sobbing so hard she couldn't speak. Finally she managed to say, "Oh, Elaine, I don't know what to do. I don't know what to do."

"I heard the news from Pam," I said. "I'm so very, very sorry. What can I do to help?" I was scheduled to pick up Shar'Day in an hour. Of course our beach trip would be canceled.

"Can we talk a little later? Me and Shar'Day are going over to Dorchester now to be with Dee Dee and the family."

I flicked on the TV. "What a loss," the commentators were saying over and over about the young Kennedy scion. "That family has endured so much."

An hour or so later Jackie called back. "Can you stand by a little longer? We're on our way to the morgue. I don't know how long it will take."

A few minutes later Shar'Day phoned, sounding cheerful. "Hi, Miss Elaine. Can you take some relatives of mine to the beach with me?"

Surprised, I said, "Of course, Shar'Day." Maybe Jackie wanted a diversion for the little ones.

Jackie phoned again and confirmed this. "If it's not asking too much, Elaine, could you come and get my baby? She needs distracting from all this." She rattled off directions to her sister's house, a route that went through a section of Dorchester I'd avoided most of my adult life. I'd last been there thirty-five years ago, when I volunteered in a Boston College tutoring program that was abruptly canceled after one of the tutors was stabbed.

Jackie's family was sitting silently on her sister Tina's small front porch on this hot, still Sunday morning. I hugged Jackie for several long minutes as she wept. Her whole body shook. When her sobs subsided, she turned to the others and said, "This is Elaine, the one I told you about, Sean's host mother from Needham."

She told me each relative's name in turn, and we shook hands. All were solemn, stricken.

"Are the other kids coming along with Shar'Day to the beach?" I asked.

One woman looked at me with a frown. "I'm keeping my kids with me," she said darkly.

"I understand," I said.

Shar'Day and I set off alone. Judy planned to join us. She had suggested we head to Good Harbor Beach in Rockport, where she'd spent her childhood summers. Judy was eager to meet Shar'Day, and we'd arranged to rendezvous after she made a brief appearance at a family brunch.

As Shar'Day and I turned onto the highway, I brought up Jeffrey's death. "It's so sad."

"I'm glad he's out of this crazy world," Shar'Day said immediately with a fierce, sidewise glance. "I can't wait to die."

I was stunned. I looked at this beautiful child, now ten—the picture of health, a girl with straight A's in school and perfect attendance who'd recently finished reading *Charlotte's Web* and three other paperbacks I'd mailed her.

"Die? Why?"

"To get out of this crazy world."

How could I deal with a child's worldview this bleak? "How old do you think you'll be when you die, Shar'Day?" I asked after some moments. She didn't answer. "About eighty?"

She nodded ever so slightly.

"Well, that's about right, because I think you have a lot of living to do yet."

She stared ahead silently but nodded a tiny bit again.

"It was a crazy gun accident with Jeffrey, but I know you're much too smart to ever play with guns, Shar'Day."

"Never! I'll never, ever play with guns," she said, her face turned fully to me now.

We pulled off the highway to meet Judy. At that moment she emerged from the restaurant, waving gaily. She poked her head into my Jeep. "Hello, Shar'Day. I'm happy to meet you!" Judy led the way in her car, and twenty-five minutes later we parked in tandem on a cottage-lined road by the ocean.

By now the sun felt hot enough to cook us. We rushed to the water. Judy and I waved and nodded approvingly as Shar'Day called to us to admire her swimming and diving skills. Within minutes she was frolicking with two other girls, sharing their inner tube.

We sat on the tranquil shore and, with eyes trained on Shar'Day, I caught Judy up on Sean's case and Jeffrey's tragedy. All the while Shar'Day swam, her energy boundless.

After several pleasant hours, we packed up our gear and drove to a nearby fish and chips joint. Shar'Day ordered a lobster roll and strawberry milk while Judy and I split an order of fried clams, hot and crumbly with squishy-soft bellies, the fare enhanced by sea air mingled with the smell of frying fish.

Rockport had brought welcome relief from both heat and horror. As darkness fell, Shar'Day and I wiped our hands and set off in my Jeep for Dorchester. The stereo piped Sarah McLachlan's ethereal voice: "In the arms of the angel, fly away from here ... May you find some comfort here."

"Jeffrey's in the arms of the angels now," I said, breaking the silence. Shar'Day nodded but remained mute.

The streets of Dorchester were pitch-black, and my Jeep's thermometer registered ninety-nine. Jackie's sister's neighborhood had a different character now from the sleepy Sunday of twelve hours earlier. A mini-skirted woman on a corner was looking to drum up business, and several young men clustered outside a grungy convenience store laughed loudly.

One car after another aggressively pulled out from side streets, cutting me off as if they had the right-of-way. The atmosphere felt chaotic and lawless. I gripped the wheel tightly. Don't piss anyone off, I told myself. I wanted to be anywhere but Dorchester in this simmering darkness. A metallic taste filled my mouth.

I glanced at Shar'Day. Sensing my hesitation on the unfamiliar streets, she perked up and began acting as lookout. At the next intersection she shouted, "Go! Now! Go!"

You had to be fierce to make your way in this traffic.

"Go—now!" Shar'Day commanded again, with an authority beyond her years. "Go left!" she barked. "Now go left again!"

Suddenly we were on her Aunt Tina's quiet street. "Good going, Shar'Day," I said. Family members were still sitting on the porch as I pulled up. I was embarrassed when the telltale "boop" of my remote revealed me locking the doors.

A boy of about eight ran up to Shar'Day, beaming. "Hi, Ma'Trez," she said, lifting him up. Recognizing his distinctive name—he was Tracy Brown's son who, as a toddler, had witnessed her murder and Celine Kirk's—I choked up. I'd thought of this boy so often over the years and never dreamed I'd encounter him. He and Shar'Day scampered off and joined their other cousins under the streetlamp.

"When are you going back to Montreal?" Jackie asked me in a low voice after I nodded my respects to the assembled family.

"Tomorrow morning. I have an appointment there. Take care," I said, hugging her tightly. "Call me when you can."

On the drive back to Quebec, I fed my morose mood by pressing repeat on my stereo to summon Sarah McLachlan singing "Angel" over and over. I knew it was cliché, but I wanted to wallow.

Five hours into the ride, bypassing my house, I headed to Rich's members-only golf club northwest of the city. As I drove down its familiar, winding driveway framed by forests carefully combed of brush, I felt gut-punched. The ultra-manicured setting, which I'd always admired, now seemed a mockery of the world I'd just left behind.

I arrived exactly on time to meet Rich for dinner with his dear friend Warren Chippindale, a much-respected businessman known across Canada. He and Rich were still dewy from their post-golf showers, their faces glowing pink from the eighteen holes and camaraderie. A cloud of aftershave hovered about them.

The sun dipped to the horizon as we took our seats on the stone patio amid the glorious summer flowers and diners murmuring in French and English. Once the waiter poured our wine, I recounted Jeffrey's death, my eyes brimming with tears.

Warren had become like a second father to Rich and me. He knew of my work with Sean. I filled him in about Joseph's drowning and Jackie's daughters' drug problems and her advanced colon cancer. "And now this grandson who Jackie brought up and loved as a son has accidentally shot himself in front of his little brother. Honestly, the things to be sad about are overwhelming. I don't know if I can do this anymore. I can't bear the suffering."

Warren comforted me. "I know. But you have important work to do. Don't lose sight of that. You must learn to pace yourself, just as those in the helping professions do, so you're able to keep fighting."

I nodded bleakly, but I wasn't sure I had the right stuff.

Most of my friends encouraged my efforts on Sean's behalf, but one long-time friend and her husband were skeptical and fearful. The week after Jeffrey died, she emailed me:

> We know you are fighting for all the right reasons, but we also see
> that you are up against some formidable foes, i.e., corrupt cops,
> morally bankrupt people, decades of poverty and poor thinking, a
> culture rife with no values, ethics or morals. More digging may put you
> at personal risk. We think you should not push any further and let
> Sean's lawyers handle the implications of what you have unearthed.

I knew my friends meant well. They were concerned about my safety, and not without reason. But to brand Sean's family with stereotypes like these was wrong. I sighed, realizing I was up against societal issues that were far bigger than anything I could solve.

Yet on a personal level, one thing was clear. I could not walk away from Sean.

CHAPTER 23

Valentine Appeal

"Sean was moved to Shirley yesterday," Jackie said when I picked up the phone in late August. "I haven't spoken with him yet, but he called Pam at 8:00 this morning. Now he'll have contact visits, meaning we'll sit right beside him." Shirley was a rural town forty-five miles northwest of Boston that housed the Souza-Baranowski maximum security prison. It was reputed to be rough but a step up from Walpole.

"How are you doing these days, Jackie?" I asked. I knew Sean had written a eulogy for Jeffrey that Pam delivered.

"Not so well. Elaine, I prayed during Jeffrey's funeral that I'd have no adverse side effects from all the stress, given my chemotherapy treatments. But this month, after the chemo, I've got the mouth sores again. My face broke out, and I had to take to my bed for three days."

Trying to cheer her up, I asked, "How's Shar'Day?" Thanks to Jackie's prowess at procuring financial aid, this coming year Shar'Day would be attending a private, Christian school.

"Good. She's busy catching up in math. And blessedly, her family down south sent one hundred dollars for school supplies and new shoes."

My thoughts flickered to Alison. Over the summer she'd been hired as an extra in a Leslie Nielsen movie being shot in Montreal. Her blonde, blue-eyed looks got her selected as a go-go dancer in a cage. "Don't worry," she told her father and me, "there's a lot of hip thrusts, but I'm not humping a guy, just a pole." (Rich found no particular comfort in that!) And when her first paycheck arrived, it was for $900.

A few weeks later I drove to Boston to take Jackie and Shar'Day out to visit Sean. It would be their first physical contact with him in five years. Souza-Baranowski prison turned out to be a one-story, cinder-block sprawl that, apart from high fences topped with barbed wire encircling the complex, could be taken for a modern elementary school.

Because there was no barrier between inmates and their visitors, the prison's pre-visit inspection was even more invasive than Walpole's. We were commanded to surrender our shoes, pull up our socks as high as they could go, roll down our cuffs, lift up our sleeves, pass our thumbs around the inside of our waistbands, open our mouths, and stick out our tongues. We then walked singly through a metal detector and had one hand stamped with invisible ink, to be read by sensors at the conclusion of our visit.

A third set of doors then opened, and we walked in silence down a long corridor with gleaming linoleum tiles. Two guards sitting at a high entry desk buzzed the three of us into the visiting room and assigned us to a row in the theater-style seating. The COs walked up and down the aisles, eyeing visitors for infractions. I soon learned, courtesy of their shouted rebukes, that you weren't allowed to cross your legs.

After several minutes Sean walked in. Jackie leapt up, and the two embraced for a long moment.

Shar'Day was excited to see her brother. Jackie had never taken her to Walpole. She bubbled over about the brown-and-white cows we'd seen on the drive out. Sean and Jackie talked about her cancer and family news. During a lull, I said, "This prison is bright and clean, compared with Walpole."

"Yeah, but the people are awful," Sean said. "They play mind games constantly with the population. I've been spending a lot of time in the prison law library. I can't stop thinking about the Walgreens videotape 'not working' that day."

"What would the videotape show?" I asked.

He shot back, "That I wasn't wearing a green sweatshirt like Rosa testified. It also might show that all the witnesses who said they were in the store were not actually there."

"The sweatshirt colors that witnesses described were all over the place," I said. "So were the hats—stocking cap, baseball cap, no hat . . ."

Sean and Jackie looked at each other knowingly. Seeing my puzzled expression, Sean explained that the idea he'd worn a hat with a Buffalo Bills logo, as Rosa Sanchez testified, was ridiculous. "Not my style," he said with disdain.

"Sean was not wearing hats in those days," Jackie said. "Patterson did though—baseball caps turned backwards." She demonstrated with her hands.

Suddenly Sean looked down. After a long pause, with voice quavering, he said, "When Rosa testified about the Buffalo Bills logo, I was so happy. Because I knew my mother, hearing it in the courtroom, would finally know Rosa was lying. There's no way I would ever, ever wear that. And my mom would know it."

Sean was near tears. Jackie nodded vigorously.

The February air was crisp and the sky a bright blue when I set out for my next visit to Sean. David Duncan had visited him the previous week with the final draft of his ninety-page brief for the appeal. He planned to submit it this week. The "worst-case timetable" was seven months until Judge McDaniel read it and up to four more months for a decision. That took us to January 2001.

The pulsing rhythms of U2 on my Jeep's sound system matched my mood: "Let go, let's go, discotheque. Go, go, go, discotheque." The lyrics' fierce momentum complemented the tape playing in my head: "We've got to get Sean out of prison...we've got to get Sean out of prison..."

As I drove over the Mystic-Tobin Bridge, diamond lights from Boston skyscrapers glittered in the cold night air. This time down I planned to stay with my sister Janet. She'd just lost her husband to a sudden heart attack, and I wanted to spend time with her.

After a restless night's sleep, I picked up Jackie and Shar'Day for a Sunday afternoon prison visit. They were waiting outside their building in the winter sunshine, Jackie in a purple crushed velvet skirt and matching jacket and Shar'Day in a pink floral skirt and white sweater. Now going on eleven, she'd grown noticeably taller. I was astonished to learn that our visit last fall was the last time they'd been out to Shirley. To reach the rural setting, you needed a car.

We signed in at the reception window only to endure an interminable wait while the guards chatted and joked with one another and shuffled papers. Once admitted to the visiting room, we waited some more for Sean to appear. He finally strode in wearing a glum expression. The white of his left eye was red, and he whispered he'd been "poked" by the inmate sitting in the row across from us. He hugged Shar'Day a few times and kissed her on the forehead and began teasing her about her peeling fingernail polish.

When we began talking about the case, I told him how the sidebar transcript and Rosa Sanchez's police interview made it clear that three guys, not two, were seen outside Walgreens. "Duncan tried hard to get this fact into evidence when he questioned Rosa–because it would mess up the Commonwealth's case theory. It got excluded as hearsay, so jurors never heard it, but Duncan got it preserved for the record."

Sean made a grimace, his default reaction whenever Rosa's name came up. "I have nothing to contribute about that. But even if I did, I wouldn't be able to talk about it. I'd be accused of being a snitch."

I stopped him. "You mean even if you knew something that police would want to know, you couldn't say it because you'd be a snitch?

"Yes," Sean said. "'No snitching' is an honor code that's binding where I come from. People's lives have been spared because of it. This even happened to me."

"Your life was in danger?"

"Yes. One day I was sitting in a car with Tia. We were discussing our relationship when we were accosted by two guys who wanted a question answered. I was stupid, caught asleep—meaning I'd let down my guard. And a 'yes' answer was going to be dangerous for me. It was a life-or-death situation. But still, I said 'yes.' I said it to keep the code not to reveal information. And because of this stance, my life was spared.

"The guys recognized my honor, even though the issue was one they were on the other side of. The phrase we use is, 'right recognizes right.' The men respected me for not snitching, and out of that respect they didn't kill me. And this incident taught me the importance of keeping to the code, of not wavering."

I was aghast. "Life-or-death situation," Sean called it. That he dealt with pressures this huge as a teenager pained me. I thought about the violence in his world. So many people close to him had been murdered: Celine Kirk and Tracy Brown. Curt Headen and Kevin Chisholm. If there was a deeper truth entombed in this case that Sean knew, who was I to judge him if he wanted—needed—to keep his mouth shut?

My moral code was 'always tell the truth.' For Sean, the truth might be too expensive.

I urged him gently, "If you do know something that could help your case, you should tell us about it. You have to believe we'd never let information get out in a way that would jeopardize your safety. Maybe it could get revealed through an investigator. That way you'd be protected; you wouldn't have snitched.

"You have to trust us," I pleaded. Jackie sat there, nodding.

"Trust?" he said with contempt. "I've had experiences in my life that make that difficult."

Just then, a CO shouted "Ellis!" It was Sean's turn to have Polaroid pictures taken. Photos were clearly a morale booster. The inmate photographer, a genial-looking friend of Sean's named Will, took shots of all of us, plus two shots of Sean to mail to Pam.

On the ride home, Jackie and I hashed over the visit. I asked for her thoughts about the no-snitching code, and she said her life experience had taught her there was no going against this rule of the streets. In their Dorchester neighborhood, honoring the code was a condition of survival.

I remembered Jackie's admonitions a year ago about Patterson potentially "raising a gang" in prison against Sean, and how Sean would not snitch even if he knew something to snitch about. I'd heard that inmates consider snitches, along with rapists and child molesters, the lowest forms of life, putting their security in prison at risk.

I shuddered at these realities.

When I dropped Jackie and Shar'Day off, we all hugged. Shar'Day thanked me three times and said, "Last night in bed I was excited, thinking, 'Miss Elaine's coming tomorrow.' Do you know what I like best about your visits?"

"What, Shar'Day?"

"The conversation."

Duncan filed Sean's Supreme Judicial Court appeal on Valentine's Day 2000. I happened to be in Boston the next day, having driven Janet down for a medical school interview. "Come on over," Duncan said when I phoned.

Prominently on display on the law office reception desk was the *Boston Herald*, its entire second page devoted to Sean's appeal, headlined "Cop killer convict wants his fourth day in court, Lawyer claims evidence tainted." A large photo showed Sean in shackles, being led off to prison in 1993 by the now-incarcerated Kenneth Acerra and Walter Robinson. My mouth

AFTER HIS 1993 ARRAIGNMENT, SEAN WAS ESCORTED TO JAIL BY DETECTIVES KENNETH ACERRA (LEFT) AND WALTER ROBINSON. *BOSTON HERALD* PHOTO.

dropped at the image. I'd not seen it before. "This is great," I said to Duncan, holding up the newspaper.

He beamed. "I'm very happy with the play and with the content. It's been all over local TV."

We sat down in the conference room, and Duncan said, "Norman thinks the double jeopardy argument is strong. He thinks Judge McDaniel manipulated the jury by not giving straightforward answers to their questions about joint venture in trials one and two." He sounded angry.

I told Duncan I'd been turning over the idea of writing a book about Sean and his case. Duncan quickly cautioned me: "I'd prefer that you and Sean not discuss any details about the night of the murder or about his relationship with Terry Patterson. Talking about anything else is fine."

"I understand," I said.

Duncan handed me Sean's appeal and its three-inch-thick appendix. "Sean has the strongest issues for appeal I've ever dealt with," he said.

As I left the law office and strode to the harborside parking lot, my mood lightened. Duncan's confidence buoyed me up. Maybe this time Sean would get out of prison.

PART 4

Uphill Climb

CHAPTER 24

"Just Life"

2000

One chilly morning in April I set off from Montreal for the six-hour drive to Souza-Baranowski prison. It would be my first solo visit with Sean. I wanted to learn more about his life, to better understand his thinking.

He ambled into the visiting room, and after we went through the usual pleasantries I said, "Tell me about your teenage years in Dorchester, Sean. You hung out with friends on Hansborough Street, I know. What was your life like?"

He smiled and got a dreamy look in his eyes. "It was at 12 Hansborough.

A nice lady lived there. She was just like one of the guys. She even let us have parties. We'd hang out on her front porch, on her steps. Sometimes guys would drink beer from coolers. There was a liquor store on the corner." He laughed. "I remember the first time I tried moonshine."

I had to ask the question. "Was this a gang?"

"Well, at one time we dressed in the same sports attire. 'The Hansborough Steelers' we called ourselves. Then we put that aside and just identified with being Hansborough."

"Who were the guys?"

"There were five or six. Terry, a guy named Sean Dookie, Jerrold Green, Rob Matthews."

"Were Curt Headen and Kevin Chisholm part of it?"

"No, Curt lived down the street." Then he blurted out, "I sold drugs." He looked sheepish but seemed relieved to put it out there.

"I figured that, Sean. Marijuana? Crack?"

He nodded.

"Did you make a lot of money?"

"I didn't make millions, but I dealt in the hundreds. I'd give Celine money whenever she needed it. And at the time I was looking out for a woman I was involved with and her child."

I knew it was Tia Walker. "How did the business work?"

"I wore a beeper, and when people wanted drugs, they'd beep me."

"Where did you get the drugs?"

"You establish a connect. Generally, once you do that, you only need to deal with him."

"Was Hansborough Street your territory?"

"I had customers from all over, but locally, yes. No one else, for example, would be allowed to come on Hansborough Street and sell. My cousin Tracy used to get after me. She'd say, 'You can't sell drugs forever.' She was pushing me to get a degree, but I was interested in working with my hands. I was interested in an auto mechanics program at Mass Bay Community College, and I was looking into that ... but in the meantime selling drugs was earning me money."

"What about your arrests, Sean? I think the paper said you had six."

He shut his eyes to remember. "The first arrest was when a friend and I stole a car from a crackhead, and we got pulled over. Then we found out the crackhead stole it from a lot."

"How old were you?"

"Young. Could be sixteen. We got brought to the station, booked, and sent home."

"Were you scared?"

"Yeah. After that I got arrested for attempted murder."

"What?" That was one I hadn't heard about.

"Curt and I had an incident. Whenever the guys were over at my house and we'd want to go to the store for a snack or something, they'd take one of my mother's kitchen knives along for protection. Eventually there were no knives left. So, when Curt came over next, I told him, 'We're going to the store to buy my mother a set of kitchen knives.'

"He refused, and we argued. After that he started beeping me all the time—while I was in school, over and over. Like fifty times. So, me and another guy went to see Curt, and he came at me with a twelve-gauge and fired it several times."

"He actually aimed at you?"

"Yeah. I ran out to the car and was trying to get away, but the car wouldn't start. He was standing there, pumping it full of lead. Ultimately, I did get away. Curt's mother came home and saw shotgun holes in her ceiling and called the cops. Curt blamed me, and I got arrested. But then he showed up in court and said it wasn't me who shot up the ceiling."

"That sounds awful, Sean."

"Well, I just thought it was, like, part of life. I mean, you see all this happening around you, and then one day it's you, and it doesn't feel outta the ordinary. It's just life."

"Did you stay friends with Curt?"

"Yes. I respected him because of what he did."

After a silence I asked, "How different are you now, Sean, from in 1993?"

He thought about this for a long moment. "In those days I didn't know anything about life. Now I do. In the early '90s I was just a Black kid from Dorchester. I didn't know about the detectives' history of corruption. Everybody in law enforcement knew about these things at the heart of my case. But I remained in the dark."

"You mentioned having trust issues the last time I visited. What did you mean?"

"Well, when I was young, my older sister Dee Dee had an experience with the police. I witnessed it, and it made a huge impression on me. Someone came to her house and took a kitchen knife and went out and used it. Because my sister knew the perpetrator, and police wanted the information, they promised her protection. They hid her in motels and squeezed it out of her. But after they got what they wanted, they said, 'OK, well, you can go home now.'"

His voice rose an octave higher: "And she was still in danger! The police didn't care at all about her. They just dropped her. And this made me not trust people or their assurances."

Visiting period was drawing to a close, and I didn't want to leave without asking Sean about an astonishing anecdote Pam had recently related. "Is it true that Mulligan opened the Walgreens door for you?"

"I think he might have." Sean smiled slightly and gave a rueful laugh. "When I was going into the store, a cop was leaving, and he held the 'out' door wide open, like in a big sweeping motion, to let me walk through. And later I realized it was probably Mulligan."

Leaving the prison bundled up against the April wind, I recalled a detail from the testimony of Walgreens clerk, Stephen Bannister. He said the diaper aisle trasher in the dark T-shirt came into Walgreens through the 'out' door. I'd suspected the cops planted Bannister's story, right down to the dark T-shirt, because Sean told them that's what he wore.

But how would they know about the kid's unconventional entrance?

A few weeks later, I drove down to visit Sean again. I found him in an unusually good mood and soon found out why. "My father is coming out with my mother on Sunday. I haven't seen him in years. There's a lot of stuff I want to ask him about—family stories, how far back our family goes, things like that. Five or six years ago we had a little tussle, a physical thing. I didn't hit him or anything, but he's been holding a grudge."

I wanted to continue our conversation about his life in Dorchester. "Can you tell me more about the 'no snitching' code?"

He shrugged. "It's just basically how you live. It's what you do. It's a bond between people. And like I told you, because of this, because of not giving anyone up, people have survived.

"The thing is, you grow up together in the same neighborhood, and you have loyalties to each other. I'm a very loyal-type person. You'd sleep in the same bed with these guys, and they'd watch your back. You owed your life to them. We all looked out for one another."

"What do you mean, 'looked out'?"

"I'd sleep at Hansborough sometimes, and I'd know I'd be safe, that the others would not allow anything to happen to me. I was arguing with my mother then, because I didn't like her boyfriend, Willie Taylor."

"Shar'Day's father?"

"Yes. Maybe it was because I didn't like the way he looked, sitting in the foyer when I'd come in. Maybe it was because I wasn't used to seeing my mother with a man. It had been so many years. But I just didn't like him. My mother would criticize me about hanging around with the Hansborough guys, but I'd tell her, 'There's things I see you doing at home that I don't approve of, so who are you to criticize me?' So, I'd hang out on Hansborough. Sometimes I'd be the only one there. But I'd know someone would eventually show up."

I wondered what Sean meant by 'things I see you doing at home,' but I didn't want to go there. I didn't want to invade Jackie's privacy.

"My relationship with my mother has come a long way since then," he continued. "I love her to death now." He gave me a long look. "Those years she was with Shar'Day's father were not her best."

He clearly wanted to talk about it. I gave in. "Drugs?"

He nodded. "I knew what I saw on the street, and then to come home and deal with it, to see it there, in my mother, was hard. I couldn't stand

Willie. He even tried to get me to sell for him! I said, 'No, I'll sell for myself.'"
Sean's scowl was intense.

"Wasn't there a kidnapping incident involving you around that time?"

"Yes," he said, "I was always very close to Shar'Day when she was little. I'd come home and find her in her bedroom, and I'd bring her out and play video games with her. She didn't know what she was doing!" He paused to smile at the memory.

"One day there was a big argument going on in the house, and Shar'Day was crying. So, I scooped her up and brought her outside. I was wiping away her tears and walking around the block to calm her down. Suddenly I looked over my shoulder and saw a cop. 'Give me the kid,' he said, and I said, 'No, she's my sister.' My mother had called the cops, and they booked me for kidnapping. It was a betrayal."

"I guess your mom was trying to teach you a lesson," I ventured.

"So, what's the lesson? If there was one, I didn't get it. I didn't get it then, and I don't get it now." Sean was visibly angry, but he quickly calmed himself. "I totally admire my mother now for how far she's come in her life. It's amazing, because I've seen her on the bottom, when she was having her struggles, and now she's at the top. And I tell Shar'Day she should be grateful, because our mother is putting her all into raising her—though I never mention my mother's past struggles."

"All her effort shows, Sean. Shar'Day is a lovely child."

Sean now brought up another accusation that rankled him. "Some family members think it was me who found Celine's and Tracy's bodies—that I had Ma'Trez call 911 and then took off."

David Murray told me this a year ago.

"It still upsets me that members of my own family say this. How could they believe I found my cousins' bodies, saw the children there, and just walked away and left them? I never could've done that. It's not in my character. If I find Celine, even if I'm dirty—that means in trouble—I still have a duty to stay with my cousins. I never would've left!"

He described how he learned about his cousins' murders. "Terry and I went to the mall where our friend worked at an auto shop." I knew from my reading of Patterson's police interview that this friend was Rob Matthews, Patterson's cousin.

"We hung out, and then our friend drove us to Tracy's apartment. It was surrounded by police cars and ambulances. I said, 'Go around the back, because then I can look inside. They're in my cousin's apartment.' I demanded to be let out of the car, but Terry objected."

I knew they'd driven to Patterson's girlfriend's house nearby and Sean taxied back.

"Eventually I spoke with an ambulance driver," he continued. "I asked him what was happening. He told me they'd found the bodies of two young women." He looked agonized.

"Someone did call 911 from Tracy's apartment," I said. "Do you think Ma'Trez could have done that?"

"Well, I don't know. I think Tracy might have trained him."

I wanted to get Sean's thoughts on something Murray told me the day we met. "Do you think Kevin's and Curt's murders were connected to the case? Your Uncle David said they are."

Sean grimaced at my mention of Murray. Once he discovered his uncle was a police informer, he had no use for him. He would not even speak Murray's name. If he acknowledged his uncle at all, it was as "my mother's brother."

Now he said, "I don't know. I heard the police gave chase both times, but they never caught the assailants. I've wondered about that."

"No, the *Globe* reported that a teenager is doing time for Headen's murder."

Sean shook his head. "The guy who's in prison for Curt's murder is not the guy who killed him. The real killer is still out there."

Seeing my doubtful look, he explained: "The guy they arrested and convicted was *not* the killer. But he kept silent. He wouldn't snitch, squawk, or complain. Though he was wrongfully accused and convicted, he wouldn't give up information. He held to the code. But he's innocent." Sean said all this in a voice full of admiration, even awe. "What happens on the street stays on the street," he added firmly.

He stared straight ahead for a few long moments, and then slowly and deliberately he said, "For me, I think being in prison is God's way of putting me on a new path. Because otherwise, I'd be dead."

Otherwise dead. Did Sean mean he would've been a casualty of Dorchester's violence? Or, given the street's suspicions about cops being behind Chisholm's and Headen's murders, did he mean dead at police hands? I was about to ask, but then I recalled Duncan's admonition against discussing sensitive matters.

Jackie set up interviews for me with Sean's sister Laselle, his father, and his friend Harriet Griffith.

Laselle Ellis lived in a neat white townhouse nestled in the woods in Boston's Hyde Park section. She answered the doorbell holding a baby girl with enormous brown eyes who looked to be about nine months old and was dressed head-to-toe in pink. Her tiny pigtails were tied with pink bows and she wore gold studs in her pierced ears.

"Ooh, what's her name?"

"Klassique," Laselle said, leading me into her small living room. She was a young woman in her mid-twenties and wore a pink Tommy Hilfiger sweat suit. A little boy sat on a couch in front of a giant TV. "He's two," she said, "and I have an eight-year-old in school."

"I have three kids myself," I said, volunteering their ages. "It goes by quickly."

Sitting down, Laselle said, "Mulligan was a dirty cop. I know lots of guys, contacts of mine, who say, 'Yeah, he was robbing us all the time, taking our money.' They said they were glad he was blown away. Besides stealing from kids, he had a reputation for having sex with girls in the projects. They'd give him blow jobs up against the wall."

It was more confirmation of the rumors. I said, "I'm interested in Tia Walker and how the cops treated her during the investigation. I hear you stay in touch with her."

"Yes, Tia still calls me. She was afraid of the cops in those days. She said they would bang on her door and say they'd take away her son if she didn't cooperate. They also made promises to her they didn't keep. They said if she cooperated, she'd get a new identity. They said they'd move her, see that she was financially secure, and give her immunity. She got the immunity, but that was it."

"Police aren't supposed to make threats or promises. Do you think Tia would sign an affidavit about that? It could help Sean."

"I don't know. Word came to Tia a while back that 'Terry wants to see you when he gets out.' Bear came around to tell her that.

"Bear?"

"Yes. She's the mother of Terry's cousin Rob Matthews's baby. She intimidates Tia, and Tia wants to move because they know her address and phone number. She wants nothing to do with them."

Laselle leaned forward. "My theory is the cops killed Mulligan. Maybe he wanted to get out of what they were all in, dealing drugs. But he knew too much, so they had to kill him."

I left Laselle's townhouse with more questions than I had when I arrived.

Sean's father, John Ellis, was sick with a stomach bug on the day we'd arranged to meet, but we talked by phone. When his call came in, I was on the road, so I pulled my Jeep into a Home Depot parking lot. The cold April rain pelting the metal roof was background music to our conversation.

Ellis expressed no interest in me or why I might be involved in his son's case. I inquired about his health and got a lengthy answer involving his inability to get warm, even under several blankets. Then he got right to it. "Sean swore to God to me, 'I didn't kill no one.' Sean felt Patterson was family. But he's not family, and I told him that."

"Patterson was selling for Mulligan," Ellis added matter-of-factly.

This sparked a thought. "If Mulligan supplied Patterson, wouldn't Sean know him? He said he didn't."

"Not necessarily," Ellis said. "You wouldn't know all the contacts." Then he echoed Laselle's angle on the murder: "The street says the police killed Mulligan. Nobody liked him."

"Do you think the murders of Sean's two friends were connected?"

Ellis' answer was immediate. "Yes. It's all connected. They had to die. They knew too much. Both boys were shot in the head, to make sure they would die."

The observation gave me pause. "Were Celine's and Tracy's murders connected as well?"

"Yes," Ellis said, again without hesitation. So much for the gold chain argument, at least in Sean's father's mind.

"I was embarrassed to give my testimony when I saw a woman from my building sitting as a juror," said Harriet Griffith when I phoned her.

"Embarrassed? Why?" I asked.

"Well, because, you know … Sean's calls to me were booty calls."

Suddenly it clicked as never before. Booty calls.

Harriet explained that she met Sean in eleventh grade at Dorchester High. "We went out, and we graduated together, but then we broke up." They remained friends. She'd attended his trials and regularly visited him in prison.

She said her first phone call from Sean that morning was between midnight and 1:00 a.m. "He said he was going to the store for diapers. He didn't say what store or with who."

I was confused. Harriet's times seemed off. "Between midnight and 1:00 a.m." would mean Sean called her before leaving Hansborough Street. But he told the police he called her around 3:00 a.m. from Walgreens and left the message, "I'll call you back when I get home."

Did Sean phone Harriet twice? Maybe he was that persistent.

Harriet continued. "Sean's next call came in when I was asleep. He left a message that said 'Call me back. I'm home.'"

Sean's 'next call'? Harriet was skipping his 3:00 call. Yet 'I'm home' was vital information. Sean's message would pin down exactly when he was back at Tracy's apartment.

"What time was this message?" I asked her excitedly.

"I don't know, and the police didn't check the message company," she said.

A click on Harriet's line indicated an incoming call. "I have to take this," she said. "It's my social worker. I'll call you back."

A good hour later Harriet and I reconnected, and I asked, "Did you know Terry Patterson?"

"I only saw him once. Nobody liked him. He was ignorant. I used to ask Sean why he hung with him. He taunted my friend who's half Black and half Chinese, called her white girl."

"What did people say about Mulligan?"

"Everyone said he was a crooked cop, that he chased the Heath Street Project girls and made them do sexual things to him."

"I've heard that."

After we hung up, I pondered our conversation. Harriet had verified Sean's account of police not checking the time of his early-morning phone calls, information they both believed was exculpatory to him. But even more important was the new perspective she'd given me on the case. I had never once contemplated the "booty" aspect of Sean's calls, and it prompted a lightning-bolt realization:

A person intent on scheduling sex in the wee hours was not likely someone planning to kill a cop.

The solitary drive back to Montreal always afforded me fertile time to mull over the case. This trip I ruminated over what Sean's life was like at the time of his lock-up in fall 1993. He'd just turned nineteen. He was managing the relentless street violence by banding with a posse of friends. The price of their protection was a code of loyalty that, in its very rigidity, imposed a sort of order on the turmoil. But there was no imposing order on the turmoil of Sean's homelife that September.

The arguments with his mother and her despised partner sounded nasty enough, but when they escalated to Jackie's calling the police on him—something she did more than once—they threatened Sean's very freedom. "A betrayal," he called it. How sapping for his youthful spirit to have felt this way about his mother. And now, "other family members" suspected him of not doing right by Celine and Tracy; some even doubted he was innocent of Mulligan's murder. No wonder Sean nursed trust issues.

I winced to think of his personal losses. His father had long ago left the home. His adored brother had drowned; his beloved cousins were brutally murdered; his two good friends were gunned down.

"Just life" he called it.

CHAPTER 25

More Sleuthing

Jackie called me with a reminder. "Sean wants you to find out the time the last movie was shown on Saturday, September 25, 1993, at the Dedham Showcase Cinema. Was it really *The Bodyguard*, as Evony Chung and Joseph Saunders claimed?"

Pam beat me to it. She struck gold at the Boston Public Library. "*The Bodyguard* wasn't showing in Dedham that Saturday night!" she shouted excitedly into the phone. She'd scoured the microfilmed newspaper archives. "*The Fugitive* played at 12:30 a.m., *In the Line of Fire* played at 12:35 a.m., and that was the last scheduled show. No *Bodyguard!*"

"Pam, this is huge! Chung and Saunders spoke to police a week after the murder. They would not have forgotten what movie they saw."

Did it mean their entire story was fake?

Pam mailed me a photocopy of the September 1993 movie schedule from the *Globe*'s classifieds. I later learned *The Bodyguard* wasn't showing anywhere around Boston that weekend. It was released in 1992.

"Sean's sister Laselle and I have an idea," Pam said on the phone some weeks later. "We want to talk with Tia, to see if she was actually threatened by police to make her statement about the guns. I think the police used Tia big time." Suddenly her voice dropped. "I'm feeling so down right now, so anxious about the upcoming SJC [Supreme Judicial Court] hearing." Its date had been set for September 8, 2000. Then she brightened. "But Sean believes the Commonwealth is more likely to let him walk than go to the expense of another trial."

A week later Pam called to say she alone had paid Tia Walker a visit. "Listen to this. The Boston police offered her a house, a car, and money if she'd cooperate. Afterward she got nothing from the police. Nothing."

Just what Laselle had told me. "Did they threaten to take away her son?"

Pam hesitated. "I don't think they made threats, only promises. I feel sorry for Tia. She really loved Sean."

The next day Pam called again, her voice lower than I'd ever heard it. "Sean is upset with me for going to see Tia. Elaine, I can't deal with this anymore." She hung up.

At Souza-Baranowski two weeks later, Jackie, Shar'Day, and I found Sean still seething about Pam's visit to Tia. "I don't want the D.A.'s office to feel I'm trying to influence her. If Tia has a story to tell, she has to come forward on her own. Her story should come out because it's the truth, not because her arm was twisted."

"What about the police promises of a house and cash," I asked, but Sean shrugged and said prosecutors would pass them off as witness protection. "That's what they did with Rosa Sanchez."

By now I'd read David Duncan's appeal and found several issues to talk over with Sean. "Homicide police retrieved the box of Luvs diapers from Tracy's apartment, along with a photo of you, plus your Massachusetts ID, on October 1, four days before Rosa Sanchez made her photo identification of you. So your photo was floating around the homicide unit. They could have shown it to her."

I continued: "And that newspaper delivery man, Art DeSalvo? He sounded flaky, switching the time he saw the brown car run the light at the intersection—obviously to fit Victor Brown's timeline—and totally changing the color of the driver's hat."

Sean agreed. "DeSalvo is another possibly bogus witness. Because Terry recently told me he didn't even go that route. He said something about driving up a one-way street. He knew that whole area because he lived there. So unless Terry was lying to me..."

This was a stunning bit of intelligence. It confirmed that Sean wasn't in the car when Patterson moved it. And the "one-way street" detail fit: Patterson lived on one-way Huntington Avenue, a short distance from Brown's wooded area.

They were crucial details to get into Sean's retrial.

Jackie's sister Jean—Celine and Tracy's mother—was terminally ill with cancer. For months now Jackie had traveled by bus to Jean's Dorchester apartment to care for her. In August, when I was back in Boston, I drove Jackie to Beth Israel Hospital, where Jean had been admitted.

While Jackie spent time at her sister's bedside, I took Shar'Day to lunch at the food court at Boston Children's Hospital across the street. There we bumped into a cousin of hers, a young man who was working construction on a nearby Harvard laboratory building. Shar'Day, now eleven, introduced the two of us with the aplomb of a debutante. I marveled at this child.

When Jackie emerged from the hospital, she was subdued. "Jean is dy-ing," she said. "Elaine, I have a very big favor to ask of you. Would you drive me to Dorchester to my daughter Dee Dee's house? I have to pick up my two granddaughters from there, my daughter Jeanelle's girls. Dee Dee has been minding them, and they're coming out to spend the weekend with me."

I had never met Jackie's daughters, and it took me a minute to do the math: Jeanelle was the daughter who had battled drugs early on but was now a star in a law firm. Dee Dee was the daughter, I'd been told, who was struggling with ongoing substance abuse.

"No problem at all," I said, and Jackie guided me across unfamiliar city neighborhoods to a worn-out wooden two-decker on Dakota Street. When our SUV pulled up, three kids came spilling out the front door and down the steps, prompting Shar'Day to shift gears: "Whaddup?" she asked her two young nieces and nephew Aubrey—the boy, I realized, who'd wit-nessed his big brother Jeffrey's death playing Russian roulette.

The front door flung open again, and an energetic Dee Dee emerged. She was wearing an oversized housedress and greeted us loudly, with whoops and hugs, overjoyed to see Jackie, who introduced me as "my an-gel." Dee Dee reached into my open driver's window, clutched me, kissed me, and gave me a boisterous hug.

I stiffened a bit in spite of myself. Was she always so animated, I won-dered, or was she under the influence this early in the day? I felt a dis-quieting mix of concern for the kids, followed by shame for being so quick to judge.

We exited the car to join her on the sidewalk. Jackie introduced me to Jeanelle's daughters, Christina and Ashley, ages six and nine. They wore cotton sundresses and sandals and smiled shyly. Dee Dee's son Aubrey, now twelve, stood off by himself. I gave him a wave.

With all the cousins in one place, I asked Jackie and Dee Dee if they'd like me to take a few pictures to mail to Sean. They agreed, and I began snapping away with my phone, mostly shots of Christina and Ashley play-ing with Shar'Day. I grabbed one picture of Aubrey. He was a handsome child but looked sad. Dee Dee made sure I got a good shot of her arm, which was tattooed with a heart holding the name Jeffrey.

Just then a skinny woman with unkempt hair came stumbling out of Dee Dee's house and onto the porch. She held up a set of car keys and shook them aimlessly. Then she squinted into the sun, rubbed her nose, and lit a cigarette with a wildly trembling hand. I didn't know who she was, and no introduction was offered. She was clearly not family, and even I could tell she was high. Nice, I thought, glancing at Shar'Day and Jackie's grandkids laughing and playing on the sidewalk.

Dee Dee announced that the following week she planned to host a cookout in honor of Jeffrey. "It's his one-year anniversary," she chirped. Turning to me she said, "You're invited! I want everyone to come!"

On the ride back to her apartment, Jackie was silent. The three girls sat wordlessly in back. Finally Jackie spoke. "Elaine, I'm concerned about this cookout of Dee Dee's. Last week she narrowly escaped a drug bust across the street. She'd just gone over to buy, and as soon as she got back in her door the cops came. Word went out that she was the snitch, and threats were made. I want her to move, and move quickly. I don't think she and my grandkids are safe in that neighborhood now."

Once home, Jackie dug into her cupboard in her building's storage area and gave me all of Sean's case materials for my book research. We loaded box after box into my Jeep: transcripts of the pretrial motion hearings and trials; defense motions and exhibits; and assorted discovery materials, including some I'd never seen.

As I pulled onto the highway, my cell phone rang. It was Jackie: "Jean died."

The next day I began pulling documents from Jackie's boxes. Right away I spotted an area of potential significance: a computer-generated form from the Boston Public Schools documenting Rosa Sanchez's transfer out of Hyde Park High School after the murder. Her withdrawal date: October 4, 1993.

This sent me to the phone. Sanchez's photo ID of Sean wasn't made until October 5. Why would she switch high schools before she identified anyone? How would she know she would make an identification and thus need to be sequestered?

"Norwood High School, this is Gail," came the pleasant voice on the phone. I explained I was researching a 1993 criminal case and asked if I could learn the date that a certain witness had transferred into the school.

"Well, we don't usually give out information. A criminal case, you say?"

"Yes, she was a witness, and we're checking her story. Rosa Sanchez."

"Oh, I remember that case. It was a murder, wasn't it?"

"Yes, the murder of John Mulligan, a Boston detective."

"Oh, that whole situation was crazy. The girl came in real quick. She was hiding because of the case, and all the talk was about 'the case, the case, the murder case.' Let me go check."

After a long while Gail picked up the receiver again. "I found it. Rosa Sanchez registered at Norwood High School on September 27, 1993."

I was floored. It was the day after Mulligan's murder, literally hours after Sanchez gave her statement at the Area E-5 police station. Was her abrupt move to this suburban high school and town an inducement to testify? A reward?

"Did you register her?"

"No. I'm the school secretary. Our guidance director, Wally, did. But I remember that she came in with a man, an older man."

"A policeman?" It had to be Acerra.

"No, at least he wasn't wearing a uniform. I remember she was really, really nervous, and, like I said, hiding because of the case. And the funny thing is, after she registered, she never showed up here—never came to class, not even for a day."

"Never came to school?"

"Nope. She and her husband lived in an apartment building downtown. Wally was constantly calling over there and talking with her husband, asking whether she was coming to school. And the husband kept saying, 'She's gonna come, she'll be there. She'll come tomorrow.' But she never did. She was supposed to be in twelfth grade, and the reason we kept calling was we didn't want her to be a dropout in our statistics. Norwood prides itself on its very low dropout rate. So, after much discussion, we eventually crossed her off our books."

My next find in the discovery materials was a stapled packet of faint photocopied pages. I stared at it in near disbelief. It was the Walgreens cash register log of September 26, 1993. I'd wondered for ages if such a log existed, as had Sean. Now I was holding it. It had been sitting in a box in Jackie's storage unit this whole time.

Flipping through its many pages, I saw that the log detailed the time and contents of every purchase customers had made from midnight till 6:00 a.m. It also gave the ID number of the clerk ("operator") who checked the customer out. I scanned the data hungrily for times pertinent to the case, keeping in mind that the cash register clocks were off by several minutes in an unknown direction.

0:17—refund of $7.13. I recalled the Walgreens manager testifying that Mulligan came back inside for a refund shortly after signing in for his shift. This was the only refund. It had to be Mulligan.

0:19 —expense of $72.00 made by the same store operator. Was it Mulligan's pay for his shift? It didn't seem enough. I'd read he earned twenty-six dollars an hour. Then I remembered Victor Brown's words. It was probably payment for the shopping carts Mulligan shagged.

I skipped down to the approximate times Sean and Rosa Sanchez shopped:

3:01—one package of Luvs for $9.99. Clearly Sean.

3:18—Huggies and several other items totaling $14.54. This must be Evony Chung.

3:19—one bar of Irish Spring soap for 99 cents. Here was Rosa Sanchez, one minute after Chung.

I examined the log for when Stephen Bannister went out on break. He said he'd handled only two cash register transactions that morning. The only operator with just two transactions was number 124, with 3:37 the time of the second transaction. It had to be Bannister. He'd left the store at 3:30. It meant the cash registers were at least seven minutes fast.

After that store sales were continuous until 3:56. Then came a gap of thirty-six minutes. I puzzled it out: 3:56 was probably the time Bannister ran back in, shouting for his manager to call 911, which probably brought sales activity to a stop. Subtracting seven minutes from 3:56 yielded 3:49— the exact time the 911 call was made.

It was more corroboration that the cash registers were seven minutes fast.

What were the implications for Sean of a time corrected by seven minutes? I did the math. It would mean he bought the Luvs at 2:54 a.m. This matched what he told the police. It meant his brush with Mulligan at the Walgreens doors occurred a few minutes before 3:00 a.m. After exiting, Mulligan probably settled down for a nap, to be seen reclining in the driver's seat by Rosa Sanchez and Evony Chung as they walked by moments later. The adjusted time also meant Sanchez had finished her errand earlier.

Studying the times, I saw a discrepancy. David Murray testified that Patterson ran up, bloody, just as Sean exited Walgreens. If Sean's purchase was at 2:54, and Mulligan was shot at 3:45, as police said, how could Patterson be bloody this early?

Going by Murray's account and the adjusted times, Mulligan had to have been killed before 3:00. But the Walgreens clerk described him as sleeping in his driver's seat at 3:30. Had he been fooled? Was the reclining Mulligan actually dead, not sleeping? Terry Patterson's attorney, Nancy Hurley, suggested this at his trial.

Interestingly, Sean had always been eager to find the Walgreens log. He'd never shown any concern over what it might reveal about his errand. I thought about this.

Norman Zalkind had said Murray was looking for the reward money. Did the uncle make up the Patterson bloody-and-running story to earn a cool $25,000 without implicating his nephew?

CHAPTER 26

Supreme Judicial Court

As the date drew closer for Sean's September hearing on the denial of his retrial motion, Janet and I were in a whirl of preparations for her and Devin's wedding on Labor Day weekend in Montreal. She'd sailed through the medical school entrance exam and been accepted to the University of Chicago, her first choice. The two wanted to wed before setting off for the States.

On the day of Janet's final gown alteration, the two of us had lunch together in Montreal's funky Plateau section. We talked at length about her beautiful strapless wedding gown and her last-minute decision to hire a tiny florist shop she loved. Then I caught her up on Sean's case.

I zeroed in on the 2:54 a.m. time of Sean's Luvs purchase and told her about the conflict this set up between Sean's uncle's account of a bloody Terry Patterson running up exactly then and the estimated time of the murder of 3:45.

"Another wrinkle in the timeline is Sean's booty call to Harriet. He supposedly called her at 3:00, after he shopped. This, too, contradicts the uncle's story. I'm really struggling with these uncertainties."

"Are you thinking Sean did it?" Janet asked. She always went to the bottom line.

"No. I don't believe that. It could have been Patterson, or the two guys in the Walgreens woods, or someone else entirely. I don't think for a minute Sean either planned that murder or pulled the trigger. He should not die in prison for this crime. But it's got me wondering. Did the murder happen while Sean was inside shopping just before 3:00 a. m., as his uncle's testimony implied? Or did it happen forty-five minutes later, as prosecutors said?"

An overriding issue had dropped into my lap: whether I could even continue working on Sean's case. August had brought a consequential family development: Rich had accepted the position of president and CEO of the Salk Institute for Biological Studies in San Diego, and in a few weeks we'd be moving to California. Geography would present a major barrier to my Boston research and interviews.

"Well, to me the crucial issue is the possibly false evidence used in the case," Janet said, bringing my focus back to Sean.

"True," I said. "Rosa Sanchez's photo ID reeks, and so do some of the other witnesses' stories." I told her about The Bodyguard not even playing that night.

Janet said, "If Rosa's ID was not authentic and other witnesses lied, it means Sean was convicted in a trial in which prosecutors presented false evidence, knowingly or not. If so, we have to care."

This took me aback. I'd gone into this conversation anticipating a sermon about not trusting a locked-up kid who might be lying his way out.

She continued. "OK, maybe it does strain our ideals to be outraged at a miscarriage of justice for an admitted drug dealer. But it's necessary. It's our test. We have to care, even about a drug dealer, because it's about the integrity of our criminal justice system. Even if the worst-case scenario were true—that Sean actually participated in the murder—if the police framed him and got witnesses to tell a story they constructed, then justice was not served. If Sean's trial was rigged, there's no justification for him being in prison—not even actual guilt."

It was a turnabout for Janet. Now she was appealing to my better angels.

I gave all this a great deal of thought. Ultimately, I decided that despite the West Coast-East Coast challenge, I could not, would not, stop contributing to Sean's fight for freedom. I don't like to let people down. Plus, I was intensely curious. The SJC hearing was fast approaching. What would happen next?

Sean was not permitted by the authorities to attend the hearing. It seemed unimaginably cruel. To buck him up, Jackie and I planned to visit him at Souza-Baranowski just ahead of the session. The night before our visit Jackie phoned me with surprising news: Pam was gone. She'd moved back to Mobile, Alabama—permanently.

At the prison we found Sean devastated. With his head hanging low he said, "My personal problems are what's on my mind now, not the case. Isn't that ironic?"

I told him my news. "Rich has accepted the presidency of the medical research institute that Dr. Jonas Salk founded after he developed the polio vaccine. So three weeks after the hearing, we'll be moving to California."

I quickly followed up with a pledge. "Sean, I will absolutely keep in touch, and I expect to get back to Boston from time to time. Whenever I do, I'll visit you."

He nodded, wide-eyed and silent. Another female abandonment.

I was living with my own female abandonment. Alison, now eighteen, had left home in July after graduating from high school the previous year (in

Quebec, high school ends at grade eleven) and spending two unsatisfying semesters at a local junior college. Having broken up with her boyfriend, and with a few hundred dollars in her pocket, she'd set out on a sixty-hour bus ride west to the Rocky Mountain resort town of Banff, Alberta, to start a new chapter.

Rich had driven her to the bus terminal, slipped her a couple of hundred dollars more, and come home in tears. The separation was brutal to endure as parents, but we had no choice, cheered at least by her declaration of independence from her destructive romance.

Alison returned to Montreal briefly to serve as Janet's maid of honor, and the wedding proved a joyful three-day interlude with a hundred friends and family. The celebration began with an informal rehearsal dinner on our roof deck for out-of-town guests and culminated in a ceremony at McGill University's austere stone chapel followed by a reception at the nearby Museum of Canadian History.

Four days later the happy couple set off for Chicago in a U-Haul truck, and Alison returned to Banff. She'd found a job as a chambermaid at a youth hostel that also provided lodging. Rich and I could only hope it was the beginning of her onward-and-upward journey through life.

Wedding music was still ringing in my ears on September 8 as Jackie and I set out for Sean's hearing in the courthouse in Pemberton Square. As the two of us tiptoed into the courtroom, another case was being heard. We slid onto a wooden bench behind the *Boston Globe*'s John Ellement. Several people in the row in front of us looked our way, all of them white. After some whispering, they stood up and moved, *en masse*, to seats across the aisle. Mulligan supporters, evidently. Jackie's skin color gave her away.

When Sean's case was called, David Duncan stood before the seven-justice panel and said the defense was hampered at Sean's trial by not being able to "impeach" two prosecution witnesses. Judge McDaniel had prohibited them from mentioning Evony Chung's dropped drug charges, and he would not allow them to confront Rosa Sanchez with the man she misidentified as her stalker in the police photo array. They believed Sanchez's tears over his photo were a smoke screen to cover her inability to select Sean, which she was being coerced to do by Detectives Acerra and Robinson. He concluded with the double jeopardy argument based on McDaniel's "inadequate answers to jurors' questions about joint venture."

At the close of Duncan's argument, one justice asked him, "What was Robinson and Acerra's level of information about Ellis?"

"They testified they only had his name and did not know what he looked like," he said.

"So we'd have to accept their testimony," the justice said. Duncan made no reply.

I fumed. On what grounds must we accept Acerra and Robinson's word? They were convicted perjurers.

The Suffolk County assistant D.A.'s counterargument boiled down to, "Although Robinson and Acerra engaged in reprehensible conduct…there has never been any evidence that they tampered with the Mulligan investigation."

Terry Patterson's appeal was up next. Jackie and I decided to stay to hear his appellate attorney, Jack Cunha, argue for overturning his convictions. Cunha said attorney Nancy Hurley erred at trial by not recusing herself to become a witness to rebut the police claim that Patterson fingered Sean as the triggerman. He also argued that the fingerprint evidence used against Patterson was flawed and should be discounted.

On the ride back to Jackie's apartment, I told her we should be optimistic. Duncan had performed well, and the panel of judges would surely conclude that Acerra's and Robinson's patterns of misconduct cast such a shadow on the Mulligan homicide investigation that a retrial was necessary.

As I drove into Jackie's parking lot, both of us teared up. We knew it was the last time we'd see each other for a while.

Over the next month, Rich and I wrapped up our life in Montreal and flew to San Diego full of excitement. The Salk Institute for Biological Studies is one of the top medical research institutions in the United States. Its faculty in 2000 included four Nobel Prize winners, among them the biology giant Francis Crick, whose pioneering work with James Watson in the 1950s revealed the structure of DNA.

Rich's duties as CEO would include fundraising around the globe. I planned to retire from my fourteen-year editorial business to travel with him and help. I was enthusiastic about our move, ready for a new challenge, and especially ready for the warmth of Southern California.

We soon found that settling back in the States after living for fourteen years in Canada entailed more than dropping the u's from neighbour, flavour, and colour. Although Rich and I were both born in Massachusetts, our foreign residence had rendered us invisible to the U.S. banking and insurance industries as well as to California's Motor Vehicle Division. To our astonishment, we were denied credit cards because of our "lack of credit history"; we could establish checking and savings accounts only after getting a letter from our Canadian bank vouching for our "good standing." The crowning blow was having to pass both the written and road tests to procure California driver's licenses. The transition tedium was lightened by a stream of visiting family members.

A month after moving into a temporary beach condo in La Jolla, the city's northernmost district, I received a letter from Sean that had bounced from Montreal and back to Souza-Baranowski before being forwarded to California. Optimistic about his retrial and vindication, he was full of plans for life after prison and seemed to have adjusted to Pam's departure. I was pleased to note his high spirits yet taken aback by his use of mystical language, evidently inspired by a new religion he'd adopted. He'd coined new names for us all: "Godma" for me, "EarthMa" or "Ol' Earth" for Jackie, and "Jahborn" for himself.

> In the Name of God, The Most High
> Peace Godma:
>
> "As a cluster of thought agitates ethereal carnal matter to vivify an outward expression, peace is constantly captivated as the fundamental source of growth."
>
> My Ol' Earth <mother> told me you drove in for the oral

arguments [at the SJC hearing]; I want you to know that I "truly"
appreciate all your support. I was given a blurred gist of what
happened [in court] ... nothing real informative though. When I
called [Duncan's] office after the argument he had left early,
but the person I spoke to at the office said he did a great job! ...

I've begun the strategic process of formulating a defense for
a fourth trial. ... I've been working vigorously ... staying up late
(beyond 2:30 a.m.) just to get this done.

Well, jumping ahead, considering the fact that Pamela
and I aren't together; it appears like I'll be returning home to my
Ol' Earth's house. ... Although I would still be in [Massachusetts],
I would not be in the areas I was before ...
I physically depart as I appeared, in the noble name of Peace!

Truly Yours,
Jahborn (Sean)

After Thanksgiving, a letter from Jackie pricked my conscience.

Just dropping a few lines to let you hear from me and Shar'Day.
We are doing fine. How did it feel to celebrate Thanksgiving
American style again? I thought of you on Thanksgiving while
I was at my daughter's house in Boston. I prepared her turkey
and stuffing for her.

So how is life in California? Is the weather as good as I see it
on television? I hope one day to visit there now that I personally
know someone on the West Coast.

I talked to Sean today. ... His spirits sound good and hopeful.
My health seems OK. ... Right now I'm a little anxious, wanting
to know what my cancer markers are like. Shar'Day seems to be
doing well in her schoolwork.

Well, girlfriend, I'm going to close now. Hope to hear from
you soon.

I phoned Jackie right away, and we had a long, warm, catch-up conversation.

A week later, while walking on beautiful La Jolla Shores Beach, I answered my cell phone and heard Jackie's voice again. This time she was sobbing. "Sean's appeal was denied on all counts," she finally got out. "They said the defense has not met its burden to prove the detectives procured false evidence. But Terry's appeal was granted. His convictions were overturned. He's getting a new trial."

The crashing California surf went blurry. "Oh no, oh no, oh no" was all I managed to say.

CHAPTER 27

Two Worlds

The SJC's December 2000 denial of Sean's appeal was a knockout punch. After spending more than seven years in prison, he'd reached the end of the legal road in Massachusetts. His only recourse now was at the federal level.

> *Peace Godma,*
>> *By now you've heard about the devastating and unjust ruling that the SJC came down with. . . . David Duncan feels that they*

applied the wrong standard to the issues pertaining to Sanchez
and Chung (at least). I'm going to the law library today to do some
research.…

I have a year to file in the Feds so I'm against time as far as my
research, [so] as far as anything that I need to do, I have to do it now.
…

I'll write again once I become more emotionally situated.
Physically I leave you as I greeted you, in the Noble name of Peace,

With Love,
Your GodSon

David Duncan and Norman Zalkind planned to submit a writ of *habeas corpus* to the Federal District Court, a civil action asking the court to determine whether Sean's imprisonment was lawful or whether his trial judge made a reversible error either in procedure or the application of the law.

Jackie wrote:

I know he didn't kill that cop. All through the day I be
thinking about him being in jail for a crime he didn't commit.
And now it seems like it's too late to do anything about it.
I pray every night asking God to reveal the truth to the powers
that be.

I miss him so much and I can't get up there to see him.
I just don't know what to do with myself. Pam seems to have
deserted him … Elaine, I'm all he has. … Oh, well, I just thank
God he can talk and share with me. Better late than never.

It was the most despairing I'd ever heard Jackie. I picked up the phone to reassure her: "Jackie, I'm all in for Sean. I might be in California, but I'm as committed as ever."

A few weeks later the Salk Institute flew Rich and me to London for our first European fundraising trip. I routed our itinerary through Boston, eager to see Sean. A Souza-Baranowski prison guard had a different idea.

Recipe for Frustration, January 2001

1. Fly 3,000 miles from California to Boston.
2. Rent a car and drive the forty-five miles to Shirley in the twenty-hour window the day before your scheduled departure for London.
3. Wait more than an hour in the Souza-Baranowski reception area while the COs chat loudly, shuffle paper, and generally waste your time.
4. Know that Sean is suffering greatly on the other side of the wall.
5. Stand when your name is called, get inspected, and suddenly hear "Contraband!" shouted by a female guard. She is pointing to a tiny safety pin, the smallest size made, replacing a missing button on the waistband of your slacks.
6. Be told, "Come back tomorrow" and get tossed out of the visiting area. There will be no admission for you today, not even if you throw away your tiny pin. No second chances.
7. Know that there is no tomorrow for you, and you won't be back in Massachusetts for months.
8. Drive away, seething, under the steely January sky.

Sean was outraged that I'd been barred:

> *Truly, I was looking forward to seeing you and I was inwardly affected.... Considering that you traveled significant distance, their denying our visit further shows their heartlessness.*
>
> *I'm still reviewing the court's decision, which leaves me bewildered. I'm trying to do the impossible and that's [to] understand an injustice.... I should have been able to argue to the jury my defense theory ... Godma the court hampered my defense!*

While Sean's case seemed fixed in amber, Rich's and my horizons were widening. Our new roles as the Salk Institute's president and "first lady" swept us into a whirlwind of social events. One task we faced was to elevate the Institute's profile in Southern California. To our surprise, although world-renowned for its scientific output, the Institute was shrouded in mystery for many San Diegans. If they thought about "the Salk" at all, they pictured an aloof community of scholars perched on a distant ocean bluff.

After a "revolving-door presidency"—three CEOs had come and gone in the last five years—Rich had been welcomed by the *San Diego Union-Tribune* as the "warm and charming leader" the Salk Institute needed. The two of us went on the social circuit and began attending every major charity ball in the region, intent on becoming the face of the Institute and attracting support.

Soliciting funding for basic research studies can be challenging. In contrast with applied research, whose goal is to develop marketable products and therapies, basic biological research seeks only to expand the world's knowledge base. Basic scientists follow their curiosity, devising experiments that probe the inner workings of cells. Their findings take years to come to fruition but form the essential foundation for future therapies and cures. Donors who appreciate this and are willing to invest "patient money" must be cultivated.

Rich adopted the tagline "Where Cures Begin" to explain the Institute's mission. He took to the podium and proved a natural explainer-in-chief, making complex scientific issues understandable through everyday analogies and clever diagrams. He would demonstrate how Watson and Crick's research into the structure of DNA launched a revolution in cell biology that led to treatments for cancer, cystic fibrosis, and other diseases. By showing a gripping, time-lapse film of dividing cells in a tiny worm, he explained how studies by Salk Nobelist Sydney Brenner laid the groundwork for sequencing the human genome and identifying disease-causing genes.

I contributed my editing skills to Rich's speeches and, based on his public lectures, published my own op-ed in the *San Diego Union-Tribune* to dispel myths about how stem cells are derived and explain how they might elucidate pathways to therapies and cures.

Fundraising rests on developing relationships. This aspect of our work was a pleasure for us. We initiated a series of donor dinners at the Institute featuring lectures by Salk scientists and also hosted private dinners in the home we'd bought in Rancho Santa Fe just north of San Diego. Entertaining philanthropists and world-renowned researchers in beautiful Southern California was a unique privilege. I often pinched myself.

The most fabulous of all our professional duties was the extensive European travel. The Institute had many devoted supporters in Great Britain and on the Continent, and we set out to revive relations with the Europe-based Salk International Council, which had lain dormant during the leadership-turnover years. The council was a star-studded group of sixty or so prominent individuals, including the owner of France's Chateau Margaux vineyard and the business manager of the Rolling Stones.

Salk scientists helped the Institute's fundraising team plot out conferences for council members highlighting advances in biological research, always explained in lay language. During the 2000s these conferences alternated between La Jolla and London, Stockholm, Vienna, and Bordeaux. They were held in the finest hotels, with generous time allotted for social events and excursions.

Rich and I became accustomed to being picked up at airports and hotels by uniformed drivers in limousines and ferried to and from glitterati-studded events. I felt honored to represent the Institute and ended up developing lifelong friends.

Whenever I could I routed our European business travel through the East Coast so I could visit Sean. The contrast of Sean's tense Souza-Baranowski prison and my new, jet-setting Salk Institute world was decidedly head spinning. Overnight I would transform from being the object of respectful, first-class pampering to being growled at and shuffled along by guards who were clearly disdainful of me, the "cop-killer visitor."

In spring 2001, on the heels of my January disappointment at being barred from visiting Sean, Rich and I made another trip to Europe, first to Dublin and London and then on to Turin, Italy. A highlight of our stay there was being accompanied by Italian-born Salk Nobelist Renato Dulbecco and his Scottish wife, Maureen.

With the Dulbeccos, we dined in the Turin home of their friends, Fiat-Ferrari magnate Gianni Agnelli and his elegant wife, Marella, a legendary beauty and 1960s Vogue model. After an apéritif, our distinguished host wielded his gold-topped walking stick to lead us into the family's formal dining room, where the Agnellis' white-gloved butler served us, European-style, from silver platters. I tried my best to appear used to such treatment.

In June Rich and I were back in Massachusetts for his thirty-fifth Holy Cross reunion. Afterward I picked up Jackie for an important meeting with David Duncan. It had been nine months since I'd seen her, and we rejoiced at her cancer's remission. "My doctors call me a walking miracle," she said, smiling and shaking her head in wonder.

Duncan brought us down to earth.

"With Sean's case now at the federal level," he said, "we'll be submitting a *habeas* petition, but you should know there's only a slim chance the judge will choose to hear it. Only three percent of submitted cases get heard. The system works like a chance tree, with the chances of getting a hearing growing thinner as you go up the tree."

I frowned and shot a glance at Jackie; she looked crushed.

We drove out to Souza-Baranowski to report on what Duncan had said. After passing uneventfully through the metal detector, I was approached by a corrections officer who asked whether I'd be willing to take a voluntary test for drugs and explosives to help them check their equipment. "Sure thing," I said, thinking, "Who better to test than ol' Miss Goody Two Shoes?"

Handing me a small white paper disk, the officer commanded me to rub it over the tops of each hand, between my fingers, and across the tops of my shoes. Then he inserted the disk into the machine. While it processed he explained, "If it comes up positive, you will be able to make your visit, but only after you pass another inspection. And if it happens again…"

I cut him off. "You don't need to go through all that for me. It won't be positive."

"That's what they all say," he said with a snort.

I'd grown used to being snarled at by the guards. Just then the machine registered its finding: "Cocaine!" the officer trumpeted. My knees went weak. I'd never seen this drug, except in the movies. So this is what it felt like to be framed.

"That's impossible," I shouted as the guard and others around him shrugged. "Look, I'm sure 'that's what they all say,' but trust me. I have never *seen* cocaine, let alone touched it. This result is completely impossible." I was close to crying, which made me doubly furious.

"If you want to make your visit, you'll have to submit to a pat-down examination," the guard said. So, as a wide-eyed Jackie proceeded to the visiting room, I trotted behind a young female corrections officer to a private anteroom. As she moved her gloved hands under my shirt and around the edges of my bra, searching for hidden drugs, my mind flew back to my most recent encounter with gloves—on the hands of the waistcoated butler who'd served me dinner at the Agnellis' home in Italy.

I laughed aloud at the absurd contrast between the two life paths I trod.

The guard was professional and reassuring: "A positive result doesn't mean you're a user," she said. "It just means that somewhere in the environment you've come in contact with the drug." A friend later told me that twenty-dollar bills from ATMs are well-known carriers of cocaine residue.

When I finally walked into the visiting room, Jackie and Sean looked up. Jackie said, "I thought, 'Oh no. Not Elaine.'" We shared a good laugh.

Jackie and I conveyed Duncan's *habeas* reality check, but Sean brushed it off: "That's how 'The Hurricane' was freed, at the *habeas* level by the federal judge." The release of celebrated prizefighter Rubin "Hurricane" Carter, wrongfully convicted of murder in New Jersey, had inspired Sean ever since I'd sent him Carter's autobiography, *The Sixteenth Round*.

Sean was still fixating on the court's barring his attorneys from im-peaching Rosa Sanchez by bringing into the courtroom Alfred Glover, the man she'd misidentified as her stalker. All winter long he'd mailed me citations of cases supporting his view. Now he wanted to hire a private investigator: "I've been having dreams about a scenario where Glover would walk past her on the street, and the private eye would hide nearby and note her reaction."

Jackie and I sat in silence. The issue was a dead horse.

"Do you think Duncan is sufficiently motivated anymore?" Sean asked abruptly. He said he'd seen a change in attitude in his lawyers from the first trial until now. "They were very charged up in the first trial, a bit notched down in the second, and noticeably less so in the third. And may-be less now? I'm thinking of switching counsel. What's your opinion?"

"Well, Duncan described the *habeas* as an uphill battle, but he was trying to be realistic, not to give us false hope," I said.

"I don't think you should switch lawyers now," Jackie said firmly.

Sean nodded. "I'm just thinking."

On the ride home Jackie wept. "He's my baby, and he tells me he didn't do it. That's all I have to go on. I can't give up hope."

The previous April Rich and I had moved from our rented beach condo in La Jolla to a spacious home in the community of Rancho Santa Fe. Built of white stucco with a terra-cotta roof and nestled on a hillside surrounded by three acres, the dwelling seemed a castle to me. Its large entry foyer and adjoining living room and patio were ideal for hosting Institute events. Though the house had good bones, its interior looked tired, a result of back-to-back divorces. This had been reflected in the listing price, so we'd pounced and were now coexisting with painters and scaffolding, tilers and sacks of grout. The spruce-up had to be finished by Labor Day, when our three kids would visit for the first time.

Come September our family visit unfolded just as I'd envisioned: four days of swimming in our beautiful pool under Rancho Santa Fe's blue sky, followed by dinners under the stars, talking, talking, and talking some more. Alison, now nineteen, was on hiatus from her new hostess job in Banff's Rimrock Hotel. We hadn't seen her in a year. Janet and Devin were enjoying their new life in Chicago, she deep in her medical studies and he grinding out his accounting duties as an associate. Mark was busier than ever, building his software consulting practice and dating an aspiring Broadway singer. I'd kept him apprised of Sean's case, for he very much cared about his old friend.

This visit Mark mused about the defense tactics: Why were all three of Sean's juries empaneled in roughly a day? Did his attorneys not raise challenges or reject jurors? Why was there no forensic evidence—no mention of hair or fibers found in Mulligan's SUV that matched or didn't match Sean or Terry Patterson? Why was there no testimony from ballistics experts on whether the shots were fired from the passenger seat or through the driver's window?

I liked and respected Sean's lawyers. They were sharp, kind, and clearly devoted to him. I was no expert in the law, but should they have been more aggressive?

At visit's end Alison surprised us all by announcing, "I'm ready for school." She wanted to live with us in California and enroll in the community college down the road. It made Rich's and my contentment complete.

The afterglow of our visit was shattered on September 11. Slated to give a speech to the Salk Wives Club that morning, I was about to get out of bed to rehearse when the telephone rang. It was the Salk's chief fundraiser, her voice strangely shrill: "Turn on your TV!" she commanded. "We are under terrorist attack!"

Mark's Astor Place apartment was near downtown Manhattan, and he regularly commuted past the World Trade Center to his Brooklyn office. Alison immediately began dialing his cell phone, only to hear "all circuits busy." Jackie telephoned us, concerned about Mark's whereabouts and safety. The gesture deeply touched me; our East Coast relatives hadn't even called. Soon afterward Pam phoned from Alabama, similarly worried.

After more than five hours of dialing, Alison finally got through to Mark. He was sitting, stunned, with his coworkers in a Brooklyn park across from their evacuated building, the site of real-time data processing for the New York and American Stock Exchanges.

He told us that on his way to work that morning, he'd stopped to vote in the primary election in Manhattan and a cop told him "a small plane flying off course" had hit the World Trade Center's north tower. He proceeded on his usual subway commute, and as he walked into his office, the second plane hit the south tower. Everyone instantly realized the truth.

Mark described confetti-like paper falling from the sky. Dust-covered pedestrians were returning on foot to Brooklyn from Manhattan.

It was dawning on all of us that the world would never be the same.

Rich, Alison, and I stayed glued to the TV for days. Who knew what terror would strike next, or where? West Coast bridges were rumored to be targets.

Life calmed down, but it was decidedly not sunny in our California household. Rich and I slowly realized Alison hadn't registered for school. One day she announced she wasn't ready to study after all and had procured a hostess job at a seaside restaurant. She settled into a lonely routine of tanning and smoking cigarettes by day and working restaurant shifts at night.

By Christmas she was gone. She'd gotten her old hostess job back in Banff in time for the busy ski season. The coming holiday would be the first we'd ever spent apart.

It was with mixed feelings of sadness and disappointment, joy and delight, that I set out twenty red poinsettias against the white stucco pillars lining our front walkway to greet the hundred faculty and guests Rich and I expected for our first Salk Institute Christmas party.

The seasons passed. Sean frantically searched for cases to support his forthcoming *habeas* appeal. He had Jackie email me research requests on tangents that reached as far as corruption in the Los Angeles Police Department:

Please respond ASAP. Sean wants to know if you have any way of
finding out information on this case—U.S. vs Mendelsohn C.D.
Cal.,1969 Crim.#4337-California District. Also he wants you to look
up a few addresses for him. Gregory Moreno, [Winston] Kevin
McKesson, and Johnnie Cochran. He's on to an angle that he hopes
might work for him.

Rich's and my fundraising travels kept expanding. We began 2002 with an extended stay at a donor's weekend hunting lodge near Dusseldorf, Germany, doted on by the family's chef and house staff. Afterward we flew to Lyon, France, and then on to Milan, Madrid, and Barcelona.

I knew this luxurious life was temporary, a chapter to be savored until its inevitable close. I was determined to enjoy every minute. There was no chance that either Rich's or my head would be turned by the splendor. Neither of us worshipped money. We considered hard-won achievements and personal integrity the measures of success. The highest achievement of all? A happy family life, something money couldn't buy.

After a year of flailing, Sean announced in January 2002 that he was "full of majestic vigor" and ready to fight. To my relief, he'd let go of his fixation on Rosa Sanchez and viewed Acerra's and Robinson's corruption as the "best route ahead" for his retrial.

Sean and his lawyers believed the Commonwealth had committed a Brady violation[2] in holding back information about the two detectives' misconduct in prior criminal cases. To support this claim, the defense had to show evidence of their untruthfulness or corruption prior to Sean's 1995 trial. Figuring there was a lot of rich material to choose from, Sean and I had begun reaching out to *Boston Globe* reporters when a June letter to Sean from David Duncan brought our research to a halt—and our *habeas* hopes crashing down.

---

2 In Brady v. Maryland 1963, the U.S. Supreme Court ruled that prosecutors in a criminal case must release all evidence favorable to a defendant. Any suppression of exculpatory evidence, willful or otherwise, is a violation of due process.

Duncan wrote:

> *I discovered, to my chagrin, that the Supreme Court has held*
> *that* habeas corpus *does not include claims of newly discovered*
> *evidence as a ground for relief....*
>
> *You had wanted me to raise the [Robinson and Acerra*
> *corruption] issue as a Brady violation, but it is a requirement*
> *of a* habeas corpus *petition that claims raised have been*
> *exhausted, i.e., litigated, up to the highest state court....*
>
> *The bottom line is, I did not raise the Brady issue in the*
> *SJC, and so it was not exhausted ... so there is no way to raise*
> *the Robinson and Acerra material in federal court.*

It was a devastating legal setback.

My faith in the justice system had been flickering. Duncan's letter all but extinguished it. What kind of justice was it when adherence to procedure trumped the search for truth?

The upshot was that on June 24, 2002, Duncan submitted Sean's federal *habeas* petition citing just two timeworn issues: the violation of his Fifth Amendment right not to be put twice in jeopardy by a third trial, and the denial of his Sixth Amendment right to confront witnesses because of restrictions placed on the cross-examinations of Rosa Sanchez and Evony Chung.

And there the matter sat.

CHAPTER 28

"Attorneyless"

2002-2003

Over the next year and a half I kept in touch with Sean through letters and visited him when I could. Upon landing in Boston or New York, I'd rent a car and take to the highway, nearly always picking up Jackie and Shar'Day to take them out to Souza-Baranowski.

Jackie's cancer markers kept testing normal. She often wore a wig of one kind or another—my favorite had short, straight black hair with magenta streaks—which got her sent to the entrance anteroom for wig inspections. Though her health and energy were good, Jackie's limp had worsened, but she chose to forgo her knee brace rather than tangle with the prison's metal detector.

Shar'Day was now taller than I. Watching her develop was bittersweet, for her blooming beauty and maturity testified to the mounting years of Sean's captivity. She clearly idolized her big brother. The two usually held hands during our visits and hugged for a long while at their close.

Whenever I had time in Boston I'd go back to the Old Federal Courthouse in Post Office Square. Sean's case file drew me like a magnet. I always hoped to find something new, and I often did. On one such occasion I came upon the several-page log of police actions taken in the Mulligan homicide investigation. One item jumped out.

The entries for Rosa's and Ivan Sanchez's interviews at the Area E-5 station house were recorded out of sequence. All the other police activities were listed on the day they occurred, in chronological order. But the Sanchezes' September 26 interviews weren't logged in until a week later. Was it significant?

I also came across an investigative action I'd not known about. On Wednesday, September 29, three days after Mulligan's murder, Sean's friend and Patterson's cousin, Rob Matthews, was questioned by the police. His cell phone was confiscated and its records subpoenaed.

Matthews was at the Hansborough Street get-together that Saturday night. The early date of his interview was perplexing. It was a day before the police questioned Sean and four days before they picked up Terry Patterson. Matthews was the first of the Hansborough kids investigators approached. This got my wheels turning.

What put the police on his trail? Was Matthews a drug dealer, and did his phone number turn up on Mulligan's cell phone? This was impossible to know.

I had another thought. Patterson stashed his VW Rabbit in Matthews's Stratton Street driveway. I checked the police log: Officers Waggett and Fratalia reported finding the car there on Sept. 28. Matthews was interviewed by the police on the 29th. Bingo.

Matthews' name appeared in the log again on October 13. This time detectives picked him up, brought him in, read him the Miranda warning, and arrested him. The log did not specify the charge. He gave a taped statement. I'd never seen it.

I shot Jackie a quick email to ask what she knew about Matthews. She replied:

> *Sean and Robert Matthews were best friends in Dorchester High*
> *School. For their prom tuxedo both Rob and Sean had their suit*
> *special made. They got the tux jacket with the tails and had the*
> *pants made just below the knee … they wore this outfit with white*
> *Adidas socks and white Adidas sneakers. They was the talk of the*
> *prom with the girls.*

At Souza-Baranowski, I updated Sean on my findings, starting with the Sanchez interviews. "The delayed log entry makes me wonder if Rosa and Ivan really were interviewed at the E-5 station house the afternoon after the murder. Remember the timing irregularities your mother and I found on their transcripts? How Rosa's interview started three and a half hours after Ivan's, and Ivan's interview started at 4:00 p.m., the exact time Elvis Garcia said Rosa called him?"

A thought occurred to me: "I wonder if Rosa's and Ivan's Humboldt Avenue police interview even occurred. Did Acerra and Robinson bring them in first and afterward set up Rosa's phone call to Garcia? Rosa's phone tip never got documented at the time. It was backfilled by Garcia a year later."

Sean pondered this.

When I related my findings about Matthews, he was surprised. I tackled it head on: "Did Matthews deal with Mulligan?"

Sean said, "I have no knowledge of that. And I haven't seen or talked with anyone from the old neighborhood in years."

Our whirlwind California life continued apace. In November 2002 Rich's and my Salk fundraising mission hit a new high when we brought a rollicking busload of fifty donors to the San Diego Sports Arena to take in the Rolling Stones' "Forty Licks" concert, courtesy of tickets donated by the Stones' distinguished elderly business manager, Prince Rupert Loewenstein, a member of the Salk's International Council. (A scion of the royal houses of Wittelsbach and Loewenstein-Wertheim, Loewenstein emigrated to England as a child in 1940 with his part-Jewish mother.)

Prince Rupert engineered a wonderful surprise for Rich and me. During Sheryl Crow's opening act, he had a concert official summon us from the audience and usher us to a black-curtained area behind the stage. To our astonishment, Mick Jagger pulled aside the curtain with a cheery "Hello!"

Clipped to Jagger's shirt was a lighted Rolling Stones red-lips logo, flashing on and off. He and Rich chatted amiably for several moments. Starstruck, all I could do was gasp and stare at the rock giant's diminutive frame and exceedingly narrow hips. Then, with a swirl of the curtain, Jagger vanished. Moments later he pranced onstage, seeming seven feet tall and singing "Start Me Up." Meeting Mick Jagger remains my greatest-ever celebrity thrill.

Some weeks later, Rich and I were introduced to retired federal Judge H. Lee Sarokin by mutual friends who knew of my work with Sean. Sarokin had overturned the wrongful triple-murder conviction of Sean's hero Rubin "Hurricane" Carter in New Jersey. He'd retired to San Diego, and our meeting was the beginning of a lovely friendship with him and his wife, Margie.

When I wrote to Sean about both these brushes with luminaries, he wrote back, *Godma, Mick Jagger is nothing much … Judge Sarokin is the real rock star!*

In May 2003 Rich and I again flew into Boston. A cold rain was falling as I drove out to Souza-Baranowski, but I felt warm inside. The *Boston Globe* had heralded a new development in the case of Shawn Drumgold, a Black man from Dorchester who'd been convicted in 1989, at age twenty-three, of the 1988 murder of a twelve-year-old girl hit by gang crossfire in Roxbury. Drumgold claimed innocence and had been fighting for his release for years. It was an uphill battle, for his conviction was considered "settled," having been affirmed by the SJC. But *Globe* reporter Dick Lehr, working with Drumgold's defense attorney, Rosemary Scapicchio, had reexamined the eyewitness testimony against Drumgold and found serious misconduct. Suffolk County District Attorney Daniel Conley was going to reopen the case.

The news would cheer Sean.

When he came into the visiting room, I saw that he'd beefed up. His head was shaved, and he had a nasty-looking rash on his cheeks. But his spirits were good as we discussed the Drumgold case details and what they might mean for his case. The wrongdoing dug up by the reporter and defense attorney involved police strong-arming eyewitnesses to tell the story the police wanted to hear and a witness whose pending cases were dismissed after he testified against Drumgold.

It all had a familiar ring.

Over the past few years a mounting tally of wrongful murder convictions had gripped Boston, generating a groundswell of interest that encouraged us all. It started in 1999, when two prominent cases were resolved. The first was of Marlon Passley, a Black man convicted in 1996 of the drive-by murder of a Dorchester teen. When new information surfaced disproving the eyewitness testimony at Passley's trial, he was exonerated and released from prison. As with Drumgold, Passley's appeal had earlier been denied by the SJC. Like Sean's.

Following his release, Passley sent money to Sean for his prison canteen. Sean choked up when he told me about this gesture of solidarity: "'Smiley' Passley and I sat at the same table in chow hall at Walpole."

In September of that same year, new evidence emerged indicating that another Black lifer, Donnell Johnson, was not responsible for the stray-bullet killing of a nine-year-old Roxbury boy in 1994 for which he'd been convicted. Johnson was just sixteen at the time of the murder. As with Passley, the eyewitness evidence used against him was untrue.

Johnson's trial was also marred by police lying. Detectives claimed Johnson did not provide an alibi when, in fact, he did. The two cops implicated in the false narrative both went on to investigate Mulligan's murder:

Sean's chief questioner, William Mahoney, and Daniel Keeler. Mahoney's "testilying" in the Johnson case got him suspended without pay for thirty days; Keeler went unpunished.

On this day, as Sean and I discussed the wrongful conviction cases, he shocked me by saying Mahoney "testilied" in his case too—about his questioning session in homicide. He grimaced at the memory. "I was upset that night about my cousins, and they took advantage of my emotional state. They called me a crackhead, and they accused me of killing my cousins. They made up some ridiculous story that I killed Tracy because she was going to start charging me rent. That was when I said, 'Stop. I want a lawyer.'"

"Mahoney testified that you didn't," I said.

"Right. But I did. I asked for a lawyer a few times. They just laughed it off, ignored it."

"Sean, why didn't your lawyers contest this?"

"They said it was basically my word against theirs and hard to prove."

Hearing this made me furious. No way in the world would this happen to me, a white woman. If I were being questioned and requested a lawyer, no cop would dare block me. That Sean endured this treatment and shrugged it off as a matter of course spoke volumes about our two worlds. How utterly powerless Sean must have felt; how utterly powerless he was. It was un-American. It was heartbreaking.

As our conversation wound around to other subjects, I asked him how things were going with a young woman from his old neighborhood who'd begun visiting him. He made a thumbs-down gesture. "She has a different attitude than me. She says I'm too serious."

Then he unloaded: "People ask me, 'Why are you always so serious?' But they don't understand. Yes, I'm serious—because there's nothing for me to laugh and take joy in, due to my circumstances. There's no reason or occasion to laugh and play. I'll never again feel the mud between my toes."

It was the most emotion Sean had ever expressed about being incarcerated. His nutshell distillation of life spent in a sea of concrete was poetry. Sad poetry.

"In here you gotta be serious," he continued. "It's how you get respect. You have to act serious, not the clown. Then people let you alone. It creates a line, and people don't cross that line. You live in peace. I learned early on that you have to make eye contact to protect yourself. Always. You do not look down."

As the visiting hours came to a close, I asked, "Have you heard from your father?" To my knowledge, John Ellis had not once visited Sean. He'd recently skipped a prison visit Jackie had arranged at Sean's request. She and Shar'Day had waited on a street corner in a cold April rain for Ellis to pick them up, but he never showed.

Sean shook his head. "It's too late for the father-son thing," he said. "But I wish he'd come and see me, so we could be friends."

Sean then brought up his former girlfriend Tia Walker. He sounded wistful. "I really cared for her. I still care. She had a little six-month-old baby, Ricky, and we got together and were like a little family. We'd go to the grocery store to buy food for the baby. When he was sick and got his tonsils out, Tia and me took turns staying overnight at the hospital." In recalling these memories, Sean smiled.

"Sometimes I lie in bed and see Tia's face. I can't get her face out of my mind. But I don't talk or tell anyone about it," he said, looking sheepish.

"A person's first love is always intense," I said. "The memories stay with you."

In summer, Rich and I traveled East to spend lazy days with family members in a rented cottage in New Hampshire. While there, I drove to Massachusetts to take Shar'Day and Jackie out to Souza-Baranowski for an unaccustomed evening visit. When we stopped for gas, they both went into the station saying they wanted a snack. Instead they came out with a single red rose for me.

The guards in the reception area dawdled even longer than usual when processing our paperwork, so it was close to 7:00 before we got in to see Sean. Visitors' long waits were totally at the whim of the COs and seemed designed to harass. There was nothing you could do but sit there and take it. Complaining would probably trigger even longer waits.

Sean beamed as he walked in, and then he turned to serious matters. Jackie's sister Rae, an Army veteran, had been in a car crash that rendered her quadriplegic, and Jackie had recently undergone training to become Rae's caregiver. Sean was close to his aunts, and it pained him to be away from the family at these times.

He turned his attention to Shar'Day and began teasing her about her social life. "Any boys callin' you?" This caused his little sister to dissolve into giggles. Sean giggled along with her.

When we got onto Sean's case, Jackie said, "Elaine tried to talk with Tia, but she didn't show." It was true. Inspired by the Drumgold witness recanting, I'd hoped Tia might tell me the cops strong-armed her as well. Laselle had set us up, and Tia had been pleasant on the phone. She'd agreed to meet me for lunch, and I'd waited for forty-five minutes at the Au Bon Pain restaurant near Boston's Symphony Hall before giving up.

Sean already knew about it. Tia had been out to see him some days earlier. Their visit hadn't gone well. She told him she was "scared" by my phone call and didn't want to talk about the case.

That same week I'd looked up ex-detective John Brazil. Finding he still lived outside Boston, I dropped him a note requesting an interview. When I told Sean this, his mouth dropped open. I explained, "I thought maybe all these years later something might motivate Brazil to tell the truth. People get cancer. They get religion. Or they just want to relieve their consciences of dark secrets."

Brazil never responded.

When the guard shouted "five more minutes" at 8:25, it was dark. On the drive home the three of us pulled into an Italian restaurant, and over spaghetti Jackie described her grueling schedule of caring for the paralyzed Rae seven days a week. Shar'Day bubbled about turning thirteen in a few days and how she loved her weekends at her Aunt Rae's Dorchester house with Jackie and Rae's daughter, Puddin, whom she idolized. "Puddin did my hair up in cornrows! She's gonna bring me to a rock concert!"

I asked Shar'Day her thoughts on attending college, and she piped up with her aspirations: "I love literature, plus singing and performing."

She said she'd heard of two state colleges in Tennessee she was eligible to attend, since her father lived there. "I want to go down and see him next year, and check out the environment, and see if it's something I'd want."

"That sounds wonderful," I said halfheartedly. Sean had told me Willie Taylor was still doing drugs. I glanced at Jackie. She sat silently.

At summer's end Sean wrote me, energized. He'd learned of another avenue available to him to pursue the withheld evidence of Acerra's and Robinson's perjury in prior criminal cases. He could petition the federal court for permission to raise the issue under "Procedural Default Cause & Prejudice." The only drawback was that he'd have to dismiss David Duncan and Norman Zalkind for ineffective counsel because they did not preserve the issue for federal review. This would put him in legal limbo.

A month later he phoned me seeking advice. He sounded stressed. "I need to decide by Thursday whether to have Duncan and Zalkind withdraw from the case."

I'd spoken with an attorney friend of mine about the issue, and he'd advised that Sean should do it. Dismissing counsel wasn't an acrimonious move, he explained; it was a legal strategy. Appellate law is a highly specialized field, so perhaps it wasn't a good thing Sean's trial lawyers had stuck with him. It was better to make the move now, before more doors closed in the legal system.

I passed on my friend's counsel to Sean. He listened hard.

Fall brought one of the most fascinating Salk social events to date: a private screening of *My Architect*, a brilliant documentary film produced and directed by Nathaniel Kahn tracing his quest to understand his largely absent father, Louis Kahn, the Salk Institute's genius architect.

In the early 1960s, Kahn had worked closely with Jonas Salk to design a research facility that captured the ambiance of a French monastery that was Salk's inspiration. The complex born of their collaboration is perched on land donated by the City of San Diego, its stunning courtyard fronting the Pacific. It is considered one of America's finest architectural achievements.

"Lou" Kahn kept a dark secret: He maintained three separate families in Philadelphia. He and his wife had a daughter. He and a colleague also had a daughter. And he and a second colleague had Nathaniel. Nathaniel spent his childhood tucked away in a corner of the city. His father was kind and loving toward him, but he visited only occasionally. Nathaniel was just eleven in 1974 when Lou Kahn was found dead of a heart attack in New York's Penn Station.

My Architect went on to win multiple awards and was nominated for the 2003 Academy Award for best documentary. After the screening Rich and I hosted a formal dinner in our home for fifty of the Institute's major donors. I sat next to Nathaniel, who'd become Rich's and my friend. Knowing of my work with Sean, he asked for an update. Then he challenged me: "Elaine, why are you interested?"

I began rattling off my usual answer about our family's friendship with the young Sean, but Nathaniel stopped me. He shook his head. "It's gotta be more than that. Why stay with it all these years?" Sweeping his arm in a gesture that took in our large foyer and living room filled with tuxedoed waiters, elegant guests, linen-draped tables, and formal flower arrangements, he said, "Is it because all this isn't enough?"

I thought about it. "All this" related to Rich's world, the world of science and Salk Institute fundraising. I was Rich's helpmate, which I considered a worthy undertaking, given the mission. But Nathaniel's point was sharp. Perhaps Sean and his case absorbed me so much because the stakes could not be higher: justice denied, a young man's life unjustly snatched away. Sean's fight for freedom was a cause where my own skills and talents— and frankly my privilege—might make a difference.

But why stay with it all these years? I'd thought about this numerous times. A literary parallel seemed pertinent. As a teen, I was obsessed with Edgar Allan Poe's tales of being buried alive. To me, wrongfully serving life without parole would feel like that. I'd want someone to help me dig out.

Going deeper still, my motivation likely came from the wellspring of my childhood. Freedom vs. constraint has been a major current in my life ever since my father became a virtual prisoner in our home, locked in by mental illness. "Your father was a powerhouse," his brother Frannie, the priest, told me one day sadly, referring to Dad's days as an influential *Boston Globe* editor in the era before TV news. But after his collapse and homecoming on a stretcher, Dad's ventures to the outside world were limited to a small handful of experiences he adjudged safe: driving to Scituate's fish pier to watch the boats, coaching youth baseball, hurling horseshoes at the Scituate Beach Association's ballfield. Dad never again returned to the newsroom, nor did he ever go back to Fenway Park, Boston Garden, or any of the other places he loved.

My father's liberty was stolen by illness. Sean's freedom was stolen by corrupt police who framed a nineteen-year-old Black kid because they could. Both losses haunted me. Only one could I hope to influence.

Some days later, a letter came from Sean:

> *Dear Godma,*
>
>   *My biggest news is I asked Duncan to withdraw from the case,*
> *[and] he filed a motion to oblige my request . . .*

Pinned to the letter was a note marked "*Addendum*":

> *To my chagrin, Godma, yet paradoxical, I'm relieved that the*
> *federal court has granted my stay, which clears the way for me*
> *to preserve the issues in hand. But with Duncan relieved of his*
> *duty, the Court has declined to appoint New Council [sic]. Thus,*
> *as I write you . . . I'm attorneyless.*

In early November the murder-one conviction of Dorchester's Shawn Drumgold was reversed, and he was freed from prison. This latest wrongful conviction received extensive coverage in the Boston media, with Drumgold's attorney, Rosemary Scapicchio, heralded for her dogged, impassioned defense work.

On Christmas Eve 2003, Sean penned a letter to Scapicchio: "Will you represent me?"

CHAPTER 29

The Same Uniform

2004

We all held our breath and waited for Rosemary Scapicchio's response. After several weeks went by with no word, Jackie called the attorney's office. Her assistant urged patience, explaining, "Since the Drumgold case, our phone has been ringing off the hook."

In spring 2004 Scapicchio contacted Sean. She told him she was quite interested in his case but because of her busy court schedule couldn't get to it for some time. She suggested another defense attorney, but Sean demurred. He'd done his research around the prison. "I'll wait for you," he said.

Meanwhile, Terry Patterson's case was heating up. With his retrial looming, his attorney, Jack Cunha, had filed a motion to dismiss his fingerprint evidence. In a May 2004 hearing Cunha brought in an expert witness to support his contention that "the science of matching fingerprints left at crime scenes to those taken from suspects" is "junk science."

By now I'd begun writing this book about Sean. Feeling restless over the standstill in his case and wanting to find more people to interview, with Rich's blessing I sublet a Harvard graduate student's apartment for the summer.

When I arrived in Boston from California in early June, I found a city suffering its worst gang violence in a decade. A barrage of headlines from Sean's Dorchester neighborhood and adjacent minority areas described a toxic mix of murder, violence, and handguns.

The newspaper accounts were devastating. Two stabbings had occurred in broad daylight at Jamaica Plain T stations. Random gunfire from gangs was so frequent in Roxbury's Bromley-Heath housing development that children living there couldn't play outside. A Dorchester teen wiped away tears over the shooting death of his fourteen-year-old friend—a star athlete who'd been gunned down as he walked to a convenience store for popcorn—and said, "I guess this is it. This is the life for us. This is Dorchester, and none of us are going to catch any breaks."

The violence and the young man's resignation to it horrified me. I'd been traveling to Boston to work on Sean's case for five years now. The brutal conditions in these neighborhoods had only worsened.

Jackie told me the recent violence had touched Sean. One of his best friends from Hansborough Street, Sean Dookie, had been shot and killed, and no one knew why. When I talked to Sean on the phone, he was crushed by Dookie's murder. Indeed, the Dorchester community was shocked. Once a young offender, Dookie had turned his life around and become a responsible father and popular neighborhood coach. It made no sense.

My rented Cambridge digs turned out to be a cramped, nearly windowless studio apartment. The upside: It was near the Harvard Square T station, and I was dependent on public transportation.

I rode the T to Boston's Old Federal Courthouse, intent on sifting through Sean's case file for the names of potential witnesses. Afterward, in the dark of my rented room, using an online people-finder and searching deep into the night, I located the addresses of fifteen such individuals. I mailed them all postcards explaining my book project and requesting an interview.

I received just two responses via my attached reply card: Walgreens clerk Stephen Bannister indicated he did not wish to be contacted. But a man named Pablo,[3] who'd been described as a "concerned citizen," was willing to meet.

After several last-minute cancellations phoned in by Pablo's wife, he and I were finally sitting next to each other on a shiny green bench in Boston Common, having removed a "Wet Paint" sign after agreeing the bench was dry.

It was a searing day at the end of June. I'd arrived fifteen minutes early for our 4:00 p.m. appointment toting a small box of Godiva chocolates I'd purchased for Pablo's wife, to thank her. I'd given Pablo my description, down to a white sweater draped over my shoulders—unfortunate, for the temperature was ninety-seven degrees.

I waited for him at the intersection of Park and Tremont Streets and sweated. And waited. And sweated and waited some more. The waiting got so long that I sat down on the hot curbstone with city traffic whizzing by.

At 4:40, nearly an hour after I'd arrived, a soft voice behind me said, "Hello, ma'am." I whirled around and was surprised to see a slight man in his early forties. I'd pictured the "concerned citizen" as old and sturdy. Pablo had a thin mustache, brown hair, and brown eyes. He was dressed like a teenager in baggy cargo shorts, sneakers, and a red-and-white head bandana. He seemed skittish.

Right away he announced, "I'm from the neighborhood. You don't have my real name. It's false. I go by many. And the address you reached me at is only a drop box." He said he had to "determine if he felt comfortable" with me before he'd talk.

---

3 a pseudonym

I gave him my personal card and explained I'd known Sean as a child. "I don't think the right people got convicted for Detective Mulligan's murder."

Pablo shrugged. "I don't know what went down that night, because I wasn't in the car with those two guys. They were always together. But now they're each blaming the other for the murder." He waved his hand in disgust. "There's a lot more to this murder, a lot more. The real story is, why was Mulligan killed? Do you know why?" He looked at me expectantly.

"Well, I figure it must involve drugs," I said. "I've heard Mulligan was dirty. Maybe he got greedy, and that's why he ended up dead."

Pablo smirked. "Mulligan was killed because someone higher up—much higher up—ordered it." He made this announcement with considerable swagger and repeated, "Much, much higher up." After a pregnant pause he added, "The person who ordered Mulligan killed wore a uniform just like Mulligan's. I know this for a fact, because I was told it by the guy I deal with who's also a man in uniform."

"The guy you deal with?"

"Yeah. I sell, and he supplies me. Mulligan was making steady money from drugs. He and the other cops each had their territory, and they respected these boundaries—but not Mulligan." He elongated the words "not Mulligan" and wagged his forefinger as he pronounced them.

I sat, wide-eyed, and Pablo continued. "Three or four nights before his murder, Mulligan did something to some people over across from Walgreens—it was in a brick building with porches around it. That pissed off some people—really, really pissed them off, and it resulted in his murder. It was all about territory. He'd gone into the others' territory more than once. He thought he was bulletproof."

"Is it still active out there—I mean drugs, with the cops supplying?"

Pablo threw his head back and laughed without mirth. "Drugs have always been, and continue to be, brisk business." He pointed to the Massachusetts State House atop the hill. "See that building with the gold dome? The flow of drugs comes from high up. Right from there.

"I don't mean the governor," he added quickly, "but high up, very high.

Every now and again, the authorities crack down. They'll arrest a few street sellers, but that's all. Only the little guys get stopped. Nothing stops the main flow. There's too much money in it."

I absorbed this grim assessment. Then I asked Pablo about the murder. "Is the word on the street that another guy or guys were with Sean and Patterson that night and were involved in Mulligan's shooting?"

Pablo seemed surprised by the question. "I don't know," he said.

"Do you know anything about Celine Kirk's murder?"

"She was killed to shut her up. She knew too much."

"But Craig Hood confessed to that murder," I said. "It was supposedly an argument about a gold chain."

"You ask Craig Hood how much he got paid."

"How about the two murdered guys, Curt Headen and Kevin Chisholm?" I asked.

"They thought they were bulletproof too," Pablo said. "You know, they get a cocky attitude. They start thinking they can get anyone."

I was growing confused. "They" ... "get anyone" ... Did Pablo mean the cops?

"It was other teenagers who shot Headen and Chisholm," I protested. Pablo nodded but remained mute. "They might have been paid to do it?" He nodded again.

Referring to Sean and Patterson, Pablo said, "Those two guys were next in line to get shot, I can tell you that." He accompanied this assertion with a clean-sweep arm gesture, as in, have the cop murdered by kids, then get rid of the kids, end of story.

I sat on the bench trying to digest this information. It was like something out of a gangland movie. Then Pablo blurted out, "I'm the one who told the cops where the car was." He meant Patterson's VW Rabbit.

"I always figured the cops were tipped off," I said. "How else could they find the car?"

"Yeah. My guy was pulling something tricky on me, something sneaky," Pablo said, referring to his uniformed drug supplier. "And so I said, 'All right,

I'll tell you where the car is. I'll give you that.' My brother-in-law needed a bumper for his VW, and he was told he could take it from Patterson's car stashed on Stratton Street."

"Did you get the reward money from the police?"

"No," Pablo said, again looking surprised. "I wonder who did?" His tone abruptly changed. "Looking back, the one regret I have is that I told the cops where the car was." He gazed into the distance, and then he turned back. "No, on second thought, I don't. Because the reason those two guys in prison are breathing today is they were lucky enough to get arrested."

The words chilled me. Sean had said if he weren't in prison, he'd be dead.

Pablo abruptly stood up. We shook hands, and he strode over to the Park Street T station, with me a careful dozen steps behind.

As I clutched the overhead strap of the packed, swaying T car hurtling toward Cambridge, I was in a daze. "What have I walked into?" I thought. Here I was, a lone writer, naïve, trying to cast light on Mulligan's murder. And the crime turns out to be the tip of a police drug-corruption iceberg that involves "high-up" politicians?

Get a grip, I admonished myself. Maybe Pablo was just repeating street rumors. Maybe he invented the tale for shock value. His account could be true, or partly true, or wildly untrue. Besides, wouldn't Pablo's supplier—the dirty cop—want Pablo to lie to me, to throw me off the scent?

Pablo didn't hit me up for money though. And he stayed anonymous. Moreover, he didn't pump me for information. But what made him give me the information he did? Did he want to burn the cops, maybe burn his supplier? It was all so confusing.

Sailboats bobbed and dipped in the Charles River as the sweltering T car crossed Longfellow Bridge. The undelivered Godiva chocolates melted in my purse, and the informer's words rang in my ears: "The person who ordered Mulligan's killing wore the same uniform as Mulligan"…Sean and Patterson were "next in line to get shot."

Sean's father's words came back to me: "The street says the police killed Mulligan. Nobody liked him." As for Headen and Chisholm? "It's all connected. They had to die. They knew too much. Both boys were shot in the head, to make sure they would die."

The gravity of my situation hit me. Pablo's "guy in uniform" must have sent him out to find out what I knew—the lady writing the book about Mulligan's murder. Maybe he'd been lurking nearby watching us. Of course! That was why Pablo was late. I was being surveilled as I sat on the curb.

Damn! I'd given Pablo my card with my California home address. Even worse, the postcard I'd mailed him indicated my Cambridge return address. Rookie mistakes.

Rich was waiting at my Cambridge sublet, having flown in from California a few days earlier to attend a friend's surprise sixtieth birthday party. When I told him Pablo's story, I felt dizzy. It would take time for all this to sink in.

Not for Rich. "You're out of here," he said. "You're coming home. You're too exposed. You have no institution backing you up. This is way too big an enterprise for you to be tackling alone."

I tossed sleeplessly all night next to Rich. The next morning, while retrieving my *Boston Globe* from the front steps, I scanned the street for stakeouts. This was crazy. It was time to get others involved. If Pablo's lead had meat to it, the *Globe* would be interested. Maybe I could hand it off to them.

I emailed metro editor Steve Kurkjian, expressing "personal fears stemming from a new development in the Mulligan case." Fifteen minutes later Kurkjian phoned. He wanted to meet.

The following day Kurkjian greeted Rich and me in the *Globe*'s lobby and led us up the escalator to the cafeteria. We were joined by a young man with the bluest eyes I'd ever seen. It was Ric Kahn, the reporter who'd broken the 1996 story revealing that the Boston Police Department was investigating allegations that Mulligan robbed two drug dealers with Robinson. As Kahn and I shook hands, I referenced this article and told him, "It was critical to my research."

Kahn smiled and said, "I got a front-page headline out of it."

I told the journalists I was writing a book about Sean's case and had unwittingly dug up the informer who told the police where to find Patterson's car, a man who used the pseudonym "Pablo." Then I explained Pablo's angle on Mulligan's murder. "I have no idea why he gave me this information," I concluded, "but he seemed to enjoy watching my reaction."

"A little guy with big ideas," Rich interjected.

Kahn said he'd gone after Mulligan's search warrants in West Roxbury Court. When I told him I'd done the same, he was surprised. We laughed over Mulligan's pitiful write-ups and his dismal record of finding drugs or money, at least on the record.

"We've always known there was more to the Mulligan murder story," Kurkjian said. "But we could never plumb the depths. Try as we might, we could never get past 'about here.'" He held his hand mid-chest.

"Yeah, we've been all over this," Kahn said. "We never bought the simple robbery theory. We knew Mulligan was killed for more than his gun." He said they'd interviewed Craig Hood. This made me envious. I hadn't thought of approaching Hood in prison.

"What did he tell you?" I asked.

Kahn shot a glance at Kurkjian. "You know, consistent with the stuff you've been telling us, but again, just up to here." He made another mid-chest gesture. "We could never take it home."

Kurkjian said, "Maybe, just maybe, if you tell us how to reach this informer you spoke with, his information could get us over that hump finally."

"I can't give you his phone number," I said. "I promised I'd keep his identity confidential."

They understood. Kurkjian was also a lawyer, and he theorized that if Patterson would "tell all" at his retrial, he could possibly cut a deal. "If he admitted to being just a pawn in this conspiracy, perhaps he could walk out for time served. That would benefit Sean, because then Patterson would no longer have to point the finger at him as a means of getting out. Then Sean could cut his own deal."

They asked about Sean's lawyer situation. When I told them Rosemary Scapicchio was potentially coming on board, they were enthusiastic. "I know Scapicchio," Kahn said. "She's a bulldog. She'll leave no stone unturned."

"What does Sean think of what you're doing?" Kurkjian asked, referring to my book project. "What's his attitude toward things?"

"He wants to get his story out, particularly the reasonable-doubt issues," I said.

Kurkjian nodded and said, "Guys like Ellis and Patterson focus on reasonable doubt. They absolutely cannot snitch their way out of prison. They'd be dead meat."

It was an about-face from the editor's dismissive stance in 1998, when I'd first met him with trial reporter John Ellement. Then they'd insisted that if Sean were innocent, he would have cooperated with the police.

Rich cut in: "Sean's attorneys have asked Elaine not to discuss the events of the murder night with Sean."

"Pablo's tale reveals nothing about Sean's guilt or innocence," Kurkjian pointed out. The cops could have hired or coerced the kids to do the job."

It was a sobering thought.

He added, "We're after the untold story about Mulligan. That's our angle on this. And what I like about this story is that it's the same cast of characters, only more." He said that to convince his editors to put significant resources into pursuing Pablo's tip, he'd need to speak with the informer directly: "I want to give him the sniff test."

Still frightened, I reiterated my pledge of confidentiality. "Pablo and his Boston police drug supplier know where to find me—on both coasts!"

Kahn reassured me: "Rosemary Scapicchio will track down every person in the file. She will find him. That would give you cover."

Kurkjian offered to write out a script for me, patter aimed at convincing Pablo to speak anonymously and confidentially with the two of them.

"OK, I'll do it," I said.

The meeting over, we left for the airport. Rich was right. It was too dangerous for me to stay in Cambridge alone. I emailed a quick excuse to Jackie about "family business" taking me home, and we boarded our flight to San Diego.

Kurkjian emailed me a script to use with Pablo. I took a deep breath and phoned him. "Would you consider talking with two trusted reporters at the *Boston Globe* who will positively keep your identity confidential?" I assured Pablo I hadn't revealed his contact information.

"I'd like to think it over," Pablo said. "I will call you back."

A week elapsed with no call. I mailed him a note containing the journalists' phone numbers and implored:

> *Here's something to think about. Two kids are in prison for life*
> *without parole. . . . Although they don't know it, they can thank you*
> *for breathing today. They surely would have been killed by others*
> *if you'd not passed along your car tip. . . .*
>
> *These two investigative reporters at the* Boston Globe *can*
> *follow this up. . . . They will guarantee that your identity will never*
> *be revealed. They have the legal right to keep sources confidential.*
> *You've already saved Sean's and Terry's lives once. Won't you help*
> *save them again?*

Weeks went by with my repeated phone calls to Pablo unanswered. Finally he picked up. "I really can't get involved with that. I really don't want to, ya know? Thank you. Goodbye."

It meant the *Globe* wouldn't be getting involved.

The first week of October Rich and I returned to Boston to celebrate his dad's ninety-second birthday at a festive dinner party in Boston's North End. I made time to visit Sean.

I found him looking older and even more serious. He sported tortoise-shell glasses and a thin mustache. "I just spent nearly two months in solitary confinement," he said. "A dispute arose between a corrections officer and three inmates. I tried to smooth it out, but all four of us were thrown in the hole. I just got out.

"There are really crazy guys up there in the hole. It's located on the roof, and I saw things there that changed my view of the world." He bent over and held his head in his hands and shuddered. "Some guy tried to throw feces into the cell of another guy, and people stop up their toilets and the stuff goes all over the floor."

I shuddered along with Sean, knowing how fastidious he was.

I launched into my mission, saying under my breath, "I met with a police informer whose name I found in your case file. He said Mulligan's killing was set up by a person who wore the same uniform as Mulligan."

Sean looked stunned.

I continued whispering. "I want you to know that this is what they're saying out there. This is the word on the street. So, if there's any truth to it, and if you know something about it, don't sit here quietly. Because if I was able to learn this, the knowledge must be widespread."

He nodded ever so slightly. Then he glanced up at what appeared to be air vents in the ceiling and muttered, "Those are actually cameras that read lips, so we must be careful."

Oh, no. Was Sean growing paranoid?

I told him about my visit to the *Globe* and described the reporter and editor as guys on the investigative Spotlight Team who'd helped bring Acerra and Robinson down. "They really know this world and weren't surprised at the informer's tip." I passed on Kurkjian's lawyerly advice that if Patterson would work with prosecutors he could possibly cut a deal—and then maybe he, Sean, could cut a deal as well.

Sean looked at me in disbelief. "Me, cooperate?" He laughed with disdain.

"Yes," I said firmly. I wanted the thought to sink in. This time it came from an experienced newsman, an investigative journalist with a law degree who'd been around the block once or twice.

The guard shouted, "Time's up!" Inmates and visitors stood, and the room was awash in embraces. Sean grabbed me and hugged me fiercely, tighter than ever before. The desperate quality of his clutch startled me.

Then he pressed his lips to my ear and hissed something that sounded like, "We're on the same path."

"What?" I said, pulling away. "What did you say?"

"We're both on the same path," he whispered, this time clearly. His whole being was intense, his arm muscles tight and his posture ramrod straight. "Keep on. Keep on."

Jackie emailed me news that would rock our world:

Rosemary Scapicchio has signed on to Sean's case.

PART 5

Back on the Path

2004–2014

CHAPTER 30

Rosemary

2006

"This murder was not done by teens. A cop killing goes over the line. I do not believe Sean is guilty of this crime!" Rosemary Scapicchio spat out her words, dripping broad Boston r's (ah's) in a voice brash and loud. Her eyes flashed with resolve.

It was early January 2006, and I was finally face to face with Sean's new attorney. We were standing in her cramped Boston office amid a hodge-podge of boxes on the floor—Sean's case files. Rosemary had begun visiting Sean and working on his case back in fall 2004, and he was ecstatic.

"Her energy is real intense ... an automatic attraction because [it's] consistent with mine," he'd written.

Sean was right. Rosemary was a dynamo, a buxom woman with platinum-blonde hair worn short and spiky. Early on I'd mailed her a letter introducing myself and explaining my work on Sean's behalf, but this past year my schedule had kept me far from Massachusetts. Now, in the dead of winter, I'd flown in to help Janet out.

She'd graduated from medical school the previous summer and had moved to Boston, having matched for a residency in internal medicine at Massachusetts General Hospital. Besides her academic accomplishments—she'd been inducted into the elite Alpha Omega Alpha medical honor society—she'd taken a year off from school to deliver our first grandchild, the adorable Nicolas. I'd offered to help care for "Nick" during her busiest hospital rotations.

Connecting with Rosemary Scapicchio was my next priority.

After her impressive victory in the Shawn Drumgold case, the *Boston Globe* had run a lengthy feature article on her titled "She's on a roll!" Born Rosemary Curran, the fourth of six sisters, she'd grown up in the projects of Boston's working-class Brighton section. She'd commuted to Suffolk University in downtown Boston for both undergraduate and law degrees. Now forty, she'd recently argued her first U.S. Supreme Court case and won, achieving loosened guidelines for federal sentences. She and her husband, Ralph Scapicchio, had three children under ten, and Ralph stayed home to care for them. Presently, however, he was deployed in Iraq with the Army National Guard, so they'd hired a nanny whose husband was likewise serving.

Rosemary's office in a high-rise near the Suffolk County courthouse looked to be a room rented within a larger firm. She apparently worked solo, the captain of her ship. The *Globe* said her specialty was eviscerating "misconduct and slipshod work" in police investigations. This boded well for Sean.

Now she took her seat behind her desk and motioned for me to sit across from her. She resumed her rapid-fire monologue: "Look, the whole theory of the case doesn't make sense. To murder a cop takes much more violent criminals. Even those who kill a cop will say 'This is a big step.' Just shooting at a cop is big. You know you won't live if you do it. So to decide to cop kill is huge, and you certainly don't do it casually, at the last minute. You don't see a sleeping cop and decide you'll kill him for a gun."

She explained how she approaches appeals. "First, I look at the physical evidence. In Mulligan's murder, it was the angle of bullets, as seen in the autopsy photos, and the fact of multiple shots."

She'd reached firm conclusions. "It was a message. I mean, five bullets? Also, I don't believe Mulligan was sleeping. I've examined the autopsy photos and seen the angle of entry. No way could you do that by inserting a gun in the driver's window opening. There was a case to be made that Mulligan's girlfriend set him up or even killed him herself. They were having problems in their relationship. One theory is she came over and gave him oral sex in the car—that Mulligan had his head thrown back, and then she shot him. That explains the bullets' angle of entry."

The theory was tantalizing and in line with the rumors of Mulligan's pants being found around his ankles.

She ticked off more issues. "How did they get Mulligan's service pistol out of its holster? He was right-handed, and that gun was buttoned into a right-sided holster."

I'd thought of this too. Mulligan's body was found leaning against the driver's door. The first officer on the scene was afraid it would tumble out if he opened the door. How could the killer have opened the driver's door and grabbed the gun without disrupting the body? It seemed more probable that he, or she, fired from the passenger seat, then locked the door when leaving.

Rosemary went on. "I don't believe Terry Patterson and Sean had the weapons. I don't believe Mulligan's gun and murder weapon were for real. They were probably planted."

This astonished me. Norman Zalkind had conceded that Sean handled the guns. I'd never questioned it.

As if reading my thoughts, Rosemary said, "Zalkind definitely should have contested the weapons. The police expert's assertion that the bullets came from that .25-caliber pearl-handled gun was based on a shear-mark analysis of the firing pin aperture. I don't buy it." She explained that scientific studies have discredited the procedure: Recently manufactured guns no longer have identifying marks.

"As for the nonexistent Walgreens videotape, why not get the previous four nights' videos to check out who Mulligan might be dealing with? Maybe we'd find some of the same cast of characters."

"You mean the witnesses in the case might have been dealing drugs with him?" I asked. I'd suspected this was why so many people came to Walgreens for curious 3:00 a.m. errands, particularly after I learned Evony Chung had gotten busted for possession.

Rosemary nodded. "Exactly. Plus, there were outside videos of the parking lot. The store kept a mounted exterior camera aimed down on the sidewalk, mainly to protect against bogus drop-and-sue incidents on the winter ice. Why didn't the police get those?"

I pondered this. Terry Patterson told detectives he assumed the parking lot was under video surveillance.

"I think Acerra and Robinson pulled the Walgreens videotape," Rosemary continued. "Acerra was definitely at the murder scene early. When I reviewed the TV tapes and the news video, I saw him standing outside the store." She didn't know exactly what time this was.

Given the suspicions that Acerra took Mulligan's cell phone from his SUV after the murder, it was significant to know he'd been at Walgreens.

"Second, the way the murder was investigated? I don't buy it. I think the timing of Rosa Sanchez was concocted. I think the Sanchezes weren't slotted in until later."

This piqued my interest. I told Rosemary that Rosa's and Ivan's police interviews weren't logged in for a week, and Ivan's starting time of 4:00 p.m. conflicted with Rosa's 4:00 p.m. phone tip to Officer Garcia.

She leaned forward: "Robinson, Acerra, and Mulligan were all profiting from drugs. And when Mulligan was killed, the other two didn't want their activity found out. So they developed this witness and this story so the police wouldn't investigate further."

I was thunderstruck. "I've theorized that since 1999!" I exclaimed. "They were all in it together. And Acerra and Robinson were afraid that the digging into Mulligan's police work would expose them!"

Rosemary said, "I don't think the police just got lucky when they found Patterson and Sean so quickly. I always look at the path, what led the police to my guy?"

I told her about the informer Pablo's statement that the person behind Mulligan's murder "wore the same uniform." "He told me it was about drug money, that Mulligan didn't respect the boundaries the cops had agreed on and was grabbing more than his share. He also said all the other murders—Curt Headen, Kevin Chisholm, Celine Kirk, and Tracy Brown—were connected with Mulligan's."

Rosemary listened intently. Then she threw out a jarring theory: "What if Acerra and Robinson did Mulligan?"

She explained her plan: "To get a successful retrial motion for Sean, we have to uncover either new evidence or withheld exculpatory evidence. The first track I'm pursuing is to seek documents through the Freedom of Information Act. I'll target the state police, the crime lab, the FBI, and more. If you go to all the places, you invariably find one or two reports."

The point of the exercise was to find out whether Zalkind and Duncan had all the information prosecutors had. If not, it was a Brady violation.

Her second track was to interview witnesses again. "The Drumgold witnesses eventually talked. Sometimes it takes three or four tries, but eventually they'll talk. They want their moment of fame. And it's my hope in Sean's case that Rosa Sanchez will finally talk. She, of course, is key, being the only eyewitness who connected him to the scene.

"I'm going to look into every single witness who incriminated Sean—to the point of going to criminal court and pulling files—because promises to witnesses are often physically written on their file folders before they get computerized into the docket sheet."

I began telling Rosemary about my own witness interviews and research. She occasionally jotted notes. When I got to Rosa Sanchez's drug overdose, I confessed I'd wanted to interview Sanchez but, given her importance to the case, held back lest I screw something up for Sean. "Also, I was afraid," I added, feeling sheepish.

Rosemary laughed. "I only travel to such interviews with a gun-carrying assistant."

She asked me what I thought of David Murray's story. I said I'd believed it at first, since Jackie told it to me, but I'd come to have doubts. "Jackie was just echoing what her brother told her. She didn't talk to Sean directly about that morning."

I asked her, "What do you make of Tia Walker's testimony about Sean and the guns?"

Rosemary shrugged.

I continued. "Sean's girlfriend Pam told me the cops promised Tia a house, a car, and money in return for her cooperation. His sister Laselle said in addition to immunity they promised her they'd relocate her and give her a new identity. Laselle also said they threatened Tia with taking away her baby boy if she didn't cooperate."

Rosemary wrote this down.

"Who got the $25,000 reward?" she asked abruptly. I told her I'd called the Boston Police Department looking for that answer, but no one would tell me. "We'll find out!" she vowed.

We began discussing Patterson. His retrial was now scheduled for March 9. After Christmas Jackie had written me that his fingerprints had been disallowed as evidence by the Massachusetts Supreme Judicial Court. Attorney Jack Cunha, backed by over a dozen experts, had successfully argued that the method Boston police used to match Patterson's prints with prints on the door of Mulligan's SUV—counting ridge characteristics from three fingers—was unscientific and unreliable, "a house of cards," Cunha said.

The resulting SJC ruling banned any fingerprints collected and analyzed by this method from being used as evidence in Massachusetts. It stood to affect nearly 1 percent of criminal cases.

Rosemary made a startling prediction: "With the fingerprint evidence now unable to be used, I think the Commonwealth will offer Patterson a plea deal for time served."

I rode down the elevator smiling. Rosemary had tossed out creative new perspectives on Sean's case like a baseball machine throwing pitches. Any one of them might be a home run. She had the aura of a street fighter, and her zest for the coming battle was staggering.

Attorney Rosemary Scapicchio was exactly who Sean needed.

CHAPTER 31

Exit Patterson

A month after I met Rosemary, Rich and I flew to balmy Monaco on Salk Institute business. It was one of our more relaxing, enjoyable foreign trips. As we walked back to our Monte Carlo hotel after a delicious dinner of mussels and French wine, Rich phoned his mother in Massachusetts to say hello. Moments into the conversation, his expression turned grim. "Tell Elaine," he said, passing me his cell phone.

"Did you hear about that boy pleading to manslaughter in Sean's case?" my mother-in-law said. "A good-looking boy too."

My heart began pounding. I'd been checking the *Boston Globe* online for such a development since my conversation with Rosemary.

Back in our hotel suite I logged on and found the report, dated February 8, 2006: "With plea deal, man convicted in officer's slaying may be freed":

"Five weeks before he was to be retried in the notorious 1993 killing of a Boston police detective, a former Dorchester man pleaded guilty yesterday to manslaughter and received a prison sentence expected to result in his release this summer.... Terry L. Patterson, who has spent more than 12 years in prison, agreed to a plea deal with the Suffolk district attorney's office after the state's highest court recently barred prosecutors from presenting fingerprint evidence that tied him to the gunshot execution of Detective John J. Mulligan."

It was just what Rosemary had predicted. Without Patterson's fingerprint evidence, the Commonwealth had no case. I read on:

"Suffolk District Attorney Daniel F. Conley and Boston Police Commissioner Kathleen M. O'Toole said afterward that they were satisfied the triggerman in the slaying—a friend of Patterson's who fired a gun five times into Mulligan's face as they stole his handgun—was convicted of the murder in 1995 and is serving a life sentence.... Patterson's lawyer said [Superior Court Judge Margaret] Hinkle recognized that Patterson had ... limited culpability."

"Limited culpability," I read aloud to Rich, enraged. "That's how the Commonwealth spun it about Patterson—that the real killer, Sean, is behind bars."

"Ass covering," Rich said. "It's public relations. They have to say Sean was the triggerman to make the plea bargain palatable."

"How can Patterson snitch and survive in prison?" I said. "They'll have to let him out right away. Maybe after he gets out he'll be the hero and say Sean had nothing to do with it."

"Don't hold your breath," Rich said.

After we landed back in the States, I called Jackie. "How are you doing?"

"OK," she said with a heavy sigh, her voice a monotone. "It kinda knocked me for a loop when I read about it, but then I talked with Sean and Rosemary. She said Patterson basically signed whatever he had to, to get out of prison. Black kid, white cop. He didn't want another jury trial. Rosemary didn't like the idea they fingered Sean in the plea deal, but she said it wouldn't deter her from taking his case."

"Well, that's great news at least. What is Sean thinking?"

"He evidently expected it."

My mood worsened when I got an email from Rosemary. *Terry had to agree that Sean gave him the gun ... Sean can't understand why he'd do that.* She thought the plea deal stunk.

"Mulligan was a dirty guy," Jack Cunha said as we sat down to talk in his Boston office. It was late February, and I was back East again to help out Janet during one of her grueling residency rotations. Upon arriving in Boston, I'd phoned Patterson's attorney, and he'd agreed to an interview. He was a genial man—slim, attractive, and youthfully dressed in a tailored blue shirt with black suspenders, his graying hair slicked back. He turned out to be a fellow Boston College alum.

"Mulligan bought four cell phones for Acerra, himself, and Brazil," he pointed out. "I think they were all in the drug game together. Acerra may even have been dealing."

He explained Patterson's plea process: "For a plea to be valid, you must show you're knowing, willing, voluntary. And there must be a factual basis for the plea. The facts as presented by the Commonwealth were that Terry Patterson participated in a plan to steal Mulligan's firearm, and in the course of the subsequent robbery Ellis shot Mulligan. Terry needed to say one word, 'Yes,' in answer to this theory of the case. And he did. In saying 'Yes,' he conveyed that Sean Ellis was the man who shot Mulligan.

"It could never be used in court against Sean," Cunha quickly added. "Patterson could still be liable for conspiracy to commit murder or for the federal charge of depriving an individual of his civil rights. So I would counsel him to plead the Fifth. By the way, the effect of this plea on Sean was of considerable concern to Terry. I assured him there would be none."

Cunha said the Commonwealth required nothing further of Terry regarding Sean—no future testimony, no giving of evidence—and this had surprised him: "All they wanted was a clean admission that he, Patterson, participated in a plan to steal Mulligan's firearm, and in the course of the subsequent robbery Ellis shot Mulligan."

I was heartsick.

Cunha was frank about the challenges in both Sean's and Patterson's cases. "The problem, the real question, was the guns: How did the kids come into possession of the handguns? Also, they were both at the store. My strategy for Sean would be to attack Acerra and Robinson regarding their distortion of the truth regarding witnesses. Brazil, too, because he interrogated Terry with Detective Harris and distorted his statement."

Cunha floated an alternative theory of the murder he'd planned to present at Patterson's retrial. "A case could be made that someone else shot Mulligan and that afterward the kids came upon the guns and took what they could get. That way the purpose of Sean's crouching could be debated. Was it to case the car and develop a murder plan, as the Commonwealth said? Or was it to see 'Is the cop dead?'"

"What if the killer was Mary Shopov?" he said, referring to Mulligan's girlfriend. "The five shots to Mulligan's face were in a deliberate cross. It was personal, definitely a 'fuck you.' A girlfriend would do that. Plus, the .25-caliber gun was a lady's gun. Some people said Mulligan gave Mary the pearl-handled gun for protection."

I mulled this over. Shopov was cleared early on by the police.

"Let's face it, if these two Black guys hadn't materialized, the police would have looked a lot longer and harder at Mary Shopov. There had been plenty of evidence to support a case against her. Police went out to question her three times. She lied repeatedly to them."

"Lied?"

"Yes. They went to her condo between 4:00 and 5:00 a.m. to inform her of Mulligan's death. She told them she didn't go out at all that night. But they found that the hood of her parked car was warm, and the pavement beneath it was wet—and it was raining. Also, her windshield showed a drier area where the wipers had been engaged."

This was all news to me.

"In Mary's police interviews, it came to light that she'd been lying to Mulligan about an affair she was then having with a man her age named Bobby." Mulligan had been nearly twice Shopov's age.

Cunha continued. "She and Mulligan fought bitterly over Bobby right up until his death. Her roommate confirmed this, and a fellow police officer saw Mary and Mulligan arguing loudly in public the week before his murder."

Recalling the testimony in Patterson's trial about a woman with stringy blonde or brown hair sitting in Mulligan's passenger seat, I asked, "Do you think the woman in Mulligan's car was Mary?"

"Yes," Cunha said without hesitation.

"And do you think it's possible that Mulligan was shot earlier than the police estimated—somewhere between 3:00 and 3:45 —and people assumed he was asleep?"

"Absolutely."

I shared my doubts about the killer firing through the slightly open driver's window. Cunha agreed and simulated the awkwardness of angling a gun through the three-inch opening to pull off shots. He said, "What if Shopov drove to Walgreens early that morning, gave Mulligan a blow job, and during sex reached up and killed him with the .25?"

It was exactly what Rosemary speculated.

Cunha continued. "[Prosecutor] Phyllis Broker told me she heard Mulligan was found with his pants down, though she could never get it corroborated. Broker told me this herself! She wasn't trying to hide it."

He described some physical evidence I hadn't known about: "There was a blood spatter pattern on the near side of the passenger seat—the side near Mulligan. So if the killer was sitting there, his or her leg wasn't on that part of the seat. It could have been Mary—or someone—leaning down during sex . . . and reaching up to fire the shots."

I knew Cunha was setting up a scenario to sow doubt in jurors' minds. That's what defense lawyers did. "How do you explain the murder weapon turning up in a field?" I asked.

He had a ready answer. "Mary dropped it at the scene. She freaked out. She wasn't a professional killer, after all. And the kids came along and found it and took Mulligan's gun too. It's not a big deal for kids to pick up the guns."

That same theory, of kids happening upon the dead detective and stealing his guns, had been bandied about in the press following the murder. The oral-sex theory had circulated on the street. But the street had Sean's cousin Celine Kirk as the female, not Mary Shopov.

I asked Cunha what he thought about the murders of Curt Headen and Kevin Chisholm. "It's violent out there," was his take. As for Celine's murder, he believed the story of Craig Hood and the necklace.

We agreed that Patterson's trial attorney, Nancy Hurley, did "a noble thing" by contesting what she deemed inaccuracies in Detectives John Brazil's and Dennis Harris's report of Patterson's interview. I asked him, "Why did Phyllis Broker allow Harris to testify that Patterson fingered Sean as the triggerman, even though Hurley sent her a letter saying the police account wasn't true?"

"Broker had to assume Harris was telling the truth," Cunha said. "Remember, she'd had trouble with the detectives union earlier over Acerra and Robinson. The union's attack on her was festering in the background. She *had* to take the police at their word."

I stood up to shake Cunha's hand and thank him for his time, and he made a parting observation: "I think Sean Ellis' chance of a retrial is a long shot. A real long shot."

When Sean came into the Souza-Baranowski visitors' room, his face looked fuller and somehow more mature. "How are you doing?" I asked.

He managed a weak smile. "OK. Better than I was." He was astounded to hear I'd met with Cunha. When I told him Patterson had signed an affidavit naming him as the perpetrator, he recoiled as if punched in the stomach. "He said *I* did it?"

"Yes. It was part of the plea." I quickly told him of Cunha's reassurances. "The good news is, it won't be used against you in court. Cunha won't let him testify. He'll have him take the Fifth. He told me that the effect of the plea on you was of considerable concern to Patterson."

Sean was unmoved. "Terry still hasn't written to me. If he was a stand-up guy, he'd write me and say, 'This is what I have to do, and I want you to know.'" He sounded perplexed and deeply hurt. "I've been losing sleep," he said.

We sat for a while in silence.

"I could never do that," Sean said. "I mean, Terry was going to trial, and he could not blow trial—that's what we say in here, meaning he couldn't lose. Without the fingerprints, he could not blow trial. So why not go to court and take your shot? Why plead out and say that?"

"Pleading was a guaranteed way out of prison, that's why," I said, seizing the moment to lobby him: "You've been going by a strict code of conduct all these years, staying loyal to the code, to your friends..."

Sean hung his head, anticipating my usual sermon.

"...and as I've said before, nobody else is playing by those rules. Terry did what he did to get out of prison. The newspaper said he'll be free by summer."

My speech only spawned another of Sean's soliloquies on why it wasn't in his nature to snitch: "Not snitching is a core value that I can't violate and still look in the mirror. I just couldn't do it. This code is what I've learned it takes to be a man. I didn't have a father around to teach me about being a man. I learned it from the streets."

I quietly absorbed Sean's view of his reality. It made me sad.

Changing the subject, I told him about the defense strategy implicating Mary Shopov that Jack Cunha had developed for Patterson's retrial. To my surprise, Sean knew about Shopov's incriminating car evidence. He had the transcripts of her three police interviews in his storage area. He said he'd mail them to me.

I left wondering why Sean had never mentioned Shopov as a potential killer.

After this prison visit I spoke with my close friend Kay about Sean's firm commitment to the code of the streets. Kay was a psychiatric social worker and one of the wisest people I knew.

"Don't push him on this, Elaine," she said right away. "Sean's code of conduct is his source of integrity. It gives him meaning. Don't take it from him."

Terry Patterson walked out of prison in May 2006, having been credited for time served.

CHAPTER 32

Stirrings

Rosemary had dug up buried treasure. She'd found statements from three witnesses that undermined the prosecution's case. Sean mailed me the transcripts of their police interviews.

In the early morning hours of September 26, 1993, Deborah Cox shopped at Walgreens. Detectives interviewed her and her companion, Leon Nelson, shortly after the murder, and Cox's account of her time inside Walgreens blew a hole in Rosa Sanchez's story.

The explanation Sanchez gave at trial for why it took her twenty minutes to buy a bar of soap was that she first browsed for greeting cards. But Cox was in Walgreens from 2:45 to 3:14 that morning, overlapping Sanchez and, coincidentally, shopping for greeting cards as well.

Cox never saw Sanchez.

Cox shopped alone in the Walgreens greeting card aisle for twenty minutes. She sat on the floor and read cards. She had the whole aisle to herself. She told police she never saw another card shopper. She never saw a Hispanic teenager.

Ultimately Cox selected several greeting cards and charged them on her Visa. The purchase was made at 3:14 a.m. Immediately afterward she and Nelson drove off.

I digested Cox's statement. Sanchez went into the store just after 3:00 and bought one bar of Irish Spring soap at 3:18, cash register time. If she'd browsed cards ahead of that, she would have tripped, or at least stepped, over Cox sitting on the floor. And Cox would have seen Sanchez. The incorrect register times didn't change anything: Four minutes were all that separated the women's check-out times.

Broker did not call on Cox to testify. And with Zalkind and Duncan not mounting a defense, Cox wasn't called by them, either.

Cox's companion, Leon Nelson, waited in the car while she shopped. He told police he saw five or six other cars in the parking lot and a red SUV in front of the store.

Nelson did not see a Black man crouching by the SUV. He did see activity at the phone bank: "One young person—a black male—used the telephone ... the youngster was pleading with a lady friend to allow him to visit at 'this late hour.'" He left the area in a dark-colored car, possibly "an '84 or '85 Olds."

After waiting for twenty minutes or so for Cox, Nelson grew impatient and went into Walgreens to hustle her along. It was then about 3:05. He found her reading greeting cards. After prodding Cox, he returned to his car and moved it to the fire lane about twenty feet away from Mulligan's

SUV. He eyed the policeman inside. "From my vantage point, it appeared that the officer was sleeping, as he would periodically raise his head and body, and then re-assume the reclining position."

I gleaned two main things from Nelson's statement: First, Mulligan's raising his head precluded the murder from happening before 3:15 a.m. Second, Nelson's Black youth at the pay phones pleading with a woman for an early-morning visit sounded like Sean making his booty call to Harriet Griffith. The message was right. The physical description was right. The timing was right. But the car, an '84 or '85 Olds, was wrong.

Or was it?

By now my research had thrown shade on the assumption that Sean was in Patterson's VW Rabbit when Patterson moved it to Victor Brown's street. If the young man Nelson saw on the pay phone was indeed Sean, then whose '84 or '85 Oldsmobile did he jump into?

The third potential witness buried in Sean's case file was Tony Pungitore, manager of the Dedham Showcase Cinema. Pungitore had been ready to testify that on the evening of September 25, 1993, *The Bodyguard* was not showing at his theater, as witnesses Evony Chung and Joseph Saunders claimed—the information Pam had discovered on the Boston Public Library's microfilm.

Jackie's voice on the phone was weary. Drugs were taking their toll on her family. One of her daughters—the responsible one who worked at the law firm—had relapsed: "Two days before Christmas, DSS [the Department of Social Services] came and took the two kids away, and they've been in foster homes ever since." Jackie had petitioned for custody of these granddaughters, but the father of one girl was fighting it. They had a court date coming up.

Jackie hadn't spoken with this daughter in six months; her arthritis was flaring; and she was worn down from riding to Dorchester every day to care for Rae. On top of it all, Shar'Day, now in high school, was having "teen problems."

"She had words with a gang of ten girls, who jumped her," Jackie said. The police had been called. Shar'Day had a court date coming up.

"Oh, no, not Shar'Day," I cried out.

CHAPTER 33

Gun Conundrum

2007

After seven years of heading the Salk Institute, Rich retired in July 2007. He created a consulting firm to advise academic institutions on their medical research programs, and I became his office manager and editor. Rich's first assignment was the interim directorship of the newly created California Institute for Regenerative Medicine (CIRM), a voter-funded initiative to finance research studies employing human stem cells. CIRM was in San Francisco, so we rented out our Rancho Santa Fe home and took an apartment near that city's scenic Embarcadero.

At August's end, before our move to Northern California, we rented a New Hampshire lakeside cottage to decompress and spend time with our East Coast family. When I caught up with Jackie by phone, she sounded chipper. This time she had good news to report: "Shar'Day's high school run-in was resolved by a mediator, and her court date was called off. It was agreed that the girls overreacted, and they all ended up with three-day suspensions."

There was more: "I won custody of my two granddaughters."

With Terry Patterson's case now settled, Jack Cunha gave Rosemary Scapicchio access to a raft of taped police interviews from his case file that neither she nor I had ever listened to. One beastly hot day I drove into Boston and, with the help of one of Rosemary's law-student interns, picked through the materials in the basement of Cunha's office building. We filled a rolling suitcase with tapes, and I also scooped up transcripts from the October 1993 grand jury that indicted Sean and Patterson. I'd never read them.

The police audiotape cassettes were old, and we had to locate a vintage machine to play them. I piled everything into my car and drove back to New Hampshire. For the next week, while my family frolicked in the lake, I sat in a corner of the rustic living room wearing headphones and typing furiously. Rosemary wanted me to search out every gun reference.

The guns troubled me. If Sean and Patterson had left Walgreens with the murder weapon, how could they say they were not involved in the murder?

Curt Headen and Kevin Chisholm

It was eerie and sad to hear Headen's and Chisholm's youthful voices on tape. Interviewed separately, the teenagers gave near-identical accounts of finding and hiding the guns.

Chisholm's interview cleared up one issue. He could not have been one of the Black men in the Walgreens parking lot the morning of the murder.

He was incarcerated that weekend in the Billerica House of Corrections and was not released until Tuesday, September 28.

At the start of Headen's October 13, 1993, interview, his questioner carefully noted that the teenager had already spoken to police "freely and voluntarily" the previous day. Headen agreed, and he also agreed to the statement, "Last night you had the opportunity to be involved in a phone call with … Officer Fratalia, late. And you told him you wanted to come in again, [to] tell us more about what you knew."

My radar pinged at the formal phrasing: Drug dealer Headen "had the opportunity to be involved" with a detective?

He was asked about Celine Kirk's murder. Interestingly, the first thing he said was, "Celine Kirk was my girlfriend."

That was news to me.

The day after Celine's murder, he phoned her friend Nikki Coleman. Nikki told him she'd been talking on the phone with Celine just before her murder. Craig Hood was in the apartment, and she heard him and Celine arguing. Then the phone was abruptly disconnected. After learning this, Headen tried to get Hood's address from one of Celine's other sisters, who lived near Hood in Brockton.

Asked to describe hiding the guns in the Mulligan case, Headen said the episode began at noon on October 1 outside the courthouse. Sean was inside being arraigned on a charge of kidnapping for an incident involving his cousin a few weeks prior. (The charge was later dropped). "[I]t was me, Kevin [Chisholm], Tia [Walker], and Sean's mother, like in a circle, we was talkin'. Tia was crying. And Sean's mother said to Tia, 'If you've got anything in your house, you better get it out.' Then she said to me, 'They're onto Patterson.' At first I didn't know what she meant; then I pulled her aside, just me and her, and [asked] what you mean by that? And she told me she thinks Terry killed the cop, and she thinks Terry had something to do with her nieces being killed."

This gave me pause. Seeing Jackie in this courthouse conversation was surprising. It was the day after Sean's questioning by police. According to

Sean's uncle, Sean was distraught and crying at this point but wouldn't open up to Jackie. Were her suspicions based on what Celine told the family about Walgreens?

It was clear there were depths in this case I'd never to be able to plumb. I resumed reading.

Tia then asked Headen and Chisholm to drive her home. They took Chisholm's car. No one was home at Tia's house. They went upstairs to her bedroom, and under the nightstand they saw two guns: a "small, nickel-plated .25-caliber with an empty clip … and an all-black Glock with a full clip." Chisholm said Headen put socks on his hands and placed both guns on the table to "admire" them. When he saw "Boston Police" written on the side of the Glock, he said to Headen, "Yo, that's that cop's gun, and that's that .25 that killed him! Yo, put it down! Put it down!" He said he and Kevin were both "scared" when they figured this out. Tia began crying and said, "I don't want nothing to do with this!"

For the next half hour the teenagers discussed what to do with the guns. According to Chisholm, "Curt wiped them off, because his fingerprints were on them, and [Tia] said she'd touched them … that Sean had put them there."

Headen said, "… I put them in my pants … left the house … went up the street … on the path into the field, into the bushes [and] put them there, kicked some leaves over them."

Afterward the three friends drove back to the courthouse to wait for Sean.

Detectives asked Headen if he'd ever seen the .25 before. He said yes, it looked familiar: "Kevin was like, 'Terry had a .25, Terry had a .25, yo, like that right there, like that right there.' And I was like, 'Yeah,' cause one day I went down … Hansborough and Sean was out there … and some Willcox [Road] kids came down on the block, so Terry came out [of] the bushes and he had the .25, the same one that was at [Tia's] house."

Headen's questioners asked him to confirm that the .25-caliber gun at Tia's house was the same gun he'd seen Patterson take from the bushes. Headen said, "Yeah, looked like the same."

Headen said that six days later, on October 7, he told Sean's uncle, David Murray, where he'd hidden the guns. Asked to describe the circumstances, he said that he and Chisholm and Tia were back outside the courthouse together while Sean was being arraigned for Mulligan's murder: "We was leaving West Roxbury Court, and Sean's uncle pulled up. And he asked to speak to me. He got out of the car. And he pulled me aside, and me and him was talking. And he asked me where [the guns] was at. And I told them they was in a field down the street ... right there on Callendar and Floyd Street."

David Murray

Sean's uncle's voice on tape was snarly and deep. He agreed he'd been having confidential discussions with police. In the first of several recorded interviews, he said he first spoke with detectives on September 29, at the scene of Tracy Brown's and Celine Kirk's homicides, and by October 1 he'd discussed the sisters' double homicide *and* Mulligan's murder with them "multiple times."

In a lengthy discussion about his conversations with Sean in the week after Mulligan's murder, Murray gave the same information he later testified to. Detectives asked him to describe how he learned the guns' hiding place, and Murray said he got the tip while waiting with Sean's family outside the courthouse on October 7.

Yet Murray's account of how the gun tip got revealed was strikingly different from Headen's.

Murray said a youth drove by the courthouse in a "small [VW] Rabbit ... red in color." He was "one of Sean's friends. I don't know his name.... And the person says, 'The guns are in the field,' and he drove off.... [He] said the guns could be found within three fields of [Sean's] house. He didn't give me no indication of which field the guns were in.... I called Officer Brazil and I relayed this message to him." Murray later met with Brazil and drew him a diagram.

I paused the tape and stared out at the sparkling lake. This was new.

Sean's uncle told police the guns' hiding place? I'd always thought it was Headen and Chisholm. The newspaper said they received immunity in exchange for their cooperation. But it was actually Murray? I was shocked.

Who was Murray's tipster in the red VW Rabbit? Terry's maroon Rabbit had been impounded by then. I knew of one other VW Rabbit in the case. In my courthouse digging, I'd seen a police report stating that Sean first told detectives that Rob Matthews drove him to Walgreens that morning in his VW Rabbit. Sean described Matthews's car in detail, calling it rust-colored and saying its broken front seat forced him to sit in back. Nothing much was made of this first story of Sean's; I'd been troubled that he gave more than one story to police but ultimately dismissed the Matthews angle as Sean's vain attempt to distance himself from Patterson.

Tia Walker

I had no tapes of Sean's girlfriend's police interviews, only transcripts of her October 21 and 28 grand jury appearances. At the start of her first appearance, prosecutors reviewed the terms of her immunity deal, underlining that "perjury committed during the course of the testimony of a capital case carries with it a term of imprisonment of up to life." Tia said she understood. Her testimony included details that did not come out at the later trials.

Tia and her baby lived in Dorchester with her mother, sister, and six-year-old brother. On September 25, the Saturday night before John Mulligan's murder, she waited in vain for Sean to call her. The next day he phoned explaining, "Late last night I had to go get Tracy some diapers."

She said she did not see him until Wednesday, September 29, when he came to her house at 11:00 p.m. and spent the night. The two "discussed their relationship" and then fell asleep. They were awakened at 2:45 a.m., when Curt Headen and Kevin Chisholm came to her window to tell them about the double murder of Sean's cousins. "[Sean] started crying and stuff."

At this point I paused. Here was an entirely different account of how Sean learned of his cousins' murders: He was sleeping at Tia's house, and

Curt and Kevin came to the window?

Sean himself had told me an ambulance attendant gave him the dreadful news outside Tracy's building. Terry Patterson separately told the police roughly the same thing.

Tia's account didn't ring true. Having learned such horrendous news from the emergency worker about the two cousins he loved, how could Sean waltz into Tia's at 11:00, talk with her about their relationship for a while, and then fall asleep?

I resumed reading.

Tia said the next morning she and Sean taxied to Tracy's apartment: "He just said, 'I have to go get a couple of things ... I have to go get a gun.'"

As Tia waited in the apartment building's hallway, Sean entered Tracy's apartment. She heard him yell out in shock. After "maybe three minutes" he emerged with a backpack.

Tia didn't see what was in the backpack until they'd taxied back to her house. There, in her bedroom, "I seen a little gun and a big gun ... I believe it was a .25 and ... [the other] looked like a cop's gun. It was black and it had like a rubber handle." She'd never seen either gun before.

Sean put the weapons under her nightstand and said, "Don't touch them. Don't mess with them." He told her that the guns were Patterson's and that "he got them the night the cop was killed." He said Patterson told him, "Here, hide these guns."

"I'm not saying that it's right," Tia told the grand jurors. "But, you know, mostly every Black male has a gun. So if your friend asks you to hold a gun, you're not going to think nothing of it. You're just going to take the gun and hide it."

She said she asked Sean, "Did you kill a cop?" and he denied any involvement and said he didn't even know if Patterson had done it.

"Did he tell you why he was moving [the guns] to your house?" prosecutors asked.

"He said because he had touched the guns too, and his fingerprints might have been on there. He didn't want to be getting in trouble for the murder of a police officer."

Tia was asked about Headen taking the guns from her house on October 1 and hiding them in the nearby vacant lot. Her account mirrored Chisholm's and Headen's exactly.

Her testimony before the grand jury a week later, on October 21, mainly covered the harassment she was receiving from friends and relatives of Terry Patterson. They called her a snitch for linking Patterson to Mulligan's murder. Her main accuser was Rob Matthews. He'd accosted her in the courthouse after her previous grand jury appearance, saying, "People better learn to keep their mouths shut, because if my boy gets locked up, there's going to be on people." Back in the neighborhood, Matthews warned her twice more to "keep her mouth shut."

"Rob is a real sneaky person," Tia said. "And him and Terry is real close, you know. He'll do anything for Terry. I don't know, you know, exactly . . . what extremes he'd go through [sic]. But he'd do anything for him."

She related another courthouse encounter she'd had, this time with Matthews' friend Lew Richardson. "He's fat," Tia volunteered. "He asked me what was I up here for . . ." Not wanting to tell Richardson her reason for being in court, she lied about having a car accident. "And Lew said, 'Well, they got me in, and they asked me all kinds of questions. But you know, we just got to . . . stick together on this. Because . . . we know Terry didn't [do it].'"

She'd told Sean about these threats from Patterson's friends, and Sean urged her to call Sergeant Detective Tom O'Leary [head of the Mulligan homicide investigation] and report the incidents. So Tia reached out to O'Leary, leaving a message. "He didn't call back."

I noted one other interesting fact from Tia's testimony. At the close of her October 21 appearance, she was told she had to give her fingerprints the following day, so police could compare them with prints found on the weapons. Tia objected strenuously: "I have to get fingerprints? I am not a criminal here!"

The date was puzzling—and it seemed important. The police didn't have Tia's prints until October 22. Wasn't her print on the gun clip the stated reason she began cooperating with the police? But that was in early October. It didn't compute.

Mary Shopov and Tina Erti

Police conducted separate interviews of Mulligan's girlfriend, Mary Shopov, and her roommate, Tina Erti, on October 2 and 3. I had only transcripts of those interviews, not tapes.

Shopov and Erti shared a condo upstairs from Mulligan's in the same West Roxbury complex. Shopov, in particular, was well-acquainted with both Kenneth Acerra and Walter Robinson, given the men's friendship with Mulligan. She and Mulligan had attended Robinson's wedding together.

Both women told their questioners that Robinson visited Mulligan's condo shortly after the murder. They said Shopov let him in, and he proceeded to take money out of a jacket hanging in the detective's bedroom closet.

Shopov said she told Erti about this money. She'd seen it while searching Mulligan's pocket for an address book to notify his relatives, and after Robinson left she noticed it missing. She said she later questioned Robinson about it, and he'd told her he turned the money in to the Boston Police Department.

I paused to reflect. Robinson made a beeline for Mulligan's jacket. I wondered how much money was in it. It was clear Robinson knew the cash was there and wanted it—or else wanted to make sure no one else found it.

Erti confirmed that Shopov told her about Robinson taking the money. The detectives then probed Erti at length about Shopov's relationship with Mulligan. She revealed that Shopov had confided that the fifty-two-year-old detective was "too old for her" and she felt "boxed in." She said Mulligan kept phoning Shopov, which aggravated her. He'd recently taken her shopping for a "surprise" two-carat marquis diamond ring and was pressuring her to get married.

Erti said Shopov occasionally went to Walgreens to keep Mulligan company during his details. Then she confirmed what attorney Jack Cunha had told me: For the past seven months, Shopov had been two-timing

Mulligan with a younger boyfriend named Bobby. Bobby visited Erti and Shopov's apartment when Mulligan was working.

A few months before the murder, Mulligan had found out about Bobby after he left several phone messages for Shopov, and Mulligan and Shopov had a blow-up. "[Mulligan] came up to the apartment with Mary, saying he wanted to listen to the messages. One of them pulled the phone out [of the wall]. ... It sounded like the phone was thrown ... it was a violent argument—though he never hit her, never."

Bobby then arrived at the complex to see Mary, and he and Mulligan had a face-to-face confrontation in the parking lot.

The next day Mulligan took away the car he'd given Shopov and parked it outside the Area E-5 station. Erti arrived home to find a desk, a computer, and a chair of Shopov's that she'd been using in Mulligan's apartment "outside our door, in the hallway ..."

"Mary and John made up after that," Erti said, yet Shopov continued seeing both men and hiding it from each of them.

Detectives asked Erti about the day and night of Mulligan's murder. Erti said Shopov told her they had a "really good day" on Saturday. They went out for dinner, then watched a movie and the news in Mulligan's apartment before he left for his Walgreens detail. Shopov then came upstairs to their apartment. Mulligan called her about 1:00 a.m. and told her to wake him up the next morning at 10:00 so they could shop for a dress she needed for a wedding.

After that, "she was on the phone with Bobby. ... Mary would always talk to Bobby late at night. I want to say [till] three, three-thirty ... they talk a long time. ... Because she said she had fallen asleep around four."

Erti knew Shopov had told police she'd read in bed till 4:00 a.m. She asked Shopov why she didn't just tell the police she was talking to Bobby, by way of an alibi. But Shopov didn't want to expose their relationship. "She was scared ... [she] knew police were gonna drag Bobby into it, and then everybody would know about Bobby and her cheating on John."

Rosemary had asked me to look out for gun information. In the women's interviews, I found perplexing questions that the detectives put to each of them about Mulligan owning a gun "with pearl handles":

From Erti's October 2, 1993, interview:

Q: "Have you ever seen John with a small-caliber gun with pearl handles?"

A: "Never."

Q. "Have you ever seen Mary with a firearm of any type?"

A: "Never."

From Shopov's October 3, 1993, interview:

Q: "Did you ever see John with a small-caliber gun?"

A: "No. The only other gun I've ever seen John with, other than the Glock, would have been the gun he had before that, that was issued through the department."

Q: "Did you ever see John with a small-caliber gun with pearl handles?"

A: "No."

I pondered this. The alleged murder weapon was a .25-caliber Raven with a pearl handle. Police found it buried under leaves on October 7. The women's interviews were on October 2 and 3. Why were police asking questions about a small-caliber, pearl-handled gun nearly a week before a gun *of this exact description* was pulled from the Dorchester vacant lot?

After Labor Day, before heading to San Francisco, I went to Rosemary's office to brief her on what I'd learned about the guns. She was as surprised as I'd been to learn that Sean's uncle was the person who told police the guns' hiding place—specifically, John Brazil. It was yet another instance of either Brazil, Acerra, or Robinson being in the exact right place at the exact right time to pull in key evidence. Wizards.

Rosemary was familiar with most everything else I'd found. "There was no report of any money being turned into the police department," she said acidly of Robinson's money grab from Mulligan's closet.

I told her I found it noteworthy that Tia hadn't given her fingerprints until the end of October, *after* she testified to the grand jury: "If the police didn't have Tia's prints on the gun clip before her testimony, what motivated her to talk about Sean and the weapons?"

"I don't know," Rosemary said.

She did know about the clairvoyant questions that detectives posed to Shopov and Erti about a pearl-handled .25-caliber gun. She sat back and announced, "I think the pearl-handled gun was Mulligan's. I think he was shot by his own handgun."

I was confused. "But Headen said the pearl-handled gun was Patterson's. He told detectives he saw Patterson pull this gun out of some bushes on Hansborough Street a couple of weeks before Mulligan's murder."

Rosemary threw back her head and laughed. "I don't believe that for a minute! The police made Curt say this. I'm sure of it. They had to put that gun in Terry's hands before the murder."

Her voice got steely. "Did you know that Headen's gun-hiding story emerged for the very first time at his 'voluntary' (Rosemary made air quotes) questioning session in homicide? And do you know who drove him there that night?"

I didn't know.

"Acerra and Robinson. The two of them, with Sergeant Lenny Marquardt, picked up Headen after learning that Rob Matthews paged him at midnight, a few hours before the murder. But detectives never asked Headen one question about Matthews's page in that interview. They only talked about the gun-hiding."

It was true. There'd been zero mention of Rob Matthews on Headen's tape.

Rosemary drove her point home. "It was at Headen's October 13 interview session, after he was alone with Acerra and Robinson in the car, that he first talked about finding the guns in Tia's bedroom and hiding them. That was plenty of time for those guys to feed him a story. And one week later Tia told the identical story to the grand jury. That was the first time she'd ever mentioned her role in the gun-hiding. The subject of guns never came up in her police interviews."

Rosemary then repeated what she told me the first day we met: "I think the guns were planted." She meant planted by the corrupt cops.

On my flight back to California, I tried to make sense of all I'd learned. Until now I'd more or less blown off Rosemary's gun theories. They'd seemed rather wild, given Tia's trial testimony that Sean accepted the weapons from Patterson, and Norman Zalkind's concession of this at trial. Yet Rosemary had long been skeptical of this scenario.

Rosemary was famously street-smart. In her two decades of practice, she'd seen it all. And she was right: the gun-in-the-bushes story could be a calculated setup of Patterson by the police, a story fed to Headen to parrot on tape.

But if the cops planted Mulligan's service revolver and the gun that killed him, how did *they* come into possession of the weapons?

The implications were mind-boggling.

CHAPTER 34

"I Forgive Her"

2007–2008

No sooner had I landed from Boston and opened the door to our San Francisco apartment than the phone rang. It was Jackie. Her family was in an uproar. Rosemary had told Sean it was his uncle who tipped the police about the guns, and everyone was furious with David Murray. "Could you talk with Sean's cousin Puddin about it?" Jackie asked.

"Of course," I said, thinking, "Here it is, 2007. These events occurred fourteen years ago, and they still have the power to enrage."

Suddenly Puddin was on the line. I'd met Jackie's niece just once, at the hospital after her mother, Rae's, paralyzing car accident. Over the years Puddin had been a regular visitor to Sean at Souza-Baranowski.

"From what he's telling me, it's based on Tia and David that he's in there," Puddin said. "And Sean feels hurt that they put out the information they did, because it isn't true. It isn't true Sean went to Celine and Tracy's apartment and took out the guns, the way Tia testified. That's ridiculous! That apartment was a crime scene!"

I tried to wrap my mind around Puddin's words. "You're saying Tia lied about the guns on the stand?" I was dumbfounded.

"Yes, she lied. Sean did not get the guns." Puddin sounded disgusted.

I was doubtful. Tia had immunity. The only crime she could be prosecuted for was perjury. "Why would she lie about Sean and risk a perjury charge?" I asked.

"Because she was offered a new life to tell that story," Puddin said, distaste in her gravelly voice. "Also, Tia was a young mother then. I think police threatened her with the loss of [her son] Ricky."

I'd always believed the police arm-twisted Tia. But I'd thought it was to squeeze out whatever she knew about the guns. I'd never imagined the police pressured her to lie about the guns—lie to implicate her boyfriend.

It made sense. It had always seemed preposterous that the police could have overlooked two guns in Tracy Brown's apartment, the scene of a double homicide. Improbable that Sean could have just walked in and taken out guns the morning after the murders. Detectives would have scoured that apartment.

At this point Murray knocked on Puddin's door. She'd demanded that he come over and explain the gun tip. She said she'd call me back in an hour.

When Puddin called back I asked, "So, why did your uncle tell Brazil where the guns were hidden?" I was thinking about the $25,000 reward—setting aside for the moment Rosemary's theory of the cops planting the guns.

Puddin's answer surprised me. "He told that story because he was on parole. My Aunt Jackie asked him to come over and assist her, but by rights he shouldn'ta had any interaction with Sean, because Sean had the open kidnapping case. But he did. And the police spoke to David multiple times about his parole problem, saying they could send him back to prison. He told me Brazil was a jerk—that wasn't his word—about the whole situation. He said the police stayed on him like glue."

Who was telling the truth, and who was lying? At this point I had no idea. I was ready to conclude "everybody lies."

March 2008 found me back in Boston, and I took time to dig into another gun question that had long gnawed at me. At trial, David Murray had agreed with Phyllis Broker that Sean had "a good hide" for the weapons in Tracy's apartment. Didn't this prove that Sean brought the guns home after the murder? I pulled out the trial transcripts and found the exchange between Broker and Murray in Sean's second trial:

Broker: "Do you remember having some conversation with Sean Ellis about 4 Oakcrest Road [Tracy's apartment] relative to the guns?"

Murray: "I cannot—I can't answer that ... "

Broker then showed Murray a transcript of his October 8, 1993 grand jury testimony and said, "Read that to yourself, please, sir." [Pause] "Mr. Murray, did Sean Ellis tell you that he had 'a good hide' at 4 Oakcrest Street?"

Murray: "Yes"

I re-checked the police transcripts of David Murray's interviews. His October 1, 1993, meeting with Detectives Brazil and Mahoney was eye opening:

Murray: "[Sean] told me he came back to the apartment yesterday [September 30], and he had got that gun. And I says to him, 'You mean to tell me the police didn't find the gun?' And he said, 'No.'"

Detective: "Now are you aware that Sean had a very good hide in that apartment, and where that gun could have been?"

Murray: "He had, whatever, he had to have a good hide—um, somewhere in that apartment, because he went to that apartment and he got the gun."

Detective: ..."Was he referring to a .38-caliber revolver?"

Murray: "[Yes], a .38-caliber. . .revolver."

This was disturbing. It appeared Broker was playing a shell game. The gun Murray was talking about with Brazil and Mahoney was a .38-caliber revolver, not the 25-caliber pearl-handled gun that police said killed Mulligan. All along I'd thought Murray's "good hide" referred to the murder weapon. The jurors likely did too.

The chief prosecutor had to have seen the transcript of Murray's police interview, in which case she knew his questioner specifically asked about a .38-caliber gun. But Broker fudged the issue at trial—whether by design or not, only she could say. She'd left the caliber unspecified and framed her question in such a way that jurors might conclude the "good hide" was for the murder weapon. The exchange surely fooled me.

It gave me one more reason to wonder about Broker's moral compass.

In the end, Murray's "good hide" gun information was a cul-de-sac, case-wise, for he did not testify in trial three. But I was glad to sew up the loose end in my own search for the truth.

Exploring it set up further questions in my mind about Sean's uncle. In agreeing with Broker about the hidden gun—when he knew the actual weapon was a .38—did Murray get confused? Or did he deliberately go along with prosecutor's story line?

If so, what else did he go along with?

When Sean entered the Souza-Baranowski visiting room I saw that he had neat cornrows ending in fluffy bits at the nape of his neck. He carried new, burgundy-framed eyeglasses in his shirt pocket. As always, his white running shoes looked fresh out of the box.

"How are you?" I asked.

"I'm growing as a person and as a man," he said with pride. "Recently there was an incident here, a fistfight among several inmates. A guy named Thief told me to get involved, but I didn't. I just watched. And later Thief commanded me to participate in a follow-up, but I didn't. I didn't think the cause was just. They'd already settled it cleanly."

He shook his head in disgust: "It's really hard to grow in here, hard to resist the peer pressure. The guys have an adolescent mindset. I'm just focused on my case and getting my freedom—and getting transferred to Norfolk."

Norfolk was a far less restrictive prison, considered the best in the state.

I hadn't seen him since the previous summer, when I'd transcribed the tapes of Headen's and Chisholm's police interviews. It had seemed a bad idea to put anything in a letter. Now I launched into a full debriefing: "Headen's voice sounded reluctant and unhappy…" I began.

When I got to Headen's description of Patterson pulling the pearl-handled gun from the bushes to brandish at the Willcox boys, Sean couldn't contain himself. "No! Things didn't happen that way on the street. First of all, if it had happened, I would have heard about it. And I didn't. Second, this was the early nineties. No one 'brandished' a gun. If guys harassed you, you took a shot."

"Don't worry," I said. "Rosemary considers the gun-in-the-bushes story a lie that the police fed to Headen."

I took a deep breath. "Sean, I need to talk with you about some gun testimony. First of all, I dug deeper into your uncle's statements about a "good hide" you had for a gun at Tracy's apartment. But it turns out David was referring to a .38 caliber gun you'd hidden there, not a .25. I cross-checked this in the transcripts of his police interviews.

Sean looked blank.

"Then there's Tia's damning testimony about you getting the two Mulligan guns from Tracy's apartment and bringing them to her bedroom. That's been bothering me, because Puddin told me it's not true. She said you never brought the weapons to Tia's house. So why would Tia say that on the stand?"

After a long moment, with eyes lowered, Sean said almost in a whisper, "Aspects of what Tia said at trial were not true."

I blinked. "Not true?"

He spat it out. "Yeah. I didn't take guns from Tracy's apartment."

"What?" I stared at him. I felt gut-punched. Sean's words upended everything. Here it was, 2008. I'd been fighting for his retrial for the past ten years. And this was the first time he was telling me what he'd known all along—that Tia flat-out lied on the stand?

I thought about my drives from Montreal to Boston and back, six hours each. The countless itineraries from San Diego to Europe routed to include a Boston stop. The hours of combing through transcripts, articles, documents, and files. The interviews of witnesses, relatives, and friends. The prison visits, with their maddening delays and hostile guards. And through it all Sean had withheld this important truth?

Forcing the words out, I said, "If you didn't retrieve the guns from Tracy's apartment, then where did Tia get that story?"

"I think...something like...a cop...I don't remember who...came up behind her...in a car maybe, pulled her over, I dunno...and basically told her, 'This is the story you're gonna tell.'"

I felt the blood rush to my face. For ten years I'd looked for flaws, contradictions, lies, anything that could get Sean a retrial. And all that time he'd been sitting on the one big lie that could do it. If we could show that the police coerced false testimony from Tia, his case would be reopened.

No one had followed the wrongful conviction cases of Marlon Passley, Donnell Johnson, and Shawn Drumgold more closely than Sean. All these men had been freed from prison because of false testimony by witnesses. And here Sean sat, holding the key to unlock his cell. Yet he wasn't using it.

Fury welled up in me. "Why didn't you tell me this before?"

Another long silence. Then Sean said, "Tia lied, like my Uncle David. But, unlike my uncle, she didn't do it willingly. I know that. She was coerced by the cops. And, having lived through the same experiences as Tia, I understand her position, why she did what she did. And I forgive her. Before, I might not have. But I can now."

I felt the floor drop away. Didn't Sean get it? He'd been deceiving me. For years.

The rest of the visit was a blur.

My thoughts whirled as I drove back to Janet's. Sean was all about respect. What about respect for me?

In the weeks that followed, my emotions ran the gamut from scalding anger to bitter cynicism. Sean had destroyed the trust we'd built over a decade. I felt betrayed, and my enthusiasm for his cause dimmed. I talked to Rich about it. He couldn't understand Sean's rationale either.

He'd sat mutely through all three trials, fully knowing that Tia's gun testimony was false. He'd apparently kept this from his lawyers. Of course, this was when they felt confident that there was insufficient evidence to convict him. Yet he was convicted. And throughout the decade-plus since, the fact of Tia's false testimony might have undone that.

Sean's silence about that testimony was inscrutable.

Discouraged, I wrote down my feelings:

> *The culture of the street keeps Sean imprisoned, both physically*
> *and mentally. He will not, cannot bust out of it. Not snitching is*
> *his code of honor, and I think applying this code to Tia makes him*
> *feel heroic and noble.*

I kept trying to formulate what to say to Sean in a letter. I wanted to sound philosophical, not hostile:

> *I'm ending my participation in your case. I'm frustrated and*
> *disappointed and angry that you never told me Tia lied in her*
> *testimony about the guns. I guess this was so you wouldn't snitch*
> *on her, but this stance has likely kept you from gaining the*
> *freedom you deserve. I don't see how any further efforts of mine*
> *can help you.*

And yet…I cared about Sean and cared deeply. Plus, I believed that his adherence to the street code stemmed at least partly from fear.

I never mailed Sean my thoughts. Even though he'd not been fully honest with me, I believed he'd been terribly wronged by the criminal justice system. I'd put ten years of my life into his case, and I believed the effort was justified. My empathy toward him overrode any hurt that I felt.

CHAPTER 35

Roadblocks

2008–2010

I rejoiced in August when I received Sean's news:

> *8/13/08*
>
> *Peace Godma,*
>
> *I have transferred to [Norfolk] ... [and it] is truly a culture shock. This compound is its own community ... [with] its own political structure. They have good programs here: AACC (African American Coalition Committee), Family Awareness, Young Fathers, L.A.C. (Legal*

Advisory Committee) which is the legal arm of the prisoner/inmate
counsel, and more. . . .

> *This prison allows for the establishment and advancement*
of a progressive mind, to say the least . . . committees here have
by-laws and everything. The population has a constitution.
It's crazy in a good way.

> *Well Godma, I miss you! . . .*

With Love, peace and happiness,
Jahborn,
Ur Godson

When I drove out to Norfolk Prison for my first visit later that month, I was impressed. The small, semirural town of Norfolk was about thirty miles southwest of Boston, and the prison's multiple brick buildings were scattered over a several-acre campus. Despite the crumbling cement steps at the entrance and a waiting room and visitor restroom that looked untouched since the 1930s, the tension in the air that was ever-present at Souza-Baranowski seemed much reduced here. The CO's who processed visitors' paperwork were respectful. Some actually smiled.

Sean walked into the freestanding, octagonal visiting rotunda wearing horn-rimmed rectangular glasses. He still had cornrows, but he'd grown a slight beard and mustache. His size-thirteen feet were encased in his usual pure-white sneakers, but he was wearing dark jeans and a black, short-sleeved shirt over a white T-shirt. It brought me joy. Up till now I'd seen him only in prison jumpsuits.

"I have some exciting news," he said. "Rosemary called me to say she was contacted by Rosa Sanchez."

Sean sat back and smiled at my widening eyes. He continued. "She asked Rosemary to represent a friend of hers who's in trouble. And she told Rosemary, 'I'm willing to talk.'"

I was openmouthed. Rosa Sanchez, ready to confess that her "Uncle Kenny" rigged her photo ID? It didn't get bigger than that.

"I had this intense physical reaction of a huge weight lifting off of me," he said. "It was amazing, so powerful. And the feeling lasted the whole day. But after a while I talked myself down. 'Don't get excited,' I told myself. 'There's a long way to go. She hasn't talked yet or given an affidavit. She might change her mind.'"

For these reasons he hadn't told his mother about Sanchez, and he asked me not to either.

When I commented on the improved surroundings at Norfolk, he said, "There's a lot of politics here, but good politics—prisoner groups that elect representatives and have a voice." He'd already been elected chairman of the activities committee in one group, and his whole being was animated as he described their work: "Time was, I'd be OK with 'Whaddup dawg' or 'Nigga' as a greeting, but no more. I'm not a dog. I'm not a nigga. I'm a man. Black men have to reexamine their values, or otherwise they'll never get ahead."

His energy, enthusiasm, and attitude all hinted at a new era opening up for him. There were programs in this place, I thought, pleased. At Souza-Baranowski, whenever Sean had tried to take a course, he'd been refused.

At the end of our visit, when I asked if he needed anything, he said, "Could you send me *Robert's Rules of Order*? It would help me deal with some of the personalities in this place."

I hadn't seen Rosemary for a while. When I went to her office to catch up, I vented about my anger and frustration at finally hearing from Sean that Tia's testimony about him and the guns was a lie. As she heard me out, Rosemary's expression remained neutral. I knew she couldn't violate the attorney-client relationship, and I didn't know what Sean had told her about the guns.

I said that, after seething for months, I'd reconciled myself to it. "I think Sean has held in Tia's lying because he wanted to shield her from perjury charges." Protecting Tia was the only way I could fathom Sean's silence. By now I'd concluded it was more than faithfulness to the code. It was Sean's faithfulness to Tia. He'd loved her once. Perhaps he loved her still. She and her baby boy, Ricky, had been his "little family." I'd slowly grown to understand and accept this. Doing so had gone a long way toward repairing the cracks in my trust.

Recently, over lunch with Jackie, I'd broached the topic of Tia, fishing for her reaction: "After all these years, Sean finally told me Tia lied on the stand."

Jackie eyed me and then said, "It took a lot for him to tell you that, because up to now he's been looking out for her, protecting her."

So, Jackie was very much in the know. She proceeded to fill me in. "Back then, when Sean was sentenced, I confronted Tia about the lying. And she told me, 'One detective told me they'd take away Ricky.' I tried to reason with her, saying that would be coercion, and there's a law against it. But Tia would have none of it."

My phone conversation with Puddin the previous fall had reinforced this. She'd told me, "Tia would need reassurance that, if she comes clean now, nothing would happen to her."

Rosemary set me straight: "The statute of limitations for perjury in a homicide case is seven years. We learned that with the Drumgold witnesses who recanted. None of them encountered any legal problems. If Tia is concerned about her legal vulnerabilities, I can get her separate counsel, free of charge, through the Commonwealth, as I did for them."

She wanted to talk with Tia, and soon, for she was more convinced than ever the guns were a police setup. "I don't believe Tia's prints were on that gun clip. I don't believe she ever handled a gun. The officer who collected and analyzed Tia's prints was Sergeant Robert Foilb—the same officer who collected the prints from Mulligan's SUV and concluded they were Patterson's."

Rosemary was deeply cynical about how Boston police handled evidence. This same Sergeant Foilb had also misidentified a thumbprint on a water glass from a 1997 shooting scene, resulting in the conviction of an innocent Boston man, Stephan Cowans, for wounding a policeman. After spending six and a half years in prison, Cowans was exonerated in 2004. The case had triggered a federal grand jury probe of the Boston Police Department's fingerprint unit and its shutdown because of shoddy practices.

Rosemary wanted to persuade Tia to give her fingerprints again so she could get them retested, to re-examine the Commonwealth's work.

In summer 2009 Rich and I sold our Rancho Santa Fe home and moved back to Boston for good. Rich could do his consulting from anywhere, and the prospect of living closer to two of our three children outweighed even California's glorious weather.

Janet and Devin had bought a house west of Boston. Their second son, Adam, had been born during Janet's final year of medical residency, and she was now a fellow in GI oncology at Mass General and Dana Farber Cancer Institute. Mark was but a train ride south. He'd graduated in May with an MBA in finance, having attended New York University's Stern School of Business part time while maintaining his full client load.

The move east also meant I could see more of Sean and his family. By now Shar'Day had graduated from high school. Jackie nearly burst with pride when, over lunch in Boston's Back Bay, she told me, "She's working on her associates degree at North Shore Community College and wants to concentrate in social work."

I shared my own proud education story: Rich and I were about to fly to Vancouver to attend Alison's October college graduation from Simon Fraser University. After spending four years in Banff, she'd declared herself "done with partying" and moved to Vancouver, where she earned a digital design certificate and then entered community college as a mature student. Her excellent grades led to her transfer to Simon Fraser, and she was now poised to receive an honors degree in commerce and a leadership prize.

For a few years Rich and I had feared Alison would never get her life together in a way that would make her happy. But, by dint of living on her own, she'd blossomed into a responsible and delightful young woman. Best of all, we were getting along.

In spring 2010, just as I was setting out to visit Sean with Jackie, Rosemary reached me with an urgent message. "Sean has been working hard to connect us with Tia, and she's agreed to visit him and talk. But I want him to know it's imperative that he *not* speak with Tia until I've had a chance to speak with her. If he speaks with her this early, the D.A. will claim he told Tia what to say. This could wreck his case." Knowing we were about to visit Sean, she asked me to deliver this message.

On our ride to the prison, Jackie gave me the bad news. "I've already patched through two phone calls from Sean to Tia."

When I delivered Rosemary's warning at Norfolk, Sean was indignant. "Tia and I spoke only about personal issues. She has three kids and just ended a thirteen-year relationship. That's what we discussed. Life. Only that. Nothing about the case."

All things Tia were nonnegotiable with Sean.

"It doesn't matter," Rosemary said when I stopped by afterward to report. "Just the fact Sean spoke with Tia looks bad."

Rosemary's usual confident manner was gone. Even her posture drooped. She had just learned Tia wasn't going to cooperate. After tracking her down through Facebook, Rosemary had sent out her private investigator, Scott, to ask if she'd come forward to get her prints retested—and admit that detectives gave her a script to recite about the guns. But Tia had refused to speak with Scott, and her boyfriend made it clear that he should leave their front porch. Immediately.

"We can submit Sean's retrial motion without Tia," Rosemary said. "But I'm afraid it isn't enough. Because this is a cop killing. And a cop killing is different."

She had more bad news to report.

"Rosa Sanchez is not going to cooperate either. We met with her, and she dropped hints about wanting money for her testimony. She was smart enough not to ask for money outright. She said things like, 'If I cooperated, I'd have to move...and I don't have the money for that.... How could I get the money to move?' and so on.

"I told her, 'We don't pay people to tell the truth.' So we're at an impasse. I still think Rosa is guilty of telling Acerra's story. But I'm going to stop pushing her. She's not going to budge. It's a dead end."

First Tia, and now Sanchez, choosing to stay in the shadows.

And just like that, two potential roads to Sean's freedom were blocked.

CHAPTER 36

Low and Lonely

2010–2011

The Monday before Thanksgiving 2010, Jackie and I made a hurried visit to Sean. She'd just been informed that Celine Kirk and Tracy Brown's killer, Craig Hood, was being transferred to Norfolk. Alarmed, she'd contacted the corrections commissioner to warn him of Sean's intense grief over his cousins' murders. There could be violence when Sean came in contact with Hood.

Rosemary also called the prison and persuaded them to interview Sean. Mystifyingly, Sean told the officials he was fine with Hood being there; he'd even signed a waiver.

Jackie was dead set against Sean and Hood being in the same prison. She wanted to speak with Sean, and time was of the essence. Hood was already at Norfolk and being segregated until the issue was resolved.

I'd just arrived home from ten days in Hawaii, where we'd flown to attend a November wedding: Mark's. He had fallen in love with a winsome Montreal elementary school teacher named Glyncora, the daughter of one of Rich's colleagues, and their courtship led to a dream wedding on Maui. We'd rented an oceanside villa there large enough to house the entire family, which now included Alison's partner, Jeremy. It was a week in paradise. Now it was back to the grim reality of Sean's life.

Jackie and I arrived at Norfolk feeling tense and worried, but only Jackie got in to see Sean. My underwire bra set off the metal detector, and the guards sent me to the reception area to await a second inspection by hand. That inspection never materialized, and I stewed.

In the end the Norfolk prison officials rejected Hood's transfer. The situation was too volatile. Later I asked Sean why he'd been OK with Hood coming to Norfolk. "I just wanted to talk with him and ask, 'Why? Why?'" he said.

The following June, when Sean walked into the visitors' rotunda, I didn't recognize him. His dreadlocks were long, and his eyes looked squinty. He didn't see me sitting in the first row, and he walked back and forth, scanning the visitors. I had to call out his name.

He was more downcast than I'd seen him in the thirteen years I'd been visiting. I soon learned that personal issues were bringing him down. He wasn't getting many visits from family. He never heard from his sister Laselle. Though he remained close to Puddin, even she didn't come see him much anymore. "She's under a lot of stress," he explained, his voice a monotone. Puddin's mother, Rae, had succumbed to complications of her paralysis, and Puddin was taking her death hard.

Not even Jackie and Shar'Day had visited Sean lately. A minor misunderstanding had created a rift between him and his mother, and Shar'Day had decided not to come: "She feels visiting me would acknowledge that the state of affairs is permanent, and she won't do that," Sean explained.

He spoke wistfully of his father, John Ellis. "I want to see him now. He's been diagnosed with Alzheimer's, and he's in a home. Time was, I didn't care if anything happened to him. I was angry that he'd had nothing to do with my life. But I don't feel like that now. Far from it. I would like to see him. My uncle was supposed to bring him out to Norfolk, but nothing came of it."

Sean again brought up Tia. He confessed he'd been dreaming about her. "We were each going through so much when we were together. We were always there for each other, and this developed a very strong bond. I imagine she thinks I hate her guts, but I don't."

He idealized Tia. I knew he longed for a soulmate, someone who understood him. I ached for him. How lonely he must be. Several women had come and gone in Sean's life, even though he was behind bars. Jackie laughingly referred to them as "the flavor of the month." No doubt about it, Sean was a handsome guy with considerable charm. Perhaps part of that charm was his vulnerability.

After Pam broke up with him, he'd had a brief flirtation with the young woman from Dorchester who pronounced him "too serious." After that, he took up with another Dorchester woman fifteen years his senior. I'll call her Darlene. He wrote,

> She says she is attracted to me. She has a hard life, works three jobs,
> the first as a kidney dialysis technician, the second as a receptionist
> in a hotel, and the third in retail. She has two children who are
> growing up, and she wants to have someone to talk things over with.

Soon Darlene was visiting him every other Friday. Their bond made him genuinely happy. Their relationship deepened, and he pronounced himself in love. (No sexual contact was allowed by Massachusetts prisons.) Being involved with Darlene "makes me a better man," he wrote.

All was good for a long while. Then I heard from Jackie that things were going south. On this visit, Sean opened up about it. Though he was totally focused on getting out of prison, Darlene was not interested at all. "She says things like, 'Why would you do that?' She seems to want to keep me in here, where she can control me." He was mystified that she took this tack. "I can't, I won't give up my focus and effort to get out, despite her pressure."

He sighed heavily. "There are jealousy issues, control issues on her part. She often comments on the young women who visit here, saying, 'They'd be all over you, if you were out.' I think she wants to keep me in a box."

His face twisted as he spoke, and when he removed his glasses I saw that he was crying.

"She hasn't been out to visit in a long, long while. I think she has made miscalculations about me, and me and her, which resulted in the radical change with us."

Pam had recently moved back to Boston and had visited him. Learning this, I said, "When Pam was with you, her sole focus was getting you out of prison, and she worked very hard."

"Yes, and she raised me in a way," Sean said. "She was the first person to get me off that old path and onto a new path. She sent me scriptures from the Bible, and we discussed them. She and I will always be bonded."

The one bright light on Sean's horizon was a former high school friend named Reynell. A busy professional with two active sons, she was also pursuing a master's degree at night. She'd begun visiting Sean on weekends and was helping him research his case.

Jackie approved: "This one's responsible."

Trying to cheer Sean up, I asked about his work in Norfolk's "Second Thoughts" program. Inmate counselors led structured sessions for offenders aged eighteen and under, who were bused to the prison. Sean had been selected as a group leader: "You have to have an impeccable disciplinary record to be a counselor," he'd told me proudly.

The counselor training he received had helped him grow emotionally. He'd acknowledged and confronted what he termed "family issues" with his siblings and for the first time in his life talked openly about his brother, Joseph's, death. He'd wept.

"I was surprised when the other trainees didn't look at me differently after that," he'd told me. "They cried, too, over their various issues. Before,

I would push my emotions down, lock them up. I thought that was good, that it meant being strong. But now I know it's better to get the emotions out, to express them. That way others can share the burden with you."

I knew Sean loved his counseling work. But today he said, "It tires me. Some kids come in hardened ... one kid in particular ..." His voice trailed off, and he looked away. Then he brightened: "But by the second-to-last visit, even he opened up and cried."

As I stood to leave, Sean said, "I just want to get out of here. I just want to go home.... I'm tired of it all, and I spend too much energy just avoiding getting tangled up in the negativity of this place."

I drove away from Norfolk thinking that, although Sean tried valiantly to hang onto hope, he was showing deep fatigue of spirit. By now he'd been incarcerated for eighteen years. I fervently hoped Rosemary's tenacity would get him freed.

In November, Sean wrote me in distress about a talk he'd attended:

> [T]wo guest speakers (women) spoke about losing their sons to gun violence. One of them, Kim Odom, whose son Stephen [sic] Philip Odom was murdered, really affected me with her testimony re: her loss, the circumstances, etc.—and she forgives the person.
>
> Godma when I look at me, Celine & Tracy ... I can't or won't forgive Craig Hood. Why am I like this?

I looked up the Odom case. Thirteen-year-old Steven Odom had been shot in the head in Boston in October 2007—a bullet apparently meant for someone else.

I immediately got in the car.

"I almost wish I hadn't gone to the talk, it affected me so," Sean said. He sighed heavily. "I went up to speak with Kim Odom afterwards and told her I was going through this issue, and I couldn't forgive. But she only said, 'I'll pray for you.' Others were standing in line behind me, so I walked away. I'm wondering if my anger at Hood is some kind of character defect."

I searched for words. "Sean, Craig Hood has never shown remorse or asked for forgiveness, correct? I'd have a very hard time forgiving him too. I think Mrs. Odom's forgiveness is extraordinary. Angelic, even. It's a pretty high standard to measure yourself by."

"I'm still trying to work through it all," he said.

Ever since Sean had told me Tia lied on the stand, I'd reflected a lot on our friendship. In a recent yoga class, the instructor had read a beautiful passage about the Japanese philosophy of embracing life's flaws. The outlook found expression in kintsugi, a technique for mending broken ceramics. When a piece of crockery broke, the Japanese would not discard it. Rather, they would piece it together with a lacquer mixed with gold, or silver, or platinum, making no attempt to hide the cracks. In fact, they illuminated the cracks, believing that imperfections sustained over the life of an object make it more interesting and beautiful.

That's how I thought about Sean's and my relationship, I reflected as I drove home from Norfolk. The cracks that were created by his withheld information were ultimately repaired through a lacquer of understanding and acceptance.

Like a broken Japanese vase, our bond had become stronger through the mending.

CHAPTER 37

The FBI Reports

2011   **FOIA MATERIALS**

Meanwhile, work on Sean's retrial motion had taken a giant leap forward. On a bright August day in 2011, with a bounce in her step and a broad smile on her lips, Rosemary ushered me into her office and took her seat behind her commodious desk. "At long last, the FBI reports have started coming in," she announced triumphantly.

Rosemary had begun submitting her Freedom of Information Act (FOIA) requests in 2004. Up till now we hadn't received a single document on the Mulligan homicide investigation or on Acerra's, Robinson's, Brazil's, and Mulligan's misconduct.

"Thirty-one pages in all have arrived," she said, "including multiple reports about Mulligan's corruption. The FBI had files dating back to 1983."

She handed me three photocopied reports:

> *[undated] MULLIGAN has a reputation ... of hustling hookers and for being a shakedown man.... Source feels the only reason MULLIGAN keeps his job is because he knows a lot of dirt on the department brass. He, in effect, blackmails the department brass with "if I fall, you fall."*

> *Dec. 19, 1983. ... MULLIGAN is known to have given [a female hooker] at least $150 and further convinced her to drop charges against [redacted]. MULLIGAN frequents the area of Westland Ave. and Hemmingway [sic] and is said to know all the hookers there. MULLIGAN allegedly does favors for these hookers and they reciprocate. MULLIGAN is also known to have been a bagman for [redacted] and is currently a bagman for [redacted].*

> *November 12, 1993. Former BOSTON POLICE OFFICER, JOHN MULLIGAN, aka ... PLAIN VIEW MULLIGAN, regularly ... "associated"/"liked," young black girls and "shook down" ... pimps, prostitutes, and drug dealers for money. MULLIGAN extorted from other police officers, and ... used every means available to blackmail people. MULLIGAN was as "dirty as they come." MULLIGAN dealt drugs extensively. ... Source has heard often that MULLIGAN committed murder as a cop. [Redacted], the author, had an intimate knowledge of MULLIGAN.*

Rosemary was elated. "All this evidence about Mulligan's criminality was known by the Boston Police Department. None of it was ever disclosed before any of Sean's three trials, before his first retrial motion, or before his appeal. And all of it suggests suspects with motives to harm Mulligan—information Sean's lawyers could have used at trial to sow doubt in jurors' minds that this murder was a random crime committed by two teens."

She smiled as she dropped another bomb: "Listen to this. During the investigation, two different Boston cops came forward to say they had reason to believe it was an inside job—that Mulligan was killed by a fellow officer."

I sat back. It was the informer Pablo's tip, come to life.

She continued: "The first FBI report about this was a tip from a named Boston police officer who accused another named colleague of killing Mulligan. Both names were blackened out in the report, but the individuals were known to Boston police." She handed me a paper bearing the FBI's letterhead dated November 1, 1993—five weeks after Mulligan's murder—and I read it:

> *Source advised that [redacted police officer] was recently disciplined for accusing [redacted police officer] of involvement in the murder of Detective John Mulligan. Source stated that [redacted police officer] is corrupt and was involved in 'ripping off' and beating up hookers while assigned to the vice squad.*

"This information went nowhere," Rosemary said. She passed me a second FBI report dated a month later:

> *December 3, 1993. Boston police Officer John Mulligan (deceased) might have been killed to keep him from talking. A Boston police Officer might have been involved in Mulligan's death. Source has told the above [redacted].*

"'To keep him from talking' probably referred to all the drug dealer robberies going on," Rosemary said. "But the main thing is, neither of these tips was given to Sean's lawyers."

I sat, savoring the moment, but at the same time thinking, "After all these years, and all the disappointments, will things really start to move now?"

Rosemary answered my unspoken question: "Withheld evidence this important should merit a new trial."

As was her practice, Rosemary set out to read "every single piece of paper" in the case. She asked me for everything I had, so I lugged in the boxes of materials Jackie gave me in 2000. For the past five and a half years I'd sent Rosemary written summaries of my investigative findings, interview notes, and timelines, and I put copies of these in the mix. A young lawyer in Rosemary's office, Dennis Toomey, transferred the materials from my trunk to their basement storeroom.

I had a good feeling. The gears in Sean's case were starting to turn.

CHAPTER 38

Teamwork

"I want action on Sean's case, pronto," Rosemary barked into the phone one day in late August. "I'm setting up a team." The flow of incoming FOIA documents had increased from a trickle to a flood and now reached critical mass.

Rich and I were just back from a trip to Canada. In July Alison had married Jeremy in a rustic yet comfortable lodge on British Columbia's Sunshine Coast. No roads led there, so guests ferried in from Vancouver. Alison was a glowing bride. Rich and I spoofed her in our joint wedding

speech, reading aloud from hilarious letters she'd written us from summer camp and framing their contents—usually transparent manipula-
tions of us to buy her things—as "advice to Jeremy." Now in her thirties,
this daughter was an abiding joy to Rich and me. We thanked our lucky
stars, realizing "luck" was a not insignificant factor in our happy ending.

The Wednesday after Labor Day I drove into Rosemary's office for our
first team meeting. I was beyond excited. It felt like the home stretch.

I'd already met Dennis Toomey. Rosemary introduced me to Amy Cadagogne, another young staff attorney, and the three of us sat across Rosemary's desk as she went over the case: "First off, Acerra and Robinson were
drug cops, not homicide investigators."

I nodded. Rosemary had emphasized this from the start. After our
very first meeting she'd emailed me, *I still cannot wrap my mind around
the idea that two dirty drug cops were the leads on a cop killing. Something
is just wrong.*

She continued. "We think Mulligan was in cahoots with Acerra, Robinson, and Brazil— that they were robbing drug dealers together. After
Mulligan was murdered, they were terrified they'd be found out. So they
sabotaged the investigation—'solved' the case quickly using Rosa Sanchez
and other tactics.

"Going forward, we need to establish Mulligan's links to Acerra, Robinson, and Brazil's drug corruption. We have the FBI reports alleging that
Mulligan shook down drug dealers. We have the 1996 *Globe* article about
the Boston Police Anti-Corruption Unit investigating drug-dealer robbery
allegations against Mulligan and Robinson. But for a retrial motion, we
need hard evidence connecting Mulligan with their crime ring."

Rosemary had recently learned that her requests for Boston Police Department files on Acerra, Robinson, and Brazil had been denied because
she'd directed the forms to Internal Affairs, not specifically to the Anti-Corruption Unit (ACU) within Internal Affairs. The administrative roadblock
had cost Sean's defense team two years.

"Pure stonewalling," Rosemary raged. Amy would now begin the process again, filling out new applications and paying yet another stiff fee.

And we'd wait some more.

Dennis would dig into the criminal records of trial witnesses to see if the police or prosecutors had made any suspicious deals or promises. I would serve as "case historian" and organize Sean's case file chronologically. All three of us would comb the FOIA documents for anything of substance not given to Norman Zalkind and David Duncan. This exercise was key. If we found something, it would constitute a Brady violation meriting retrial.

Rosemary pumped us all up: "The fact Sean Ellis is sitting there for a crime he didn't commit is horrendous. I think we're going to get him out. With what I know, if he doesn't get out, I quit!"

For some time now Rosemary had worked out of a swanky new office in a repurposed warehouse made of granite on Union Wharf, one of several historic wharves jutting into Boston Harbor dating from the Revolutionary War era. Rosemary set me up in a basement conference room with walls of exposed stone, and I began commuting in from my suburban condo, carefully timing my rides around Boston's notorious rush-hour traffic.

By now there were piles of FOIA materials to explore from the Mulligan investigation: police reports, notes of investigators' interviews, and case-related photographs. I looked through them all. When I came across duplicates of materials I'd seen in Zalkind and Duncan's office, I weeded them out. Some of the contents gave me pause, and I lingered over them.

An eight-by-ten-inch photo of Mulligan's SUV parked outside Walgreens showed the vehicle parked directly in front of the mounted pay phones. It still amazed me how close these elements were to each other. You could spit from the phones and hit the Ford Explorer.

Mulligan's autopsy photos were in an envelope. The accompanying report said the bullets "passed from front to back" on a "basically level plain [sic]" parallel to the ground. Rosemary told Dennis, Amy, and me that there was no way these wounds could have been inflicted by a gun being thrust through the car window, given the position of Mulligan's head and body. She believed the forensic evidence indicated a passenger-seat killer.

Several police photos showed the recovery of the guns under leaves in the Dorchester field, with John Brazil supervising the police cadets. What interested me most was that each weapon was wrapped in some sort of rag—definitely not in plastic bags, as Sean's uncle testified.

A memo from the Boston police homicide unit recommended that the $25,000 reward money be "shared by 6 individuals." Who were they, we wondered? Victor Brown had denied getting a share, as did the informer Pablo. Zalkind had said David Murray was ruled out. Who else was in the cast of characters? Sean had reported a prison-grapevine rumor that Rosa and Ivan Sanchez received a check for $7,000 after the trial, but we'd not been able to confirm this.

Just as in the TV-news video Rosemary saw, the police crime scene photos captured Acerra standing outside Walgreens sometime after the murder. I recalled that, when asked to recount under oath all his actions and duties that morning, Acerra never mentioned going to Walgreens. The photo of him on the sidewalk was damning, given that the crime scene technicians didn't find Mulligan's cell phone when conducting their inventory of the SUV's contents a few hours after the murder.

Two police reports I'd never seen described Acerra's discovery of the cell phone a week later. Both were written by Detective Richard Ross. Ross stated that on October 1, 1993, Acerra told him he wanted to look for Mulligan's cell phone charger in the SUV and asked him to be present. When Ross began looking in the SUV's armrest compartment, Acerra stopped him and "requested that we should look in the center console." Ross then "opened up the top of the console and removed the cash tray," and there was Mulligan's black Panasonic portable telephone. Ross contacted the ID unit to photograph and analyze the phone for fingerprints.

Two days later Ross wrote a second report documenting a subsequent interaction with Don Hayes from the police crime lab. He said Hayes asked him, "What was the story about the portable telephone?" Ross told him he and Acerra came upon it while searching for Mulligan's charger. Hayes then asked Ross "to show him what he did to the center console," so Ross re-enacted how they located the phone.

Referring to himself in the third person, Ross wrote:

> *At this time Don Hayes stated to Det. Ross that he didn't understand
> the problem because he and Dave Brody found that phone late
> Sunday afternoon, September 26, 1993, but wasn't [sic] told that
> anyone was looking for a phone. Also, Hayes stated that they were
> only looking for blood, hair, blood splattering and direction, and gun
> powder residue.*

I found the police account laughable. Cell phones were investigative
gold. Mulligan's last calls might point to his killer or to a crucial witness.
The notion that trained forensics investigators would ignore the presence
of a cell phone in Mulligan's SUV and not report it to homicide detectives
was preposterous.

Two bankers boxes piled in Rosemary's storeroom contained folder after
folder of witness testimony from the 1996-97 federal probe into Area E-5
drug corruption. The transcripts numbered perhaps a thousand pages. I
lugged the boxes into the conference room and set them on the table,
eager to get cracking. Unlike Rosemary, Amy, and Dennis, I had uninter-
rupted time. My mission: See if Mulligan was present at any of Acerra's,
Robinson's, or Brazil's crime scenes..

It had been fifteen years since that Montreal summer when I began
researching the Mulligan case in my third-floor study. The stakes now
couldn't be higher. Barring a pardon by the governor, Sean's only shot at
getting out of prison was Rosemary's retrial motion.

I felt in my bones that Mulligan had to be robbing drug dealers with
his station-house buddies. Given his own seamy reputation—the rumors
of his drug profiteering were now confirmed by the FBI—and his perpet-
ual need for money, it was hard to imagine Mulligan not plundering with
these friends. Acerra and Brazil shared a cell phone contract with him.
Acerra had his housekey. Robinson somehow knew to remove Mulligan's

wad of cash from his jacket pocket. These guys were tight.

Lurking within these transcripts might be the concrete evidence we needed to prove Mulligan was part of their criminal scheme. I just had to find it.

I took a deep breath and started reading.

CHAPTER 39

The Search for Criminal Links

Federal grand jury hearings into Kenneth Acerra's, Walter Robinson's, and John Brazil's misconduct had been held weekly from March 1996 through February 1997. The boxes before me contained thirty-five folders of testimony from selected victims. Most were drug dealers, with a smaller number of immigrants who ran illegal lotteries. All were given the extraordinary assurance that their own criminal conduct was not under scrutiny, only that of Boston police.

Acerra and Robinson's former partner in crime, Brazil, flipped on them and described their methods. Several totally innocent people victimized by the detective-felons gave testimony. A handful of Area E-5 supervisors and detectives were called to testify, but to a one they stonewalled prosecutors' questions, revealing much about themselves and the station house. Neither Robinson nor Acerra was subpoenaed, but Robinson insisted on testifying anyway.

The police informer

Enlightening perspectives on Robinson came from a jailed informer who'd worked for him. Ron Hansen was a thirty-year-old drug dealer awaiting trial on charges of assault with intent to kill. Interviewed at Nashua Street Prison in spring 1996, in advance of his grand jury appearance, he painted a colorful picture of Robinson.

Hansen and his ex-wife, Julie, were cocaine users who'd been busted by Robinson. Julie then became Robinson's informer and his occasional sex partner. She would tip him off to drug locations, and he would pay her a hundred dollars for each ounce of cocaine he seized. Sometimes Robinson paid Julie with cocaine.

"He used to like to bust Dominicans," Hansen said, "immigrants that didn't have green cards, because they would ... give up the fight. If they had twenty thousand cash and he took ten, they wouldn't say, 'ten thousand dollars is missing.' Their concern was to get off the drug charges so they wouldn't get deported.... Robinson would tell them, 'I'm a decorated police officer. You're a convicted felon. Who they gonna believe?'"

Hansen described a swaggering Robinson driving a red Corvette convertible and wearing $1,000 suits and $200 shoes. The pockets of his $500 camel hair topcoat bulged with bills. He was "always loaded," Hansen said, and generally carried $2,000 to $3,000 in cash.

"He always had this ongoing joke ... about [how] he carried money in two pockets.... He used to say, 'One's my money and one's buy money.' The buy money was the money ... he would get from drug dealers ... [that] he used to buy information or drugs.... He'd give Julie money out of his buy money for her to buy drugs from someone so he could see if they were selling ...

"Him and Kenny [Acerra] made it very clear that they were partners. If Walter wasn't around, you could talk to Kenny. If Kenny wasn't around, you could talk to Walter.... If [an informant] gave [Acerra] information, the information was passed on to Walter, and him and Kenny would work together on it."

According to Hansen, when Robinson or Acerra found a stash of drug money, they would typically split out one-half for themselves and turn in the rest. "I mean [Robinson] always made it clear that ... there was always something to be taken for him, whether it be drugs or cash. He would say, 'Oh, I just take a little off the top'... [H]e always just gave the drugs to his little snitches, that's how he worded it.... He'd give it to them instead of giving them cash."

Neither detective was particularly interested in convicting the dealers they arrested. They would "tell the person, 'Hey, if you give us a bigger fish, we won't show up in court.'"

Interestingly, Hansen was asked what he knew about John Mulligan. He said his wife had known Mulligan since she was sixteen. She'd told him Mulligan liked to bring "little girls" for rides in his car.

She'd also said Mulligan wore a .25-caliber gun strapped to his ankle.

Hansen passed on a rumor he'd heard about the murder: Mulligan "took drugs from the girlfriend of one of the killers and told her if her boyfriend wanted the drugs back, he would have to come and see him, or he'd arrest her.... One of the girls killed in Mattapan was the girlfriend."

Hansen's tip was startlingly specific—and food for thought. Curt Headen had called Celine Kirk his girlfriend.

John Brazil

Shielded from prosecution by a grant of immunity, Brazil testified in December 1996 about Robinson's and Acerra's illegal tactics and his own. His work with them began in 1989, when he rejoined the Boston force after a lengthy absence because of a car accident and was posted to Area E-5. Right away station supervisor Lenny Marquardt told Brazil he should take lessons on writing search warrant applications from the "in-house experts," Acerra and Robinson.

Brazil said Robinson showed him "word for word, as I sat at a typewriter," how to fake the informants and the surveillance activities they were supposed to have conducted before searching each address. "There was absolutely particular words to use.... When I asked, 'Well, who do I use for the informant?' [Robinson] would indicate ... 'Don't worry about it, just use, use the people that we [arrested] the other night.'"

When it came to executing the warrants, Robinson "ran the show." "I would recover drugs or money...[and] Robinson would say, 'I'll take care of that.... I'll hold onto the money until the case comes up.'"

Brazil said Robinson instructed him to omit any mention of money in their police reports.

He said Robinson paid hush money to certain Boston defense attorneys to keep quiet about the false records.

The victims

Questioned by Assistant U.S. Attorneys Theodore "Ted" Merritt and Kevin Cloherty, the detectives' victims gave vivid accounts of bullying cops in full uniform bursting into their apartments and workplaces and grabbing cash and drugs. I quickly learned Acerra, Robinson, and Brazil hadn't worked alone. Victim after victim described other Area E-5 detectives stealing with them. Sometimes these detectives were named, but other times they were merely described.

I scoured the pages for mention of Mulligan, convinced he'd been in the mix. Several accounts of a paunchy, gray-haired, middle-aged cop present at various robberies buoyed my hopes of nailing him.

Reading through the three-score cases was deadening. One disgusting robbery began blurring into the next. But the scenes of innocent people caught in the mayhem gripped me:

- Acerra forcing his way into a woman's apartment in a residence for the disabled where she cared for her wheelchair-bound son, "tearing it apart" and grabbing her $960 rent money—all because her daughter dated a dealer.

- Acerra and an unnamed detective bursting into a young mother's bedroom as she sat nursing her newborn baby, "throwing things about" and grabbing $3,900 cash from her bureau drawer—"money that [my mother and father] had been collecting to do repairs in the house."

- Robinson and a companion entering a man's apartment in Jamaica Plain, "destroying it," tying the man to a chair as his girlfriend crouched in horror, taking $2,300 cash he'd put aside for a used car, and then hauling him to the Area E-5 station and demanding he give up "someone big." When he could not, pulling out a large bag of cocaine and subsequently using it as "evidence" against the innocent man in court.

- Acerra and Robinson stealing $25,000 from the currency exchange business of a Dominican immigrant family—money earmarked for delivery to their customers' Santo Domingo relatives; the thirteen-year-old son giving testimony, since his mother didn't speak English and three months earlier his father had "died of a self-inflicted gunshot wound" after becoming "extremely depressed" over being wiped out by the detectives.

Acerra and Robinson's denouement began with their overreach in a 1990 kidnapping case. A Boston hospital chaplain had agreed to pay $8,000 ransom to the captors of his teenage son after they abducted him in a dispute. The clergyman went to the police, and Acerra, Robinson, and Marquardt accompanied him to the money exchange and arrested the kidnappers. The father got his son back but not his money. "That's evidence," Acerra said.

After six years of spurned requests for his $8,000, the chaplain lodged a complaint with Internal Affairs—and this was the spark that ignited the investigation into Area E-5 that the department said was ongoing at the time of the *Globe*'s 1996 expose.

Other Area E-5 detectives

Several Area E-5 supervisors and colleagues of Acerra and Robinson were called to testify. Not one could remember a single detail of any drug search originating from the station, even when they were shown search warrants bearing their names. The officer responsible for documenting Area E-5's seized money and drugs admitted he kept no records of money.

He seemed unconcerned.

"Everything [at E-5 was] absolutely on the up and up," insisted one detective who'd been named by several victims as one of their robbers. Asked about a $15,000 cash deposit to his Florida bank account made during the period, this detective could not recall it. Neither could he remember any phone calls he ever had with Robinson, Acerra, or Marquardt regarding seized money or station procedures, even when prosecutors confronted him with phone logs showing a flurry of calls among the four after the *Boston Globe*'s Spotlight Team began pulling warrants in 1996.

Reading this, I was disgusted. I was witnessing the infamous police "blue wall of silence" play out in the hearing room.

No legal actions were taken against any of Acerra and Robinson's fellow Area E-5 officers.

Robinson and Acerra

Despite being warned by prosecutors that his words could be used against him, Robinson demanded a grand jury appearance. He swore he never once failed to turn all seized drugs and firearms into the department; likewise, he always noted all seized drug money on the police reports.

Questioned at length about specific searches in which victims had named him, Robinson remembered little or nothing or else shrugged them off with "That was Acerra's case" or "That was Brazil's case." When prosecutors brought up several cases of Robinson's that had been dismissed when he failed to show up in court, he said, "I didn't do it on purpose."

Acerra did not testify, but his actions in one prominent case had a starring role in the 1998 Change of Plea hearing at which he and Robinson finally admitted guilt in return for reduced sentences. Assistant U.S.

Attorney Merritt told the judge that Acerra, like Robinson, not only robbed people but also fabricated evidence.

To illustrate, Merritt detailed Acerra's 1996 recovery of the missing police department share of $43,830 in cash that he, Robinson, and others had seized from drug dealer Humberto Guzman in 1992. (By custom, the proceeds of drug busts were split equally between the police department and the D.A.'s office.)

Acerra had taken custody of the department's $21,915 portion, but he never logged it in. The proceeds vanished … until the *Boston Globe* publicized the missing Guzman money in its 1996 Spotlight series.

Miraculously, a few days after its mention in the newspaper, Acerra found the Guzman cash and turned it in. He explained he'd stashed it in a locker years before and forgotten it. Now, spurred on by the *Globe*'s reporting, he'd commandeered fellow detective Kenny Beers to help him find it. Lo and behold, they opened a long-locked storage closet and spied the money sitting there in a heat-sealed plastic bag.

Or so Acerra said.

I laughed aloud when I read prosecutor Merritt's statement: "The evidence would show, Your Honor, that the majority of the bills … in that heat-sealed envelope were not in circulation at the time of the [Guzman] search."

The similarity of Acerra's M.O. in discovering the "missing" Guzman cash and discovering Mulligan's "missing" cell phone was not lost on me.

In pleading guilty to conspiracy, and civil rights and tax violations, Acerra and Robinson admitted they faked more than thirty warrants and stole over $200,000 in illegal searches between 1990 and 1996. The change in their pleas undid all of Robinson's perjured testimony.

Every one of their victims was awarded restitution, to be paid in full by the two of them. I scanned the list of victims in the Change of Plea document, looking for the innocents they'd targeted. I smiled:

- The mother of the disabled boy got her $960 rent money back.
- The nursing mother got her parents' $3,900 home-repair money back.

- The chaplain got his $8,000 ransom money back.
- The bereaved family received the $25,000 stolen from their currency exchange business.[4]

This concluded my reading. Discouraged, I put the folders back and closed the boxes. In a thousand pages, I did not come across Mulligan's name.

It took me four and a half days to get through the hearing transcripts, meticulously reading each case and filling a small spiral notebook with my left-handed scrawl. I packed sandwiches each day, not wanting to leave the office for lunch. I packed a sweater, too, since Rosemary's basement, so near Boston Harbor, always felt cool and clammy. I took very few breaks and lost all track of time in the damp room, my back stiffening up. And I came up dry.

The grand jury testimony gave me a bird's-eye view of the wholesale corruption at Boston's Area E-5 station house. But the gray-haired, middle-aged cop involved in multiple robberies was never pinned down by name.

My instincts told me he was Mulligan. And by subtracting out the names and descriptions of the other, named Area E-5 detectives, I deduced it was Mulligan. But the man remained an unnamed specter. I had no proof.

I lugged the boxes back to the storeroom with a pit in my stomach and climbed the stairs. The office was deserted. It was Friday afternoon, and the only person left was the receptionist.

I drove home.

---

4 One year later, in 1999, the city of Boston awarded a $62,500 settlement to the tied-up, framed Jamaica Plain man, confirming his false arrest by Robinson and Acerra and clearing his name.

CHAPTER 40

Smoking Gun

"I just know Mulligan was wrapped up with those guys," I said to Rich over my second glass of wine. "I can't imagine his friends were pulling in all that cash from drugs and him not getting a piece of the action."

I stewed all weekend. Rosemary was pursuing other investigative angles, but none would be as valuable as hard evidence of Mulligan's criminal activity with Acerra and Robinson.

By the end of the weekend I'd made my decision: I would not give up. Ask my family: I'm nothing if not persistent.

On Monday I found Rosemary at her desk. When she looked up expectantly, I said, "Nothing to report yet, but I'm not done. I need to reread some of
the transcripts."

I descended the wide wooden steps to Rosemary's basement, took a
deep breath, pulled out the boxes, and began plowing through the transcripts a second time. By now the names seemed like familiar characters
in a crime novel.

The morning's work was a repeat of last week's. Nothing.

After lunch I started rereading the transcript of Robert Martin's September 9, 1993, drug bust on Boston's Commonwealth Avenue. Five detectives
led by Robinson and Acerra had taken all of Martin's drugs and money.

Martin was part owner of a Boston jewelry store. On the side, he ran a
thriving business supplying marijuana to dealers in pound lots at $1,400
each. He lived in downtown Boston at 208 Commonwealth but stored
most of his drugs and money in a safe in an apartment leased by two of
his friends at 373 Commonwealth.

Testifying on October 3, 1996, Martin described a police drug bust of
both apartments three years earlier. Though Martin's section of Boston
was not under Area E-5 jurisdiction, the five detectives who ripped him off
were all from E-5.

Martin had arranged to sell seven pounds of marijuana to a dealer
named Mike. He stuffed the marijuana in a backpack and, leaving his girlfriend and another friend waiting in his apartment, went down to Mike's
car parked in the back alley. Martin got in, and Mike gave him $9,800 for
the drugs plus $5,200 he owed him for a previous transaction. Suddenly "a
bunch of police officers came running down the street from both sides...
with their guns in the air..." Martin testified.

The first officer identified himself as Walter Robinson. He showed Martin a search warrant. A second officer said he was with the Immigration
and Naturalization Service (INS) and gave his name as "Lt. McCarthy." A
third officer "was an older gentleman named Beers." Also in the group was
station supervisor Lenny Marquardt.

Acerra and Robinson took the knapsack, the money, and Martin's keys, which they used to get into the back entrance of Martin's 208 Commonwealth apartment. They left Martin and Mike in the car, guarded by the fifth officer.

Half an hour later Acerra and Robinson came back to the car. Robinson told Martin they'd found his safe: "He wanted me to open it." Martin told the detectives that first they would have to let his girlfriend and his other friend go because "they had nothing to do with the drugs."

"[Robinson] said, 'Well, you do the right thing, and we'll see what we can do.'"

So Martin went up to his apartment with Robinson and Acerra and opened the safe. Inside were twenty-two pounds of marijuana packaged in five-pound lots. Street value: $30,800.

Leaving Beers and the fifth officer in Martin's apartment to guard Martin and Mike and the two hostages, Acerra, Robinson, and Marquardt left to search 373 Commonwealth. Before long Robinson phoned 208 to say they'd found Martin's second safe and wanted him to open it.

Martin told Robinson that for him to do that, his friends definitely had to be released.

Robinson then put Marquardt on the phone with Martin. Marquardt said, "Well, we only found $8,000 in your top drawer. There better be more than that in the safe, or we're not letting [your friends] go."

"There's more than $8,000 there," Martin assured Marquardt.

So Robinson came back, picked up Martin, and drove him to 373 Commonwealth, where he opened the safe. Acerra "reached in, grabbed out ... a bag full of stones which we used to make jewelry with ... silver bars we used to melt down ... a lot of keys ... a Ziploc bag full of money ... $18,000 to $20,000...."

The detectives left without searching further.

"Then they drove me back to 208," Martin testified, "and they let me watch ... as they uncuffed Mike." Unknown to Martin, Mike had informed on him. Martin's two friends were let go.

"[T]hey drove me to West Roxbury, Area E-5," Martin continued. There the detectives weighed the marijuana and then "ordered Chinese and had dinner." Afterward they took Martin's photo, and Robinson wrote the police report and drove Martin to the police station covering Commonwealth Avenue. Martin was locked up and charged with possession of marijuana with intent to distribute.

The five Area E-5 detectives had robbed Martin of twenty-nine pounds of marijuana that night and upwards of $26,000 cash. On their police report they listed "several pounds" of marijuana and no money. The report was signed and submitted by two officers: Walter Robinson...and John Mulligan.

Mulligan was the fifth detective at the Martin robbery. The one who'd guarded the dealers, held the innocent people hostage, and falsified the police report.

I pounded the table with a victory drumbeat. I knew it! Mulligan was entangled in Acerra and Robinson's criminal scheme. "Thick as thieves!" I hollered, chortling over the discovery.

I couldn't believe I'd missed Mulligan's name in the Martin transcript the first time through. I checked my notebook: Yup. I'd read the file, and I'd written notes—incomplete notes. Perhaps I'd read too much, too quickly. There had been so many cases to read and so much detail to take in. Corrosive, mind-numbing detail.

And here was Mulligan, robbing Robert Martin with Acerra and Robinson. I did the math: Seventeen days before his slaying.

Sean's jurors never knew that Mulligan led a secret criminal life *with the investigators of his murder.*

CHAPTER 41

Old Angles New

I was bursting with excitement, but again, Rosemary's, Amy's, and Dennis's offices were empty. As I left I placed the Robert Martin robbery transcript on Rosemary's desk with a note: "Found Mulligan! Proof of theory!"

This night at cocktail hour, Rich clinked my wineglass in celebration, not in sympathy. He knew how much finding Mulligan's name meant to me. On a personal level, it gave me greater satisfaction than any other achievement in my professional life. It meant Sean would have a real shot at getting a new trial. I was walking on air.

I'm sure I was still smiling when I fell asleep.

When Rosemary called me, she was thrilled we now had evidence of Mulligan's criminal link to the men, but she was also tempered and strategic, cautioning that we shouldn't get overconfident. She repeated her mantra: "A cop killing is different."

"To convince a judge to reopen Sean's settled case, we have to marshal every bit of evidence we can get. You never know which finding or what argument might move the court."

Rosemary was relentlessly practical. She had zero inclination to bask in a propitious finding. Her way was to move on to the next possible finding. So we kept digging.

My second reading of the grand jury transcripts, when complete, found no additional mention of Mulligan. It was nerve-racking to think that Sean's best prospect for a retrial might hang on the one thread of the Martin robbery.

Turning to the pile of FOIA documents, I found myself viewing with new eyes some of the duplicates of documents I'd seen in Zalkind and Duncan's law office. A few items of evidence stood out. Two claimed Mulligan's killer was a fellow officer, just as the informer Pablo told me—and just as the redacted FBI reports said was rumored within the BPD.

In 1994, Massachusetts Senator Dianne Wilkerson received a phone call from a man who identified himself as an African American officer named James from Boston's Area B-2. In a rambling monologue, James told Wilkerson that other cops could be behind Mulligan's killing. A station-house colleague had told him "a group of cops were taking money," and "maybe ... they set [Mulligan] up."

James also reported hearing that Mulligan was killed because he was "messing with young black girls." He said that after the murder, "2 guys forced Armstead [presumably a fellow detective] to retire early."

Wilkerson immediately wrote to Zalkind relating James's phone call and attaching handwritten notes she'd made of their conversation. Rereading Wilkerson's letter to Zalkind and her notes now, I noticed another tip James passed on: "The .25 caliber pearl-handled gun that police recovered in Dorchester belonged to Mulligan."

It was Rosemary's theory exactly.

A further tip in this vein was contained in an October 1994 letter written to Patterson's trial attorney, Nancy Hurley. Its author said Mulligan had been shot by a fellow cop. He claimed to know why. I'd seen this letter in Zalkind's office but dismissed its contents as far-fetched. Reading it again now, I realized with a start that the letter was penned by Robert Martin, the drug dealer who was ripped off by Mulligan, Acerra, and Robinson in September 1993—the dealer whose grand jury testimony I'd pounced on.

Martin told Hurley about his 1993 drug arrest and attached the police incident report. It was actually signed by three officers, not two: Walter Robinson, John Mulligan, and "Lt. McCarthy of INS." Martin believed Mulligan's killer was this Lt. McCarthy. He'd learned McCarthy was furious with Mulligan for raping his trusted informant, a woman named Laura who happened to be Martin's friend. He wrote:

> [McCarthy] … sits in the Explorer beside him. He gets Mulligan to
> confess about raping Laura. They laugh about it. Mulligan says,
> 'What is she going to say? She's an informant!' [and] then [McCarthy]
> turns on Mulligan and pulls a 22 [sic] caliber from his pocket
> and puts it on Mulligan's forehead. He waits a second—Mulligan is
> frozen, thinking it's only a bluff. He fires the gun, holding it to the
> face so blood doesn't spatter. He puts a cross in Mulligan's face with
> 5 bullits [sic], one in each eye!

Included with Martin's letter was a police report from 1996 stating that Martin phoned Boston police to report he'd just seen a photo of Acerra in the newspaper coverage of the Area E-5 police corruption scandal—and he recognized him: Acerra was "Lt. McCarthy," the self-proclaimed "INS agent" who arrested him in 1993.

Deductive reasoning: McCarthy = Mulligan's killer; McCarthy = Acerra; Acerra = Mulligan's killer.

Rosemary had mused more than once that Acerra and Robinson might be behind the murder. She'd hypothesized two motives. "Mulligan was drinking heavily; he was quite involved with prostitutes; and he was running off at the mouth about all the drug money they were getting. So Acerra and Robinson had to shut him up. Alternatively, Mulligan was getting greedy. He wasn't giving the others a piece of the drug sales going on in the parking lot at Walgreens."

I thought about the cop-on-cop murder theories. An inside job was what the tipster Pablo told me. It was what Laselle and John Ellis theorized. Those theories came from the street, but the gist of the rumors swirling within the Boston Police Department, as reported by the FBI, was the same.

The tips about Mulligan packing a second gun were starting to accumulate. Drug dealer Ron Hansen said Mulligan wore an ankle gun. Senator Wilkerson's tipster, James, said Mulligan's own pearl-handled .25 killed him. We now read more gun information from officer Danilo "Danny" Ramirez, who'd worked with Mulligan on numerous cases.

Ramirez told investigators that Mulligan was suspicious to the point of paranoia. He "took precautions in response to perceived threats to his life, including strapping a revolver just above his ankle." Ramirez thought it was a .38.

Ramirez said he doubted "anyone could creep up on Mulligan and shoot him five times in the face.... He even took a gun to the bathroom with him. He didn't let his guard down...."

"Someone came close to John because he let him," Ramirez theorized. "If he let him, he knew him."

CHAPTER 42

Ellis Retrial Motion #2

Rosemary kept Sean in the loop about our efforts and findings. His spirits began to rise, and then they soared. On Mother's Day 2012 he sent me a beautiful handmade card:

> Godma,
> Happy Mothers Day!
>   There's not a lot in life that I'm fearful of but some of the things
> ... is you not knowing that you've had an impact on my life that I

cherish, and how special you are to me. Sometimes I have my body armor on because I'm fearful of exposing the Lil' Sean that I left behind. But Godma, know that I love & appreciate you!! Please!!!

Love Truly,
Your Godson

By October Rosemary decreed we had enough ammunition to make a strong case that Sean hadn't received justice at his trial. She, Amy, and Dennis began writing sections of his new retrial motion. The process would take many months; Rosemary emailed me drafts along the way, for comments.

As the defense team labored, Sean wrote me about a family development in December that hit him hard:

My father passed away, returning to the essence on Dec. 1. Reynell came up and told me the horrible new(s) and ended up spending the day with me, which was a comfort. The Department of Corrections has denied me to go pay my last respects, via a viewing or the funeral ... Because of the sentence!

... The issue of not going isn't sitting well with me, at all!! His death isn't sitting well with me!! I go in & out of thoughts, and in & out of emotions!! It's crazy—one minute I'm okay, then the next I'm somewhere else! My family & friends try to help but it's hard.

I really need to get out of this place. I have one parent still alive and I really can't lose both of them while I'm in this place. I can't lose you while I'm in here ... my mind is everywhere!

I rushed out to Norfolk to offer Sean my sympathy. Grateful for my visit, he explained that prisoners with life sentences weren't allowed to attend funerals, although at one time they were. His emotions were raw. At times he was near tears. He said he'd been "crying openly": "I no longer deliberately hold the emotions in, the way I once did."

I told him about my own father's death from heart disease, accelerated by smoking, at age sixty-six, when I was twenty-three. "A parent's death is a huge milestone for everyone, even when it's expected," I said.

"I was just a baby when he and my mother split up," Sean said. He said his dad had seven other kids besides him and Laselle. "I want to reach out to all my brothers and sisters. I'd like to have more family ties."

On March 1, 2013, Rosemary submitted Sean's motion to the court requesting a retrial and evidentiary hearing. She said "justice was not done" at his trial due to evidence that had been known to the Commonwealth of Massachusetts but kept from his trial lawyers:

"After spending 19 years in prison, Ellis has discovered withheld exculpatory evidence detailing that the Boston Police Department was aware that multiple police officers believed that the victim in this case, Detective Mulligan, was actually killed by another identified police officer. The Boston Police Department was made aware—before the Ellis trials—that named officers reported that another named officer was responsible for killing Mulligan . . . and yet that information was withheld from the jury, withheld from the public, and withheld from Ellis for over 19 years.

"Additionally, more withheld exculpatory evidence finally links Mulligan to the criminal conspiracy involving Detectives Acerra, Robinson, and Brazil, whereby the group of police officers would allegedly rob drug dealers and other criminals. Withheld information generated by the Federal Bureau of Investigation and uncovered by Freedom of Information Act requests paints a true picture of Mulligan and his cohorts who were simultaneously acting as detectives, criminals, and the men that 'investigated' this crime. This new evidence suggests that Mulligan himself was involved in criminal activities and reveals a new motive for his murder."

Rosemary pointed out that although Acerra, Robinson, and Brazil's criminal conspiracy was known by the public at the time of Sean's 1998 retrial motion, Mulligan's link to the conspiracy was not. Yet the authorities knew it: "The Boston Police Department was aware of this exculpatory evidence, and they were agents of the Commonwealth for discovery purposes.

... [T]he Commonwealth's failure to disclose all of [it] resulted in the trial jury not hearing the full truth, and a new trial is warranted.

"The timely disclosure of this evidence would have ... altered the theory of defense, in that Acerra, Robinson, and Brazil were involved in almost every aspect of the investigation of the murder of Detective Mulligan, including the identification of Ellis, the recovery of the murder weapon, and the interview of key witnesses placing the murder weapon in Ellis' possession ...

"[T]he trial evidence against Ellis was created by [these] powerful but corrupt Boston police officers ... [because they were] intent on covering up their own crimes and the crimes of the victim.... [Acerra, Robinson, and Brazil] sabotaged the ... investigation from the very beginning ... [and] railroaded a young innocent black teenager named Sean Ellis who was out buying diapers."

Fleshing out Rosemary's assertions was a 123-page brief, supplemented by a three-inch-thick appendix of exhibits. These included ten FBI reports documenting Mulligan's criminal history; two FBI reports of Boston police officers telling supervisors they believed a fellow officer killed Mulligan; the Wilkerson and Martin letters alleging the same; and our crown jewel, Robert Martin's federal grand jury testimony exposing Mulligan's participation in Acerra, Robinson, and Brazil's scheme of faking search warrants and robbing drug dealers.

In her brief, Rosemary detailed questionable investigative conduct by Acerra, Robinson, and Brazil:

- Acerra's alleged tampering with Mulligan's cell phone.
- Robinson's theft of money from Mulligan's closet.
- Star witness Rosa Sanchez's family ties with Acerra and all three detectives' actions in bringing her forward.
- Acerra's and Robinson's roles in Sanchez's questionable photo ID of Sean.

She tackled the gun evidence straight on. Charging that "corrupt police orchestrated the weapons to implicate Ellis," she described Brazil's role in the recovery of the weapons and Acerra and Robinson's involvement in the guns being "coincidentally found by young people linked to Ellis":

"Notably, each of the young men allegedly linked to those guns has been killed. Further, the sole female [gun] witness, [Tia] Walker, was vulnerable to police pressure and coercion because she had a young child, and a common police tactic was to threaten to get DSS to take a child if a witness did not say what police wanted the witness to say.…

"[T]he claims purporting to link Ellis to the guns [must be] re-examined in light of the new exculpatory evidence."

Citing the questions that detectives had asked Mary Shopov and Tina Erti about Mulligan owning a pearl-handled .25, Rosemary said the fact detectives "somehow knew" the gun they were looking for had a pearl handle buttressed the theory that Mulligan was murdered by a fellow officer. She alleged that Acerra, Robinson, and Brazil had "the greatest motive to kill Mulligan": "to keep him from talking," just as the in-house BPD tip said, because "his increased criminality put their criminal conspiracy at risk of being discovered."

Ultimately the detectives' efforts to frame Sean kept other viable suspects from being pursued, Rosemary charged. Chief among these suspects were the drug dealers Mulligan ripped off (she pointed to Robert Martin) or any of the prostitutes and young girls Mulligan harassed and assaulted (she pointed to the woman seen arguing with Mulligan in his car before his murder).

At the close of her motion, Rosemary cited multiple errors in the conduct of Sean's trial: unreliable, inadmissible ballistics testimony (supported by exhibits of scientific studies); inadmissible fingerprint evidence (supported by an exhibit of the SJC's 2005 ruling excluding Terry Patterson's prints); the denial of Sean's right to confront Rosa Sanchez and Evony Chung (by not allowing information to impeach them); the denial of Sean's right to a public trial (since spectators were excluded from the courtroom during jury selection); and the denial of effective assistance of counsel (due to his "trial counsel's inactions"). She concluded:

"The combined effect of all the new evidence and errors makes it impossible to say justice was done...[This] can best be viewed by considering what would happen if all of the withheld and newly discovered evidence was presented to the jury at the time of trial.... In that scenario, it cannot be said with any confidence that the jury would have come back with a unanimous guilty verdict ... at least some of the jurors would have had serious doubts as to whether someone else killed Mulligan and doubts as to whether Ellis is innocent....

"Ultimately, the claimed evidence that led to Ellis' conviction was a cover-up of distorted and misleading facts that omitted withheld exculpatory evidence regarding the investigating police detectives, who were themselves criminals and who may have been involved in Mulligan's murder. Justice dictates that we discard that corrupted history to get at the truth.

"And the truth is that Sean Ellis is innocent."

In May, Superior Court Judge Carol S. Ball was assigned to read the motion, and the waiting commenced.

CHAPTER 43

The Longest Year

2013–2014

May 26, 2013

Dear Godma,

> *...I did some research on [Judge Ball], and I learned that she worked as a clerk in the Middlesex D.A.'s office. After that she worked as a defense attorney for several years. I've heard she's a good judge and she's fair!! Unlike McDaniel ...*

Fair or unfair, the likelihood was high that Judge Ball would dismiss the motion outright. The majority of retrial motions were dismissed in Massachusetts.

In my spring and fall visits to Sean, his spirits were high, and he looked wonderful. In May he'd begun jogging on Norfolk's track with no ill effects on his bum knee. We discussed the Boston Marathon bombings of three weeks prior. They enraged him. "This doesn't happen in Boston," he said. "I'm a proud Bostonian! It was done for no reason to innocents out to enjoy a fun day."

In October he was taking vitamins again and lifting weights. This time he related an interesting development in the case. Rosemary's private investigator, Scott, was working on a cold case for Norman Zalkind when he ran into a woman who'd been involved with Mulligan. And in this serendipitous encounter, Scott dug up evidence about Mulligan's cell phone.

Michelle "Misty" Hagar told the private eye that Mulligan phoned her after midnight the morning of his murder, looking for sex. She told Mulligan she was "busy cooking up some drugs" but would send a friend. Mulligan agreed. The woman Hagar sent was accompanied by a man. According to Hagar, the two returned from Walgreens "breathless."

Some hours later that morning a cop appeared at Hagar's front door. He said, "You were the last person Mulligan talked with on his cell phone. What do you know?"

Sean had no details about what Hagar said to the cop.

"Who was that cop?" I asked Sean. "And what do you think 'breathless' means?"

"I have no idea." Sean said. "But it's proof Mulligan's phone wasn't overlooked."

With his friend Reynell's help, Sean flung himself into efforts aimed at drumming up interest in his case. From late fall into winter 2013 he peppered Rosemary and me with exuberant suggestions for a "PR plan" targeting "the media—print, TV, radio, internet, and community/pressure groups":

> *I'm trying to galvanize support by way of family, friends, and*
> *organizations or community leaders/activists that I should reach*

(out) to. . . . I truly believe that my time is coming when I'll be
able to spend birthdays and holidays with family and friends. When
I'll be able to pay my respects to my father and other loved ones!!!

Godma, I've been racing, and unable to slow down, but I've
definitely been striving to be more disciplined, mentally! . . . Honestly,
I feel like I am overwhelming you! I feel like I am overwhelming
Rosemary as well!

Jackie and Sean began urging me to create a website, something we'd long discussed. Sean wrote:

It's about humanizing me and fixing connecting/speaking to the
false perception of me [in the press]. If I am seen as a monster or a
criminal, and if people are afraid of me via the perception/image
given by the Commonwealth, will they care enough?!?! Will they
want to get involved or want to help?"

I ran the website idea by Rosemary, and she agreed the time was right. I reached out to Mark to secure a domain, and justiceforseanellis.com was born.

On the site I described key elements of the case and poured out all the reasonable doubt I'd found in my two decades of research. I portrayed Sean as I knew him, a young man who'd struggled to survive adolescence in a violent corner of Dorchester amid a then-disturbing family life.

It was a huge relief to finally get these thoughts out of my head and into the world.

Next Sean composed a letter describing himself and declaring his innocence and mailed it to over a dozen organizations, including local churches and charities, the New England Innocence Project, and the Boston chapters of the NAACP and ACLU. I posted his letter on the website, glad to finally give him a public voice.

Rich and I followed up Sean's letter to the organizations he targeted with a letter of our own. The only feedback we received was from the ACLU's

Boston attorney, Carl Williams, who phoned me to say that while the organization could not take a position on Sean's guilt or innocence, the issue of whether he'd received a fair trial was of great importance to them. Williams told me Judge Ball had a reputation for being smart and fair. "It's a shame she's not about to retire," he added, "because she'd need to be at the end of her career to buck the Boston police."

"Now is the time to get Sean's story in the press," Rosemary urged me by phone one December day. The *Boston Globe* rebuffed us, but the editors of *Dorchester Reporter*, a well-regarded neighborhood weekly, invited me to a meeting. I asked Rich to come along.

We met with the paper's founder, Ed Forry; his son, editor/publisher Bill Forry; and their associate editor, retired *Boston Globe* managing editor Tom Mulvoy. All three said they'd long doubted the official "random robbery" motive for Mulligan's murder. They agreed to publish my article on Sean's retrial bid.

After reviewing my draft, Bill Forry asked me to add background information on Sean: Did he have a criminal record? What was his status at the time of his arrest?

I called Rosemary to verify that Sean's charge of kidnapping his cousin had been dismissed. "Why would you mention any of his arrests?" she erupted in volcanic rage.

"I have to include the information for the *Reporter* to publish my piece," I shot back. "Sean's arrest record was covered by the Boston papers in 1993, but that one case was open."

"Just because something's in the paper doesn't mean it's true," she shouted.

Actually, she screamed.

She continued at high volume: "Why would you do their work for them? Why? Why? They only want to sell papers by being negative!"

Her words flowed on like hot lava ... and on and on. I held the phone away from my ear, put it on speaker, and walked downstairs to Rich's basement office. Janet happened to be there. When they heard Rosemary's voice spewing nonstop venom, their mouths dropped open. We made hand gestures to each other. WTF?

In spite of myself, I laughed.

"Rosemary! Rosemary!" I said, forcing my way into her word torrent. "Listen to me. No one else who's writing about Sean will take as neutral a view as I will."

Another outburst ensued. Then I heard a click.

She'd hung up.

"Fuck you!" I thought. I was furious. Rosemary's reaction was over the top. Sean's previous arrests were something readers would wonder about. Forry's request was Journalism 101.

As annoyed as I was, I realized Rosemary was just doing her job. Her dedication to her clients was legendary. She had to portray Sean in the best possible light. But I had to follow the conventions of fair journalism.

I had a brainstorm. I could resolve the issue by quoting the words Sean used to describe himself in his letter, now published on my website: "While growing up, I had a few run-ins with the law. However, this is my first and only incarceration." This satisfied the editor, and my article describing Sean's retrial bid made the *Reporter*'s front page on January 14, 2014.

Sean later told me Rosemary was satisfied with the piece. But it was many long weeks before she smiled my way again.

"We got a hearing!" Rosemary crowed when I picked up the phone in May. "Judge Ball called a status hearing for June 5 to consider the issues in Sean's motion."

It was the miracle we'd hoped for: Rosemary's arguments had persuaded the judge to take the next step. Crowning it all was learning that Ball planned to retire in spring 2015.

The challenge ahead was immense. To rule favorably for Sean and throw out his convictions, Ball would have to determine that his 1995 trial had been unjust, either tarnished by the bias and possible misconduct of corrupt investigators or skewed by the withholding of exculpatory evidence from Sean's lawyers by Boston police and Suffolk County prosecutors—or both, as Rosemary alleged.

If Ball saw merit in Rosemary's arguments, she would be disagreeing with every ruling of every prior court, including the "final" ruling of the Massachusetts Supreme Judicial Court in 2000.

It would be the judicial equivalent of a takedown.

PART 6

Justice

2014–2021

CHAPTER 44

All Rise

2014

Rich and I arrived an hour early for Sean's June 5 preliminary hearing at Suffolk County Courthouse. We found Rosemary sitting on one of the wooden benches outside the locked courtroom. Beside her, wearing earphones and wielding a microphone, was Boston Public Radio WBUR reporter Delores Handy Brown. Catching sight of us, Rosemary waved a sheaf of papers in the air and beckoned us over.

"These papers were faxed to my office at 9:00 last night by Linn," Rosemary said to the three of us. Paul Linn was the Suffolk County assistant district attorney assigned to the case.

Rosemary was triumphant. "It's a 1993 Boston police report written by Mulligan homicide investigator Dan Keeler, plus additional supporting documents. And they all affirm our claim that a Boston police officer accused a fellow officer of setting up the murder and because of this the accusing officer was disciplined—and that this information was withheld from Sean's trial lawyers."

In in a voice dripping with outrage, she said, "Remember? Prosecutors said I should be disciplined for charging the police with this!"

I didn't remember, but I nodded anyway.

"I just met with Judge Ball to inform her about this now-released information," Rosemary concluded with a satisfied air.

In the FBI reports we received through FOIA, the names of the accusing and accused Boston officers were redacted. Linn's faxed documents named names.

When the courtroom doors opened, Rich and I took seats on a first-row bench, and I powered up my laptop to take notes for my next *Dorchester Reporter* article. Jackie sat down across the aisle with two of her daughters, but when she saw us she stood up and moved beside me. Settling in, she squeezed my arm and held on tightly, murmuring over and over, "You've been here since the beginning." She was a basket of nerves.

The courtroom fell silent when Sean, shackled and handcuffed, was led in by two guards. He was wearing a tan suit, white shirt, and dark tie. He looked gaunt. His dreadlocks were gone, and his head was shaved. His expression was stony, and he gave only the barest flicker of a glance at the courtroom spectators.

The guard unlocked his handcuffs, and Sean sat down at the motioning attorneys' table, his posture stiff and his leg shackles engaged. Rosemary took her seat next to him, accompanied by Jillise McDonough, a meticulous young attorney who was now assisting her with the case.

Sitting at the prosecutors' table were Linn and Suffolk County's chief of homicide, Edmond Zabin. Linn was a hulk of a man with perpetually squinty eyes and an expression of cheery bemusement. Zabin was short and slim, with close-cropped graying hair and a calm, deliberate manner.

"All rise," said the court officer. In walked Judge Ball with a brisk, no-nonsense air. She appeared to be in her sixties and had wavy salt-and-pepper hair. The first order of business was the newly released discovery material. "Why did you release the information at this late date?" she asked Linn, her voice commanding.

SUPERIOR COURT JUDGE CAROL S. BALL, 2014. PHOTO COURTESTY OF THE SCHUSTER INSTITUTE FOR INVESTIGATIVE JOURNALISM, BRANDEIS UNIVERSITY.

"Until yesterday the Commonwealth did not know this report existed," Linn explained. "Boston police just sent it over. Since the information related to a central defense claim, we wanted to do the right thing."

The information in the report was explosive.

According to Detective George Foley, in August 1993 a Boston corrections officer named Ray Armstead Jr. told him Detective John Mulligan was going to be killed. The prospective killer? Armstead's father, Boston police officer Ray Armstead Sr.

The details of the son's tip were eerily prescient. Foley said Armstead Jr. told him, "My dad's got a beef with Mulligan...he won't leave my fourteen-year-old sister alone.... He's gonna kill him.... They have checked on him at Walgreens. He sleeps in the car. They have shaken the car. You are gonna read about it in the papers. Shot between the eyes at Walgreens."

But Foley did not immediately report this dire warning. In fact, he did not report the tip until September 30, four days after Mulligan's murder.

When Foley did report Armstead Jr.'s information to his superiors on the Mulligan task force (by then Foley was a member), it was greeted with skepticism. Doubts grew when Detective Daniel Keeler and lead investigator Sergeant Detective Thomas O'Leary questioned Armstead Jr., and he denied tipping off Foley.

Foley stuck to his story. Keeler then branded him a liar, stripped him of his gun and badge, and recommended that he be admitted to a hospital for a month-long psychiatric evaluation. Foley's lead about Ray Armstead Sr. possibly killing Mulligan was pursued no further.

Rosemary leaped from her chair. "They called me crazy—crazy to say that a Boston cop accused another cop of the murder." She pointed out that the D.A.'s office had consistently denied that evidence of another police officer being involved in Mulligan's death was "ever in the custody or control of the prosecution." They'd also denied that "any of [the FBI] sources was a Boston police officer or reported his or her beliefs to the Boston police before trial."

Standing before Ball, Rosemary was exultant. "And now we have the allegation of just that, in black and white. An allegation that was never adequately investigated and that Sean's trial lawyers never saw because it was covered up by Boston police. Here we have motive, opportunity, and a third-party culprit, but Keeler decides it's nothing." Rosemary's voice rose higher with each sentence, her manner that of a person vindicated at long last.

"Now, now, Rosie, calm down," Ball admonished, her manner firm but kindly. She turned to Linn and asked if, by today's standards, prosecutors would have turned over the Foley tip to the defense, given that the report had come from the police department's closely guarded Internal Affairs (IA) files.

Linn said they would have turned it over but stressed he was not ready to concede that this report or any other evidence had been suppressed by the Commonwealth. He felt sure the Foley tip had been known to Norman Zalkind and David Duncan. Characterizing the twenty-one-year-old Mulligan case record as voluminous, encompassing four trials, multiple hearings, and three Supreme Judicial Court cases, Linn pleaded with Ball for more time to assess the evidence. He argued that this just-released report would not have altered Sean's verdict: "There was evidence that one of them did it. Ellis and Terry Patterson were seen on a footpath near Walgreens."

Not so fast, I thought, furiously typing notes. Sean was not positively identified by Walgreens neighbor Victor Brown.

Suffolk County prosecutors had submitted a motion asking Ball to restrict the hearings to the contested withheld tips. They wanted all references to Kenneth Acerra's and Walter Robinson's crimes excluded, since previous courts had concluded these "had nothing to do with the murder investigation."

Ball denied the motion. She said she wanted to take a "broad view" of the issues: "Previous courts did not know what we know now—that Acerra and Robinson, who investigated Mulligan's murder, were actively engaged in crimes, and Mulligan was tied in with them." Had the Supreme Judicial Court known this in 2000, Ball noted, it would have given rise to a whole new theory, the "perfectly logical argument" that while serving on the Mulligan task force the two detectives might have been "serving two masters: covering up their own stuff and finding the killer." Mulligan's cell phone was found only later, she pointed out, and was possibly wiped clean by Acerra; money was removed from Mulligan's apartment by Robinson soon after the murder.

Rosemary jumped up: "And Acerra and Robinson brought forward the one and only witness who ID'd Ellis."

I wanted to jump up too. Here was the judge stating her intent to consider in full our theory about Acerra's and Robinson's motives and misconduct during the Mulligan murder investigation. I blinked back tears.

Ruling that the issues in Rosemary's motion merited a full evidentiary hearing, Ball set August 25 as the starting date and told all concerned,

"Block off the week." She tasked prosecutors and defense with making a complete inventory of the evidence shared between them.

I felt downright giddy. An evidentiary hearing. It was a miracle, what we'd worked for all these years. Sean's case would be reopened. Rosemary would get to question key figures in the Mulligan homicide probe about actions never before scrutinized. All would be viewed through the lens of Mulligan's criminal entanglement with his friends, the corrupt investigators Acerra, Robinson, and Brazil.

After spending more than two decades in prison, Sean finally had cause to dream of freedom.

CHAPTER 45

Mulligan's Cell Phone

The first matter Judge Ball took up on August 25 was "outstanding discovery." Rosemary stepped up to the podium. Her voice firm, she complained of her zero success in obtaining investigative files on Kenneth Acerra, Walter Robinson, John Brazil, and John Mulligan from the Boston Police Department's Anti-Corruption Unit. She said she'd been trying to access this information since 2004, but her efforts had been consistently denied, just as every one of Norman Zalkind and David Duncan's motions for the same materials had been denied. She said that in 2012 she'd filed a civil lawsuit to procure the materials, with no results. "The Commonwealth has stonewalled this information for twenty-one years," Rosemary told Ball.

Ball turned to prosecutor Paul Linn and in a crisp staccato said, "I want those documents put in [attorney Scapicchio's] hands by tomorrow afternoon."

Ball appeared exasperated, even angry, to learn of the police department's intransigence. She asked Rosemary if she'd like to delay the hearing to vet the documents upon their release. But with precious days blocked off in the court's packed schedule, Rosemary opted to forge ahead.

The evidentiary hearings would end up encompassing three days in August, three in November, and one in December—seven days in all in 2014, with final arguments presented in April 2015. Rich and I attended every hearing, bristling with excitement from start to finish. I summarized them all for the *Dorchester Reporter* and posted reports on justiceforseanellis.com. Alison flew in from Vancouver and attended a November session with us; in December and April my Boston friend Judy joined us in the front row.

In each drama-packed session, Rosemary called witnesses and methodically eviscerated the conduct of the Mulligan homicide investigation and the Suffolk County prosecutors' case against Sean. Her minute knowledge of case details fueled her legendary courtroom swagger.

Rosemary led off the first hearing by probing the mystery of Mulligan's missing-then-recovered cell phone. Her first witness was a blowsy, middle-aged woman who approached the stand with mincing steps. Appearing terrified, she melted into the witness chair and in a trembling, barely audible voice identified herself as Michelle "Misty" Hager.

She was the woman Rosemary's investigator, Scott, had stumbled upon, the woman Mulligan phoned just before his murder.

It was evident Hager wanted to be anywhere but in court. Ball gently coaxed her to speak up for the stenographer. Under Rosemary's noticeably temperate questioning, Hager said she'd "dated" Mulligan around the time of his death. She admitted she was addicted to heroin and crack at the time and dealt drugs to support her habit.

"He gave me one thing and I gave him another," Hager said of their relationship. Asked by Rosemary to explain, she said she often gave Mulligan the "favor" of sex, and he gave her the "favor" of getting her drug charges dropped.

"Within days of Mulligan's death," Hager testified, two Boston police officers tracked her down at her mother's house and questioned her, saying she was the last person Mulligan called from his cell phone that night.

Two officers. Were they Acerra and Robinson? They were not identified.

"So someone had those cell phone numbers," Rosemary said, ending her brief questioning of the skittish woman. Besides exposing Boston cops' possession of the call record from Mulligan's cell phone, Hager's testimony drove home Mulligan's criminality.

Prosecutor Edmond Zabin asked Hager the nature of her phone call with Mulligan that night, but Hager could not remember the details of their conversation. Neither could she recall the names of the two officers who paid her the call, nor the date of their visit.

Immediately after testifying, Hager quickly tottered out of the courtroom.

Rosemary wrote in her post-hearing memorandum:

"Not only was the fact that [Michelle Hager] was the last person called by Mulligan never disclosed to Ellis, [but] neither was the visit by two Boston Police Department officers to Hager, to question her about this.... Apparently no reports were ever written relating to this visit ..."

Rosemary traded the kid gloves she'd used on Misty Hager for boxing gloves when questioning Sergeant Detective Thomas O'Leary about Mulligan's cell phone. Though a detective of only six months' standing in September 1993, O'Leary had been assigned to head the Mulligan homicide investigation because he was on duty when the 911 call came in. Now in his early sixties, O'Leary was a short, strong-looking man with thinning, spiked hair gelled straight back and a confident, Marine-like manner. His testimony filled two and a half days.

O'Leary emphasized that his role as lead investigator was in name only. The Mulligan case was so high profile that "many sets of eyes" watched over it. Police Commissioner William Bratton and chief prosecutor Phyllis Broker were the decision-makers in the case, he said; his own role was merely to "shepherd" the information and evidence to them.

Rosemary held up a copy of the police inventory of the contents of Mulligan's SUV and began naming the items found in its center compartment, down to several small bits of plastic. They did not include a cell phone. How did the lead detective explain that one week later, while the SUV was at the crime lab undergoing forensic analysis, Acerra found the phone in the console?

O'Leary gave the police party line: "The crime lab people told detectives, 'The phone was there. We saw that phone on Sunday night, but we didn't know anyone was looking for it.'"

"You mean the crime scene investigators missed it?" Rosemary asked, her voice dripping with sarcasm, the words tossed over her shoulder as she whirled around and walked back to her seat at the table.

O'Leary then admitted he did not question Acerra after he found the phone, nor did he recall if anyone "went into the cell phone to see the numbers."

Zabin downplayed the importance of the cell phone as evidence. Although today's cell phones contain vital data, he pointed out, this was not the case in 1993.

Maybe so, I reflected, but 1993 phones did keep a record of calls made and received. And police told Misty Hager her number was the last one called from Mulligan's phone.

The search of Mulligan's SUV was further explored in December, when Sergeant Robert Foilb, now retired, took the stand. Balding and paunchy, he said he'd spent ten years in the department's ID unit processing fingerprints and photographing crime scenes. He was the technician who'd inventoried the contents of Mulligan's SUV and took the prints from its doors—the fingerprints the police claimed were Patterson's.

Foilb, the notorious bungler, I thought, remembering the other crime scene fingerprint he'd misidentified, sending the innocent Stephan Cowans to prison.

Foilb admitted he didn't secure Mulligan's vehicle at Walgreens until 8:30 a.m., almost five hours after the 911 call came in. He made his inventory after the vehicle was towed to the D Street police facility in South Boston. His method was to list each item he found and bag it separately. In the vehicle's center compartment he found nine Dunkin' Donuts napkins, six small pieces of plastic, a key chain, a Panasonic battery, sunglasses, and an open pack of Lucky Strikes. No cell phone.

Knowing Mulligan carried a personal phone, police declared it stolen.

Foilb agreed that in making his inventory he "would have opened up everything, to do his job properly." He said he did this "absolutely and thoroughly."

I sank back from the edge of my seat, relieved. Here was the "gotcha" moment. The phone was not in Mulligan's SUV by 8:30 a.m. The crime scene technician himself was saying this, under oath.

Then came a turnaround. Foilb blithely announced, "I was not aware of a second compartment between the two seats. I was told the phone was there later." He delivered his statement with a Cheshire Cat smile. Calling this second compartment a "cash tray ... more or less a secret compartment," Foilb said that because he did not see it while making his inventory and was unaware it existed, he failed to find the phone. He seemed to enjoy the effect his pronouncements had on the courtroom.

"Did you document the secret compartment in any of the reports?" Rosemary asked Foilb in undisguised disbelief.

"No," Foilb said.

"Did you photograph it once [the phone] was found?"

"I was not asked."

He estimated this compartment was four inches at bottom and six inches at top. He admitted he did not know if the 1993 cell phone "even fit" the space. He dusted the phone for fingerprints but found none. He did not find this unusual.

"Not even by the person using the phone each day?" Rosemary asked, her tone incredulous.

"No," Foilb said. He was not directed by his superiors to check for any phone numbers.

Foilb's satisfied smile never left his face as he walked out of the court-room, flanked by several fellow officers. Were they there to lend moral support to their brother, I wondered? Or to ensure he toed the line?

CHAPTER 46

Elevator Surprise

At the conclusion of the August 25 hearing, Rich and I were filing out of the courtroom with the crush of spectators when a man's voice behind me said loudly and sarcastically, "I heard there was this lady writing a book about this case. Can you imagine that? A book. Can you imagine?"

The voice came from a large man with flowing yellowish-white hair and wearing a white Tommy Bahama-style shirt and khaki pants. He walked uncomfortably close to me and glared down with piercing, yellowish-green eyes. It was Mulligan's brother, Richard. Giving me a long, disdainful look, he shook his head in disgust.

I murmured "Good afternoon" and walked away quickly.

Rich and I entered the elevator, and as the doors began closing, someone stuck a hand in, forcing them to reopen. In walked Sergeant Detective Thomas O'Leary, fresh off the witness stand. With him were Richard Mulligan and a third man who looked like an O'Leary clone—same body type, same slicked-back, spiky hair. Surely a Boston cop. Like Mulligan, he wore a short-sleeve cotton shirt, in contrast to O'Leary's witness-stand sports jacket.

O'Leary pointed his finger, first at me and then at Rich, and said mockingly, "Oh, I recognize you two. You're the court observers." He'd shed his altar boy witness-stand demeanor.

What did O'Leary mean, "court observers"? Was he referring to Rich's and my attendance at Sean's June status hearing? "No, we're not court observers," I said.

The third man said, "She's the lady with the book."

"No, there's no book," I said, thinking "as yet."

"Oh," they said in unison.

The third man said, "The website, then."

"Yes, I've done a website."

They exchanged glances and nodded in an exaggerated way.

Then Mulligan stepped close to me. Leaning down, he positioned his face inches from mine and asked, "Did you know my brother?"

When I murmured "No" he boomed, "Then how could you write those things about him?"

"I just write based on the evidence I have before me, in black and white." My eyes locked in with his. No way would I flinch. Who did he think he was?

"You're defending a fucking cop killer, that's what you're doing," Mulligan screamed, all the while staring me down.

I won't let this man intimidate me, I thought, holding my gaze steady.

Mulligan's two comrades leered at me, their body language and grunts egging him on. I couldn't believe these men were behaving this way in a public space. Two or three people standing behind Rich and me in the elevator were witnessing it all.

Seeing Mulligan's and my fierce eye-lock, Rich addressed him. "Are you trying to intimidate us?"

At this, the third man began shouting at Rich. "If I wanted to intimidate you, pal, I'd throw you on the fucking floor right now." He said this again, louder. Then he affected an abrupt, exaggerated, full-body startle and said with utmost drama, "Did you just take a step toward me, pal? Did you just take a step toward me?"

His tone was chilling. This was nuts. Rich hadn't moved an inch. I could picture the police report, with the O'Leary clone proclaiming, "He came at me, so I had to take necessary action in my own defense."

The elevator doors blessedly began opening. I took a pronounced step toward them and said to the threatening man: "Uh, the door opened?"

Rich followed me out, and the doors shut behind us. We didn't know what floor we were on, nor did we care. It turned out we were at the second-floor snack bar. At least we were free.

On the drive home Rich and I dissected the incident. We were each most amazed at O'Leary. He'd initiated the attack and then sagely stood back while the others executed it. That a Boston police detective still on the force had the gall to intimidate civilians in this public space was breathtaking. "Just imagine if we were a couple of Black kids," Rich kept saying.

That night I searched my computer for case notes containing "O'Leary." As lead homicide investigator, he was everywhere:

He'd questioned the FBI informer, Anthony Gonsalves, whitewashing on tape all of Gonsalves' prior claims about Mulligan's drug dealing.

During Rosa Sanchez's first viewing of the photo array, he'd sat in the room with Acerra, Robinson, and Ross.

After Tia Walker told grand jurors she'd been harassed as a "snitch" by Rob Matthews and Lew Richardson, Sean told her to call O'Leary and report it. Tia had left O'Leary a message; he'd ignored it.

O'Leary had prepared witnesses for trial with chief prosecutor Phyllis Broker. He'd sat beside Broker, advising her, throughout Terry Patterson's trial and Sean's three trials.

"This was a man I loved," O'Leary said of Mulligan in September 1995, as he and his colleagues celebrated Sean's conviction.

CHAPTER 47

Ignored Tips

"It's a beautiful morning, " Sergeant Detective O'Leary chirped to Judge Ball and the courtroom audience the morning after our elevator encounter. I looked over at Sean, seated at the defense table in shackles, his whole life at stake. This day may be beautiful to you, O'Leary, I thought with fury, you who can come and go. But how is it for the kid you helped railroad, a kid who for the last twenty-one years has not had a moment of freedom? Over my shoulder I saw O'Leary's police colleagues take their places in the back row of the courtroom.

Before the session, I'd buttonholed Rosemary in the foyer and told her about the elevator experience with O'Leary and the others. Rosemary strongly felt Judge Ball should know about it, so Rich and I gave her permission to relate it.

It turned out the judge already knew: Two people at the back of the elevator were court workers, and they'd immediately reported the incident.

Ball made a statement to the full courtroom acknowledging the "high emotions" on both sides of this case and instructing each side to remain separate while entering and leaving. From then onward, Sean's supporters remained in a carefully sequestered herd.

The police hotline tips

Rosemary resumed her questioning of O'Leary by grilling him about his handling of nearly sixty detailed tips about Mulligan's murder that came in over the police telephone hotline. I knew about the hotline but had never seen the reports; prosecutors had only recently disclosed them in full.

Rosemary charged that the phoned-in leads were not only withheld from Sean's defense counsel, apart from one they were not followed up by investigators, even though several tips named individuals with motive and intent to kill Mulligan.

She read a few aloud:

> *September 26, 1993: Det. Cullinane called and stated that his brother, Bobby Rowland, a prison guard at South Bay House of Correction, told him that an inmate, William Bell, told him that a drug dealer named Armstead had a contract out on Mulligan.*

My ears pricked up upon hearing "Armstead." It was the name of Detective Foley's tipster. Not Smith, not Jones: Armstead.

> *September 27, 1993: Councilman O'Neil came by the homicide unit and indicated that someone detained at South Bay Cove [sic] named Blair may be responsible for the murder.*

> *[undated]: Caller saw Detective Mulligan giving a ticket to and arguing with a black male outside of the Bradlee's [sic] parking lot in Roslindale on September 25, 1993, at 5 p.m.*

> *September 30, 1993: a cab driver claimed he drove Mulligan's girlfriend to the parking lot the night of the murder where she shot him with a .25 caliber weapon Mulligan had given her for self-defense.*

Mary Shopov again.

Two tips stated:

> *...Royce Hill was an accomplice to Mulligan's murder.*

O'Leary said he organized the telephone tips into two piles: one for general tips on the homicide, the other for information relating to a brown car containing two African American youths that was seen near Walgreens the morning of the murder.

This began the prejudice, I reflected. The VW's sighting was given equal weight with all the other leads combined.

The sole hotline tip O'Leary did assign for follow-up was the one from South Bay about the drug dealer Armstead. The task force members he assigned to investigate? Kenneth Acerra and his supervisor, Lenny Marquardt. O'Leary could not recall receiving any report of the men's investigation, nor whether any follow-up had been done.

O'Leary's memory frequently faltered when he was responding to Rosemary's questions, and he would claim "no recollection." Yet when questioned by prosecutors, he was a practiced witness, comfortable and articulate, and he recalled everything in detail.

Asked at length about the coding system he devised to show that the hotline tips he "shepherded" had been turned over to Sean's lawyers, O'Leary said he handwrote numbers atop the reports, circled the numbers on the tips he gave the chief prosecutor, and noted these numbers on an index. Yet when Rosemary showed him his two indexes, one numbering each incoming tip and the other recording the tips turned over to prosecutors, O'Leary admitted the numbers on the two lists did not correspond.

The Foley tip

O'Leary was one of the detectives who questioned Detective George Foley about his clairvoyant tip from Ray Armstead Jr. that John Mulligan would be shot "between the eyes" outside Walgreens by his father, Boston officer Ray Armstead Sr. Under Rosemary's questioning, O'Leary said he gave no credence to Foley's information: "It was so detailed it was crazy."

He said when he, Sergeant Detective Daniel Keeler, and Captain Ed McNelly, the head of homicide, pressed Foley about the tip, Foley had "a breakdown." "He had his head down, distraught.... He went back and forth with his story.... He was a mess." McNelly immediately took Foley's gun and had him transported to a hospital for thirty days' psychiatric observation.

Characterizing Foley as an alcoholic who was "beset by mental illness," O'Leary offered his own theory: "Foley began drinking that Wednesday... and had a vision."

In earlier testimony O'Leary had said his first order of business upon taking charge of the Mulligan investigation was to select fifty elite officers for the task force. He'd proudly described meeting with Police Commissioner Bratton and McNelly over dinner at a suburban restaurant and choosing "only the best and brightest."

Rosemary seized upon this now, pointing out that Foley was one of the officers they'd handpicked. "'The best and the brightest,' you say? This 'alcoholic'?"

Returning to her seat, she hurled further taunts at O'Leary: "The 'best and brightest' on the task force? Acerra? Robinson?"

I stifled laughter as I typed the exchange into my laptop. Touché!

Rosemary presented for exhibit a statement Foley signed for Internal Affairs a month after his interrogation and hospitalization. Foley swore that at no time did he deliberately misstate information regarding his tip from Armstead Jr. He said that after his hospital release he was immediately reinstated to active duty, with gun.

"To get your gun back you have to have a disciplinary hearing," Rosemary said to O'Leary. "Was there ever such a hearing or report?"

O'Leary could not recall.

In November, Sergeant Detective Daniel Keeler testified about the Foley tip. I was interested to see Keeler in the flesh. I knew of his checkered career, and I knew he and Rosemary had a bitter history together. Their mutual disdain soon became evident.

Keeler wore spiked, gel-slicked hair in the style of O'Leary and the cop who accosted us in the elevator. Although he'd once been dubbed "Mr. Homicide" for his investigative prowess, Keeler's hard-driving manner and tactics had led to a raft of controversial police actions and several lawsuits with him as subject. His star lost luster in the Donnell Johnson wrongful conviction case in the late '90s, when he and Sergeant Detective William Mahoney (Sean's chief interrogator) were exposed as having failed to disclose the alibi Johnson gave police.

Keeler's fall from grace came in 2004, when he was forced to admit at a murder trial that his claim of videotaping the crime scene was false and that he'd lied about interviewing a witness in his police report. Rosemary was the defense attorney who pried these admissions from Keeler. He subsequently left homicide and was reassigned to beat work in Boston's South End.

Under Rosemary's questioning, Keeler, like O'Leary before him, said he and his colleagues had so little confidence in Foley's information that they didn't follow it up. However, he was "tasked with" (he spat out the phrase) interviewing alleged tipster Ray Armstead Jr. He said he did so only reluctantly: "Imagine me having to face someone like you if I didn't?" he shot at Rosemary. The stance played well with Keeler's fellow officers sitting together in back; their titters rippled through the courtroom.

Keeler said he told Armstead Jr. straightaway he didn't believe Foley. This drew an expression of horror (or mock horror) from Rosemary: "Is it your usual practice to tell those you interview all the information you have ahead of time—and tell them you don't believe it?"

"No," Keeler grunted.

Armstead Jr. denied making the tip, and Keeler confronted Foley: "I said to him, 'You're full of shit, George.'" Foley then had a "meltdown." In his telling, Keeler was the hero of the story. Saying he "felt fear" when he saw a crying George Foley sitting "in his shirtsleeves and carrying a gun in a shoulder holster," he "scratched a note" to Ed McNelly saying, "Get his gun now," and they called in the stress unit.

Prosecutor Linn disputed Rosemary's claim that Foley's tip had been withheld from Sean's lawyers. He said multiple copies of Keeler's report on the tip were noted on three separate lists as having been turned over. He said Sean's attorneys probably forgot about the tip or discarded it, since it did not fit their defense strategy of blaming Terry Patterson.

In preparation for these hearings, Linn's team had reached out to Ray Armstead Sr. (George Foley and Ray Armstead Jr. were now deceased). Armstead told them that in 1993 his family lived in central Massachusetts, not near Mulligan, and he had no biological daughter.

Rosemary countered this with evidence that the Armstead family had two foster daughters living in their home at that time, one age twelve or thirteen. She drove home her point: Mulligan task force detectives never investigated the substance of Foley's tip in 1993, not even whether Armstead Jr. had a sister who was being victimized by Mulligan.

They never interviewed alleged killer Ray Armstead Sr.

Former chief prosecutor and now-retired district court judge Phyllis Broker testified about the disputed tips via video from her home. A pleasant-looking, mature woman with a crisp manner and short, light-brown curly hair, she came off as eminently reasonable, a witness ready to cooperate. She made clear at the outset she had "no memory of any individual documents that twenty years ago were turned over to defense counsel" and could testify only about her "standard discovery practices and how she typically handled her cases."

She had a "vague recollection" of the Foley tip and believed that it, as well as all the police hotline tips, had been turned over to Sean's lawyers.

A lengthy description ensued about Broker's record-keeping system, the gist being she coded all documents with circled numbers on top, kept a list of all turned-over documents, and wrote cover letters to defense attorneys referencing this list.

She said that in deciding which reports to turn over, her unwavering policy was "When in doubt, give it out," something she did no matter how "believable" she might have deemed any particular tip: "Who was I to judge that it might not be important to them? They could make of any of it what they want...they had their job. I had my job."

Yet the police hotline tip reports were not marked with Broker's circled numbers, giving credence to Rosemary's claim they'd been withheld. Further, Keeler's report of the Foley tip bore the circled number 186. Broker conceded there was no cover letter in evidence specifying any document higher than number 184.

Norman Zalkind and David Duncan testified about the tips on successive days. Duncan looked thinner and even more serious than he had thirteen years earlier. Zalkind, now in his eighties, appeared aged, his manner at times distracted but other times sharp and canny. Both attorneys categorically denied ever receiving any of the contested tips.

The Commonwealth provided the discovery materials in "trickles or floods," Duncan said. He was certain he and his partner reviewed every bit of discovery prior to Sean's trial because "it was a very important and highly publicized case, and we were looking for anything that we could find to defend our client with."

Having now been apprised of the substance of the Foley and hotline tips, Duncan was definite: The defense never received them before Sean's trial. Given how "sensational" the tips were, he said, he and Zalkind "most certainly would have tracked them down" by filing discovery motions and sending out an investigator to follow up each.

Zalkind echoed Duncan's testimony. Calling Foley's tip about Officer Ray Armstead Sr. "pretty incredible," he said he "absolutely" would have remembered it had they received it and "absolutely" would have sent out their investigator: "The Mulligan murder case was extremely high profile, the kind we obsessed over.... We didn't have any evidence of other parties killing Mulligan."

As for the hotline tips, Zalkind insisted that had they received them, they would have requested the phone numbers and locations of each tipster, the length of the call, who took the call, information about that officer, and what exactly was said. He pointed out that had he filed such discovery motions, "it would have been all over the press," and this might have generated valuable follow-up information from the public.

To demonstrate Duncan and Zalkind's thoroughness in following up tips, Rosemary introduced the discovery motion they filed in February 1994 requesting more information about former State Senator Wilkerson's tip from Boston police officer James. Duncan agreed this was the exact kind of motion they typically filed—and would have filed to pursue the Foley/Armstead tip and the hotline tips had they known about them.

CHAPTER 48

Corrupt Detectives

Judge Ball's August court order prompted the release of approximately five hundred pages of police documents detailing allegations against Acerra, Robinson, Brazil, and Mulligan—records that had gathered dust for two decades. In them was confirmation of the Internal Affairs investigation of Robinson, launched in November 1993, for allegedly robbing two Brighton drug dealers with Mulligan in 1991. The police had been tipped by a known source whose credibility was rated "good."

It was proof positive that when Robinson testified at Sean's pretrial hearing, he was being investigated for a crime he allegedly committed with the victim in the case. The police upper ranks knew this. Sean's trial attorneys did not.

Made aware of this now, Duncan and Zalkind said they'd tried in vain to obtain such information from the police files, but their motions were consistently opposed by Suffolk County prosecutors as "too broad" and "immaterial" and denied by judges as "irrelevant to the case." Zalkind sounded furious: "[T]hey were fighting me tooth and nail!"

As for the Robert Martin robbery two and a half weeks before Mulligan's murder in which Mulligan was Acerra and Robinson's accomplice, Duncan said he and Zalkind were "not made aware" of Martin's October 1996 grand jury testimony. Zalkind called the Martin testimony "the most important information I've read in the case." "We got two hung juries," Zalkind stressed. "If I'd had [this information] during my examination of Robinson in the trials, I don't think we'd be here today."

Prosecutor Zabin countered that the defense attorneys almost certainly knew from "rumors and newspaper articles" that Mulligan was "controversial."

Zalkind admitted hearing rumors about the slain detective and also about Acerra, Robinson, and Brazil, but stressed that his and Duncan's hands were tied, for they had nothing beyond newspaper accounts: "Judges … respect, you know, police reports, witness statements, investigative statements. They don't respect the press statements," he said.

Zabin sought to minimize Mulligan's complicity in the Martin robbery, saying he may well have believed the search warrant his comrades used was legitimate. Mulligan's name was not on this warrant, nor was it on any other falsified warrant submitted by the later-disgraced detectives in 1992-93.

Zalkind laughed this off: "Mulligan was a bad cop, the most likely person in the world who'd be involved with Robinson in a crime … a rampant criminal.…It looks to me that Robinson and Mulligan were into [the Martin] crime together: [Mulligan is] holding that guy [in the car] while others go in and rob.... I certainly would have motioned."

Rosemary questioned Broker about the Martin robbery. The former chief prosecutor said she did not receive documents from the federal government relating to Mulligan's corruption or any other acts of his wrongdoing, either prior to Sean's trials or prior to his 1998 motion for a new trial. Asked if she was aware of reports in the *Boston Globe* about Acerra's and Robinson's corruption, Broker said, "I had a vague, somewhat distant relationship with all that was going on with Robinson and Acerra. I didn't want to know about it. It didn't affect me, so I didn't pay much attention to it."

Watching Broker calmly declare she'd purposefully kept at arm's length from Robinson and Acerra and "all that was going on" with them was infuriating. The men handled nearly every piece of evidence she used against Sean. Their corruption "didn't affect" her?

Rosemary bore in, asking Broker about her 1993 demand that Acerra "provide a statement relating to both [Rosa] Sanchez's identification [of Sean Ellis] and Acerra's discovery of Mulligan's cell phone."

Broker's response was a curt "I have no memory of that."

Rich and I exchanged shocked glances. How could Broker forget this career crisis? She'd almost lost her job over having Acerra and Robinson questioned on tape, a nonnegotiable demand she'd made within the hour of Sanchez's photo session, I'd learned. Now Broker was forgetting she'd suspected Acerra of evidence corruption? Forgetting that the powerful detectives union had objected to her actions, and Commissioner Bratton had ordered her to cease and desist?

That was a lot of forgetting.

Rosemary persisted. "Did you ask the Boston Police Department to take Kenneth Acerra or Walter Robinson off the Mulligan investigation?"

Broker did recall asking that Acerra be removed. Her reason? "I had no use for him. I thought he was incompetent. I didn't want anyone incompetent anywhere near my cases."

SEAN WITH CO-COUNSELS JILLISE MCDONOUGH (LEFT) AND ROSEMARY SCAPICCHIO AT THE AUGUST 26, 2014, EVIDENTIARY HEARING. PHOTO COURTESY OF THE SCHUSTER INSTITUTE FOR INVESTIGATIVE JOURNALISM, BRANDEIS UNIVERSITY.

Rosemary reprised that Acerra's removal had been bitterly opposed by the Boston detectives union, whose president had written a letter to D.A. Ralph Martin II demanding that Broker be fired. Broker countered, "I don't know why the letter was sent." But she admitted that "communications were not good" between the agencies: "It was a very difficult time. A police officer was killed ... my boss was standing for election ... there were strained relations between my office and the Boston Police Department ... and all of those things together created the perfect storm."

In a further sharp exchange, Rosemary reminded Broker she'd blocked every one of Zalkind and Duncan's motions for further discovery, including their requests for Internal Affairs records for Acerra, Robinson, Brazil, and Mulligan.

Broker shot back that she'd never had the requested documents in her possession. "I'm not doing that without a court order.... I was of the opinion they weren't entitled to it."

So much for Broker's stated policy: "When in doubt, give it out."

Another item of interest in the Anti-Corruption Unit files released by Judge Ball was a 1998 subpoena issued to American Airlines by the federal grand jury investigating Area E-5 corruption. It requested "records relating to all travel by ... Kenneth Acerra, Elizabeth Tejeda and Rosa Sanchez made for the period January 1, 1990, to the present, including but not limited to trips ... from the Dominican Republic on 8/5/95 and 10/15/94."

Elizabeth Tejada was Rosa Sanchez's mother, the sister of Acerra's domestic partner, Lucy Delvalle, and a friend of Acerra's. If these trips together occurred, they would refute Acerra's sworn testimony that he was not close with Rosa Sanchez and saw her only occasionally at family events.

Also disclosed was that Rosa Sanchez's maternal Uncle Hector was a paid informant of Acerra's who possibly lived with Ivan Sanchez's family on Humboldt Avenue, yet another tie between Rosa and Acerra.

Acerra, Robinson, and Brazil were subpoenaed to testify at the retrial motion hearings. They chose not to appear, invoking their Fifth Amendment right against self-incrimination through their attorneys.

Several other matters covered in the evidentiary hearings were noteworthy.

Armstead three times: In Rosemary's questioning of Keeler she asked, "Were you aware, sir, in the context of your investigation, that at least one person was aware of the name Armstead early on in the investigation?" She showed him the notes Wilkerson had taken of her phone conversation with Boston police officer James, which included the information that Armstead was forced to "retire early."

Keeler said he was not aware.

The Wilkerson tip was the third mention of Armstead in the tips, the first being the hotline tip from South Bay House of Correction on the day of the murder and the other, Foley's tip about Ray Armstead Sr.

The pearl-handled gun: Asked why detectives quizzed Mulligan's girlfriend and her roommate about a pearl-handled gun five days before it was found, Sergeant Detective Thomas O'Leary waffled and finally responded that the police department "never conclusively determined the origin of the pearl-handled .25 Raven" later identified as the murder weapon.

This unsatisfactory answer was apparently all we were ever going to get.

Courtroom fireworks: Given Rosemary's role in Sergeant Detective Keeler's comedown, he made no effort to hide his dislike for her. Their exchanges were at times fiery, and Keeler milked them for their dramatic impact. When asked why detectives never followed up the hotline tips, he extended his arm, pointed to Sean, and shouted, "Police took no further action when it became clear that the shots were fired by your client!"

The detective's outburst drew murmurs in the courtroom, some from Sean's family, others from fellow officers. To me, Keeler's antics were aimed at the video camera recording the proceedings.

Moments later Keeler grandstanded again. With voice rising, he said it was easy to dismiss Foley's tip when "it became evident *that* man (pointing to Sean) was responsible for the murder of John Mulligan!"

AT TIMES EMOTIONS RAN HIGH IN THE COURTROOM. JACKIE ELLIS IS HUGGED BY SHAR'DAY. PHOTO COURTESY OF THE SCHUSTER INSTITUTE FOR INVESTIGATIVE JOURNALISM, BRANDEIS UNIVERSITY.

"You have no idea what happened that night, Detective Keeler," Rosemary snapped back, leaping to her feet, her voice as loud and sharp as the cop's. She set upon Keeler like a vulture pecking on prey: "Were you there that night, sir? Did you see the murder? Were you there, sir?"

Rat-a-tat-tat came Rosemary's questions, all of them unanswered.

CHAPTER 49

Decision

2015

Rosemary charged into her final argument in April 2015 like a racehorse hearing the starting gun. Judge Ball stopped her and admonished her with a smile, "Slow down! You're even worse than me!"

Curbing her speed only slightly, Rosemary listed three "overshadowing issues" that required that Sean receive a new trial: Kenneth Acerra's, Walter Robinson's, and John Brazil's conflicts of interest as homicide investigators, given their history of robbing drug dealers with Mulligan; the withheld tips from the police hotline and Detective Foley; and the lack of an adequate police investigation into other possible suspects.

Rosemary proceeded to connect the dots between the three corrupt detectives and virtually every piece of evidence used against Sean, from interviewing Rosa Sanchez several hours after the murder occurred and later shepherding her through the photo ID procedure, through driving Curt Headen to the homicide unit the night he delivered his gun-hiding story.

She said Boston detectives' questions about the pearl-handled .25-caliber gun five days before it was recovered, plus multiple witness reports of Mulligan wearing a .25-caliber gun on his ankle, showed that police believed the gun was stolen from Mulligan's body the morning of the murder. This indicated the murder and robbery were not committed by random teens. Kids would not know of the hidden gun's existence. The perpetrator had to be someone who knew Mulligan.

Citing Robinson's removal of cash from Mulligan's closet and Acerra's alleged tampering with Mulligan's cell phone, she charged that the corrupt detectives tried to "cover tracks of what Mulligan was doing" and "scapegoated an innocent Black teen."

She said Robinson never should have been on the task force in the first place, given the ongoing Internal Affairs investigation into his and Mulligan's alleged robberies together in Brighton. Had Police Commissioner Bratton and his staff disclosed this information as they were obliged to, "It would have blown the top off" the detectives' corrupt scheme.

She reprised that task force detectives never followed up the viable third-party culprits named in the withheld tips, even when the name "Armstead" came up three times. This showed a rush to judgment.

"There never was overwhelming evidence of Sean Ellis' guilt," Rosemary concluded, citing Sean's two hung juries. The Commonwealth has "only a general description of two Black males, one taller, one shorter," with the only person to identify Sean Ellis "the niece of [an] officer who had an absolute conflict and who wanted to close the investigation. That's their case.

"Give [Sean Ellis] the opportunity to have a fair trial," she implored Judge Ball.

Delivering the Commonwealth's rebuttal, prosecutor Paul Linn said nearly all the evidence cited in Sean's retrial motion had been previously litigated, with only three matters of fact remaining: Did the Commonwealth turn over the hotline tips? Did the Commonwealth turn over the Foley tip? And did police visit Michelle Hager? "The answers are yes, yes, and no."

Dismissing Foley's tip about Ray Armstead Sr. as "patently absurd," Linn insisted that this and all tips received over the police telephone hotline had been disclosed by prosecutor Phyllis Broker to trial lawyers Norman Zalkind and David Duncan, but now, twenty years later, they simply forgot they'd received them.

While acknowledging Acerra's and Robinson's corruption, Linn called the robberies Mulligan allegedly committed with them "isolated instances," not proof he was deeply involved in their criminal conspiracy. He said the 1991 Brighton robberies did not involve search warrants and thus were unrelated to the ongoing criminal scheme. As for the September 1993 Martin drug bust, he reiterated his claim that Mulligan may have believed it was legitimate.

Linn accepted as fact the police description of Acerra finding Mulligan's cell phone in the SUV's "cash tray" and said there was no evidence the phone numbers had been erased. He called Hager's testimony "vague and unconvincing."

Whether Sean Ellis himself shot Mulligan is "a very contested issue," Linn admitted. But he reminded Ball that Terry Patterson admitted that he and Sean drove to a side street and walked into the woods; Victor Brown saw two men walking onto the path toward Walgreens; and parking lot witnesses saw "two Black men whose physical appearances matched Terry Patterson and Sean Ellis." All this caused jurors to conclude the men were in a joint venture, Linn said. "There is almost no new evidence, and what is new does not add anything material to what we know."

The minute Linn finished, Rosemary was on her feet.

"What we did not know before was the Martin robbery and Mulligan's participation in it. That was the link the SJC [Supreme Judicial Court] did not have in 2000. We knew Acerra and Robinson were ripping people off…

but we did not have the link with Mulligan. And that's the purpose of this hearing. We've linked every important piece of evidence to Acerra, Robinson, and Brazil, and now we've linked these men to Mulligan. If we'd had the information then, it would have changed everything."

I felt goosebumps. Thank God I'd reread those federal transcripts.

She concluded: "The issue is, did Sean Ellis get a fair trial? And a trial today would look a lot different than it did then. Because we didn't have that connection then ... not in front of the jury. And that's why Sean Ellis should get a new trial."

Judge Ball did not interrupt Rosemary's presentation, but she posed several challenges to Linn. Two stood out:

When Linn insisted that, despite Zalkind's and Duncan's assertions to the contrary, prosecutors did turn over the Foley report and hotline tips, Ball brought up the trial attorneys' motions for further discovery concerning Senator Wilkerson's phone call from James. "Why would they have followed up that tip energetically, but not follow up the Foley tip?" she asked.

She also noted the defense team's failure to catch the mention of Armstead in the Wilkerson tip, which indicated to her they'd not seen the hotline tip with the same name: "'Armstead' again, and they did nothing? I don't know ..."

When Linn backed the police explanation of Acerra finding Mulligan's phone, the judge cut him off. "[Phyllis Broker] herself suspected that phone was planted. It's hard to imagine that cell phone was overlooked.... I saw the pictures. That tray covers only half the hole.... You could see stuff on the bottom."

In closing, Ball observed, "If a Boston police officer were, God forbid, murdered today, close friends and colleagues of the victim would not be allowed to investigate."

Linn agreed.

We were ecstatic. Rosemary had done a spectacular job. She was a dynamic, colorful presence in the courtroom, and her precise questioning showed a comprehensive and detailed grasp of the evidence. Quick on her feet, she'd followed up witnesses' answers and challenged prosecutors' assertions.

Prosecutors Linn and Zabin appeared to be honorable public servants. They did their jobs; it was a cop killing, after all. But, to my mind, they were tasked with defending the indefensible.

Despite the positive signals I parsed from Judge Ball's questions and comments, I was on edge. On May 5, I drove out to Norfolk to visit Sean. His spirits were excellent as we spoke of Rosemary's smarts and her stellar courtroom performance. We also discussed, cautiously yet optimistically, what he would do if granted a new trial. I came home feeling upbeat.

No sooner had I walked in my door than my cell phone rang. It was Rosemary.

"We won!" she shouted.

At first it didn't sink in. "We won!" she repeated. "Sean's getting a new trial. His conviction was vacated. Judge Ball agreed with every major argument we made!"

She was phoning me from her car, having just driven out to Norfolk to tell Sean in person. We'd literally passed each other on the road. My knees went weak as I shouted out the news to Rich.

"Sean cried for ten minutes," Rosemary said.

> The court concludes that the newly discovered evidence of Detectives Robinson, Brazil and Acerra's conflict of interest and the BPD's failure to follow up on leads implicating third-party suspects is material, credible, and would have been a real factor in the jury's deliberations in the Commonwealth's case against Ellis.
>
> Indeed, even without the third-party culprit evidence, in this judge's opinion, the evidence of Detectives Robinson, Brazil and Acerra's bias would have played an important role in the jury's deliberations.
>
> Accordingly, the court concludes that this is a case where justice has not been done.
>
> — Judge Carol Ball, May 5, 2015

CHAPTER 50

Free

On May 12, 2015, a week after vacating Sean's convictions and over the strong objections of prosecutors and Mulligan's family, Judge Ball granted him $50,000 cash bail and sent him to Boston's Nashua Street Jail to await release pending presentation of bail. She required him to wear a GPS monitoring device on his ankle while awaiting retrial.

I visited Sean at Nashua Street and was horrified. He shuffled into a one-person visiting room wearing an orange jumpsuit, his legs and hands shackled. Glass separated us. An open slot beneath the glass theoretically permitted us to hear each other, but it was difficult to access and speak into. There was so much noise from inmates milling around behind and below the mezzanine area, I couldn't hear Sean.

The scene was dehumanizing, shocking. Sean had come so far, working his way up the prison ladder to Norfolk and earning respect as a peer leader along the way. This was a big step down. I prayed that Jackie and the family would raise bail soon.

"How are you doing, Sean?" I asked, trying to sound cheery but dreading his answer. To my surprise, he shrugged and said he was taking the Nashua Street experience as a "learning opportunity": "The guys here are mostly young guys just off the street, awaiting trial. They have different ways of talking from the days I was out there. So I listen to them. I want to find out what issues they're talking about, what's going on."

After a short while we were told our time was up. I hoped my visit was a comfort to Sean, but it left me shaken.

The bail-raising continued, and the days turned into weeks. Jackie was waging an all-out, grassroots effort to come up with the cash, even going on the radio. She was helped by Shar'Day, now twenty-two. After graduating from college with a degree in social work, she'd been hired by the Commonwealth of Massachusetts. Pam helped a great deal as well, hosting several fundraising events in Dorchester's parks and pubs. Having moved back to Boston from Alabama in 2014, she had resumed visiting Sean. (He and Reynell had amicably parted.)

I drove Jackie to her local savings bank and helped her establish an escrow account. The court had strict requirements: She had to keep a careful list of donors, for contributions would have to be returned after the case was settled unless the giver specified that Sean could keep the money. Rich and I held back, waiting to see if bail could be raised without our help. We planned to be a financial and emotional support for Sean during his readjustment.

Rich wrote to Sean for the first time.

5/20/15

Dear Sean,

Congratulations on all the good things that have happened to you over the past month. The last chapter isn't yet written, but we look forward to your release and to your getting your life back on track. I'm writing now to let you know that I fully endorse the financial plan for your support over the next year that Elaine has proposed to you. We hope that plan makes sense and is acceptable. . . .

I also want to offer you my personal availability in helping you acclimate to life on the outside. Mentors can be extremely important, and I'm happy to serve in that capacity for you, if you think I can be helpful. Throughout my career, I was blessed by surrounding myself with experienced elders who I sought out for advice and guidance. They provided me fresh perspectives on the personal and professional problems that I was facing, and their advice was always helpful in my making informed decisions, whether or not I agreed with them. . . .

I agree fully with the advice Elaine and Rosemary have given you to go slowly in making the important decisions you will face during the next number of months. As you know, the challenges will be significant and not easy to overcome. You'll need time to acclimate to today's technologies, to find a job, to make friends, and to make the transition from who you were as a 19 year old put in prison to the 40 year old you are now on the outside. But what an exciting opportunity that is: a new beginning designed by and for you, not by others. . . .

You were fortunate to have Elaine by your side for the past 20 years, but we were also fortunate as a family to have you as a friend. Your cause became our family's cause. We all look forward to your release and, with your permission, to helping you during this difficult, challenging but exciting transition period.

Sincerely yours,
Rich Murphy

Sean wrote Rich back from his Nashua Street cell:

> *June 1, 2015*
>
> *Dear Mr. Murphy,*
>
> *Thank you for the "congratulations" for all that has happened over the past month. It has definitely been an overwhelming and emotional month. I'm unable to explain, but to go from being told that I'm going to die in prison, to being told that I have another chance at life. . . . Three trials, a motion for new trial, a direct appeal, a federal [habeus], all either denials or setbacks.*
>
> *Each denial, each setback tightens the grip on you. Imagine the life being squeezed out of you, and then one day the giant that was squeezing it out of you just drops you. Imagine the happiness & fright you'd feel. That doesn't capture it. . . .*
>
> *Try to understand, I often said that if Massachusetts had the death penalty, I would have been on death row! Now think about everything Godma has done! It makes me "very" emotional! Godma is actually an Angel!*
>
> *. . . I thank you so much for all of the support that you have given to me and to Godma over the years! I also thank you for and accept your mentorship, which, to me, will be extremely important. I grew up in a single parent household, and for the most part I was the only male child in the house. On top of that, at 19 years old, I was arrested. So, at this point I have more time incarcerated on this earth than I do as a free person. . . . my point is, there's a lot that I do not know about life as a free person. Therefore, your advice and your guidance will be needed.*
>
> *Before I left MCI-Norfolk a correctional officer told me to take charge of my life. Once I reflected on those words (as well as things that Godma & my attorney has said) . . . I can only say Wow! It's Scary! I have to "LEARN" to take charge of my life and live in a world that I don't know. I will really need you!*

Again, thank you so much for everything!

Truly yours,
Sean

Beyond requiring bail, the court would not release Sean until he had a place to live. Moving in with Jackie was out of the question. She lived in subsidized housing, and the rules wouldn't allow it.

Pam came forward, pronouncing herself Sean's fiancée. To my astonishment, he went along with it. She wanted Sean to move in with her in her aunt's basement. But when the aunt learned Sean's story, she gave a firm "No!"

It was back to square one, but this came as a relief to Rosemary and me. We'd questioned the stability of the suddenly revived romance and the cobbled-together living arrangement.

Rosemary and I began furiously working together to find Sean an apartment, comparing notes in a flurry of phone conferences during her morning commute. We reached out to every nonprofit and charitable organization we could find and learned firsthand how difficult it is for ex-inmates to get housing.

We were always transparent about Sean's story. Every agency we approached turned him down when they learned it, even those whose stated mission was to house the homeless. One Boston agency, Caritas Communities, initially seemed a port in the storm. But after I had two weeks of encouraging phone conversations with their agent, filled out the required paperwork, and pledged monthly financial support for Sean, they denied his application at the eleventh hour. Their stated reasons: "No letter from a previous landlord. No credit rating."

"Who do these groups try to place," Rich said, exasperated. "CEOs?"

Blessedly, Bishop André Bennett of Jackie's church stepped up. He was a kind man in his forties who'd been a great support to Jackie and Shar'Day. "You are as welcome in my house as family," he told Sean. And Sean found his haven.

The next challenge was getting Sean signed up for counseling. This was vital, Rosemary said: "These guys haven't made a decision on their own for all the time they've been incarcerated. They have not turned a doorknob on their own or decided when to wake up, when to eat, when to turn out the lights, or when to go to bed. So when they're released, they truly don't know how to put one foot in front of the other on their own. They may be big, strong guys, but they're terrified of independence."

After weeks of searching, we connected Sean with Span, Inc., a well-regarded Boston transition counseling service that helped released prisoners adjust to life outside. The timing was fortuitous: They'd just received federal funds to initiate a program to collectively embrace people affected by murder, both the families of victims and the people convicted. Sean was their first enrollee.

By the first week of June, Jackie had finally raised the needed bail from relatives, friends, and even a few Norfolk inmates. The waiting was over.

On Wednesday, June 6, 2015, the Suffolk County courtroom was packed. Sean, natty in a dark blue suit, sat on a spectator bench with his family— for the first time not at the defense table with shackled legs. After a brief statement from the hearing judge (not Judge Ball), Sean walked out a free man, escorted by Rosemary, Jackie, and Shar'Day. Other family members and friends followed.

Outside the courtroom the lobby scene was chaotic joy. A crush of Sean's supporters jostled with reporters carrying microphones and cameras. Aunts, uncles, and cousins whom I'd never heard of, plus a group of people from Jackie's church, swarmed around Sean and Rosemary, visibly elated. Several members of Minister Don Muhammad's Mosque #11 in Roxbury, wearing their Nation of Islam black suits, white shirts, and red bow ties, stood close to Sean, protecting him. Jackie had called them in, worried about his safety.

Sean was physically steered through the press scrum by Rosemary. He seemed terrified. A microphone was thrust in his face, and he gave a sober, halting statement thanking Rosemary, his family, and his many supporters.

SEAN WALKS FREE HOLDING HIS MOTHER JACKIE'S HAND ON JUNE 6, 2015.
GETTY IMAGES.

He asked the press to give him time and space to reconnect with his family.

I videotaped his speech, but Rich and I stood back. We couldn't get close to him in the bedlam. He knew we were there. That was enough.

After a brief stop across the hall to fill out paperwork, Sean disappeared into the elevators clutching Jackie's hand, with Shar'Day close behind. He'd been in prison for twenty-one years and eight months—more than half his life, as he'd noted to Rich. Now, surrounded by his protectors, he emerged from the Suffolk County Superior Courthouse and strode off to meet the first day of the rest of his life.

Rich and I walked in silence to our car, smiling all the way. We didn't need to talk. Everything felt surreal. I was floating.

When we got home, life suddenly seemed flat. I went out to my garden and began weeding in the warm sunshine. As I worked the soil on this beautiful day of days, I reflected on the decades I'd spent on Sean's case.

My cell phone rang. It was Sean, phoning me from the car on his ride to his new home at Bishop André's. "I had to call you to say I would not be where I am today without you," he said, his voice woven with smiles.

His call at that moment meant the world.

CHAPTER 51

Adjusting

The first week after Sean's release he phoned me three times on his new smartphone, a gift from Shar'Day. We talked for nearly half an hour each time.

The day after his release he called me after leaving the grocery store with Jackie. He wanted to tell me how good it felt "being able to help her out…just being a son."

His story had been all over the Boston news. Shar'Day, interviewed on TV the night of his release, struck just the right note: Their family planned no big celebration, she said. "We want just to love him and make him feel comfortable."

I asked Sean if they'd seen the newspaper coverage. They had not, so I told him to go back into the store and buy the *Boston Herald* and *Boston Globe*. "How do I do that, Godma?" he asked. So I walked him through how to bring the papers to the check-out clerk and get them scanned. Later that evening I saw a photo of him on Facebook at a restaurant with Jackie, Shar'Day, and Pam.

On Friday he phoned me again, bubbling over. He now had an email address and was learning how to use it.

The following weekend Mark came up from New York, and he, Sean, Shar'Day, Rich, and I held a celebratory dinner on an oceanside patio. We presented Sean with a new Microsoft tablet from the Murphy family.

MARK MURPHY AND SEAN REUNITE THE WEEK AFTER SEAN'S JUNE 2015 RELEASE.

A few days later I picked Sean up for a computer training session at the Microsoft store at Burlington Mall west of Boston. Looking handsome in a pale blue shirt, black pants, and black leather shoes, he climbed into my passenger seat. Then he turned to me and grinned. He held that grin for a long minute and then said, "I'm here!" I'm sitting *here!*" He laughed and shook his head in wonderment.

I passed him a hand-me-down Tumi backpack to hold his computer and equipment. As we approached the mall, he grew serious and said, "I recognize this. I've been here before. I was here the day Celine was murdered. It was at Sears. I was at my friend's job. And when the police accused me of murdering my cousins—I said, 'What? That's my family! I love my family!'—I told them where I'd been. The police checked with my friend's boss, and he confirmed it. So they dropped it."

After a moment he said, "Celine and I were each going through problems at that time, at home, and this bonded us even closer. We confided in each other. She was always there, from birth, and we were always close. I remember standing on the corner of Blue Hill Avenue and Callender Street and thinking, 'I don't want to live if Celine is dead.'"

We parked, and as we walked into the mall I slipped Sean two twenty dollar bills. "Walking-around money," I said. "Stick it in your wallet."

"Wallet? I've never had a wallet," Sean said.

I quickly detoured him to Macy's and bought him his first.

After his training session we had lunch at the Cheesecake Factory. He was flummoxed by the oversized menu with its myriad choices and unfamiliar terms. Tapas? Crostini?

I saw what Rosemary meant: Being confronted with a sea of choices was overwhelming for a guy who, for nearly twenty-two years, had been handed food on metal trays. I suggested a salad topped with scallops. He nodded his agreement to the waitress, relieved.

He confessed he was self-conscious about eating in public. "Norfolk was just a bunch of guys," he said, motioning shovelfuls of food going into his mouth. I laughed.

I asked how things were going at the bishop's house. It was on a busy thoroughfare, so I was surprised to hear him say, "I find it quiet. I like to get up early in the morning and just sit on the front steps and watch the cars go by."

When we finished lunch he said, "I have to go back to Norfolk Prison soon to pick up my property. And I want to go there dignified, wearing presentable clothes, not jeans. Because I left in shackles."

Sean passed his first free summer soaking up nature: walking the beach, perching on an ocean jetty with a friend to watch the waves, gazing at a pond in a nearby park. "It's ironic what a hold water has on me," he told me with a slight grimace. "Ironic, because of my brother, Joseph."

Rich began regularly taking Sean to Costco, where they would fill a flatbed wagon with meat and staples to take back to the bishop's house. When Rich and I compared notes, we realized that whenever either of us dropped Sean off after an outing, he always said the same two things: "I love you" and "Stay safe."

SEAN VISITS ELAINE AND RICH MURPHY IN THEIR HOME OUTSIDE BOSTON, 2016.

Ever mindful of how lucky in life we've been, Rich and I continued to "pay it forward" by equipping Sean with two essential tools for success in civilian life: a car (a used Nissan) and driving lessons. When his six-week driver's ed course was finished, and Sean walked back into the DMV office after passing his Massachusetts road test, the entire waiting-room crowd stood and applauded. A beaming Shar'Day had tipped them off.

His case was still not settled. The Commonwealth immediately appealed Judge Ball's ruling, and a court battle lay ahead. If prosecutors won their appeal, the police would immediately pick up Sean and take him back to prison to serve out his life sentence. If they lost, they planned to retry Sean for murder one and robbery. It would be his fourth trial.

These grim possibilities loomed in the back of all our minds.

After Sean was freed, he and Pam tried and failed to rekindle their romance. Then he ran into Tia Walker's son Ricky, now in his mid-twenties, at a Boston mosque. And Sean and Tia reconnected.

Because of his 1995 gun convictions and uncertain future, it was difficult for Sean to get a job. At first all he could find were occasional shifts on a demolition crew. But ultimately he got a full-time position on the shipping dock of Community Servings, a respected Boston nonprofit whose mission was to prepare and deliver medically tailored meals to critically and chronically ill individuals and their families. In his job interview Sean was frank about his story. He expected to be turned down yet again. But the director said, "I admire your honesty. Here, we believe in second chances."

Over lunch one summer day he told me about some of his biggest post-prison challenges. "I had to ask André, 'How long does a shower take?' I really had no idea. In prison, showers are where you're most vulnerable. So you're in and you're out, quick....

"I also have trouble when strangers stand too close. I don't know how to react. When I first got out, I was in a CVS, shopping, when I noticed two guys watching me intently. One was looking me up and down, up and down. And then he walked over and got into my personal space. My heart began pounding. My first thought was, 'Defend yourself!' And then the guy lunged at me. He gave me a big hug and said, 'Oh, man!' Turns out he recognized me from TV."

"When did you start to relax and feel comfortable with your freedom?" I asked.

Sean searched his mind for a minute. Then he smiled. "It started at the birthday party my family threw for me in July, about a month after I got out. I was playing a laser-light game with one of my sisters. We were laughing a lot. That's when I realized I could be silly."

On a warm afternoon the following October, Sean and I sat together in a Waltham, Massachusetts, deli eating sandwiches. We'd just taken part with Rosemary in a Brandeis University panel exploring his case.

"Godma, did you ever think you and I would reach this moment?" Sean asked. He smiled broadly. "I remember how scared you seemed the first time you came to see me at Walpole. I remember getting your letters and cards when I was inside, and how you'd say, 'This will be our year.' You always said *our*."

"You reminded me of Buddha," I said. "I couldn't believe how serene you were—then and always, really. You've never seemed bitter."

"I was bitter for a while, and then I stopped," he said.

An hour earlier, the Brandeis students had been attentive and respectful. Sean was feeling the glow. "It was therapeutic to do the panel," he said. "In prison you have to disconnect from certain parts of yourself. Experiences like this give you the chance to reconnect with those parts."

"What parts?" I asked.

"The parts that make you human. Your emotions, your compassion, your instinct to help a guy in need."

That morning, I'd watched Sean pull into the Brandeis guest parking lot and marveled at how he'd found his way to campus by virtue of his brand new driver's license and Google Maps on his smartphone. I pictured him hurtling through lost decades, catching up with the modern world.

He'd walked into the classroom, handsome in his tan summer suit, crisp white shirt, and tie, which made an interesting counterpoint to the ripped jeans and T-shirts worn by the two dozen fresh-faced students.

Rosemary kicked off the presentation with an overview of the prosecutorial flaws and police misconduct in Sean's case, the challenging FOIA request process, and her strategy in arguing for his retrial. I spoke on the importance of advocacy and the power of grit—of never giving up when you think you're right. I applauded the influence of investigative journalism:

Were it not for the *Boston Globe*'s exposé of the three detectives who were criminals, Sean probably would be languishing in prison like so many other wrongfully convicted men, most of them Black.

At the Q&A afterward, the students mainly wanted to hear from Sean. The last question they asked him was whether he "holds a grudge" against the prosecution and the police.

After a long pause Sean said, "I don't hold a grudge. My personal disposition is that it's too heavy to carry. I just want to put my life back together, and I can't do that bearing a grudge."

My heart swelled. This was the character of the man I went to bat for all those years ago.

CHAPTER 52

Moving On

2016–2021

Sean's case

On May 5, 2016, a year to the day after Sean's convictions were overturned, five justices of the Massachusetts Supreme Judicial Court took their seats behind their long bench to hear the Commonwealth's challenge to Judge Ball's ruling. (Two justices had recused themselves because of conflicts.) The courtroom galleries overflowed with Sean's family members and supporters, and the media presence was considerable.

Rich and I sat in the second row of a side gallery. I craned my neck and caught sight of Sean in the main section facing the justices. Wearing a dark blue suit, pale blue shirt, and navy-and-red striped tie, he looked composed. I was consumed by nerves. If the Commonwealth prevailed, Sean would go back to prison forever. How did he bear the pressure?

Assistant District Attorney Paul Linn and Rosemary again faced off. Linn began by saying, "Judge Ball's decision was riddled with error."

Big mistake, I thought. Carol Ball was much respected by her colleagues.

Linn rehashed the Commonwealth's claims: The hotline and Foley tips had in fact been turned over to Sean's trial lawyers. The new evidence of Mulligan's criminality "added nothing material" beyond what was presented in Sean's 1998 retrial motion. Even if Judge Ball's findings were accurate, there was still no justification for a retrial: "Despite all that the defense raises," the evidence "keeps coming back to Ellis and Patterson." Citing Tia Walker's fingerprint on the gun clip, he said, "Once you have Ellis in possession of the guns, you have overwhelming evidence that the murder was committed by either Ellis or Patterson or both of them in combination."

Rosemary responded with confidence and energy. She stressed that Acerra, Robinson, and Brazil were the ones who gathered the evidence "from beginning to end," and it, like them, was corrupt. She disputed Sean's possession of the guns and cast shade on Tia Walker's account that he'd pulled the weapons from the scene of a double homicide the previous day. She said for a retrial she would investigate "what the police officers did to get her to tell that story" and also retest the gun clip: "I don't believe Walker's print was on it."

She homed in on detectives' prescient questions to two witnesses about a pearl-handled .25 caliber gun five days before a gun of this description was recovered and declared the murder weapon. "How did people involved in this investigation know it had a pearl handle?" she asked.

In a flourish she answered the question: "The guns were absolutely planted."

She concluded by imploring the justices to "...[L]ook at the entire record here.... There's no way Ellis got a fair trial."

Four months later, on September 9, 2016, the SJC upheld Judge Ball's ruling in every respect. The decision was unanimous. Chief Justice Ralph Gants wrote the forty-page opinion, contrasting this ruling with the court's 2000 denial of Sean's first retrial motion:

> *We did not know [in 2000] that [Detectives Acerra, Robinson, and Brazil] had been engaged with [victim John Mulligan] in criminal acts of police misconduct as recently as seventeen days before the victim's murder. The complicity of the victim in the detectives' malfeasance fundamentally changes the significance of the detectives' corruption with respect to their investigation of the victim's murder. ...*
>
> *[T]hese detectives would likely fear that a prolonged and comprehensive investigation of the victim's murder would uncover leads that might reveal their own criminal corruption. They, therefore, had a powerful incentive to prevent a prolonged or comprehensive investigation, and to discourage or thwart any investigation of leads that might reveal the victim's corrupt acts.*
>
> *—Massachusetts Supreme Judicial Court, 2016*

This certification by the Commonwealth's highest court of the injustice done to Sean was thrilling—and thoroughly satisfying. Deep down I'd felt things would go our way ever since Gants, in a riposte to Linn at the hearing, revealed his personal assessment of the new evidence showing Mulligan robbing a drug dealer with his friends:

"A game changer," Gants said.

Suffolk County D.A. Daniel Conley responded to the SJC's ruling by pressing murder one and armed robbery charges against Sean. His retrial was set for September 2017.

At the end of 2016 prosecutors offered Sean a plea bargain: If he would admit to manslaughter, they would credit him for time served and release him, and he would face no further charges. Sean refused the deal, choosing to place his fate in the hands of a fourth jury rather than "plead guilty to a crime I didn't commit." He told me later he did not spend a minute entertaining the D.A.'s offer.

Sean's fourth trial date was moved to May 2018. Then it was moved twice more, to October 2018 and ultimately to September 2019.

In February 2018 Conley "stunned the political world" in Boston by announcing he would not stand for reelection come November. Seven months later, in another stunner, Conley resigned three months before the end of his term. John Pappas was named interim district attorney.

In November Conley's handpicked successor for D.A. was roundly beaten by Rachael Rollins, an attorney who'd run on a reform platform. During Rollins' campaign, when asked about the Sean Ellis case, she pledged to review it and consider dropping charges. On January 1, 2019, Rollins would become the first woman of color to hold the office of Suffolk County District Attorney.

Three weeks before Rollins' swearing in, on December 17, 2018, D.A. Pappas and Boston Police Commissioner William Gross (who'd assumed the post four months earlier) convened an unusual afternoon live-streaming event. Fifteen minutes before they took to the podium, they contacted Rosemary to say they were dropping all charges against Sean.

Rosemary phoned me to alert me. "Are you sitting down?"

I was bowled over. Sean would now be truly free.

As I watched the press conference, however, my excitement dimmed. In announcing the dropped charges, the D.A. and police commissioner pointedly refused to exonerate Sean. They stressed that they and the victim's family believed Sean "had a role" in John Mulligan's murder, but they'd concluded a retrial was unlikely to result in his conviction. They attributed this to the "fading memories" of witnesses and "the corruption of three investigating detectives ... inextricably intertwined with the investigation and critical witnesses in the case."

There was more. Pappas and Gross both stated they believed Suffolk County prosecutors had maintained "impeccable conduct throughout" the Mulligan case. They also wanted it known they did "not believe that Detective Mulligan was complicit in the crimes" of investigators Acerra, Robinson, and Brazil.

My outrage mounted as I watched this online spectacle. What were these men talking about? Two courts had found prosecutorial misconduct amounting to Brady violations. We'd shown documentary evidence of Mulligan robbing with Acerra and Robinson.

These officials weren't just papering things over. They were rewriting history.

The next day, in a brief court hearing, Sean's charges were officially dropped, and his GPS ankle bracelet was ordered removed. Outside the courtroom Rosemary sounded off to reporters:

"The district attorney's office held that press conference yesterday to get out ahead of what we think Rachael Rollins would have done when she took over on this case. We think Rachael Rollins would *not* have praised the district attorney's office for their work on this case. And by issuing [their statement] yesterday, three weeks before Rachael Rollins takes office, they were able to get their version of the story out there. And their version of the story conflicts absolutely with what Judge Ball found and what the SJC found."

In December 2020 Rosemary filed a retrial motion to overturn Sean's 1995 firearms convictions on the grounds that Detectives Acerra's, Robinson's, and Brazil's corruption, including their criminal collaboration with Mulligan, had not been disclosed to jurors. Rather than fight the motion, District Attorney Rachael Rollins affirmed it, commenting, "Corruption at the root tainted every branch of the investigation into Detective Mulligan's murder, including the gun possession charges." Calling Boston detectives' conduct in Sean's case and prosecutors' withholding of evidence "disgraceful chapters in our history," Rollins became the first Boston law enforcement official to affirm that Sean did not receive justice.

On May 3, 2021, at a virtual meeting, Judge Robert Ullmann announced his approval of the firearms retrial motion:

> *I decide today that justice was not done at Mr. Ellis's January 1995 trial, and on that basis a motion for a new trial is allowed ... This whole case is a very sad chapter in the history of our criminal justice system. Thankfully, this chapter seems to be nearing its conclusion.*
>
> *— Judge Robert Ullman, 2021*

The following day D.A. Rollins filed a *nolle prosequi*, formally dropping the charges against Sean and wiping his record clean.

A stunning development occurred in 2021: Sean received a $16 million payment from the city of Boston, described by the *Boston Globe* as "monetary atonement" for wrongdoing by the Boston Police Department. It was the largest such payment ever made by the city.

Sean's personal life

After enduring twenty-one years, seven months, and twenty-nine days of wrongful incarceration, Sean is living an admirable life. He is a familiar presence on Boston's public TV, speaking about his experiences and the need for criminal justice reform, and he is frequently invited to speak at community forums, colleges, and law schools in and around the city.

He enjoys the steadfast love and support of his large family, whose heartbeat remains Jackie Ellis. Her triumph over adversity and her long-ago flirtation with drugs is complete, and she's an inspiration to all who know her.

Soon after his release from prison, Sean and Tia Walker reunited as a couple, which made him very happy. Though gripped by emotional fallout from the trauma of prison, he channeled his energy into his advocacy work and his employment at Community Servings, where he quickly moved from the loading dock to the reception desk and ultimately to a management position in fundraising and community outreach.

Shar'Day is a social worker. Following years of employment by the Commonwealth of Massachusetts, she took a position with a school system near Boston. A self-described activist and community organizer, she occasionally joins Sean in discussions hosted by universities and social service agencies. She remains as bubbly and upbeat as the newly baptized nine-year-old I met in 1998.

In 2016 Shar'day bought a multifamily home in a community north of Boston, and Sean energetically launched into renovations and repairs. Sean and Tia and her youngest child soon moved into its second-floor apartment; Shar'Day and Jackie took over the first floor; and Sean's sister Jeanelle's two daughters, whom Jackie raised to adulthood, took up residence on the third floor along with little Maddy, Jackie's great-granddaughter and the light of her life.

In spring 2017, with the permission of the court, Sean took his very first flight, with Shar'Day, to tell his story at the Innocence Network's[5] national conference in San Diego. He went on to speak at the Network's 2018 and 2019 conferences in Nashville and Atlanta.

In fall 2017, as Sean faced the prospect of a fourth trial, independent film producers from Toronto became aware of his plight (my website, justiceforseanellis.com, played a part). They sought and received permission from Sean and his lawyers to document his story, and I was asked to sign on as well. After months of research, in summer 2018 a Paris-based crew began filming what would become an eight-part Netflix series titled *Trial 4*.

---

5 The Innocence Network (as distinguished from the Innocence Project affiliated with Yeshiva University's Benjamin N. Cardozo School of Law) is an affiliation of organizations dedicated to providing *pro bono* legal and investigative services to individuals seeking to prove their innocence of crimes for which they have been convicted. Its membership comprises organizations from all 50 states as well as Canada, Australia, and the United Kingdom.

Spring 2019 brought both ups and downs in Sean's life. He enrolled in his first college course at the University of Massachusetts Boston and earned an honors grade; but after three-and-a-half years of living together, he and Tia parted ways.

The year 2020 ushered in a series of momentous events for Sean. His friendship with a work colleague named Toka blossomed into romance. In September he took his place among two dozen "rising social change leaders" as a community fellow in Tufts University's Institute for Nonprofit Practice. He became a trustee of the New England Innocence Project (NEIP), a regional social-justice nonprofit whose mission is "to correct and prevent wrongful convictions and fight injustice within the criminal legal system for innocent people imprisoned for a crime they did not commit." And Netflix released *Trial 4* informing the world about the Mulligan murder and Sean's wrongful conviction. The docuseries quickly became one of the media giant's most-streamed programs.

As a result of Netflix's international reach, more than 350,000 people from around the globe have visited justiceforseanellis.com over the past few years, and warm words of support for Sean have poured in. Many messages express admiration for the dignified way Sean has carried himself throughout his ordeal.

Following his multi-million-dollar payment from the city of Boston in 2021, Sean made exciting turns in his life. He and Toka married, and he resigned from the board of the New England Innocence Project to become a full-time employee. At NEIP he co-founded and now directs the Exoneree Network, dedicated to supporting "the practical, emotional, and spiritual reentry needs of exonerees as they work to rebuild their lives in freedom."

At this writing (2023), Sean is financially secure, happily married, and engaged in meaningful work. Still, the trauma of being wrongfully accused, convicted, and incarcerated shadows him. Perhaps it always will. But Sean is a survivor, and he draws inspiration from his oft-cited mantra, "Wounded but not broken."

CHAPTER 53

My Journey

1995–2022

I'll never cease being amazed at how, living in Canada, I learned of Sean's murder conviction in 1995. And I'll never cease being amazed at how things turned out.

Seared into my memory are the bleak years of Sean's incarceration, when I was one of his few visitors. Year after year, out of public view, he endured denial after denial from the courts. In those desolate times, the prospect that he would gain his freedom seemed an unreachable dream. The notion that untold numbers of people around the world would learn his story through a Netflix documentary series was unimaginable. And the idea that Sean would be made a multi-millionaire by the city was in the realm of fantasy.

Netflix's *Trial 4* also brought me out of the shadows, but apart from doing a media interview now and again, I'm retired. Sadly, in 2022 I lost my husband of 53 years. Rich was diagnosed with a glioblastoma brain tumor in June 2021 and died the following March. Despite the challenges thrown us by this cruel disease, we squeezed happiness out of his final months with time lavished upon us by our kids and grandkids. Since Rich's passing, family togetherness continues to sustain me, as do my friendships on both sides of the 49th parallel. All told, I appreciate every moment of this fleeting life.

A big part of that life for the past twenty-five years has been Sean. I often reflect on the chance intersection that brought him into our family's orbit. Were it not for Boston's METCO school integration program, we never would have met him. What a loss that would have been.

I reflect, too, on the ups and downs of the years I devoted to Sean's case, starting with my 1995 *Boston Globe* op-ed recounting memories of an adorable schoolboy in a party hat. I was turning fifty when I wrote that essay; I turned seventy the year he was freed from prison.

Why did I become so invested in Sean and his cause? I'd never been a firebrand. During the anti-Vietnam War demonstrations of the 1960s, you'd sooner find me researching a paper on J. D. Salinger in the Boston College library than marching in the streets. And, as I've none-too-proudly admitted, I was oblivious to race for the first half of my life. But in the 1980s, when Mark struck up his friendship with Sean—one of two Black students imported to his classroom—I was shocked to learn that some of my neighbors weren't pleased with school integration. Jack, across the street, frequently bellyached, "The teachers spend too much time helping the Black kids at the expense of *our* kids."

I never confronted this neighbor or corrected his misperception. I should have. And now I would add, "Jack, they are *all* 'our kids.'"

The same with Greta, my Boston teacher aide in the late 1960s. I lacked the experience, and maybe the courage, to cut into her racist diatribes. I would just change the subject. After all, we had to work side by side, and her views were her own business...

But really, they were not.

Learning in 1995 that the Sean Ellis we'd known was destined to die in prison shook my world. I ended up crusading for him because he was a young man with the deck stacked against him who said he'd been denied justice. Once, Sean was a child visiting my home. We were connected. My unquestioned assumption was that his life on earth is equal in value to my own, and the fact he would never move about and freely live that life resonated deeply with me. I had the crazy, outsized notion, 'Maybe I can help.'

Along the way, I came to see how integral Sean's Blackness was to the Boston murder investigation. At the outset, I didn't understand much about the Black experience, but as my commitment to Sean deepened, I became increasingly aware of the searing challenges the Black community faces.

In the 1970s, as a Harvard graduate student doing coursework in developmental psychology, I was steeped in the theories of Erik Erikson, who taught that the first task in a person's psychosocial development is to develop trust—a core belief that the world is safe and one's basic needs will be met. Sean's pocket of Boston was anything but safe and trust inspiring. Readers of this book have seen how commonplace guns and killings were in Sean's world. A horrifying six people close to him died violently and young: two cousins, a nephew, and three friends. This backdrop was the genesis of Sean's behavior on the Dorchester streets and his adherence to the no-snitching code: adaptations made to survive.

'Just life.' That's how Sean shrugged off the perils of his world.

That was not life for my kids.

Mark spent his childhood earning jarfuls of quarters at summer lemonade stands. Decorating his bike for the Fourth of July parade. Learning to swim. Taking piano lessons. Playing Little League baseball. As a teen he studied guitar, jammed with friends, tended to his tropical fish, and played more baseball. His biggest worry was not being popular, his greatest sorrow having a pet goldfish die.

The naked truth of the two Americas hovers over the pages of this book. My kids looked toward a future of unlimited possibilities. Sean and his Dorchester friends, equally American, summed up their prospects in four words: "Dead or in jail."

The legal injustices Sean endured eventually did get righted, but the societal injustices at the heart of his story persist. I'm not the first to observe and comment on the two Americas. My heart hopes I'll be among the last. My head knows this is fanciful.

In my life I've done a fair bit of traveling, for the Salk Institute in the 1990s and also well before that. Following my 1967 college graduation, a thirst to see the world led me to a stint as a flight attendant for Pan American Airways. My Pacific routes took me from Hong Kong to Tahiti, with perilous trips in and out of Vietnam during the conflict, transporting soldiers to R&R vacation spots. But my journey with Sean carried me into worlds I found even more foreign—the U.S. legal system and prison system.

I saw how police and prosecutors operate, and my eyes were opened to their failings. I saw not only corrupt police, but also the blind eye given police misconduct by supervisors and senior officials. I saw prosecutors who put winning ahead of getting at the truth. I saw that most of Sean's fellow prisoners were Black or brown.

I also saw good folks, bright spots in the system that gave me hope: *Boston Globe* investigative journalists. Ethical prosecutors who admitted their mistakes and freed the innocent. Brave and principled judges. And dedicated defense attorneys like Norman Zalkind, David Duncan, Jillise McDonough, and Rosemary Scapicchio—especially Rosemary, whose legal work for Sean can only be described as brilliant.

I grew in courage during the decades I spent working with Sean in his quest for freedom. His plight got me to stretch myself further than I'd ever stretched before: meeting with lawyers and *Boston Globe* editors and reporters, interviewing witnesses and jurors and private investigators and police informants, demanding answers.

THE AUTHOR IS INTERVIEWED BY MEMBERS OF THE BOSTON MEDIA FOLLOWING SEAN'S OVERTURNED CONVICTIONS.

The work pushed my security envelope too. I was terrified when driving into high-crime neighborhoods, nervous when facing hostile corrections officers while visiting Sean in prison. I expected that my website and newspaper articles might anger certain Boston police and officials, but being verbally assaulted by law officers in a courthouse elevator was unexpected, ugly, and disturbing.

Yet all these experiences were broadening. They popped the bubbles that for decades had wrapped me in a comfortable, oblivious world.

Looking back, I see that helping Sean helped *me*—to become braver and more determined. More broadminded and socially aware. More intolerant of structural inequalities. More tolerant of hard choices taken to survive.

My friendship with Sean changed my life.

AFTERWORD

The question remains: Who killed John Mulligan?

Who would kill a uniformed police detective with five shots to the face, arranged in a cross? Mulligan's murder was surely a message, but from whom, to whom? Was it a disgruntled drug dealer lurking about the Walgreens parking lot? A fellow corrupt Boston officer looking to cut Mulligan out of the drug profits? Someone with an entirely different beef with Mulligan, like the mysterious "one-eyed Mr. C" iintroduced in the Netflix documentary series *Trial 4*?

After twenty-two years of research, I acknowledge I still do not know. What I do know is there's a murderer out there, either above ground or below.

AUTHOR'S METHODS & ACKNOWLEDGMENTS

Methods: Having discovered Sean's plight only after his 1995 conviction, I first resorted to researching the *Boston Globe*'s 1993-95 coverage of Detective John J. Mulligan's murder, homicide investigation, and ensuing four trials; in 1996 I learned about the related Boston police corruption scandal and began following it in real time (1996-98).

Primary documents then became my chief sources: the transcripts of Sean Ellis' and Terry Patterson's trials; Sean's Suffolk County case file; all the police reports and discovery materials that Sean's attorneys made available to me; and the FOIA materials procured by Rosemary Scapicchio that ultimately resulted in Sean's overturned convictions and release.

For every phone call and in-person discussion I had with Sean's family members and lawyers and all those I interviewed about the case, I took contemporaneous notes—a practice I'd honed over my decade-long career as a writer and editor in Canada.

When visiting Sean in prison I was barred from bringing in writing materials. But I made it a habit to document the key points of our discussions either immediately afterward or that evening, latest. I found our conversations so interesting and enlightening that I never shirked from this task, always amazed at how clearly I remembered Sean's words. I literally heard his voice in my mind as I typed my notes. The conversations I've reconstructed on these pages are based on these notes and my memory. I know I have conveyed their essence.

For privacy's sake, I elected to use pseudonyms for three individuals in this book, confident that their actual identities were immaterial to the story.

While writing I worked solo for an embarrassing number of years, discarding many an early chapter before settling on what I hope became the proper blend of documented fact and personal reflection. It was lonely work.

Midway through the process I conferred with the marvelous David Corbett, a San Francisco-based mystery writer and former private investigator who advised me on emphasizing character and honing the narrative arc. As I neared final-draft stage, in a monumental stroke of good fortune, family friend and literature professor Sara Rutkowski connected me with book editor Linda Kulman. Additional polish was provided by copy editor Paula Southerland, a consummate professional, and by crackerjack proofreader Bonnie Lynn Bailey. I am fortunate to have had the counsel of all these fine editors in shaping the product that came to be.

Thank yous: I will forever be grateful to Sean Ellis and his family for trusting me and opening their hearts during some of the most difficult years of their lives. Sean bestowed the honorific "Godma" upon me in 2000. I wear it with utmost pride and hope to always remain worthy of it.

Over the years, as I pursued my work on Sean's case and my writing, a constant source of strength has been my extended family in Massachusetts and my friends and colleagues in Canada, California, Massachusetts, and beyond. They cheered me on, propped me up, provided me lodging, and always expressed genuine interest in the case—even when I rambled on far too long. Sincere thanks go out to family members Ken and Rosemary Murphy, Mike Murphy and Cheryl LeFave, and Janet Carroll; to my dear friends Judy Saide, Bruce Stevenson and Kay Towers, Gerri and Brian Monaghan, Amy and Rob Singer, Rich and Jean Hand, Joe and Karen McGraw, Barbara Cook, Maybeth and Ken Shockey, Tanja and Steve Dorsey, Barbara Zack and Bill McDonough; and to my esteemed former colleagues John LeBaron, Connie Louie, and Susan Foote in Massachusetts and David Steiner, Louise Rousseau, and Peter McBride in Montreal.

There are special places in my heart for Patricia DeWilde, who gave me meticulous and important feedback on early drafts, and to Rich's and my lifelong friend, Rich Hand, Esq., for generously sharing the legal wisdom he gained during his successful advocacy for Billy Wayne Sinclair, convicted as a teen for an unintended, scattershot Louisiana murder.

I'm particularly grateful for the calming words and peerless empathy of Kay Towers, whose insights from her social work practice guided me through several rough patches, and for the eloquent words of encouragement from Toronto author Scott Thornley, OC. His words meant more to me than he knows.

I am thankful also for the the sage and kindly guidance of my attorneys Joseph Steinfield, Brian McMenimen, and Jeff Pyle. Much praise is also due the brilliant and fearless journalist Florence Graves, founder and director of Brandeis University's Schuster Institute for Investigative Journalism, who became my trusted adviser and friend.

From the bottom of my heart, I thank my children, who have lived with me (if not physically) through the entirety of this work. Mark started things off through his friendship with and affection for Sean. As two decades passed, Mark was busy with college, graduate school, career, marriage, and parenthood, but his interest in Sean's welfare never flagged. Janet, with her own fond memories of Sean, was not only a supporter of my efforts, but also an adviser, reader, and critic—a genuine colleague.

Alison, with her unbending desire for justice and social change, has long been the conscience of our family. Her support for this project was unwavering, and she magnanimously gave me permission to describe our relationship struggles during her teens.

I'm grateful as well to my kids' fantastic spouses, Glyncora, Devin, and Jeremy, for their interest and forbearance through the years, fully aware that talk about Sean's case became the main course of too many family dinners.

Finally, my late husband Rich was my anchor and shelter for more than five decades. We married in our early twenties, and his presence beside me made everything possible in my life. His steadfast love for me and his unwavering support for my work—both the justice-finding enterprise and the writing—were my mainstay. His fondest wish for me was to complete and publish this book. I know that somewhere in the universe he is smiling.

LIST OF CHARACTERS

Acerra, Kenneth: Boston detective and John Mulligan's friend and Area E-5 colleague; accused by the chief prosecutor of mishandling evidence and witnesses in the Mulligan homicide investigation

Alphonse, Joseph: Walgreens night manager

Armstead, Ray Jr.: Told Boston detective George Foley that his father, Boston police officer Ray Armstead Sr., planned to kill John Mulligan outside Walgreens

Armstead, Ray Sr.: Boston police officer in 1993; according to Boston detective George Foley, Armstead's son told him in August 1993 that Armstead Sr. planned to kill John Mulligan outside Walgreens

Ball, Carol S.: Suffolk County Superior Court judge who was assigned in 2013 to read Sean Ellis' second retrial motion

Banks, Robert: Suffolk County Superior Court judge who presided over Sean Ellis' pretrial motion hearing in December 1994

Bannister, Stephen: Walgreens night clerk; discovered John Mulligan dead outside Walgreens

Barnicle, Mike: *Boston Globe* columnist who wrote opinion pieces about John Mulligan's murder

Beers, Kenny: Boston Area E-5 detective; helped Kenneth Acerra recover the "missing" $21,915 cash forfeited in the 1992 Humberto Guzman drug raid

Bennett, André: Pastor at Zion Baptist Church, Lynn, Massachusetts

Boykin, Pam: Sean Ellis' girlfriend beginning in 1993

Bratton, William ("Bill"): Boston police commissioner in September 1993

Brazil, John: Boston homicide detective and John Mulligan's former Area E-5 colleague who investigated Mulligan's murder

Broker, Phyllis: Assistant district attorney and chief of homicide in Suffolk County; chief prosecutor in the Mulligan murder case

Brown, Ma'Trez: Son of Sean Ellis' cousin Tracy Brown

Brown, Tracy: Sean Ellis' cousin who was murdered at age twenty-four by Craig Hood three days after John Mulligan's murder

Brown, Victor: Trial witness who identified Terry Patterson's VW Rabbit; lived on a residential street adjacent to the Walgreens strip mall

Cadagogne, Amy: Attorney in Rosemary Scapicchio's law office in 2011

Chisholm, Kevin: Sean Ellis' Dorchester friend; murdered in 1994 at age eighteen

Chung, Evony: Walgreens shopper who testified at Sean Ellis' three trials

Cloherty, Kevin: Assistant U.S. attorney; with Theodore Merritt conducted the 1996-1997 federal grand jury inquiry into Boston Area E-5 drug corruption

Conley, Daniel: Suffolk County district attorney from February 2002 to September 2018

Cox, Deborah: Walgreens shopper; not called to testify in Sean Ellis' trials

Cunha, Jack: Terry Patterson's appellate attorney

Darlene (pseudonym): Woman with whom Sean Ellis had a personal relationship for several years while incarcerated

Dee Dee: Jackie Ellis' daughter; Sean Ellis' sister

DeSalvo, Albert "Art": Newspaper deliveryman in the vicinity of Walgreens on the morning of the murder

Devin (Advani): Author's son-in-law; married daughter Janet Murphy in 2000

Dookie, Sean: Sean Ellis' Hansborough Street friend

Dorch, Kenneth: Boston detective, one of the first officers at John Mulligan's murder crime scene

Dowd, Tom: Supervisor at the U.S. Department of Treasury's Bureau of Alcohol, Tobacco, and Firearms; met with the author

Duncan, David: Sean Ellis' trial lawyer, with Norman Zalkind

Ellement, John: *Boston Globe* reporter; did lion's share of reporting on the Mulligan case

Ellis, John: Sean Ellis' father

Ellis, Mary ("Jackie"): Sean Ellis' mother

Ellis, Sean: Convicted of Boston detective John Mulligan's 1993 murder and robbery

Erti, Tina: Lived in same condominium complex as John Mulligan; roommate of Mulligan's girlfriend, Mary Shopov

Evans, Paul: Succeeded William Bratton as Boston police commissioner in February 1994

Foilb, Robert: Boston Police Department fingerprint expert; testified that Terry Patterson's fingerprints were on John Mulligan's driver's door

Foley, George: Boston detective who reported the tip that John Mulligan was going to be killed by Boston police officer Ray Armstead Sr.

Forry, Bill: Editor/publisher of the weekly *Dorchester Reporter*

Gants, Ralph: Chief justice of the Massachusetts Supreme Judicial Court; in 2016 wrote the ruling affirming Judge Carol Ball's 2015 reversal of Sean Ellis' murder and robbery convictions

Garcia, Elvis: Ivan Sanchez's brother-in-law and Boston police officer; testified that Rosa Sanchez phoned him to report what she saw outside Walgreens

Glover, Alfred: His photo in a 1993 police array of mug shots brought Walgreens eyewitness Rosa Sanchez to tears when she mistook him for a man who'd once stalked her

Glyncora (Murphy, née Weir): Author's daughter-in-law; married Mark Murphy in 2010

Gonsalves, Anthony: FBI informer who gave information about Sean Ellis and John Mulligan's murder that was later deemed unreliable

Griffith, Harriet: Sean Ellis' high school friend whom Ellis said he phoned outside Walgreens the morning of Mulligan's murder

Gross, William: Boston police commissioner from August 2018 until January 2021; dropped murder and robbery charges against Sean Ellis in 2018

Hager, Michelle ("Misty"): Had sexual relationship with Mulligan in 1993; testified at August 2014 evidentiary hearing of Sean Ellis' retrial motion

Hansen, Ron: Drug dealer who shared his knowledge of Detectives Acerra, Robinson, and Mulligan with Boston police investigators and federal grand jury

Harris, Dennis: Boston homicide detective who interrogated Terry Patterson; accused by Patterson's lawyer of making false statements about the session

Headen, Curt: Sean Ellis' Dorchester friend; murdered in 1994 at age eighteen

Hood, Craig: Convicted killer of Sean Ellis' cousins Celine Kirk and Tracy Brown

Hurley, Nancy: Terry Patterson's trial lawyer

Jean (Kirk): Sean Ellis' maternal aunt; mother of Sean Ellis' cousins Celine Kirk and Tracy Brown

Jeanelle: Jackie Ellis' daughter; Sean Ellis' sister

Jeffrey: Sean Ellis' nephew who died at age seventeen in a gun accident in 1999 in his Dorchester home

Jeremy (Byrgesen): Author's son-in-law; married Alison Murphy in 2011

Johnna: John Ellis' daughter; Sean Ellis' sister

Joseph (Moody): Jackie Ellis' son; Sean Ellis' older brother, who drowned in a Needham, Massachusetts, classmate's pool in 1984 at age 12

Kahn, Ric: Former reporter for the *Boston Globe* who wrote about Mulligan case; met with the author

Keeler, Daniel: Boston detective who investigated Mulligan murder

Kelly, Stephen: Boston police officer who was first to arrive at the Mulligan murder crime scene

Kirk, Celine: Sean Ellis' seventeen-year-old cousin who accompanied Sean and Terry Patterson to Walgreens the morning of John Mulligan's murder; was murdered three days later by Craig Hood

Kottmyer, Diane: Suffolk County Superior Court judge

Kurkjian, Steve: *Boston Globe* metro editor in the late 1990s

Laselle (Ellis): John Ellis' daughter; Sean Ellis' sister

Layne, Eugene: Walgreens shopper; testified in Terry Patterson's trial

Linn, Paul: Suffolk County assistant district attorney; with Edmond Zabin represented the Commonwealth of Massachusetts in opposing Sean Ellis' 2013 retrial motion

Mahoney, William: Boston detective; led interrogation of Sean Ellis on September 30, 1993

Marquardt, Lenny: Boston detective and Area E-5 supervisor; interviewed Rosa Sanchez several hours after John Mulligan's murder regarding her phoned-in tip

Martin, Ralph II: Suffolk County district attorney from 1992 to 2002.

Martin, Robert: Boston drug dealer; testified about being robbed in September 1993 by Area E-5 detectives including John Mulligan

Matthews, Robert ("Rob"): Sean Ellis' Hansborough Street friend and Terry Patterson's cousin

McCarthy, Lt. of INS: False name used by Detective Kenneth Acerra when he participated in the September 1993 robbery of drug dealer Robert Martin

McDaniel, James D. Jr.: Suffolk County Superior Court judge; in 1995 presided over all three Ellis trials and Terry Patterson's trial

McDonough, Jillise: Attorney in Rosemary Scapicchio's law office; co-counsel with Scapicchio in the preparation and defense of Sean Ellis' 2013 retrial motion

McNamara, Eileen: Pulitzer Prize-winning *Boston Globe* columnist; recommended a retrial for Sean Ellis because of the potential "taint" of the investigators of John Mulligan's murder

McNelly, Ed: Boston detective; headed the homicide unit in 1993; questioned detective George Foley about the Armstead tip

Merritt, Theodore ("Ted"): Assistant U.S. attorney; with Kevin Cloherty conducted the 1996-97 federal grand jury inquiry into allegations of drug robberies by Boston Area E-5 detectives

Mulligan, John J.: Boston detective; murdered on September 26, 1993, at age fifty-two

Mulligan, Richard: Brother of John J. Mulligan

Murphy, Alison: Author's daughter

Murphy, Janet: Author's daughter; knew Sean Ellis and his brother Joseph Moody as students in Needham, Massachusetts

Murphy, Mark: Author's son; Sean Ellis' friend during the 1980s at Mitchell Elementary School, Needham, Massachusetts

Murphy, Richard ("Rich"): Author's husband; neuroscientist and academic administrator

Murray, David: Sean Ellis' maternal uncle

Nelson, Leon: Walgreens shopper; not called to testify in Sean Ellis' trials

Nikki: Friend of Sean Ellis' cousin Celine Kirk

O'Connor, Gerald: Walgreens neighbor who identified Terry Patterson's VW Rabbit

O'Donovan, Brendan (pseudonym): Boston defense attorney; advised author

O'Leary, Thomas: Boston detective; lead investigator of the Mulligan homicide squad; took control of the Mulligan murder crime scene

Pablo (pseudonym): Listed as a "concerned citizen" and potential witness in Sean Ellis' Suffolk County case file

Pappas, John: Interim district attorney in Suffolk County from 2018 to 2019

Patterson, Terry: Sean Ellis' friend; convicted in February 1995 of John Mulligan's murder and robbery

Puddin: Sean Ellis' cousin; daughter of Jackie Ellis' sister Rae

Pungitore, Tony: Manager of the Dedham Showcase Cinema in 1993

Rae: Sean Ellis' maternal aunt, who was paralyzed in a 2003 car accident; mother of Puddin

Ramirez, Danilo ("Danny"): Boston officer who occasionally worked with John Mulligan; told investigators Mulligan was "paranoid" about his personal safety and strapped a hidden revolver on his ankle

Reynell: Sean Ellis' high school friend who helped him research his case from about 2010 to 2013

Richardson, Lewis ("Lew"): Rob Matthews's in-law and friend

Robinson, Walter F. Jr.: Boston detective and John Mulligan's friend and Area E-5 colleague; accused by the chief prosecutor of mishandling evidence and witnesses in the Mulligan homicide investigation

Rollins, Rachael: Suffolk County district attorney; took office January 1, 2019

Ross, Richard: Boston detective; one of the first detectives to arrive at the Mulligan murder crime scene

Saia, Joseph V. Jr.: Boston police superintendent, chief of detectives and head of the Mulligan task force

Samuel, Joanne: Walgreens shopper; testified in Terry Patterson's trial

Sanchez, Ivan: Walgreens shopper and husband of Rosa Sanchez

Sanchez, Rosa: Walgreens shopper and wife of Ivan Sanchez; positively identified Sean Ellis in police photos

Saunders, Joseph: Walgreens shopper

Scapicchio, Rosemary: Sean Ellis' appellate attorney starting in 2004

Scott: Private investigator who worked for attorney Rosemary Scapicchio; discovered witness Michelle Hager, who testified about her relationship with John Mulligan in Sean Ellis' August 2014 evidentiary hearing

Shar'Day (Taylor): Jackie Ellis' daughter; Sean Ellis' youngest sister

Shopov, Mary: John Mulligan's girlfriend

Toomey, Dennis: Attorney in Rosemary Scapicchio's law office in 2011

Ullmann, Robert: Suffolk County Superior Court judge; presided over the 2020 appeal of Sean Ellis' 1995 firearms convictions

Walker, Latia ("Tia"): Sean Ellis' girlfriend at the time of John Mulligan's murder in 1993

Wilkerson, Dianne: Massachusetts state senator in 1993; received phoned information about John Mulligan's murder from a self-described Boston police officer

Zabin, Edmond: Suffolk County assistant district attorney and chief of homicide; assisted Paul Linn in opposing Sean Ellis' 2013 retrial motion

Zalkind, Norman: Sean Ellis' trial lawyer, with David Duncan

NOTES

THE MURDER

Description of John Mulligan's murder scene in Roslindale, MA: Testimony of Walgreens clerk Stephen Bannister, Walgreens store manager Joseph Alphonse, parking-lot witness Joseph Saunders, Boston police officer Stephen Kelly, and first-responder paramedics at Sean Ellis' January and March 1995 trials; *Boston Globe*, "As one officer falls, others rise, salute," September 27, 1993; *Boston Globe*, "Stuart errors not forgotten," October 3, 1993.

moonlighted ... extra cash: *Boston Globe*, "City police detective slain execution style," September 27, 1993; *Boston Globe*, "Assignments a part of police work in city," September 28, 1993; *Boston Globe*, "Downturn in real estate market left Mulligan in a financial bind," September 29, 1993.

"Call 911 ... Mulligan": Testimony of Walgreens manager Joseph Alphonse at Sean Ellis' January and March 1995 trials.

Bratton ... "execution-style assassination": *Boston Globe*, "City police detective slain execution style," September 27, 1993; *Boston Globe*, "A force of 65 sifts details of victim's life," September 28, 1993; *Boston Globe*, "Revenge is the theme of police-slaying leads," September 28, 1993; *Boston Globe*, "Reward set in officer's death," September 30, 1993.

sixty-five member task force: *Boston Globe*, "A force of 65 sifts details of victim's life," September 28, 1993.

"We are going to go the extra mile on this one": Boston police Commissioner William Bratton quoted in *Boston Globe*, "Revenge is the theme of police-slaying leads," September 28, 1993.

Description of Mulligan's funeral and burial: *Boston Globe*, "2000 Police mourn one of their own," October 2, 1993.

"What a beautiful day ... paid detail": Richard Mulligan, quoted in *Boston Globe*, "2000 Police mourn one of their own," October 2, 1993.

died blue: *Boston Globe*, "As one officer falls, others rise, salute," September 27, 1993.

CHAPTER 1: VISITING SEAN

He says he didn't do it: *Boston Globe*, "Detective's conviction sparks move for new trial in slaying of officer," October 1, 1998.

Three articles on the verdict: *Boston Globe*, "Ellis convicted on 3d try in murder of detective," September 15, 1995; *Boston Globe*, "Police: Justice is served by verdict," September 15, 1995; *Boston Globe*, "After sentencing, Mulligan family visits cemetery," September 15, 1995.

recent retrial motion: *Boston Globe*, "Detectives' conviction sparks move for new trial in slaying of officer," October 1, 1998.

CHAPTER 2: BAD NEWS TRAVELS NORTH

I faxed it in ... run it on Thursday: *Boston Globe*, "What went wrong in the life of Sean Ellis?" September 21, 1995.

Full text of the article: Our weekend guests arrived from Maine with laughter and greetings and tales of getting lost. Along with their bags they plopped down the morning's *Boston Globe*. I glanced at the familiar nameplate with affection. For displaced Bostonians, the *Globe*'s front page is visual comfort food. I couldn't wait to sit down later and digest the local news.

But what does that headline say? "Ellis convicted on 3d try in murder of detective." Pictured alongside it is a downcast young black face.

Funny. We once knew a Sean Ellis, about a dozen years ago in Needham. He was a quiet, sweet African American boy from the Boston projects. The Metco Program bused him each day to our local school. That Sean Ellis had become our son Mark's friend in the third and fourth grades.

Who could this Sean Ellis be?

Eyes dart down the column, looking for identifying features. "21, of Dorchester." Omigod! Same age as Mark. Could this convicted cop killer be that polite, painfully shy Sean Ellis? That impeccably clean Sean Ellis, with a mother's loves and hopes so evident in his crisply ironed shirts?

By now the young visage looks familiar. Nausea rises as the truth sinks in. The two Sean Ellises are one and the same.

The memories flood back. The Needham Sean Ellis had a disabling speech impediment. His stutter mortified him, and he hardly ventured a word. The statement in the *Globe* takes on new meaning: "Ellis never testified in any of the trials..."

What could have gone wrong in this man's life and mind to transform the agreeable child we knew to a convicted murderer?

My husband and I recall Sean's several visits to our home, occasions the whole family enjoyed. He was a reserved boy. Some details come back: the time Sean slept over so he could sing in the Christmas concert, his next-day's clothes neatly folded for school. At Mark's birthday, Sean shyly presenting his gift: a paperback book, clearly used and clearly adult in subject matter—all the family could muster. That paperback is still on our family's bookshelf.

The time Mark went to Sean's birthday party in the projects and came home dazzled. The occasion had given rise to a neighborhood barbecue. There were chicken and ribs and music and dancing. "Why don't we have a party like that?" Mark wanted to know. A loving mother was behind it all.

"Ellis' mother, Mary, had attended each day of the three trials, but was absent yesterday when the verdict was returned..."

Our older daughter also knew Sean. With Mark away, she was the first to hear of the ghastly Boston murder and Sean's conviction. She blurted out, "It must have broken his mother's heart!"

We recalled that tragedy had visited Mary Ellis before during those Needham days. Sean's older brother, Joe Moody, was also a Needham-Boston Metco student. One hot June afternoon, a middle school classmate invited his friends over for a pool party. All the kids jumped into the back yard pool, but Joe didn't come back up. He sank like a stone and drowned, too embarrassed to admit he couldn't swim. Nobody thought to ask.

After leaving the Needham schools 10 years ago, Mark lost track of his city friend. Just this summer he mused, "I wonder what ever happened to Sean Ellis. Remember those feet?" Of course we did. They were size 10 even then, oversize anchors weighing down the slimmest of boys.

When he heard the dreadful news from Boston, Mark was stricken. To him, Sean had been a good buddy. He remembered that stand-out day my husband treated them both to a Red Sox game and McDonald's. He also remembered Sean getting into fights in school.

Life imprisonment without parole. How sad the paths of two Needham classmates could diverge so greatly. Though a world apart economically, our own son was no golden boy. He had his difficulties in school but has managed to surmount them, and it looks like he'll be a late bloomer.

Mary's 21-year-old Sean will not be blooming.

And yet as a young student he had an uncommon sweetness about him; that, and a caring family, and all the opportunity and hopes the Metco program represented. What turned him to violence?

If we knew the answer and ways to prevent it, the Mulligan family and Mary Ellis might not be grieving.

CHAPTER 3: THE VICTIM

"Who would shoot a police officer": Boston police Superintendent Joseph V. Saia Jr., titular head of the Mulligan task force, quoted in *Boston Globe*, "Revenge is the theme of police-slaying leads," September 28, 1993.

A detective killed ... summons dignitaries: *Boston Globe*, "Menino's role in contrast with Flynn," September 28, 1993; *Boston Globe*, "Despite clashes with detectives, prosecutor prevails in 2-year ordeal," September 15, 1995.

Police cruisers holding grim fellow officers: *Boston Globe*, "As one officer falls, others rise, salute," September 12, 1995.

"an old fashioned, bare-knuckles sort of cop ... blunt": *Boston Globe*, "A veteran known for toughness and, lately, for trouble," September 27, 1993.

alternately admired and loathed: *Boston Globe*, "City police detective slain execution style," September 27, 1993; *Boston Globe*, "A veteran known for his toughness, and lately for trouble," September 27, 1993; *Boston Globe*, "Revenge is the theme of police-slaying leads," September 28, 1993; *Boston Globe*, "Mulligan seldom pulled back from edge," October 3, 1993.

"chief notoriety ... for misconduct": *Boston Globe*, "A veteran known for toughness and, lately, for trouble," September 27, 1993.

"problem officer": *Ibid.*

professional consequences ... nearly nil: *Boston Globe*, "Officer's history marked," September 15, 1992; *Boston Globe*, "Wave of abuse claims laid to a few officers," October 4, 1992; *Boston Globe*, "A veteran known for toughness and, lately, for trouble," September 27, 1993; *Boston Globe*, "Revenge is the theme of police-slaying leads," September 28, 1993.

making charges disappear: *Boston Globe*, "Wave of abuse claims laid to a few officers," October 4, 1992.

whiff of drug corruption: *Boston Globe*, "A veteran known for toughness and, lately, for trouble," September 27, 1993; *Boston Globe*, "Mulligan seldom pulled back from edge," October 3, 1993.

Mulligan's past had caught up with him: Observation made by *Boston Globe* reporter Tony Locy in the Netflix documentary film series *Trial 4*; *Boston Globe*, "City police detective slain execution style," September 27, 1993; *Boston Globe*, "A veteran known for his toughness, and lately for trouble," September 27, 1993.

"It was a message": *Boston Globe*, "A break in the thin blue line," September 30, 1993.

"That's got us looking at his personal and his professional life": Boston police superintendent Joseph V. Saia Jr. quoted in *Boston Globe*, "Revenge is the theme of police-slaying leads," September 28, 1993.

individuals bent on revenge: *Boston Globe*, "Revenge is the theme of police-slaying leads," September 28, 1993.

Money was another potential motivator: *Boston Globe*, "Downturn in real estate market left Mulligan in a financial bind," September 29, 1993; *Boston Globe*, "Mulligan seldom pulled back from edge," October 3, 1993; *Boston Globe*, "Car seized in probe of police death," October 3, 1993.

hundred-hour workweeks ... 190th of the year: *Boston Globe*, "A veteran known for toughness and, lately, for trouble," September 27, 1993; *Boston Globe*, "Downturn in real estate market left Mulligan in a financial bind," September 29, 1993.

long considered a loner: *Boston Globe*, "A veteran known for toughness and, lately, for trouble," September 27, 1993; *Boston Globe*, "Revenge is the theme of police-slaying leads," September 28, 1993.

"shunned the company of ... fellow officers": *Boston Globe*, "A veteran known for toughness and, lately, for trouble," September 27, 1993.

"domineering person": unidentified neighbor of John Mulligan quoted in *Boston Globe*, "Woman reportedly sought in police killing," September 29, 1993.

"controlled any woman he ever went out with": *Ibid.*

"**John was the charmer type ... stories**": Mulligan's girlfriend Mary Shopov quoted in *Boston Globe*, "Girlfriend received call loved ones fear," September 27, 1993.

"**hard working and honest**": *Ibid.*

"**unfair blemishes ... record**": *Ibid.*

"**Up to now ... something good about him**": *Ibid.*

"**avenging officer**": *Boston Globe*, "Mulligan seldom pulled back from edge," October 3, 1993.

"**on the edge of the blue line**": *Ibid.*

died in uniform ... buried in uniform: *Ibid.*

CHAPTER 4: SEAN'S ARREST

Forensic testing ... rented Ford Explorer: *Boston Globe*, "City police detective slain execution style," September 27, 1993; *Boston Globe*, "Revenge is the theme of police-slaying lead," September 28, 1993; *Boston Globe*, "Detective and killer sat together in car, police say," October 1, 1993.

five times in specific parts of his head: *Boston Globe*, "Woman reportedly sought in police killing," September 29, 1993.

An unidentified woman ... before his murder: *Ibid.*

Mulligan reportedly had phoned his girlfriend: *Boston Globe*, "Mulligan rarely pulled back from edge," October 3, 1993.

interviewing Shopov "extensively": *Boston Globe*, "Woman reportedly sought in police killing," September 29, 1993; *Boston Globe*, "Reward set in officer's death," September 30, 1993.

Fear was palpable: *Boston Globe*, "Gun attack claims a 2d life, October 4, 1993; *Boston Globe*, "Bratton says gun violence has city disturbed," October 4, 1993.

A double homicide stirred particular horror: *Boston Globe*, "Boy, 2, alerts police to two Mattapan slayings," September 30, 1993; *Boston Globe*, "Relatives hope boy, 2, has clues to slayings," October 1, 1993; *Boston Globe*, "Slain women's kin say family knows Mulligan suspect," October 5, 1993.

"**My mommy's on the floor**": toddler Ma'Trez Brown quoted in *Boston Globe*, "Source says toddler has helped police," October 2, 1993.

"**a very dangerous felon**": *Boston Globe*, "Brockton teenager charged in 2 murders," October 4, 1993; *Boston Globe*, "Man held in slaying of officer," October 5, 1993; *Boston Globe*, "Teen-ager arraigned in double slayings," October 5, 1993; *Boston Globe*, "Suspects had eluded system," October 7, 1993.

The bullets ... did not match: *Boston Globe*, "Man held in slaying of officer," October 5, 1993.

two consecutive, fifteen-year sentences: *Boston Globe*, "Killer of 2 women in '93 makes plea agreement," June 20, 1995.

promising lead: *Boston Globe*, "Woman reportedly sought in police killing," September 29, 1993; *Boston Globe*, "Police hunt car reported at scene of killing," September 29, 1993; *Boston Globe*, "Car seized in probe of police death," October 3, 1993.

"chocolate brown" VW Rabbit: *Boston Globe*, "Woman reportedly sought in police killing," September 29, 1993.

"moments after [Mulligan] was slain": *Ibid.*

"tinted windows, custom wheel rims, and a vinyl cover over part of the hood and grille": *Ibid.*

police found the VW Rabbit: *Boston Globe*, "Car seized in probe of police death," October 3, 1993; *Boston Globe*, "Man held in slaying of officer," October 5, 1993; testimony of Walgreens neighbors Victor Brown and Gerald O'Connor at Sean Ellis' January and March 1995 trials.

On October 3 they picked Patterson up: *Boston Globe*, "Man held in slaying of officer," October 5, 1993.

"robbery, pure and simple": unidentified police official, quoted *Ibid.*

"John Mulligan was an innocent victim": Suffolk County D.A. Ralph Martin II, quoted *Ibid.*

Relatives ... said the women knew Patterson: *Ibid.*

"a close friend of [their] cousin, Sean Ellis": unnamed relatives of Sean Ellis, quoted *Ibid.*

Celine had told her family ... time of Mulligan's murder: *Boston Globe*, "Slain women's kin say family knows Mulligan suspect," October 5, 1993.

"Kirk and Ellis appeared on a store videotape": *Ibid.*

"they might have been able to implicate Patterson ... death": *Ibid.*

Patterson hung out with Hood: attributed to unnamed relatives of Sean Ellis in *Boston Globe*, "Sister's cousin held in police killing," October 7, 1993; *Boston Globe*, "Patterson drawn by gang image," October 17, 1993.

police rejected any connection ... link: *Boston Globe*, "Bratton criticizes stories on killings," October 4, 1993.

"blamed Sean K. Ellis": *Boston Globe*, "Slay suspect said to blame friend," October 6, 1993.

officials charged Patterson with murder one and robbery: *Ibid.*

The .25-caliber gun ... still missing: *Boston Globe*, "Sisters' cousin held in police killing," October 7, 1993.

October 6 ... joint funeral: *Boston Globe*, "Cries of sorrow, call for prayer punctuate funeral for 2 sisters," October 7, 1993.

summoned Sean outside and arrested him: personal communication to the author by Mary "Jackie" Ellis; *Boston Globe*, "Sisters' cousin held in police killing," October 7, 1993.

Being with Patterson ... co-defendant: October 1, 1993, police interview of David Murray; testimony of Boston detective William Mahoney at Sean Ellis' January and March 1995 trials.

jubilant midnight press conference: *Boston Globe*, "Sister's cousin held in police killing," October 7, 1993; *Boston Globe*.

"basically closed" the Mulligan investigation: *Ibid.*

"three men may have been in the [VW Rabbit]": *Boston Globe*, "Slay suspect said to blame friend," October 6, 1993.

"suspected of involvement": *Ibid.*; *Boston Globe*, "Please don't act surprised," October 6, 1993; *Boston Globe*, "Suspects' common thread: drugs, guns, violence," October 6, 1993.

"happened upon Mulligan": *Boston Globe*, "Sisters' cousin held in police killing," October 7, 1993.

"opened the passenger's side door ... five times in the face": *Ibid.*

random crime of opportunity: *Ibid.*

Sean was charged ... \\ appeared on his behalf: *Boston Globe*, "Handguns found in vacant lot tied to death of officer," October 8, 1993.

The judge denied bail: *Ibid.*

police cadets ... pearl-handled Raven: *Ibid.*; *Boston Globe*, "Police say detective was killed by gun found in vacant lot," October 9, 1993; *Boston Globe*, "Suspects' prints not found on gun in Mulligan case," December 28, 1993.

teenage friend of Sean's ... granted immunity: *Boston Globe*, "Immunity deal for witness reported in Mulligan killing," October 22, 1993.

Another immunity deal ... in the works: *Ibid.*

indictments for Sean and Patterson: *Boston Globe*, "2 in custody indicted in policeman's killing," October 28, 1993.

"significant questions" remaining in the case: *Boston Globe*, "Mulligan probe leaves many questions unanswered," October 8, 1993.

"difficult to comprehend ... kicks or a pistol": *Ibid.*

"cruelest of ironies": *Ibid.*

"All of the questions ...": *Ibid.*

"At first blush ... those doubts": Defense attorney Norman Zalkind, quoted *Ibid.*

"fast and violent crowd ... each other's backs": *Boston Globe*, "Suspects' common thread: drugs, guns, violence," October 6, 1993; *Boston Globe*, "Suspects had eluded system," October 7, 1993; *Boston Globe*, "Fear a fact of life in neighborhoods," October 10, 1993.

urban war zone: *Boston Globe*, "Suspects' common thread: drugs, guns, violence," October 6, 1993; *Boston Globe*, "Please don't act surprised," October 6, 1993; *Boston Globe*, "Suspects had eluded system," October 7, 1993; *Boston Globe*, "Where beasts prowl the street," *Boston Globe*, October 7, 1993; *Boston Globe*, "Fear a fact of life in neighborhoods," October 10, 1993.

"There's always a chance ... broken down": Frank Hart, outreach worker with Project Free, quoted in *Boston Globe*, "Fear a fact of life in neighborhoods," October 10, 1993.

"You think it's easy ... black male in America?": 17-year-old Daril Burton, Jr. quoted in *Boston Globe*, "Wise beyond their years," November 14, 1993.

"Part-time jobs are scarce ... you wind up dead or in jail": 14-year-old Charles Wilson quoted *Ibid*.

Background: Throughout the fall of 1993 and into winter 1994, youth violence smoldered in Boston's neighborhoods and was the subject of much reporting. The problem of teenagers wielding guns had percolated across the U.S. for a decade, with murders by firearm quadrupling from four thousand in 1980 to nearly sixteen thousand in 1992. Most of the violence was attributed to inner-city youths aged fifteen to nineteen. In Massachusetts blame was placed on the Commonwealth's "fragmented, antiquated and apathetic criminal justice system." A backlog of twelve thousand arraignments clogged the courts, allowing "young men with lengthy criminal records ... to remain on the streets." Violent offenders routinely dodged charges by not showing up for their court appearances, knowing there would be no follow-up; arresting police officers also frequently missed court dates, forcing judges to DWOP the cases (dismiss for want of prosecution). Compounding the problems was the lack of communication between police computer systems and those of the courts. Although Acting Mayor Tom Menino instituted "warrant apprehension teams" to search out youthful offenders, they still managed to slip through the cracks. Boston's "culture of violence" was decried in numerous *Boston Globe* articles. Sources :"Wise beyond their years," November 14, 1993; "Police, youths agree: It's too dangerous, February 10, 1994; " Slayings of young climb in in Boston," August 13, 1993; "Suspects had eluded system," October 7, 1993; "Please don't act surprised,' October 6, 1993; "Breakdowns, chaos plague court system, October 9, 1993; "Fear a fact of life in neighborhoods," October 10, 1993; "Police to target offenders on street," October 13, 1993; "Warrant team targets young suspects on lam," January 9, 1994.

Terry Patterson's family lived: *Boston Globe*, "Slay suspect said to blame friend," October 6, 1993; *Boston Globe*, "Patterson drawn by gang image," October 17, 1993.

By 1999 ... considerable police record: *Ibid*.

Sean ... lumped in with Patterson ... Hood: *Boston Globe*, "Suspects' common thread: drugs, guns, violence," October 6, 1993; *Boston Globe*, "Please don't act surprised," October 6, 1993; *Boston Globe*, "Sister's cousin held in police killing," October 7, 1993; *Boston Globe*, "Where beasts prowl the street," October 7, 1993; *Boston Globe*, "Breakdowns, chaos plague court system," October 9, 1993; *Boston Globe*, "Fear a fact of life in neighborhoods," October 10, 1993; *Boston Globe*, "Suspect veered to violence early," October 17, 1993.

"an army of sociopaths": *Boston Globe*, "Where beasts prowl the street," October 7, 1993.

"the case of the dead detective … a white person too": *Ibid.*

"I can't visualize it … take somebody's life": Mary "Jackie" Ellis quoted in *Boston Globe*, "Ellis' mother recalls efforts to teach respect for law," October 17, 1993.

"He's no killer": Mary "Jackie" Ellis quoted *Ibid.*

recent kidnapping charge: *Ibid.*

"I was just about to serve him dinner… really scared": Mary "Jackie" Ellis quoted *Ibid.*

CHAPTER 5: INVESTIGATIVE TURMOIL

two detectives … accused of mishandling crucial evidence and a key eyewitness: *Boston Globe*, "Lawyer asserts Ellis ID is flawed," October 29, 1993; *Boston Globe*, "Mulligan probe creates tensions," November 1, 1993; *Boston Globe*, "Martin, police bickering over Mulligan case," November 19, 1993.

Acerra balked and went to his detectives union: *Boston Globe*, "Martin, police bickering over Mulligan case," November 19, 1993.

second suspicion … about Acerra: *Ibid.*

union president … demanded Broker's removal: *Ibid.*

District Attorney Ralph Martin II refused: *Ibid.*

[Broker] could remain … on one condition: *Boston Globe*, "Mulligan probe creates tensions," November 1, 1993.

(BPD) was still reeling from a sensational murder case: *Boston Globe*, "Stuart errors not forgotten," October 3, 1993; "Bratton criticizes stories on killings," October 4, 1993.

St. Clair Commission … convened to examine … entire department: Background: In 1992 Boston's Mayor Raymond Flynn appointed a special commission to scrutinize Boston police operations. Composed of eight distinguished citizens and chaired by former Watergate special prosecutor James St. Clair, the panel confirmed a "disturbing pattern of violence toward citizens by a small number of officers" and also a steep decline in the department's rate of "disciplining their own": ["Officers were cleared so often that Internal Affairs simply could not be credited with performing the job properly": *Boston Globe*, "Wave of abuse claims laid to a few officers," October 4, 1992.] The commissioners recommended a complete overhaul of the BPD, including reining in its homicide unit. Sources: *Boston Globe*, "St. Clair report/Excerpts," January 15, 1992; *Boston Globe*, "Hub police internal probe of Stuart case is decried," September 8, 1992; *Boston Globe*, "Boston force is targeting 71 'problem' police," December 9, 1992; *Boston Globe*, "In court, Roache says he delegated discipline," April 8, 1993; *Boston Globe*, "Stuart errors not forgotten," October 3, 1993.

Bratton and Martin … pledged to run an impeccable, transparent probe: *Boston Globe*, "Stuart errors not forgotten," October 3, 1993.

cleanup of Boston's "rogue" homicide unit ... 1993: *Boston Globe*, "Boston police may hold the key to new DA's success," July 31, 1992; *Boston Globe*, "Bratton promises tight rein on unit," September 16, 1992.

Nancy Hurley ... charge of police misconduct: *Boston Globe*, "Slay suspect said to blame friend," October 6, 1993; *Boston Globe*, "2 in custody indicted in policeman's killing," October 28, 1993; *Boston Globe*, "Mulligan affidavit challenged," November 6, 1993.

"nodded his head in an affirmative manner": police report quoted in *Boston Globe*, "Mulligan affidavit challenged," November 6, 1993.

"Patterson was not asked ... did not nod his head": Attorney Nancy Hurley quoted *Ibid*.

Two of Sean's friends ... murdered in separate incidents: *Boston Globe*, "Trial witness in police killing is gunned down," October 8, 1994.

Headen had been poised to testify: *Ibid*.

young life ... pockmarked by violence: *Ibid*.

"We're absolutely satisfied ... unrelated to the Mulligan case": *Ibid*.

Kevin Chisholm ... killed the previous July: *Ibid*.

Chisholm ... also cooperating with the police: *Ibid*.

"failed to identify Ellis until she conferred with police": *Ibid*.

inquiries ... "evaporated when Ellis and Patterson were arrested": *Ibid*.

"The murder of another potential witness ... numerous questions unanswered": *Ibid*.

CHAPTER 6: CONVICTIONS

Sean's lawyers filed a motion to suppress ... evidence: *Boston Globe*, "Mulligan probe creates tensions," November 1, 1993.

Sean first came to police attention: testimony of Boston detective William Mahoney, Sean Ellis' pre-trial hearing, December 1994.

The women's relatives told Detective John Brazil: conveyed to the author by Sean's uncle, David Murray, December 1998.

Sean was initially a suspect in the sisters' murders: *Boston Globe*, "Accused was suspect in cousins' murders," December 9, 1994.

at the three-hour mark the subject turned: testimony of Boston detective William Mahoney at Sean Ellis' January 1995 trial.

Sean ... denied any role in Mulligan's murder ... questioning: *Boston Globe*, "Accused was suspect in cousins' murders," December 9, 1994.

"It could be viewed as exculpatory": Judge Robert Banks, cited by defense attorney Norman Zalkind in *Boston Globe*, "1st trial on track in Mulligan slaying," December 13, 1994.

The Walgreens shopper who identified Sean ... another man first: *Boston Globe*, "Suspect in Mulligan murder case was ID'ed by witness on 2d viewing," December 7, 1994.

"never saw a photograph of Ellis before ... October 5": *Boston Globe*, "Witnesses differ on naming of suspect," December 8, 1994.

"No one, at any time directed Rosa Sanchez to any photograph": Chief Prosecutor Phyllis Broker quoted in *Boston Globe*, "Suspect in Mulligan murder case was ID'ed by witness on second viewing," December 7, 1994.

"Sanchez picked [Sean's photo] ... relationship with Sanchez's aunt": *Boston Globe*, "Suspect in Mulligan murder case was ID'ed by witness on 2d viewing," December 7, 1994.

"There is no evidence before the court ... pick out Sean Ellis.": Judge Robert Banks quoted in *Boston Globe*, "1st trial on track in Mulligan slaying," December 13, 1994.

"jointly responsible": *Boston Globe*, "Lawyer: Ellis had gun, did not shoot," January 9, 1993.

proving joint venture was a challenge: *Boston Globe*, "2d jury deadlocks in Mulligan case," April 2, 1995; "Ellis convicted on 3d try in murder of detective," September 15, 1995; *Boston Globe*, "Joint venture concept confuses some jurors," April 4, 1995.

Broker outlined her case theory: *Boston Globe*, "Lawyer: Ellis had gun, did not shoot," January 6, 1995; *Boston Globe*, "Summations concluded, Ellis trial goes to jury," January 13, 1993.

Rosa Sanchez gave her story: *Boston Globe*, "Witness links Ellis to slaying of officer," January 10, 1995; testimony of Rosa Sanchez, Sean Ellis' January 1995 trial.

"lied to police": testimony of eyewitness Rosa Sanchez in Sean Ellis' March 1995 trial.

Victor Brown lived on a residential street: testimony of Walgreens' neighbor Victor Brown reported in *Boston Globe*, "Mulligan case witness: Men parked nearby," January 11, 1995.

"somewhat shorter": *Boston Globe*, "Witness links Ellis to slaying of officer," January 10, 1995.

"in the direction of the mall": *Boston Globe*, "Lawyer says Ellis had gun, did not shoot," January 6, 1993; testimony of Victor Brown in Sean Ellis' January and March 1995 trials.

Brown ... police found it parked.: testimony of Victor Brown in Sean Ellis' January and March 1995 trials.

David Murray ... conversations he had with Sean: *Boston Globe*, "Witness links Ellis to slaying of officer," January 10, 1995.

Sean's girlfriend, Latia "Tia" Walker ... agreed they were the guns: Testimony of Tia Walker at Sean Ellis' January 1995 trial, as quoted in *Boston Globe*, "Ellis hid guns in women's home, girlfriend testifies," January 12, 1995.

Zalkind ... Patterson alone killed Mulligan: *Boston Globe*, "Retrial begins for man accused in officer's slaying," March 25, 1995.

"She's putty. She'll say anything": Defense attorney Norman Zalkind, quoted *Ibid*.

"powerful evidence ... after Mulligan was killed": *Boston Globe*, "Lawyer: Ellis had gun, did not shoot," January 6, 1995.

"all over that car": Defense attorney Norman Zalkind, closing statement at Sean Ellis' January 1995 trial.

"He had the guns but that's not murder": *Boston Globe*, "Lawyer: Ellis had gun, did not shoot," January 6, 1995.

The jury deliberated for eight days: *Boston Globe*, "No verdict in Mulligan murder case," January 14, 1995; *Boston Globe*, "Jury reaches partial verdict in Mulligan murder case," January 15, 1995; *Boston Globe*, "Ellis jury reports a deadlock," January 19, 1995; *Boston Globe*, "Jury questions judge in Mulligan slaying trial," January 20, 1995; *Boston Globe*, "Mulligan case jurors give up; retrial slated," January 22, 1995.

nine jurors told reporters they'd voted to acquit: *Boston Globe*, "Vote was 9-3 to acquit Ellis or murder," January 26, 1995; *Boston Globe*, "Justice often is only human," January 26, 1995.

"[Detective Mulligan] was executed ... next jury": Suffolk County District Attorney Ralph Martin, quoted in *Boston Globe*, "Mulligan case jurors give up; retrial slated," January 22, 1995.

Description of Patterson trial testimony and verdict, January 26 to February 1, 1995: *Boston Globe*, "Trial begins for second man accused of murdering officer," January 27, 1995; *Boston Globe*, "Mulligan-trial witness says he saw a lookout," January 28, 1995; *Boston Globe*, "Brother's testimony places Mulligan defendant at scene," January 31, 1995; *Boston Globe*, "Suspect's prints on Mulligan vehicle," February 1, 1995; *Boston Globe*, "Patterson found guilty in murder of detective," February 2, 1995; *Boston Globe*, "Jury foreman: Evidence left no doubt about Patterson's guilt," February 3, 1995.

"The prints were left by someone closing a door": *Boston Globe*, "Suspect's prints on Mulligan vehicle," February 1, 1995.

"stringy blonde or brown hair": witness Joanne Samuel's testimony at Terry Patterson's 1995 trial quoted in *Boston Globe*, "Suspect's prints on Mulligan vehicle," February 1, 1995.

"moving her head animatedly": testimony of eyewitness Joanne Samuel in Terry Patterson's 1995 trial.

Description of Sean Ellis' second trial, March 24 to 29, 1995, testimony and verdict: *Boston Globe*, "Jurors chosen for Ellis murder trial," March 22, 1995; *Boston Globe*, "Defendants have the upper hand," March 23, 1995; *Boston Globe*, "Retrial begins for man accused in officer's slaying," March 25, 1995; *Boston Globe*, "2d Jury set to weigh evidence against Ellis," March 19, 1995; *Boston Globe*, "Jurors chosen for Ellis murder trial," March 22, 1995; *Boston Globe*, "Ellis trial witnesses take hostile stance," March 28, 1995; *Boston Globe*, "Final arguments today in Ellis trial," March 30, 1995; *Boston Globe*, "Of 2 accused in detective's death, prosecutor paints Ellis as shooter," March 31, 1995; *Boston Globe*, "No verdict reached in Mulligan murder retrial," April 1, 1995; *Boston Globe*, "2d Jury quits on Ellis verdict," April 2, 1995; *Boston Globe*, "Joint venture concept confuses some jurors," April 4, 1995; *Boston Globe*, "2d Jury for Ellis reversed 1st vote," April 19, 1995.

"hopelessly deadlocked": *Boston Globe*, "2d Jury quits on Ellis verdict," April 2, 1995.

Zalkind and Duncan filed a motion to dismiss charges: *Boston Globe*, "Suspect's attorneys file for dismissal," May 31, 1995; *Boston Globe*, "Lawyers want judge off Ellis case," June 1, 1995; *Boston Globe*, "Judge won't drop case against Ellis," June 10, 1995; *Boston Globe*, "Dismissal sought in 3d murder trial," August 17, 1995; *Boston Globe*, "Accused killer of officer loses bid," August 24, 1995.

Description of Sean Ellis' September 1995 trial, testimony, and verdict: *Boston Globe*, "3d Trial set to begin in officer's death," September 6, 1995; *Boston Globe*, "Arguments begin in murder retrial," September 7, 1995; *Boston Globe*, "3d Trial of co-defendant starts in detective's murder," September 8, 1995; *Boston Globe*, "Mulligan murder case goes to a 3d jury," September 14, 1995. *Boston Globe*, "Ellis convicted on 3d try in murder of detective," September 15, 1995; *Boston Globe*, "Despite clashes with detectives, prosecutor prevails in 2-year ordeal," September 15, 1995; *Boston Globe*, "Police: Justice is served by verdict," September 15, 1995; *Boston Globe*, "Jurors say evidence against Ellis overwhelming," September 16, 1995.

"virtually immobile, calm, almost stoic": *Boston Globe*, "Ellis convicted on 3d try in murder of detective," September 15, 1995.

"appeared shaken": *Ibid.*

"As he stood to be sentenced ... after the sentence was imposed": *Ibid.*

CHAPTER 8: DIRTY COPS!

more than a dozen articles: *Boston Globe*, "Corruption probe shakes up Boston detective unit: Officers are disciplined in drug-raid inquiries," February 10, 1996; *Boston Globe*, "Evans: Police district subject of probe," February 11, 1996; *Boston Globe*, "A look at 3 detectives' affidavits from '92 reveals oddities," February 12, 1996; *Boston Herald*, "Other charges expected vs. cops," February 11, 1996; *Boston Globe*, "Probe of police belies relatively good record," February 12, 1995; *Boston Globe*, "Missing raid cash forgotten, union says," February 13, 1996; *Boston Globe*, editorial, "When police break the law," February 13, 1996; *Boston Globe*, "Accused detective wants job back," February 14, 1996; *Boston Globe*, "Meeting canceled in probe of corruption," February 15, 1996; *Boston Herald*, "Three hub detectives focus of probe over returned $8G ransom," February 15, 1996; *Boston Globe*, "U.S. Attorney joins probe of detectives," February 17, 1996; *Boston Globe*, "Drug money entrusted to officer," February 17, 1996; *Boston Globe*, "1993 Charge revived in police probe," February 18, 1996; *Boston Herald*, "Ex-cop denies corruption allegations," February 22, 1996; *Boston Globe*, "Mystery lingers on drug proceed split," March 2, 1996; *Boston Globe*, "Police no-shows scuttled drug cases," March 3, 1996; *Boston Globe*, "IRS joins Boston police in tracking seized cash," March 6, 1996; *Boston Globe*, "2d detective disciplined at Area E," April 10, 1996; *Boston Herald*, "Attorney eyes cop probe to toss evidence vs. client," April 10, 1996; *Boston Globe*, "Police file sought in murder case," April 10, 1996; *Boston Globe*, "Defense attorney seeks files on officer," April 17, 1996; *Boston Globe*, "Cocaine charge dismissed after 2 ex-detectives fail to show," May 29, 1996.

"vanished as evidence...criminal proceedings": *Boston Globe*, "Corruption probe shakes up Boston police detective unit: The case of the disappearing money," February 10, 1996.

An eyewitness said $8,0000 was probably far less: *Ibid*.

Acerra was suspended ... Robinson resigned ... no mention of Brazil's fate: *Boston Globe*, "Evans: Police district subject of probe," February 11, 1996.

A Boston Police Department internal inquiry: *Ibid*.

Bill Bratton had left Boston in January 1994: *Boston Globe*, "Bratton will direct NYC police," December 3, 1993.

the 1992 West Roxbury robbery was not ... first: *Boston Globe*, "A look at 3 detectives' affidavits from '92 reveals oddities," February 12, 1996.

tied John Mulligan to Robinson in drug dealer robberies: *Boston Globe*, "1993 charge revived in police probe," February 18, 1996.

corruption scandal began undoing ... police work: *Boston Globe*, "Cocaine charge dismissed after 2 ex-detectives fail to show," May 29, 1996; *Boston Globe*, "Drug charges dismissed against 4 defendants," March 26, 1997.

statements Brazil attributed to him were false: *Boston Globe*, "2d detective disciplined at Area E," April 6, 1996; *Boston Globe*, "Police file sought in murder case," April 10, 1996.

federal grand jury was now considering indictments: *Boston Globe*, "Cocaine charge dismissed after 2 ex-detectives fail to show," May 29, 1996.

winter 1997 ... robbery allegedly committed by Acerra and Robinson: *Boston Globe*, "Grand jury focuses on drug raids in Area E," January 5, 1997.

Brazil had flipped: *Boston Globe*, "2 City detectives indicted in thefts," March 11, 1997.

The alleged criminality ... like a tsunami: *Boston Globe*, "Charges have heads shaking," March 11, 1997; *Boston Herald*, "Police pair charged in shakedowns," March 11, 1996; *Boston Herald*, "'Rogue' detectives lived the high life," March 11, 1996; *Boston Herald*, "Indictments may mean some cases no longer closed," March 11, 1997; *Boston Herald*, "Insiders surprised feds didn't indict others, too," March 11, 1996; *Boston Herald*, "Former boss of detectives 'shocked' by shakedowns," March 12, 1997; *Boston Globe*, "Police indictments could cloud 5 cases, prosecutor warns," March 12, 1997; *Boston Globe*, "Indicted cops taint Ellis trial," March 12, 1997; *Boston Globe*, editorial, "When police are criminals," March 13, 1997; *Boston Herald*, "Police indictments may cast doubt in Ellis case," March 14, 1997.

as serious a corruption case ... department's history: statement attributed to Boston Police Commissioner Paul Evans in *Boston Globe*, "2 City detectives indicted in thefts," March 11, 1997.

Eileen McNamara, immediately questioned: *Boston Globe*, "Indicted cops taint Ellis trials," March 12, 1997.

separate trials were scheduled: *Boston Globe*, "January trial set for hub officers," May 10, 1997.

the detectives had cut deals: *Boston Globe*, "Ex-police detectives plead guilty," March 7, 1998.

Seven months later ... retrial motion for Sean: *Boston Globe*, "Detectives' conviction sparks move for new trial in slaying of officer," October 1, 1998.

"would effectively end the case against Ellis": Sean's defense attorneys paraphrased in *Boston Globe*, "Detectives' conviction sparks move for new trial in slaying of officer," October 1, 1998.

CHAPTER 20: "PLAIN VIEW MULLIGAN"

Boston defense attorneys called him "Plain View Mulligan": *Boston Globe*, "2000 Police mourn one of their own," October 2, 1993; *Boston Globe*, "Man held in slaying of officer," October 5, 1993.

CHAPTER 27: TWO WORLDS

"revolving-door presidency": *San Diego Union-Tribune*, "Salk hires new CEO renowned for results," September 9, 2000; quote is from a subsequent September 2000 editorial not accessible via *San Diego Union-Tribune* archives.

"warm and charming leader": *Ibid.*, September 2000 editorial in *San Diego Union-Tribune*.

CHAPTER 28: "ATTORNEYLESS"

new development in the case of Shawn Drumgold: *Boston Globe*, "DA to eye new evidence in Drumgold conviction," May 6, 2003.

found serious misconduct: *Ibid.*

he was exonerated and released from prison: *Boston Globe*, "Man held in '95 slaying released," April 18, 1999.

Donnell Johnson ... not responsible for the stray-bullet killing: *Boston Globe*, "New evidence could help man held for '94 killing," September 22, 1999; *Boston Globe*, "Man freed in slaying of boy, 9," November 24, 1999; *Boston Globe*, "System debates informants' reliability," November 24, 1999.

Johnson's trial ... police lying: *Boston Globe*, "Boston police 'testilying' leaves trail of injustice," December 7, 1997. **Background:** At trial, Boston Detective William Mahoney falsely testified that Johnson refused to talk with police. In fact, the youth gave a full statement, with alibi, to Boston detective Daniel Keeler. Johnson's statement eventually surfaced before the trial ended, but nonetheless he was convicted. Both Mahoney and Keeler became Mulligan task force members—a team advertised by the department as Boston's "best and brightest" detectives.

CHAPTER 29: THE SAME UNIFORM

city suffering its worst gang violence in a decade: *Boston Globe*, "2 men killed, 1 hurt as more violence erupts in Boston," July 12, 2004; *Boston Globe*, "The Last Shot," August 1, 2004; *Boston Globe*, "Violence surges; city vows vigilance," August 3, 2004; *Boston Globe*, "Shootings stun, terrify children," August 3, 2004; *Boston Globe*, "Communities meet in hope, fear," August 4, 2004; *Boston Globe*, "Law enforcement agencies vow, 'We've had enough,'" August 7, 2004; *Boston Globe*, "27 arrested in violence crackdown," August 8, 2004; *Boston Globe*, "Outpouring of prayers for city peace," August 9, 2004.

"I guess this is it ... catch any breaks": Dorchester youth Job Williams, 18, quoted in *Boston Globe*, "Boy dies after street shooting," January 24, 2003.

Dorchester community was shocked: *Boston Globe*, "Slay victim said to put life of crime behind him," June 4, 2004.

CHAPTER 30: ROSEMARY

A lengthy feature article on her: *Boston Globe*, "She's on a roll," May 10, 2005.

"misconduct and slipshod work": *Ibid.*

Attorney Jack Cunha ... put it: *Boston Globe*, "SJC bars a type of prints at trial," December 28, 2005.

the method Boston Police used to match Patterson's prints: Background: Boston police Sergeant Robert Foilb testified at trial that three latent fingerprints recovered on the driver's side window of Mulligan's car belonged to Patterson. But Patterson's attorney, Jack Cunha, said that Foilb reached that conclusion by adding up matching ridge characteristics from three fingers—six on one, two on another, and five on the third: [**"The entire methodology is nonsense. You cannot make an identification of somebody from a limited number of comparison points, particularly when they're fingerprints like you find in [criminal] cases. They're partial, they're smudged, they're distorted."** Attorney Jack Cunha, quoted in *Boston Globe*, "Lawyer cites trouble with fingerprints as evidence," February 6, 2004.] *Boston Globe*, "Scientist rebuts reliance on fingerprints testifies in retrial of man convicted of killing detective," May 18, 2004; *Boston Globe*, "SJC to hear arguments on banning fingerprint evidence," September 5, 2005; *Boston Globe*, "SJC hears arguments on fingerprints," September 8, 2005.

"a house of cards": attorney Jack Cunha quoted in *Boston Globe*, "SJC bars a type of prints at trial," December 28, 2005.

CHAPTER 31: EXIT PATTERSON

Terry Patterson walked out of prison: *Boston Globe*, "With plea deal, man convicted in officer's slaying may be freed," February 8, 2006; May release of Patterson conveyed to author by Mary "Jackie" Ellis.

CHAPTER 36: LOW AND LONELY

Steven Odom had been shot: *Boston Globe*, "Amid grief, a call to action," October 14, 2007.

CHAPTER 39: THE SEARCH FOR CRIMINAL LINKS

the city of Boston would award a $62,500 settlement: *Boston Globe*, "Boston pays settlement over alleged police setup," March 12, 1999.

CHAPTER 52: MOVING ON

Suffolk County D.A. Daniel Conley ... against Sean.: *Boston Globe*, "New trial ordered for man convicted in 1993 death of Boston police officer," September 10, 2016; *Boston Globe*, "Case should be closed," September 12, 2016.

prosecutors offered Sean a plea bargain: personal communication to the author by Sean Ellis.

Conley "stunned the political world": *Boston Globe*, "Garrison may have chance to join City Council," February 23, 2018.

resigned three months before the end of his term: *Boston Globe*, "Conley taking early exit as DA," September 13, 2018.

John Pappas was named: *Boston Globe*, "Veteran prosecutor named interim Suffolk County DA," September 26, 2018.

roundly beaten by Rachael Rollins: *Boston Globe*, "Rollins rolls to victory in Suffolk County DA race," November 7, 2018.

afternoon live-streaming event: online press conference by Suffolk County District Attorney Pappas and Boston Police Commissioner William Gross, December 17, 2018, followed by a press release.

"I decide today ...nearing its conclusion": Judge Robert Ullmann at a May 3, 2021, virtual meeting quoted in *Boston Globe*, "Judge throws out remaining gun charge against Sean Ellis in 1993 killing of Boston police officer," May 4, 2021.

D.A. Rollins filed a *nolle prosequi*: *Boston Globe*, "Judge cancels another conviction in officer's death," May 5, 2021.

CHAPTER 52: MOVING ON

"monetary atonement": *Boston Globe*, "Boston police account for $31 million of city legal payouts since 2020, including $16 million for wrongfully convicted man," January 24, 2023.

ABOUT THE AUTHOR

Elaine Alice Murphy began her career in education, first teaching English in Boston and later becoming an education specialist for the Massachusetts Department of Education. Upon moving to Canada in 1986, she turned to freelance writing. The wrongful 1995 murder conviction of Boston's Sean Ellis plunged her into the world of investigative journalism and led to her appointment as a senior justice fellow at Brandeis University. She holds an honors B.A. from Boston College and an M.Ed. from Harvard University. Now retired, she divides her time between Massachusetts and New Hampshire.

COLOPHON

The text of this book is set in Mencken, an editorial, serif typeface designed in 2005 by Jean François Porchez. Originally designed for *The Baltimore Sun*, it is a low contrast transitional typeface that provides ease of reading for lengthy editorial. It was named after Henry Louis Mencken (1880–1956), an American journalist, satirist, cultural critic and scholar of American English who was known as the "Sage of Baltimore."

Subheads are set in Franklin Gothic. Franklin Gothic is a sans-serif typeface in the industrial or grotesque style developed in the early years of the 20th century by the type foundry American Type Founders (ATF) and is attributed to its head designer, Morris Fuller Benton (1902–1967). It was named in honor of Benjamin Franklin who was known to be a prolific American printer.

Titling is set in Austin, a contemporary display face originally designed by Paul Barnes for the British magazine *Harper's & Queen* in 2004. It is based loosely on the first British moderns cut by Richard Austin (1756–1832) in 1788 for the publisher John Bell in London. Elegant with a high contrast between thick and thin strokes with sharp bracketed serif, Austin has a narrow design making it perfect for headline use.